Flat Panel Display Materials

MATERIALS RESEARCH SOCIETY SYMPOSIUM PROCEEDINGS VOLUME 345

Flat Panel Display Materials

Symposium held April 5–6, 1994, San Francisco, California, U.S.A.

EDITORS:

J. Batey

IBM T.J. Watson Research Center
Yorktown Heights, New York, U.S.A.

A. Chiang

Xerox Palo Alto Research Center
Palo Alto, California, U.S.A.

P.H. Holloway

University of Florida
Gainesville, Florida, U.S.A.

MATERIALS RESEARCH SOCIETY
Pittsburgh, Pennsylvania

Single article reprints from this publication are available through
University Microfilms Inc., 300 North Zeeb Road, Ann Arbor, Michigan 48106

CODEN: MRSPDH

Published by:

Materials Research Society
9800 McKnight Road
Pittsburgh, Pennsylvania 15237
Telephone (412) 367-3003
Fax (412) 367-4373

Library of Congress Cataloging in Publication Data

Flat panel display materials : symposium held April 5-6, 1994, San Francisco,
    California, U.S.A. / editors, J. Batey, A. Chiang, P.H. Holloway.
        p. cm.—(Materials Research Society symposium proceedings, ISSN 0272-9172 ;
        v. 345)
    Includes bibliographical references and index.
    ISBN 1-55899-245-6
        1. Liquid crystal displays—Materials—Congresses. 2. Thin film transistors—
    Materials—Congresses. 3. Information display devices—Materials—Congresses
    I. Batey, J. II. Chiang, A. III. Holloway, Paul H. IV. Series: Materials Research
    Society symposium proceedings ; v. 345.
TK7872.L56F53 1994   94-37470
621.3815'42—dc20   CIP

Manufactured in the United States of America

Contents

PART I: THIN FILM TRANSISTOR MATERIALS AND TECHNOLOGY

*Invited Paper

*Invited Paper

PART III: EMISSIVE DISPLAYS

*Invited Paper

Preface

This volume contains papers presented at the symposium on Flat Panel Display Materials which was part of the 1994 MRS Spring Meeting held in San Francisco, California. This is a new symposium for the Materials Research Society, organized at a time when the flat panel industry is experiencing rapid growth. The intent of the symposium was to bring together experts from the display and materials science communities to help bridge the gap between basic materials and processing science, and the emerging flat panel display manufacturing industry.

Much of the growth in this field is fueled by the increasing popularity of notebook computers and consumer electronics incorporating high quality, active matrix addressed liquid crystal displays (LCDs). Accordingly, the first two parts of these proceedings are devoted to papers on various aspects of LCDs. Part I, "Thin Film Transistor Materials and Technology," includes papers given at a session held jointly with the Amorphous Silicon Technology symposium, together with good representation from the polycrystalline silicon community. Part II, "Liquid Crystal Display Materials and Processes," includes papers providing a broader coverage of materials issues, spanning the range from basic research to manufacturing. Part III, "Emissive Displays," covers a range of self-emissive flat panel display technologies, most of which are thin film phosphor based. These displays are better suited than LCDs for some applications and may yet challenge the dominance of LCDs if the underlying materials and manufacturing issues can be resolved.

J. Batey
A. Chiang
P.H. Holloway

September 1994

MATERIALS RESEARCH SOCIETY SYMPOSIUM PROCEEDINGS

MATERIALS RESEARCH SOCIETY SYMPOSIUM PROCEEDINGS

Prior Materials Research Society Symposium Proceedings
available by contacting Materials Research Society

PART I

Thin Film Transistor Materials
and Technology

a-Si TFT TECHNOLOGIES FOR AM-LCDS

NOBUKI IBARAKI
Toshiba Corporation, Display Device Engineering Laboratory
8 Shinsugita-cho, Isogo-ku, Yokohama 235, Japan

ABSTRACT

A technical trend for a-Si TFTs is their application to large-size, high-pixel density AM-LCDs such as XGA, EWS, and HDTV. In order to realize these LCDs, the TFT device characteristics must be improved. Future technologies, which will be necessary to fabricate TFTs with improved characteristics are as follows,
(1) Fully self-aligned TFT technology: A SA-TFT structure reduces the feedthrough voltage caused by parasitic capacitance due to gate/source overlap. This results in an improved picture quality and a higher aperture ratio. Fabrication of such a structure would require ion doping technology.
(2) Ion doping technology : This non-mass-separated implantation technique has large area doping capability and much higher doping speed compared to conventional ion implantation technique. The major problems with the ion doping technique is the implantation of unwanted species which deteriorate the quality of source/drain and channel regions of TFTs.

INTRODUCTION

Due to an increased use of portable computers, recently the market for active matrix liquid crystal displays (AM-LCDs), which use amorphous silicon thin film transistors (a-Si TFTs) array, is growing very rapidly. In addition, new TFT-LCD markets in the areas of amusement, car navigation system, avionics, and projection TVs etc are also expanding. High end products such as extended graphics array (XGA) and engineering work station (EWS) display would require high pixel density and large display size. In the case of video graphics array (VGA) displays used in personal computers, an increase in aperture ratio is needed to reduce the backlight power consumption to prolong the battery life. In the case of XGA and EWS displays, an increase in pixel density would reduce the aperture ratio. To increase the aperture ratio and to increase the display size, a-Si TFT structure and device performance must be improved. The a-Si TFTs used in these displays must have larger field effect mobility and smaller value of parasitic capacitance due to gate/source overlap. Since the mobility of a-Si TFTs is limited by material properties, an improvement in TFT structure should be made to reduce the parasitic capacitance. The parasitic capacitance due to gate/source overlap can be reduced by adopting a fully self-aligned (SA-) TFT structure [1]. A self-aligned structure will also reduce the size of TFT and increase the aperture ratio. Such a self-aligned structure would require the use of ion-doping technique to dope source and drain regions of TFTs.

In this paper, I will discuss two technologies which will be necessary to improve the device performance and increase the aperture ratio. They are as follows:
(1) Fully self-aligned TFT technology.
(2) Non-mass-separated ion doping technology which is necessary for fully self-alignd TFT fabrication process.

3

Mat. Res. Soc. Symp. Proc. Vol. 345. ©1994 **Materials Research Society**

FULLY SELF-ALIGNED TFT

Reported values of the field effect mobility (μ_{FE}) for a-Si TFTs are about $0.3 \sim 1.0$ cm^2/Vs depending on PE-CVD process conditions [1]. These mobility values are still too small for designing large size, high pixel density AM-LCDs. Alternatively, increasing the channel width (W) to get enough current requires more area, which increases the parasitic capacitance (Cgs) of TFTs. Feedthrough voltage caused by this parasitic capacitance disturbs the pixel voltage symmetry on alternative operation. Therefore it deteriorates the picture quality as flicker and after image are increased. Additional storage capacitor (Cs) which compensates the feedthrough voltage requires an additional area, which decreases the aperture ratio. Thus proper design of TFT structure is very important to increase aperture ratio and improve image quality.

Figure 1(a), 1(b) and 1(c) compare three kinds of TFT structures. Figure 1(a) shows a conventional TFT with channel length of L and gate/source overlap of ΔL, where the minimum value of ΔL due to mask alignment accuracy is about 3μ m. L is determined by the accuracy of photolithography to form the space between source and drain, and to form the overlap distance between source/drain pattern edge and channel passivation pattern edge, giving a typical minimum value of 12μ m. Figure 1(b) shows a semi SA-TFT where channel passivation pattern is self aligned by gate pattern using back side exposure of photoresist. Gate/source overlap (Δ Ls) is controlled by process conditions and it ranges from 0.5 to 1.0μ m. Therefore Cgs in semi SA-TFT can be reduced to about 2/3 compared to the conventional TFT. Figure 1(c) shows a fully SA-TFT where ion doped n$^+$ a-Si is used for source and drain regions. The channel passivation pattern is self-aligned to gate pattern in a way similar to semi SA-TFT, then ion doping is carried out with channel passivation pattern as the channel masking layer. Low resistance metal silicide layer is formed between channel and source/drain metal electrodes [2]. This silicide region is needed because the resistivity of doped a-Si film is too high to connect channel and metal source/drain electrodes. Refractory metals such as Mo and Cr are suitable since they can easily form thin silicide layer with a-Si. The metal silicide is formed by metal deposition and subsequent thermal annealing. After the unreacted part of the metal is removed by etching, the metal source/drain electrodes are deposited and patterned. The channel length (Ls) is reduced in this case and thus the channel width (W) can be reduced so that W/L is constant. Smaller values of W and L result in smaller value of Cgs, therefore Cs area can also be reduced.

Figure 2 shows the simulation results for required field effect mobility as a function of diagonal size of the display for the three TFT structures discussed above. The simulation was carried out using SPICE. In this simulation, concentrated constant circuit in two-step II ladder model was used for the gate line equivalent circuit and table look-up model was used for TFT characteristics. The modeled AM-LCD was SXGA which had 1280×3 data lines and 1024 gate lines. The following values were used during the simulations: L=12μm. ΔL=4μ m, ΔLs=0.5μ m, and Ls=6μ m. Channel width W, field effect mobility μ_{FE} and Cs were optimized to obtain maximum aperture ratio.

We can see that larger value of mobility is necessary with increasing the display size. This is because an increase in pixel size leads to an increase in the capacity in liquid crystal, resulting in large W to supply enough current to pixel capacitor. In the case of a conventional TFT structure, μ_{FE} of 0.85cm^2/Vs and 1.45 are necessary for 14-inch diagonal and 25-inch diagonal LCDs, respectively. Such large mobility values are difficult to realize using current PE-CVD process for a-Si deposition during manufacturing, as well as in laboratory. In the case of semi SA-TFT, which have been already adopted in manufacturing, the mobility values of $0.6 \sim 1.0$ cm^2/Vs are required for $14 \sim 25$ inch LCDs. For fully SA-TFTs, μ_{FE} of $0.2 \sim 0.3$cm^2/Vs are

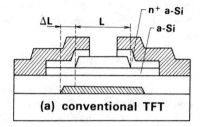

(a) conventional TFT

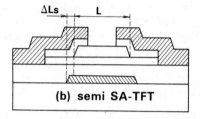

(b) semi SA-TFT

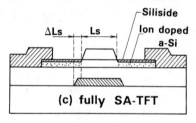

(c) fully SA-TFT

Figure 1. Cross sectional view of TFT structures.
(a) Conventional TFT,
(b) Semi self-aligned TFT, and
(c) Fully self-aligned TFT.

Figure 2. Required field effect mobility as a
function of diagonal size of the TFT-LCD
for different TFT structures. The modeled
display was SXGA.

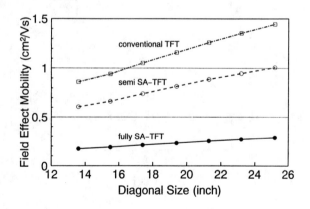

required for 14~25 inch LCDs. Therefore fully SA-TFT structure is superior compared to other structures and has potential ability for the application to larger size, higher pixel density LCDs.

ION DOPING TECHNIQUE

Doped source/drain region of fully SA-TFTs can be made by ion doping technique which is a non-mass separated implantation technique using dopant gas plasma. It offers several advantages over ion implantation technique such as simple machine system, high beam-current and large-area implantation. One of the major disadvantages of ion doping technique is implantation of unwanted species such as hydrogen during ion doping when dopant source gas (such as PH_3 for P doping) is diluted by H_2. TFT characteristics are affected by implantation of these unwanted species. Also high energy plasma and high beam current during ion doping process can cause damage to a-Si layer.

Figure 3 shows SIMS depth profiles of ion doped phosphorus (P) and hydrogen in 0.6 μ m thick a-Si layer. The a-Si layer for SIMS analysis was deposited by LP-CVD process, since hydrogen profile analysis required less background level of hydrogen in a-Si. RF discharge plasma was used for ion doping source with 5% PH_3 gas diluted by H_2. Ion energy was 30keV and P dose was 1.9×10^{16} /cm^2. The hydrogen depth profile was found to have three species, H^+, H_2^+ and H_3^+ as deduced by comparing the SIMS profile with TRIM simulation profiles [3].

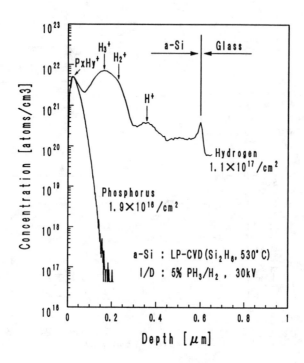

Figure 3. Depth profile of ion doped phosphorous and hydrogen in a-Si.

During ion doping of TFTs, two different regions are exposed to ion beam. One is source/drain contact region where the sectional layered structure is glass/gate/gate-SiN_x/a-Si. The other is channel region where the structure is glass/gate/gate-SiN_x/a-Si/top-SiN_x. For the source/drain region with a-Si layer thickness of $500\,\text{Å}$, the effect of ion doping is as follows: At lower ion energy, concentration of P at the surface as well as in a-Si is high enough to make good contact with metal or silicide electrodes but at the same time high concentration of hydrogen may be incorporated in a-Si layer. These hydrogen atoms may deteriorate the quality of a-Si and hence reduces the doping efficiency. At higher ion energy, ohmic property may be deteriorated because of low concentration of P at the surface, but hydrogen atoms may not affect a-Si conductivity since they reach deep in gate-SiN_x. The detrimental effect of hydrogen on a-Si conductivity was confirmed experimentally by the fact that the conductivity of ion doped samples with P dose of 1×10^{16} /cm^2 at an ion energy of 10keV was 2×10^{-6} /ohm-cm, whereas for the same P dose at an ion energy of 60keV, it was 3×10^{-2} /ohm-cm [4].

For the channel region, a deposited SiN_x layer is used as a mask to prevent the implantation of ions into the channel region. Since the hydrogen ions are much lighter compared to phosphorus ions, they can penetrate the SiN_x masking layer and can cause damage to the channel area of a-Si TFTs. The penetration of hydrogen ions will depend upon SiN_x layer thickness, the implant energy, and type of dominant species such as H^+, H_2^+, or H_3^+ present in the plasma. To study the effect of hydrogen ions on the quality of channel layer, we fabricated MIS samples having a structure, glass/gate/gate-insulator/a-Si/top-SiN_x. The MIS structures used here are analogus to a cross section of TFT. These structures were ion doped in the range of 10 to 60keV ion energy at a phosphorus dose of 5×10^{15} /cm^2. We used two different thicknesses of top-SiN_x layer, $2,000\,\text{Å}$ and $4,000\,\text{Å}$, to see the penetration of hydrogen into a-Si layer. The thickness of a-Si was $2,000\,\text{Å}$. After ion doping, the top-SiN_x layer was removed by etching and then n^+a-Si and metal electrode were deposited as contacts. The capacitance-voltage characteristics were measured at a frequency of 100kHz [5].

Figure 4(a) and 4(b) show the C-V characteristics for the MIS structures which had 2000 and $4000\,\text{Å}$ thick top-SiN_x layers during ion doping experiment, respectively. As can be seen from the figure 4(a), for $2000\,\text{Å}$ top-SiN_x layer, the C-V characteristics deteriorate as the ion energy is increased. At $4000\,\text{Å}$ top-SiN_x thickness, however, no deterioration of C-V characteristics is observed up to 60keV. To explain these results, the hydrogen ion depth profiles were simulated. The depth profiles of Fig.5(a) and 5(b) were obtained by fitting TRIM-simulated depth profiles for various hydrogen ions to total hydrogen concentration obtained by SIMS. As can be seen from figure 5(a), at 10keV ion energy, most of the hydrogen is stopped by $2000\,\text{Å}$ of top-SiN_x. On increasing the ion energy to 20keV, high concentration of H_2^+ ions and some H^+ ions are incorporated into the a-Si layer. This results in deterioration of C-V characteristics as seen in Fig.4(a). We attribute the deterioration of C-V characteristics at 20keV to incorporation of H_2^+ ions rather than H^+ ions because H_2^+ ion concentration is higher and they are heavier compared to H^+ ions. At 60keV, high concentrations of H_2^+ and heavier H_3^+ ions are incorporated into a-Si. Moreover, H_2^+ ions also reach the a-Si/insulator interface. This results in flat C-V characteristics at 60keV as seen in Fig.4(a). When the top-SiN_x film thickness is $4000\,\text{Å}$ (Fig.5(b)), H_2^+ and H_3^+ are almost stopped by SiN_x at all energies, while H^+ enter a-Si and reach a-Si/insulator interface only at 60keV. Since the C-V characteristics are not affected at 60keV, as seen in Fig.4(b), H^+ ions do not seem to contribute to damage to a-Si or a-Si/insulator interface. This happens probably because of lower concentration as well as lower mass of H^+ ions.

We also fabricated fully SA-TFTs using this ion doping technique. Figure 6 shows channel length dependence of mobilities obtained in saturation and linear regions of Id-Vd

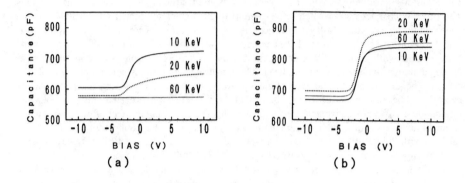

Figure 4. Capacitance-voltage characteristics of ion doped MIS structures for (a) 2000 Å top-SiN$_X$, and (b) 4000 Å top-SiN$_X$.

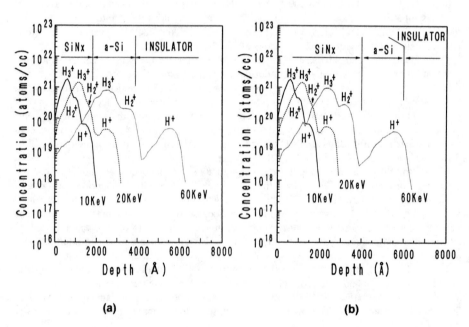

Figure 5. Depth profiles of H$^+$, H$_2$$^+$, and H$_3$$^+$ at various ion energy for (a) 2000 Å top-SiN$_X$, and (b) 4000 Å top-SiN$_X$.

characteristics. The ion doping in this case was carried out at 20keV with a dose of 1×10^{16} /cm^2. The mobilities in both regions decrease with decreasing channel length. The saturation region mobility at L=6μm is about 0.5cm^2/Vs, which is 77% of that of L=12μm. However, in spite of lower mobility at shorter channel length, the charging characteristics of the fully SA-TFT with short channel could be improved by a factor of 1.5 compared to those of a conventional TFT with twice the channel length, because the on-current of a TFT is also proportion to inverse of channel length as well as being proportional to mobility [6].

To test the performance of fully self-aligned TFTs in an actual AM-LCD, we fabricated 4-inch diagonal TFT-LCD. The size of the display was chosen by the facility limtation in our laboratory. The LCD had 480×220 pixcels. The pixel circuit consisted of a fully SA-TFT and a storage capacitor. The channel length of the TFT was 6 μm. We did not observe defects in display such as line defect, point defect, defect clustering, lack of uniformity etc. The good image quality of this display indicates that fully SA-TFT has a potential for application to high-resolution AM-LCDs.

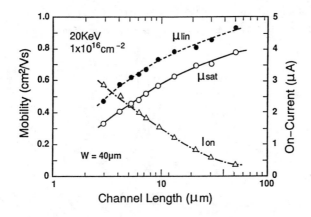

Figure 6. Field effect mobility and on-current as a function of channel length for fully self-aligned TFT. μ_{lin} and μ_{sat} were obtained at linear and saturation regions, respectively.

SUMMARY

One of technical trends for a-Si TFTs is their application to large-size, high-pixel density AM-LCDs. For these applications, the TFT performance must be improved. We discussed two technologies which will be most important for this purpose. They are
(1) Fully self-aligned TFT technology,
(2) Non-mass-separated ion doping technology,
These technologies are also suitable for current AM-LCDs such as VGA displays.

ACKNOWLEDGEMENT

The author acknowledges the colleagues, Dr. R.Kakkad, M.Shibusawa, M.Akiyama, T.Shimano for joining the research. He would like to thank Dr. Y.Ando of Nissin Electric Co.Ltd. for sample preparation and valuable discussion.

References

[1] N.Ibaraki, Proc. 12th Int. Display Res. Conf. (1992) 205, J.Institute of Television Eng. Japan, 47 (1993) 600
(in Japanese)

[2] S.Nishida, H.Uchida, S.Kaneko, Mat. Res. Soc. Symp. Proc. 219 (1991) 303

[3] TRIM 91.08 by J.F.Ziegler, J.P.Biersack, IBM-Research, 28-0, Yorktown, New York 10598 USA

[4] R.Kakkad, T.Shimano, N.Ibaraki, Jpn. J. Appl. Phys. 31 (1992) 4563, Ext. Abstract 1992 Int. Conf. Solid State
Devices & Materials, (1992) 152

[5] T.Shimano, R.Kakkad, N.Ibaraki, Ext. Abstract 1993 Int. Conf. SSDM (1993) 1008

[6] M.Akiyama, Y.Ikeda, M.Ikeda, K.Suzuki, Digest of Tech. Papers, Society Information Display Int. Symp.
(1993) 887

This article appears in Mat. Res. Soc. Symp. Proc. Vol. 336

10

AMORPHOUS SILICON ALLOY PHOTOVOLTAIC TECHNOLOGY - FROM R&D TO PRODUCTION

S. GUHA,[*] J. YANG,[*] A. BANERJEE,[*] T. GLATFELTER,[*] K. HOFFMAN,[*] S.R. OVSHINSKY,[**] M. IZU,[**] H. C. OVSHINSKY,[**] AND X. DENG[**]
[*]United Solar Systems Corp., 1100 West Maple Road, Troy, MI 48084
[**]Energy Conversion Devices, Inc., 1675 West Maple Road, Troy, MI 48084

ABSTRACT

The key requirements for photovoltaic modules to be accepted for large-scale terrestrial applications are (i) low material cost, (ii) high efficiency with good stability, (iii) low manufacturing cost with good yield and (iv) environmental safety. Thin films of amorphous silicon alloy are inexpensive; the products are also environmentally benign. The challenge has been to improve the stable efficiency of these modules and transfer the R&D results into production. Using a multijunction, multi-bandgap approach to capture the solar spectrum more efficiently, we have developed one-square-foot modules with initial efficiency of 11.8%. After 1000 h of one-sun light soaking, a stable efficiency of 10.2% was obtained. Both the efficiency values were confirmed by National Renewable Energy Laboratory. The technology has been transferred to production using an automated roll-to-roll process in which different layers of the cell structure are deposited in a continuous manner onto stainless steel rolls, 14" wide and half a mile long. The rolls are next processed into modules of different sizes. This inexpensive manufacturing process produces high efficiency modules with subcell yields greater than 99%. The key features of the technology transfer and future scope for improvement are discussed.

INTRODUCTION

There is a great need for a renewable, non-polluting energy source which can be used for generation of electricity for large-scale terrestrial applications. Photovoltaic (PV) modules are being used extensively for generation of electricity in remote areas; the cost, however, is still much higher than that produced by conventional fuels. In order for PV to be economically viable, the modules must have low material cost, they must show high efficiency with good stability and they must be easily manufacturable with good yield. Amorphous silicon (a-Si) alloys have attracted a great deal of attention [1] because only a thin layer (less than 1 μm) is needed to absorb the solar photons. The material cost of amorphous silicon PV panels is therefore low. The challenge has been how to improve stable efficiency and demonstrate manufacturability. In this paper, we describe our work to address these issues.

EFFICIENCY CONSIDERATIONS

Cell Efficiency

It is now well recognized that a multi-bandgap, multijunction approach offers the opportunity to obtain the highest stable efficiency for a-Si alloy solar cells [2]. A schematic

11

diagram of a triple-junction structure is shown in Fig. 1. The top cell which captures the blue photons uses a-Si alloy with an optical gap of ~1.8 eV for the intrinsic (*i*) layer. The *i* layer for the middle cell is a-SiGe alloy with about 10% Ge. The optical gap is ~1.6 eV which is ideally suited for capturing the green photons. The bottom cell captures the red and the infrared photons and uses an *i* layer of a-SiGe alloy with about 40-50% Ge corresponding to an optical gap of ~1.4 eV. Light which is not absorbed in the cells gets reflected from the Ag/ZnO back reflector which is usually textured to scatter the light at an angle to facilitate multiple internal reflections.

The requirements to obtain high efficiency multijunction cells are the following: (1) high quality back reflector for efficient light trapping, (2) high efficiency component cells, (3) high quality doped layers to obtain good internal "tunnel" *p n* junctions with low electrical and optical losses and (4) optimum matching of the component cells.

The back reflector should perform two important functions. It must be highly reflecting; it should also scatter light at an angle higher than the critical angle for total internal reflection which, for a-Si alloy, is 16.6°. Ag is usually used to obtain high reflectivity. The interface between Ag and Si, however, is not highly reflecting because of intermixing of the two elements, and a buffer layer of ZnO is deposited in between to prevent intermixing. The required texture for optimum scattering is obtained by depositing Ag and ZnO at a high temperature in the range between 100 to 400 °C.

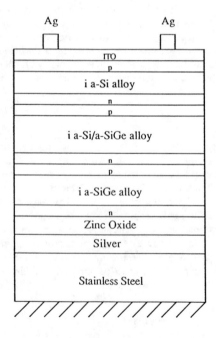

Fig. 1.   Schematic diagram of a triple-junction cell structure.

The use of Ag/ZnO back reflector has resulted in significant gain [3,4] in short-circuit current density (J_{sc}) over specular stainless steel substrate. For a 4000 Å i layer of a-Si alloy, the gain is as much as 4 to 5 mA/cm^2. Theoretical calculations, however, show [5] that there is scope for much larger gain if there is total internal reflection without any loss at the reflecting surface. Experiments with different kinds of texture with different specular to diffusive reflection ratio show a remarkable insensitivity of J_{sc} to the degree of texture once a certain amount of texture is achieved [6]. It appears that there is a parasitic loss at the Si/ZnO and ZnO/Ag interface which limits J_{sc}. Elimination or reduction of this loss will have a large impact on cell efficiency, especially for the multijunction structure.

High efficiency component cells need high quality i layers. As mentioned earlier, we use a-Si alloy for the top cell and a-SiGe alloy for the middle and the bottom cells. In order to obtain high open-circuit voltage (V_{oc}) with good stability, we use hydrogen dilution of the gas mixture. Since the first [7] report of observation of improved stability with hydrogen dilution in a-Si alloy films, significant work has been carried out [8,9] to understand the role of excess hydrogen in the growth process. It is believed that hydrogen coverage of the growing surface gives the impinging species longer time to be incorporated and as a result gives a denser structure. For a-SiGe alloy we use [10] hydrogen diluted gas mixture of Si_2H_6 and GeH_4. We have shown earlier that since dissociation rates of Si_2H_6 and GeH_4 are similar, a gas mixture of Si_2H_6 and GeH_4 produces higher quality material than SiH_4 and GeH_4. Although significant advances have been made to improve the quality of a-SiGe alloy, the best quality a-SiGe alloy still has poorer transport properties than a-Si alloy. To achieve better collection from a given material, profiling of Ge-content in the cell has been used [11] to (a) provide increased built-in field and (b) generate the holes closer to the p-contact so that they do not have very far to move.

Typical initial performances for state-of-the-art component cells for the triple-junction structure are shown [12] in Table I. Also shown are the values after filtered one-sun (metal-arc lamp), 50 °C, 600 h light soaking. In this experiment, the component cells were degraded under open-circuit condition at 50 °C for 600 h and measured at 25 °C. The top cell was degraded under one sun and measured under AM1.5 illumination; the middle cell was degraded under one sun with a 530 nm cut-on filter and measured under AM1.5 illumination with the same filter; the bottom cell was degraded under one sun with a 630 nm cut-on filter and measured under AM1.5 illumination with the same filter. The top and middle cells were deposited on textured substrate without any back reflector, since in the multijunction configuration these cells do not see much reflected light. The bottom cells were deposited on our conventional Ag/ZnO textured back reflector. We notice a degradation of 10% to 20% after light soaking. We should mention that one can improve the initial performance by making the component cells thicker, but this results in larger degradation and lower light-degraded efficiency.

All the component cells in this study show true saturation in efficiency after prolonged light exposure. A typical example for the top and the bottom cell is shown in Fig. 2. The degradation is much lower than those obtained under intense light illumination, demonstrating the importance of thermal annealing of defects under normal operating conditions.

The doped layers play an important role in terms of providing high built-in potential in the bulk and also facilitating junctions between the adjacent cells without resistive loss. Since the doped layers are inactive as far as conversion of light to electricity is concerned, they must also be optically transparent. B-doping of a-Si alloy usually results in larger absorption in the material; the conductivity is also low resulting in large junction loss between the p and the n layers. We have developed [13] microcrystalline p layer with low optical loss. The layers are also highly conducting so as to provide high built-in potential and low tunnel junction loss [14].

Table I.   Present status of typical initial and degraded cell parameters for component cells degraded and measured under conditions described in the text. The high- and the mid-bandgap cells use Cr as back reflector. Use of Ag/ZnO as back reflectors for these cells increases J_{sc} by 30% to 40%.

			J_{sc} (mA/cm^2)	V_{oc} (V)	FF	P_{max} (mW/cm^2)
a-Si	high-bandgap cell	initial	7.3	1.01	0.75	5.53
		degraded	7.2	0.98	0.71	5.01
		degradation (%)	1.4	3.0	5.3	9.4
a-SiGe	mid-bandgap cell	initial	7.02	0.77	0.65	3.51
		degraded	6.85	0.74	0.57	2.89
		degradation (%)	2.4	3.9	12.3	17.7
a-SiGe	low-bandgap cell	initial	7.8	0.67	0.64	3.34
		degraded	7.7	0.65	0.56	2.80
		degradation (%)	1.3	3.0	12.5	16.2

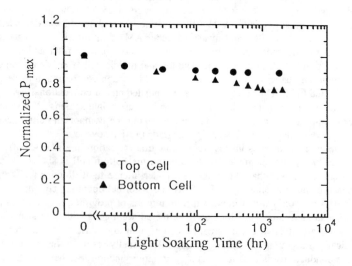

Fig. 2.   Saturation in light-induced degradation of component cells.

For the fabrication of the multijunction cell, the next requirement is the matching of the component cells. The stability of the multijunction cell is primarily dictated by the performance of the component cell that limits the current. Since the top cell shows the maximum stability, it is desirable to design the structure top-cell limited, and small-area stable efficiency exceeding 11% has been achieved [15] using this approach.

<u>Module Efficiency</u>

In order to translate the small-area cell performance into modules, several key requirements need to be fulfilled. There has to be good uniformity over the deposited area; the optical loss due to encapsulation and current carrying grid-lines and the electrical loss due to transparent conducting oxide, grid-lines, etc. should be low. We use a monolithic approach in which the unit cell is a large-area cell of one-square-foot area. The grid design and the encapsulant are optimized to give an optical loss of ~2.1% and an electrical loss of ~2.4%. The total loss from average small-area efficiency to module is thus expected to be 4 to 5%.

A large number (about 200) of multijunction modules has been made over the last two years incorporating the optimizations outlined above. This resulted in a significant progress in the improvement of module efficiency as indicated in Fig. 3. The program on fabrication of one-square foot modules on Ag/ZnO back reflector started in September 1991, and in a period of about two years, the initial module efficiency has increased from 7.5% to 11.8%. The best results achieved to date are shown in Table II where the initial efficiencies for one-square-foot modules as measured at National Renewable Energy Laboratory (NREL) under a Spire 240A simulator are shown. Also shown are the measurements at NREL on modules from the same batch which have been light soaked under one-sun condition for 1000 h at 50 °C.

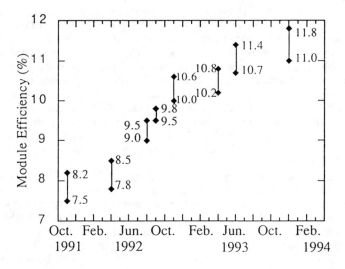

Fig. 3.   Progress in initial module efficiency.

Table II.   Summary of Module Results as Measured at NREL.

Sample	State	J_{sc} (mA/cm^2)	V_{oc} (V)	FF	η (%)
2452	Initial	7.25	2.400	0.675	11.75
2465	Initial	7.48	2.395	0.652	11.69
2437	Final	6.86	2.354	0.629	10.16
2445	Final	7.04	2.349	0.607	10.04
2447	Final	7.17	2.318	0.612	10.17

The stable module efficiency of 10.2% meets the important milestone of 10% stipulated for thin film PV modules to be acceptable for large-scale terrestrial applications. We should mention that as per NREL guidelines [16], the term "stable" refers to the performance level reached after 600 h of one-sun light soaking at 50 °C. As we have demonstrated earlier [17], our multijunction modules show saturation in degradation after about 600 h of one-sun light soaking at 50 °C. Because of thermal annealing effects, the degradation is lower at higher light soaking temperature and higher at lower temperature.

MANUFACTURING ISSUES

In order to translate the R&D results into production, the efficiency targets must be met with using a low-cost process with high yield. Energy Conversion Devices (ECD) pioneered a roll-to-roll method [18] of deposition of solar cells in which rolls of stainless steel, half-a-mile long, 14″ wide and 5 mil thick move in a continuous manner in four machines that serve the purpose of (i) washing, (ii) depositing the back reflector, (iii) depositing the a-Si alloy layers and (iv) depositing an antireflection coating. At United Solar, a fully automated roll-to-roll manufacturing line has been operational for many years [19] for depositing same bandgap double-junction cells. The coated web with the deposited cell is next processed to make a variety of lightweight, flexible and rugged products. The processing steps involve (i) cutting of the web into 16″ x 14″ slabs, (ii) scribing of ITO by screen printing, (iii) short and shunt passivation, (iv) screen printing of silver grid and (v) final assembly involving cell cutting and interconnection and lamination.

Typical stable module efficiency of the products is about 6% [20]. In order to improve the efficiency further, it is necessary to introduce many of the innovations described in the previous section into the manufacturing line. A triple-junction module manufacturing facility with an annual capacity of 2 MW has recently been designed and built [21] for Sovlux, a joint venture between ECD and Kvant, Moscow. The manufacturing line incorporated a Ag/ZnO back reflector sputtering machine to facilitate improved light trapping in the module. It also uses the triple-junction cell design in which the bottom cell uses a-SiGe alloy with bandgap profiling. The middle and the top cell use a-Si alloy deposited at different temperatures to change the bandgap.

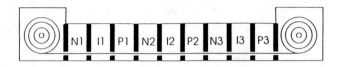

Fig. 4.   Schematic diagram of roll-to-roll triple-junction a-Si alloy deposition machine.

The schematic diagram for the a-Si alloy deposition machine is shown in Fig. 4. The machine consists of a web payoff chamber, nine plasma-CVD chambers for the nine layers of the triple-junction cell and a take-up chamber. Stainless steel web, coated with Ag/ZnO, moves continuously through the chambers depositing the various layers sequentially. The process gas mixtures in each section are dynamically isolated from the adjacent chambers depositing the doped and undoped layers by proprietary "gas gates." The "gas gates" utilize laminar gas flow through constant geometrical cross-section conduits in a direction opposite to the diffusion gradient of the dopant gas concentration. SIMS analysis shows that one can eliminate migration of dopants to the undoped layer to a level below $10^{16}/cm^3$.

One of the key features in the a-Si alloy deposition machine is the provision for bandgap profiling of a-SiGe alloy in the bottom cell. This is achieved by using a proprietary gas distribution manifold and cathode configuration so that a gas mixture containing different amounts of GeH_4 is delivered into different parts of the chamber. The design was optimized to obtain any desired profile of Ge-concentration in the intrinsic layer.

For a PV production line, it is important to have appropriate evaluation of the cell performance such as cell efficiency, yield and uniformity through the entire production run. In our quality analysis (QA) process, statistical samples of 4″ x 14″ are selected from the production roll of 2500′ at an interval of 60′. Twenty-eight test solar cells of 7.35 cm² area (7 rows and 4 columns) are processed on each sample by the following procedures: (1) TCO scribing by screen printing of etching paste, heat curing and rinsing, (2) short and shunt passivation, and (3) screen printing of Ag paste grid.

The J-V data of 28 cells in a typical sample, sample 23 of run 109, is summarized in Table III. The efficiencies of all 28 cells are above 10%. The uniformity is excellent. The average V_{oc}, J_{sc}, FF and η are 2.37 V, 6.51 mA/cm², 0.673 and 10.41%, respectively, as shown in the table. With a subcell yield criterion of FF ≥ 0.55, the subcell yield of the sample is 100%. Figure 5 is a three-dimensional plot of subcell efficiency for every cell from the statistical QA/QC samples in a production run. Out of 1176 cells, only 3 show shunts or shorts. The results represent the excellent consistency, uniformity and yield achieved in a continuous roll-to-roll manufacturing process.

17

Table III.   Performance Data of 28 Cells in a QA/QC Sample.

Cell No.	V_{oc} (V)	J_{sc} (mA/cm^2)	FF	Eff (%)	Cell No.	V_{oc} (V)	J_{sc} (mA/cm^2)	FF	Eff (%)
1	2.38	6.45	0.706	10.49	15	2.38	6.24	0.698	10.36
2	2.38	6.45	0.694	10.64	16	2.38	6.47	0.663	10.20
3	2.37	6.66	0.658	10.37	17	2.37	6.55	0.679	10.54
4	2.37	6.88	0.602	10.46	18	2.37	6.52	0.672	10.39
5	2.37	6.65	0.670	10.59	19	2.37	6.67	0.654	10.33
6	2.38	6.54	0.676	10.52	20	2.38	6.49	0.674	10.40
7	2.38	6.52	0.668	10.36	21	2.39	6.63	0.663	10.50
8	2.39	6.36	0.670	10.19	22	2.38	6.39	0.684	10.39
9	2.38	6.32	0.684	10.29	23	2.37	6.27	0.704	10.47
10	2.37	6.35	0.686	10.30	24	2.37	6.43	0.695	10.59
11	2.37	6.88	0.633	10.31	25	2.37	6.53	0.679	10.50
12	2.37	6.52	0.671	10.36	26	2.37	6.66	0.652	10.30
13	2.38	6.39	0.688	10.45	27	2.38	6.67	0.651	10.34
14	2.39	6.71	0.669	10.72	28	2.38	6.37	0.674	10.21

Average   2.37   6.51   0.673   10.41
Yield for cells with FF $\geq$ 0.55: 100%

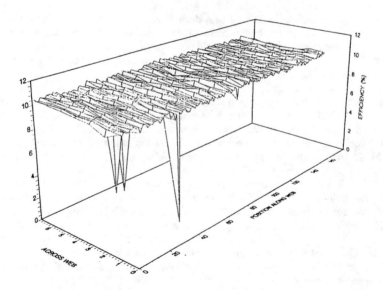

Fig. 5.   Three dimensional plot of cell efficiency of test cells in a production run.

Table IV.   Initial Module Performance Data of Four-square-
             foot Modules Produced in the Manufacturing Line.

Module	V_{oc} (V)	I_{sc} (A)	FF	η	Measurement Lab
23	21.62	2.68	0.628	9.31	ECD
	21.56	2.72	0.63	9.46	NREL
27	21.6	2.72	0.632	9.48	ECD
28	21.3	2.75	0.634	9.47	ECD
30	21.61	2.68	0.63	9.36	ECD
	21.51	2.74	0.627	9.47	NREL

Modules of four-square-foot area (1' x 4') were fabricated by interconnecting 9 strip cells for obtaining approximately 16 V at maximum power point. Typical results are shown in Table IV. Note that initial aperture area efficiencies in the range of 9.4 to 9.5% have been confirmed both at ECD and NREL. The modules were light soaked under one sun for 2000 h at a temperature between 50 to 60 °C. The degradation behavior is shown in Fig. 6. We note that the stabilized efficiency is 8%.

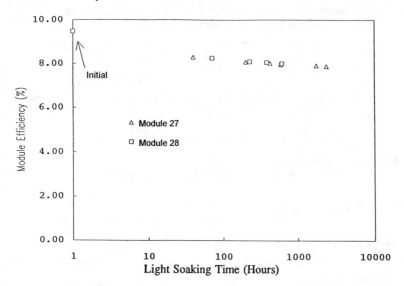

Fig. 6.   Module efficiencies of two 4 ft^2 modules as a function of light
             soaking time under one-sun illumination.

The manufacturing line is still being optimized, and it is important to discuss how the gap between 10% stabilized efficiency in R&D and 8% from the manufacturing line can be bridged. The middle cell in the latter case does not contain any germanium. This limits the short-circuit current from the cell and lowers the efficiency. The deposition rate of the top cell is high (> 10 Å/s). Use of somewhat lower deposition rate and higher hydrogen dilution as discussed earlier will improve the module efficiency further.

FUTURE DIRECTIONS

Although the achievement of 10% stable module efficiency addresses the important issue of near-term market acceptability, the multijunction approach holds promise for much higher efficiency. The component cell requirement for 15% module efficiency has been addressed by Guha et al. [17]. Typical characteristics necessary vis-a-vis the current status at United Solar are shown in Table V. Improvement in material quality, especially for the low bandgap alloy, will be necessary to meet that goal. Use of novel plasma deposition methods [22] in which the growth kinetics can be controlled by selecting suitable species to impinge on the growing surface will play a key role in improving the stable material quality. Further investigation of the role of microstructure, hydrogen bonding and impurities on stable device performance for materials deposited under different conditions will help us to have a better understanding of the issues involved. Reduction of losses in the back reflector will also improve the efficiency. With a well-focussed sustained approach encompassing both material and device research, the progress in improvement of stable module efficiency can surely be maintained.

Table V.   Component cell stabilized parameters for 15% module efficiency. (Present status at United Solar shown in parentheses.)

	Voc (V)	FF	J_{sc} (mA/cm^2)	Power (mW/cm^2)
Top Cell[+]	1.1 (0.98)	0.75 (0.71)	8.2 (7.7)	6.8 (5.3)
Middle Cell[*+]	0.89 (0.74)	0.70 (0.57)	8.4 (6.9)	5.2 (2.9)
Bottom Cell[Δ]	0.68 (0.65)	0.68 (0.56)	8.6 (7.7)	4.0 (2.8)
Devices	2.67	0.72	8.3	16.0

[+] Without back reflector
[*] Under λ>530 nm light
[Δ] Under λ>630 nm light

CONCLUSIONS

General considerations for obtaining high stabilized solar cell and module efficiencies using a-Si alloy are discussed. Using a multi-bandgap, multijunction approach, a stable efficiency of 10.2% has been achieved on a one-square-foot panel. A manufacturing line has been designed and built to translate the R&D results into a low-cost production process with high yield. Further scope for improvement in efficiency is discussed.

ACKNOWLEDGEMENT

The authors would like to thank X. Xu, A. Krisko and K.L. Narasimhan for discussions and collaboration, V. Trudeau for preparation of the manuscript, and National Renewable Energy Laboratory for supporting the program under Subcontract Nos. ZM-1-19033-2 at United Solar Systems Corp. and ZM-2-1104-7 at Energy Conversion Devices, Inc.

REFERENCES

1. See, for example, Mat. Res. Soc. Symp. Proc. **297** (1993).
2. S. Guha, Mat. Res. Soc. Symp. Proc. **149**, 405 (1980).
3. A. Banerjee and S. Guha, J. Appl. Phys. **69**, 1030 (1991).
4. A. Banerjee, J. Yang, and S. Guha (to be published).
5. E. Yablonovitch and G. Cody, IEEE ED-**29**, 300 (1982).
6. S. Guha, Optoelectronics **5** (2), 201-207 (1990).
7. S. Guha, K.L. Narasimhan, and S.M. Pietruszko, J. Appl. Phys. **52**, 859 (1981).
8. K. Tanaka and A. Matsuda, Mat. Sci. Reports **2**, 139 (1987).
9. A. Gallagher, SERI Technical Report, SERI/TP-211-3747 (1990).
10. S. Guha, J.S. Payson, S.C. Agarwal, and S.R. Ovshinsky, J. Non-cryst. Solids **97-98**, 1455 (1987).
11. S. Guha, J. Yang, A. Pawlikiewicz, T. Glatfelter, R. Ross, and S.R. Ovshinsky, Appl. Phys. Lett. **54**, 2330 (1989).
12. X. Xu, J. Yang, and S. Guha, Proc. 23rd IEEE PVSC, Louisville, KY, 971 (1993).
13. S. Guha, J. Yang, P. Nath, and M. Hack, Appl. Phys. Lett. **49**, 218 (1986).
14. A. Banerjee, J. Yang, T. Glatfelter, K. Hoffman, and S. Guha, Appl. Phys. Lett. **64**, 1517 (1994).
15. J. Yang and S. Guha, Appl. Phys. Lett. **61**, 2917 (1992).
16. W. Luft, B. Stafford, and B. von Roedern, in <u>Amorphous Silicon Materials and Solar Cells</u>, AIP Conf. Proc. No. 234, edited by B. Stafford (American Institute of Physics, New York, 1991), p. 3.
17. S. Guha, J. Yang, A. Banerjee, T. Glatfelter, K. Hoffman, and X. Xu, PVSEC-7, 43 (1993).
18. M. Izu and S.R. Ovshinsky, SPIE Proc. **407**, 43 (1983).
19. P. Nath, K. Hoffman, J. Call, C. Vogeli, M. Izu, and S.R. Ovshinsky, PVSEC-3, 395 (1987).
20. W. Luft, B. von Roedern, B. Stafford, D. Waddington, and L. Mrig, Proc. 22nd IEEE PVSC, Las Vegas, NV, 1393 (1981).
21. M. Izu, X. Deng, A. Krisko, K.Whelan, R. Young, H.C. Ovshinsky, K.L. Narasimhan, and S.R. Ovshinsky, Proc. 23rd IEEE PVSC, Louisville, KY, 919 (1993).
22. S.R. Ovshinsky, Solar Energy Materials (in press).

This article appears in Mat. Res. Soc. Symp. Proc. Vol. 336

SILICON NITRIDE OPTIMISATION FOR a-Si:H TFTs USED IN PROJECTION LC-TVs

I. D. FRENCH, C. J. CURLING AND A.L. GOODYEAR
Philips Research Laboratories, Cross Oak Lane, Redhill, RH1 5HA, England.

ABSTRACT

Multi-layer devices based on thin films in Large Area Electronics have different intrinsic and extrinsic properties that must be optimised to produce the correct physical shape of the device, in addition to having acceptable electrical characteristics. For instance it is quite easy to produce individual layers optimised for electrical performance that will physically "pull off" underlying films, or result in poor step coverage. The factors that must be considered include mechanical stress, etching rates and profiles, thickness and stoichiometry uniformity, and thermal budgets, as well as electrical characteristics. This paper gives an example of silicon nitride optimisation for use in a-Si:H TFT projection displays. Three different silicon nitride layers were included to give a storage capacitor, together with controlled etch profiles for step coverage. The layers were optimised with respect to several different parameters in the minimum number of depositions by the use of experimental design techniques.

INTRODUCTION

Devices fabricated using amorphous silicon technologies have varied in complexity from displays and sensors with few layers and four or less photolithographic mask steps[1],[2], to ones with more than seven mask steps, and correspondingly complicated structures. In displays the extra mask steps introduce storage capacitors and features to increase yield, while some types of sensors use the extra layers to integrate TFT switches and photodiodes on the same substrate[3]. These complex structures place multiple requirements on the dielectric and semiconductor layers deposited by Plasma Enhanced Chemical Vapour Deposition (PECVD). In addition to having acceptable electrical performance and stability, they must be capable of being etched to the required shape reliably over large areas, and not crack, bubble, or adversely affect other layers. The multi-factorial nature of the input parameters (deposition parameters) and responses (film properties) makes optimising the PECVD process a complicated task. An understanding of deposition processes is essential, but detailed deposition parameters for different deposition systems can only be obtained by experimentation. This is illustrated by optimisation of silicon nitride layers for use in TFTs and storage capacitors in projection LC-TVs. A deposition parameter space was explored using experimental design techniques. Curve fitting predicted film properties within this space, and based on the device specification new deposition parameters were chosen. Experiments confirmed the film properties, and then the layers were incorporated into TFTs.

TFT AND CAPACITOR STRUCTURE.

Figure 1 shows a schematic cross-sectional view through a projection LC-TV array from the ITO pixel, through the TFT, to the data line. The pixel is the bottom level of the array,

Mat. Res. Soc. Symp. Proc. Vol. 345. ©1994 Materials Research Society

and the first silicon nitride layer forms the storage capacitor dielectric between pixels and the gate line of the preceding row. An inverted staggered TFT with a top silicon nitride etch stop is fabricated on top of the capacitor array. It can be seen that the pixel, gate line, and data line are all on different levels separated by silicon nitride, even though alternative designs would save processing steps by making some of these layers coplanar. Having insulating layers between the conductors increases yield by preventing small etching faults, particularly of the ITO, causing short-circuits to rows or columns.

The metal connection between the TFT and the pixel goes over a combined silicon nitride step of 0.8 μm. For good step coverage these layers must have a bevelled edge. This can be achieved by dry etching, but wet etching is more economical. In this case the bevel is produced by introducing a thin layer of silicon nitride at the top surface of the gate silicon nitride, so that there are three different silicon nitride layers in the step. Each successive layer has a higher wet etch rate than the layers underneath, which gives enhanced lateral etching of the uppermost layers. This produced bevelled edges, and good step coverage for the metal layers that are subsequently deposited over the step.

Fig. 1 Schematic cross-section from the data line to the pixel. The storage capacitor is not shown, but it is formed by overlapping areas of Cr1 and the gate Cr.

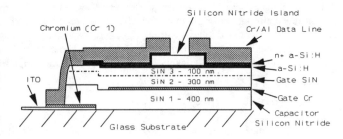

SILICON NITRIDE REQUIREMENTS.

When optimising silicon nitride layers several different material properties need to be considered. In common with some other groups[4] we find that when the gate silicon nitride is nitrogen-rich the electrical stability of TFTs at display operating voltages is dominated by state creation in the amorphous silicon[5]. For uniform TFT characteristics the silicon nitride layers must have uniform thickness and material properties. Thickness uniformity can be simply measured, but materials analysis for stoichiometry uniformity is relatively expensive and time consuming, and hence unsuitable for uniformity characterisation of large numbers of substrates. However, the optical band gap uniformity gives a good indication of the composition uniformity. The optical band gap was defined as the point where the absorption coefficient was equal to 10^4 cm^{-1}. In this application we specified that the thickness spread should be no greater than 8%, and the E_{opt} spread no greater than 4% for layers with a band gap greater than 5.3 eV. The mechanical stress of silicon nitride layers can be changed from strongly tensile to weakly compressive by varying deposition parameters. Compressive films can have poor adhesion, and strongly tensile films can damage underlying layers. Generally weakly tensile films are preferred. For mass production the deposition rate of the silicon nitride must be high enough to allow an adequate throughput in the PECVD systems. The required level is dependent on the factory set-up, but a reasonable value for in-line deposition systems would be above 200 Å/min, which gives a deposition time of twenty minutes each for the capacitor and gate silicon nitride layers, if carried out in a single chamber. Large in-line systems typically process eight substrates simultaneously, each with an area greater than 300 x 300 mm², so this would equal a throughput of 24 substrates per hour. As previously indicated, for this application well defined and controllable etch rates must also be achieved.

EXPERIMENTAL DESIGN.

In plasma deposition there are several different deposition parameters that can be varied to alter any single material property. For instance the optical band gap of silicon nitride can be increased by increasing the NH_3/SiH_4 ratio, increasing R.F. power to increase the dissociated NH_3, or increasing the gas residency time. Each of these will have different effects on other material properties. When optimising several different material parameters it is advantageous to use experimental design techniques to explore multi-dimensional parameter space[6],[7]. In this case a Box-Behnken design was chosen, see Fig. 2, to minimise the number of depositions required, while still including interaction terms of the deposition parameters in the analysis. Three deposition parameters were chosen for investigation: NH_3/SiH_4 gas ratio, hydrogen dilution, and deposition temperature. Nitrogen and hydrogen were used as diluent gases, with their combined flow being kept constant at 500 sccm. Hydrogen dilution was defined as the ratio of hydrogen over the total flow of hydrogen and nitrogen. This was chosen as a variable because it is known to alter film stress[4] and to reduce the amount of hydrogen in the deposited silicon nitride. The wet etch rate is a function of hydrogen content. Deposition parameters are shown in TABLE I.

The PECVD system used was an Anelva ILV-9104 vertical in-line system with three deposition chambers and a load-lock. The effective deposition area was 45 x 45 cm². For each deposition condition 0.4 to 0.5 μm thick films were deposited. Optical transmission measurements were carried out on quartz substrates from the centre and from the corners of the deposition area. The thickness of deposited layers was calculated from interference fringes, and once the thickness was known the optical band gap was obtained from absorbance plots. FTIR measurements were carried out on films deposited on undoped silicon wafers. Mechanical stress was calculated from the deformation of thin borosilicate glass substrates. The bending profile was measured by an automated laser profiling system. The etch rate was found by measuring photolithographically defined steps after immersion in 10:1 buffered HF (B.HF) at 25°C.

TABLE I. Deposition parameters.

SiH_4 flow	40 sccm
$N_2 + H_2$	500 sccm
NH_3/SiH_4	4 to 10
$H_2/(H_2 + N_2)$	0 to 70%
Pressure	115 Pa
Temperature	270 to 330°C
R.F. Power	0.092 W/cm²
R.F. frequency	13.56 MHz

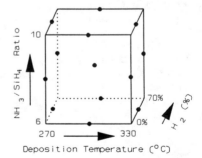

Fig. 2 Box-Behnken design used in this work. All points investigated were midpoints of lines, except for the centre point of the cube. Deposition order was randomised, and the central point repeated three times.

EXPERIMENTAL RESULTS

In order to visualise the results a series of contour plots were generated. The contours were defined by fitting polynomials (including linear, square, and interaction terms) to the measured data using multiple linear regression. Polynomials with only small deviations from measured results were produced for growth rate, growth rate uniformity, E_{opt}, E_{opt} uniformity, film stress and etch rate. A satisfactory fit for FTIR data could not be made, probably because of limited accuracy in measuring the absorption peak area. A backward elimination technique, which removed polynomial terms of little significance, was used to minimise the polynomial expression for each of the response functions[8]. For example the seven term polynomial fitted to the E_{opt} data was:

$$E_{opt} = 4.365 - (2.54 \times 10^{-4} \times H) + (2.35 \times 10^{-2} \times R) + (6.66 \times 10^{-3} \times T)$$

$$- (1.15 \times 10^{-5} \times T^2) + (3.32 \times 10^{-4} \times R \times H) - (1.17 \times 10^{-5} \times T \times H) \qquad (1)$$

Where T is the deposition temperature in °C, R the NH_3/SiH_4 ratio, and H the fraction of hydrogen in the diluent gases.

Fig. 3(a) Fitted results for average optical band gap (eV, plotted as solid line) and mechanical stress (GPa, dashed line) as a function of NH_3/SiH_4 ratio and H_2 content of the deposition gases for films deposited at 300°C. The stress was positive (tensile) for all conditions, except at the bottom right of the diagram, where it becomes compressive.

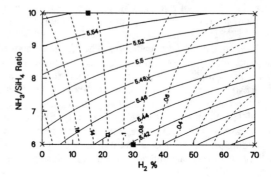

Fig. 3(b) Fitted results for deposition rate uniformity (the ratio of corner thickness/centre thickness is shown as solid lines) and film etch rate in 10:1 B.HF (Å/sec, dashed line). The crosses show the deposition parameters that were used in the initial deposition experiments, and the solid squares the deposition parameters chosen for use in the TFT gate dielectric.

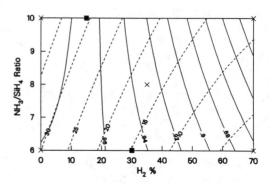

Examples of the contour plots are given above in Figures 3(a) and (b) for a deposition temperature of 300°C. For clarity the two parameters that varied least, deposition rate and

26

E_{opt} spread, have not been shown. The deposition rate had a maximum of approximately 230 Å/min for conditions at the bottom left of the graph, and fell to 200 Å/min for hydrogen dilutions in the region of 55%. The spread in optical band gap was less than 4%. All FTIR spectra had strong absorption peaks at wavenumbers of 3350, 2180 and 1550 cm^{-1}. This showed that N-H, Si-H, and N-H$_2$ bonds were all present in the films, and the (Si-H)/(N-H) ratio was always more than 10%. The presence of these high levels of Si-H indicated that the deposition did not occur in the aminosilane regime[9], probably due to a combination of low NH$_3$/SiH$_4$ ratio, high dilution levels and low gas residency times.

SILICON NITRIDE LAYERS SELECTED FOR USE IN TFT ARRAYS

The capacitor silicon nitride was deposited at 330°C, and had good uniformity with an etch rate of 7 Å/sec in 10:1 B.HF. The two silicon nitride layers used in the gate dielectric must be deposited sequentially, and therefore have the same deposition temperature. From past experience it was known that an etch rate ratio of approximately 2:1 for a top silicon nitride layer of 1 000 Å (SiN-3 layer in Fig. 1) over 3 000Å (SiN-2) of a more slowly etching material gives good bevelled edges. After inspecting the contour plots in Fig. 3, the deposition conditions indicated by the solid squares were chosen. Good agreement was found between film properties predicted by the contour plots and those measured on test layers. This is illustrated for optical band gap and deposition rate in Table II.

TABLE II. Comparison between film properties predicted by fitted parameters and measured on samples. The two silicon nitride layers are those used in the TFT gate.

	NH$_3$: SiH$_4$	H$_2$ (%)	Deposition Rate (Å/min)		Optical Band Gap (eV)	
			Predicted	Measured	Predicted	Measured
Top SiN Layer (SiN3)	10:1	15	213	221	5.56	5.55
Bottom SiN Layer (SiN2)	6:1	30	217	230	5.42	5.44

Test TFTs with composite silicon nitride had field effect mobilities of 0.55 cm^{2}V^{-1}s^{-1}, and threshold voltages of 1.8V. Fig. 4 shows the threshold voltage shift versus time for D.C. bias at different temperatures. Below 80°C the threshold voltage shift was proportional to $(t/t_0)^\beta$, where t was the stressing time. The least squares fit for 50°C had a β value of 0.25. The threshold voltage was measured using a fast technique.

The threshold voltage shift

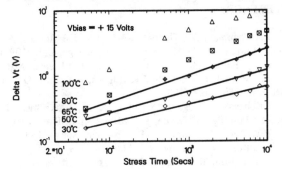

Fig. 4 Threshold Voltage shift vs. time for test TFTs with composite silicon nitride gate dielectric.

after 10^4 secs was 1.3 Volts at 50°C. Allowing for different dielectric constants, this is comparable to values shown for other a-Si:H TFTs in the literature[10].

Figure 5 shows etch profiles of test structures of the TFT gate silicon nitride layers on a silicon wafer. The bevel angle is approximately 25°, which is close to the arctan of the etch rate ratios. The films were etched in 40:1 B.HF, which gives an etch rate of roughly half that for 10:1 B.HF.

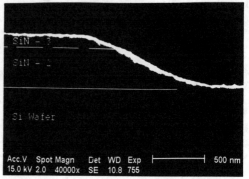

Fig. 5 SEM of bevelled edge of SiN layers deposited at 300°C.

CONCLUSION

Experimental design techniques were used to optimise different silicon nitride layers for use in projection LC-TVs. Good agreement was found between physical measurements and film properties predicted by an experimental matrix. The use of experimental design meant that comparatively few deposition runs were needed to choose deposition parameters that produced layers with: bevelled edges due to accurate control of etch rate, acceptable deposition rates, acceptable thickness and band gap uniformity, films with low tensile stress, and stable TFTs.

ACKNOWLEDGEMENTS

Thanks are due to Jim Hewett for plasma depositions and FTIR measurements, and Ron Ford and Audrey Gill for processing the structures. They are also due to Mike Pitt of Philips Electronics, Eindhoven, for discussions on experimental design. We had many stimulating discussions on the fundamental deposition process with Darren Murley of Dundee University.

REFERENCES

[1]   J A Chapman, D S George, J A Clarke, J R Hughes, A D Pearson, R V Winkle, N K Wright, Eurodisplay '93 Conference Proceedings, 275, (1993)
[2]   C van Berkel, N C Bird, C J Curling, I D French, MRS Proc. **297**, 939, (1993)
[3]   M J Powell, I D French, J R Hughes, N C Bird, O S Davies, C Glasse, J E Curran, MRS Proc. **258**, 1127 (1992)
[4]   I Kobayashi, T Ogawa, S Hotta, Jpn. J. Appl. Phys. **31**, 336, (1992)
[5]   M J Powell, S C Deane, W I Milne, Appl. Phys. Lett. **60**, 207, (1992)
[6]   P W Bohn, R C Manz, J. Electrochem. Soc. **132**, 1981, (1985)
[7]   P E Riley, A P Turley, W J Malkowski, J. Electrochem. Soc. **136**, 1112, (1989)
[8]   R L Mason, R F Gunst, J L Hess, *Statistical Design and Analysis of Experiments* (Wiley, New York, 1989) p. 574
[9]   D L Smith, A S Alimonda, C C Chen, S E Ready, B Wacker, J. Electrochem. Soc., **137**, 614, (1990)
[10]   F R Libsch, J Kanicki, SID 93 Digest, 455, (1993)

This article appears in Mat. Res. Soc. Symp. Proc. Vol. 336

EFFECTS OF N₂ PLASMA TREATMENT ON SiO₂ GATE INSULATOR IN a-Si:H THIN FILM TRANSISTOR

SUNG CHUL KIM*, SUNG SIG BAE*, EUI YEOL OH*, JEONG HYUN KIM*,
JONG WAN LEE**, CHA YEON KIM** AND DONGGIL KIM*
*LCD Research Laboratory, GoldStar Co., LTD., 533 Hogae-dong, Anyang-shi,
Kyongki-do, 430-080, Korea
**Central Research Laboratory, GoldStar Co., LTD., 16 Woomyeon-dong,
Seocho-gu, Seoul, 137-140, Korea

ABSTRACT

We fabricated the high performance a-Si:H TFT using the N₂ plasma treated APCVD SiO₂ as a gate insulator. The effects of N₂ plasma treatment on the APCVD SiO₂ were investigated by XPS and SIMS measurements. And the formation of the oxynitride interface layer between a-Si:H and APCVD SiO₂ was found in the a-Si:H TFT. From our experimental results, It may be concluded that most nitrogen atoms, which were incorporated by the exposure of SiO₂ layer to N₂ plasma, exist, not bonded to other atoms, near the surface of the SiO₂ layer and during the sequential deposition of a-Si:H on the N₂ plasma treated APCVD SiO₂ layer Si-N bonds are formed, resulting in the oxynitride layer in the interface region. This explains the high performance a-Si:H TFT with the N₂ plasma treated APCVD SiO₂ gate insulator.

INTRODUCTION

Hydrogenated amorphous silicon thin film transistors(a-Si:H TFTs) are conventionally used as the switching devices of Active Matrix Liquid Crystal Display(AMLCD), where their performance mainly depends on the quality of the interface between the a-Si:H and the gate insulator. Generally, SiN$_x$ film deposited by PECVD is used as gate insulator because of its excellant interfacial properties. The PECVD SiN$_x$ layer has some problems of electrical instability and particle induced pin-holes due to the low temperature deposition. To overcome these problems, the double layered gate insulators such as SiN$_x$/Al$_2$O$_3$[1], SiN$_x$/TaO$_x$[2], SiN$_x$/SiO$_2$[3] and the N₂ plasma treated SiO₂ single layer[4] are used to fabricate TFT arrays.

In the previous works[4,5], we reported the feasibility of APCVD SiO₂ as a gate insulator through the N₂ plasma treatment on the oxide surface. It was found that the nitrogen atoms are incorporated at the a-Si:H/SiO₂ interface, resulting in the improvement of the interface quality. The performance of a-Si:H TFT with N₂ plasma treated APCVD SiO₂ single layer is similar to those of TFTs with other gate insulators such as PECVD SiN$_x$ single layer and SiO₂/SiN$_x$ double one. With respect to electrical stability, TFT with the N₂ plasma treated APCVD SiO₂ is superior to the TFTs with other gate insulators.

In the present study, we fabricated a-Si:H TFT with the N₂ plasma treated APCVD SiO₂ single layer and the effects of N₂ plasma treatment on the SiO₂ gate insulator were investigated using the XPS and SIMS technique. The origin for the improvement of the interfacial properties between a-Si:H and APCVD SiO₂ were

29

discussed.

EXPERIMENTAL

APCVD SiO₂ layers were deposited at the temperature of 430 ℃ on the Cr patterned glass and the c-Si wafer. The thickness of SiO₂ was 3000Å. The N₂ plasma treatment was performed on the APCVD SiO₂ layers deposited on both substrates by conventional PECVD. The conditions of the N₂ plasma treatment are summarized in table 1.

Table 1. Conditions of the N₂ plasma treatment on the APCVD SiO₂ layer

Substrate Temperature (℃)	320
RF Power (W)	100
N₂ Flow Rate (sccm)	500
Pressure (Torr)	0.5
Treatment Time (min)	0 ~ 10

On the APCVD SiO₂ layers deposited on the Cr patterned glasses, a-Si:H TFTs were formed in the following sequences. After N₂ plasma treatment on the surface of the APCVD SiO₂ layer, the a-Si:H layer were deposited in the thickness of 1400Å by PECVD. n⁺-a-Si:H layers in the thickness of 500Å were successively deposited on the a-Si:H layer to make ohmic contact between the a-Si:H layer and the source/drain metal electrodes. The n⁺-a-Si:H layer between the source and the drain electrodes was etched away to open the TFT channel region after patterning the source/drain metal electrodes. For comparison of the TFT performance, the a-Si:H TFTs with a 3000Å thick SiNₓ single gate insulator and a 500/3000Å thick SiNₓ/SiO₂ double one were also fabricated. The cross-section of a-Si:H TFT studied in this work is shown in figure 1.

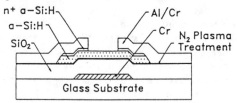

Fig. 1. Cross sectional view of a-Si:H TFT

The content and bonding configuration of the nitrogen atoms in the interface region between a-Si:H and APCVD SiO₂ was investigated by XPS. In addition, XPS measurements were performed on the N₂ plasma treated APCVD SiO₂ layer before the following deposition of the a-Si:H layer. Moreover, SIMS measurements were used to investigate the depth profile in the interface region between a-Si:H and APCVD SiO₂.

RESULTS AND DISCUSSION

Figure 2 shows the transfer(I_d-V_g)characteristics of TFTs with various gate insulators. As shown in figure 2, The threshold voltage(V_{th}), subthreshould voltage swing (S-factor), and field effect mobility(μ_{fe}) are largest in the TFT with N₂ plasma treated APCVD SiO₂ gate insulator. But the off current is smallest. Table 2 summarizes the characteristics of the TFTs shown in Fig. 2.

Table 2. Characteristics of the TFTs with various gate insulators

Gate Insulator	SiNx	SiNx/SiO2	N2 plasma treated SiO2
Field Effect Mobility (cm²/Vs)	1.04	1.1	1.27
Threshold Voltage (V)	1.7	3.3	3.5
Subthreshold Voltage Swing (V/dec.)	0.19	0.35	0.4
On/off Current Ratio	2×10^7	1×10^7	5×10^7

From table 2, it can be seen that the threshold voltage and the subthreshold voltage swing of the TFT with the SiNx gate insulator are different from those of TFT with the SiNx/SiO2 one in spite of the same a-Si:H/SiNx interface in both TFTs. Meanwhile, the subthreshold voltage swing of the TFT with N2 plasma treated APCVD SiO2 gate insulator is similar to that of the TFT with the SiN2/SiO2 one. It can be seen from table 2 that high performance a-Si:H TFT was fabricated with the APCVD SiO2 gate insulator.

Figure 3 shows the effect of N2 plasma treatment on the characteristics of the TFT with APCVD SiO2 gate insulator. The field effect mobility is nearly constant to about 1.2 cm²/Vs with the N2 plasma treatment time. The threshold voltage and the subthreshold voltage swing drop drastically with an N2 plasma treatment of 2 minutes. This result means that the interfacial property between a-Si:H and APCVD SiO2 is improved significantly by the N2 plasma treatment on the surface of the APCVD SiO2 layer. As shown in this figure, the characteristics of the TFT change little with further N2 plasma treatment time. This phenomenon will be discussed

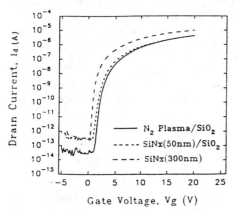

Fig. 2. Transfer characteristics of a-Si:H TFT with various gate insulators.

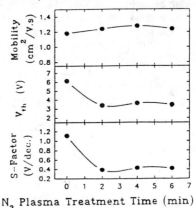

Fig. 3. Effect of N2 plasma treatment time on μ_{fe}, V_{th}, and S-factor for a-Si:H TFTs with APCVD SiO2 gate insulator.

Figure 4 shows the spectra of N1s and Si2p photoelectrons obtained from XPS measurments. These spectra were obtained on the outer surface of N2 plasma treated APCVD SiO2 layer without the sequential deposition of the a-Si:H layer. The peak positions of N1s and Si2p are 398.3, 103.9 eV, respectively. The N1s

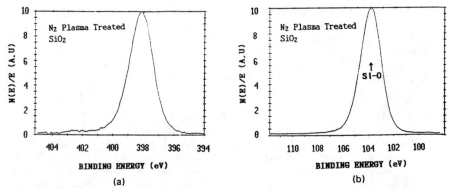

Fig. 4. Spectra of N1s(a) and Si2p(b) photoelectrons measured by XPS for
N2 plasma treated APCVD SiO2 surface.

peak due to Si-N bonds is found at 397.8 eV. The peaks due to N-H bonds appear
in the ranges of 398.5-400 eV. The peak at 103.9 eV originates from Si-O bonds.
As no Si2p peak originating from Si-N bonds, which appears near 101.8 eV, was
seen, the peak at 398.3 eV is due to N-H bonds. The content of nitrogen atoms is
about 3 at.%. Then, there are little hydrogen atoms in our APCVD SiO$_2$ film
before deposition of the a-Si:H layer. It may seem that the N-H bonds are due to
the contamination of the atmosphere. It may be thought, therefore, that most
nitrogen atoms introduced by the plasma decomposition of N$_2$ on the surface of
APCVD SiO$_2$ are not bonded to other atoms such as silicon and oxygen. Therefore,
it can be concluded that the silicon oxynitride(SiO$_x$N$_y$) layer was not formed by
the N$_2$ plasma treatment on the surface of APCVD SiO$_2$ layer.

Figure 5 shows the spectra of N1s and Si2p photoelectrons by XPS. The
sample used in this measurement is composed of three layers : N$_2$ plasma treated
APCVD SiO$_2$, a-Si:H, n$^+$-a-Si:H. These spectra were obtained in the interface region
between a-Si:H and N$_2$ plasma treated APCVD SiO$_2$. The N1s peak at 397.8 eV is
due to the Si-N bonds. In the spectra of the Si2p photoelectrons, two peaks are
found. One at 103.3 eV is due to Si-O bonds and the other at 101.8 eV due to

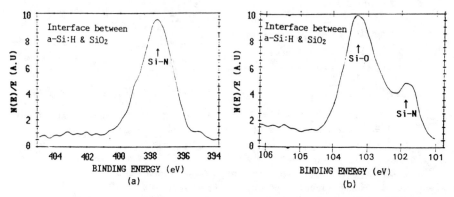

Fig. 5. Spectra of N1s(a) and Si2p(b) photoelectrons measured by XPS for
the interface region between a-Si:H and N2 plasma treated SiO2.

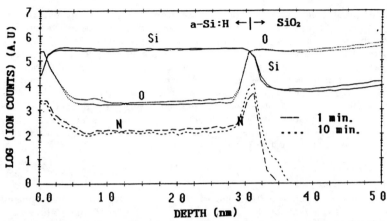

Fig. 6. SIMS depth profile of silicon, oxygen and nitrogen atoms for the interface region between a-Si:H and N2 plasma treated SiO2.

Si-N bonds, which means that the silicon oxynitride layer was formed in the interface region between a-Si:H and SiO2. From figures 4 and 5, it can be conclued that the Si-N bonds are formed by the following deposition of a-Si:H on the N2 plasma treated SiO2 layer.

It is important to know the depth profiles of silicon, oxygen, and nitrogen atoms because the interface region is roughly defined by the depth profile. The SIMS depth profile for various atoms is shown in figure 6. In this figure, nitrogen atoms are found to exist in the narrow region between a-Si:H and APCVD SiO2. Near the interface region the content of oxygen atoms decreases from the value of the bulk SiO2 to that of the bulk a-Si:H. The profile of silicon atoms, on the other hand, is found to have an opposite behavior. The content of the oxygen atoms in the bulk SiO2 is nearly constant even though the N2 plasma treatment time is increased. This result means that N2 plasma does not affect the bulk SiO2. Meanwhile, the content of nitrogen atoms increases with N2 plasma treatment time. even though the depth of nitrogen atoms does not increase much. Nitrogen atoms exist near the surface of APCVD SiO2. This is due to the low diffusion coefficient of nitrogen atoms in the SiO2. As shown in figure 6, the width of the interface region does not increase much with N2 plasma treatment time even if the nitrogen content increases. Since the performance of a-Si:H TFT is improved little with further N2 plasma treatment time as observed in figure 3. It may be concluded that the performance of a-Si:H TFT is not directly affected by the content of Si-N bonds in the interface region.

Maiti et al.[6] reported that the oxynitride layer is directly formed by the nitridation of the SiO2 layer at temperature higher than 800°C. Yasuda et.al[7] also reported the formation of the Si-N bond by N2O oxynitridation of the ultrathin SiO2 layer at the temperature of 1100°C. On the other hand, Atanassova et.al[8] presented the formation of the Si-N bond in the SiO2 layer by the NH3 soft plasma at the substrate temperature of 300°C. They confirmed their results by the FT-IR measurement. However, Si-N modes were not found in our N2 plasma treated SiO2 layer by FT-IR measurement although it was not shown in this paper. As mentioned above, it may seem that most nitrogen atoms exist ,not bonded to other atoms, on the surface of the SiO_2 layer during N_2 plasma treatment, and they combine with silicon atoms during the sequential deposition of a-Si:H on the N_2 plasma treated SiO_2 layer. During the a-Si:H deposition, Si-contained radicals, which are generated by the plasma decomposion of SiH_4 molecules, combine with the nitrogen atoms, which are not bonded to silicon and oxygen atoms on the surface of SiO_2 layer. Simultaneously, oxygen atoms exsiting near the oxide surface diffuse to the outer surface and combine with Si-contained radical, resulting in the formation of the oxynitride layer in the interface region between a-Si:H and SiO_2. This oxynitride interface layer can improve the performance of a-Si:H TFT with the APCVD SiO_2 gate insulator.

CONCLUSIONS

The effects of N_2 plasma treatment of the APCVD SiO_2 on the performance of a-Si:H TFT was investigated. The formation of the oxynitride interface layer between a-Si:H and APCVD SiO_2 was also investigated by XPS and SIMS measurments. According to our experimental results, It may be concluded that the most nitrogen atoms, which were incorporated by the exposure of SiO_2 layer to N_2 plasma, exist not bound to other atoms near the surface of SiO_2 layer and then Si-N bonds are formed during the sequential deposition of a-Si:H to make an interface layer oxyntride. This explains the high performance of the a-Si:H TFT with the N_2 plasma treated APCVD SiO_2 gate insulator.

ACKNOWLEDGEMENTS

The authors would like to thank the director Mr. C. R. Lee and Dr. W. S. Park for encouragement during this work and many colleagues at LCD Lab. GoldStar for providing samples. The authors also thank Dr. J. K. Yoon of LCD Lab. for the useful discussion.

REFERENCES

1. M. Tsumura, M. Kitajima, K. Funahata, Y. Wakui, R. Saito, Y. Mikami, Y. Nagae and T. Tsukada, Digest of 1991 Society for Information Display, Anaheim, CA. P. 215.
2. K. Fukii, Y. Tanaka, K. Honda, H. Tsutsu, H. Koseki and Hotta, Jpn. J. Appl. Phys. 31, 4574 (1992).
3. K. Fukuda and N. Ibaraki, Extended Abstracts of the 22nd International Conference on Solid State Devices and Materials (Sendai, Japan, 1990), p.1027.
4. J. H. Kim, E. Y. Oh, B. C. Ahn, D. Kim and J. Jang, Appl. Phys. Lett. 64, 1 (1994).
5. J. H. Kim, E. Y. Oh, H. S. Soh, Y. S. Park and C. H. Hong, J. Appl. Phys. to be published in 1994.
6. B. Maiti, M. Y. Hao, I. Lee and J. C. Lee, Appl. Phys. Lett. 61, 1790 (1992).
7. M. Yasuda, H. Fukuda, T. Iwabuchi and S. Ohno, Jpn. J. Appl. Phys. 30, 3597 (1991).
8. E. D. Atanassova, L. I. Popova and D. I. Kolev, Thin Solid Films, 224, 7 (1993).

This article appears in Mat. Res. Soc. Symp. Proc. Vol. 336

EFFECT OF ION DOPING TEMPERATURE ON ELECTRICAL PROPERTIES OF APCVD A-SI

KYUNG HA LEE, BYEONG YEON MOON, YOO CHAN CHUNG, SEUNG MIN LEE*, SUNG CHUL KIM, DONGGIL KIM** and JIN JANG*
*Dept. of Physics, Kyung Hee University, Dongdaemoon-ku, Seoul 130-701, Korea
**Anyang Research Lab., GoldStar, Anyang-shi, Kyungki-do, Korea

ABSTRACT

We have studied the effect of ion doping on the electrical properties for atmospheric pressure chemical vapor deposition (APCVD) amorphous silicon (a-Si) films. The room temperature conductivities after ion doping at optimum doping temperatures for n- and p-type a-Si films were found to be $> 10^{-2}$ and $>10^{-4}$ S/cm, respectively. The unintentional hydrogen incorporation into a-Si during ion doping enhances the quality of ion doped APCVD a-Si as compared to that of plasma enhanced CVD (PECVD) a-Si:H. We obtained the field effect mobility of > 1 cm^2/Vs for APCVD a-Si TFT using ion doped n$^+$-layer.

INTRODUCTION

Hydrogenated amorphous silicon (a-Si:H) is used to make thin film transistor (TFT) on glass. The advantages of a-Si:H TFTs are the low drain current at negative gate voltage and simple fabrication process, so that a-Si:H TFTs are used as switching devices in commercial active matrix liquid crystal display (AM-LCD) panels [1].

Plasma enhanced chemical vapor deposition (PECVD) is a conventional method to deposit undoped a-Si:H, n-type a-Si:H and silicon-nitride films which are used to fabricate a-Si:H TFTs [2]. However, there are drawbacks in PECVD process such as particle generation caused by the polymerization of radicals, breakdown of gate insulator film by the impinging ions during the deposition, and low throught-put of making TFT arrays due to the low deposition rate of a-Si:H [3]. Plasma free CVD process of making amorphous silicon (a-Si) TFT was developed by Matsumura's group [4]. The performance of CVD a-Si TFT is essentially the same as that of PECVD a-Si TFT. In the previous work we deposited a-Si by atmospheric pressure chemical vapor deposition (APCVD) [5]. The deposition rate of a-Si can be increased by using APCVD because it increases with the partial gas pressure of used disilane or monosilane, so that the deposition rate at 1 atm is 760 times that of low pressure CVD a-Si deposited at 1 Torr. Post hydrogenation is needed to saturate the dangling bonds in CVD a-Si.

Ion doping process can be used in fabricating a-Si:H TFTs because it gives some merits such as simple process of making doped layer and no need of n$^+$ deposition chamber [6]. Ion doping system consists of ion generating and ion acceleration parts and has no mass separation system. In the present work we studied the electrical properties of ion doped APCVD a-Si films.

ION DOPING OF APCVD A-SI

Amorphous silicon on Corning 7059 glass was deposited in a cold wall type CVD reactor. Disilane diluted in He was introduced into the reactor in

35

which the substrate holder was heated by tungsten halogen lamps located at the outside of the quartz reaction tube. The substrate temperature and the flow rate of Si₂H₆/He were fixed at 430℃ and 5 sccm, respectively. The hydrogen plasma was exposed on the surface of the deposited film at the substrate temperature of 250℃.

The ion shower system used in the present work consists of discharging tube, the diameter of which is 25 cm, and of ion acceleration tube, in which there are two mesh grids. One is grounded and the other is biased at acceleration potential. The grounded electrode is needed to reduce the secondary ions and thus to make uniformly doped a-Si [7]. The sample temperature was fixed during ion doping.

RESULTS AND DISCUSSION

Figure 1 shows the room temperature conductivity of PECVD a-Si:H vs ion dose. The acceleration voltage and doping temperature were fixed at 6 kV and 280℃, respectively. The conductivity reaches a maximum value of 4 x 10^{-4}S/cm at the ion dose of 5.4 x 10^{15}cm^{-2}. The ion damage on the surface of a-Si:H increases with ion dose, so that the conductivity decreases by increasing ion dose above 5.4 x 10^{15}cm^{-2}.

Figure 2 shows the room temperature conductivity of PECVD a-Si:H vs ion acceleration voltage. The conductivity reaches a maximum at 6 kV. The depth of ion doped impurities and the ion damage increase with the acceleration voltage, resulting in an optimum acceleration voltage of 6 kV.

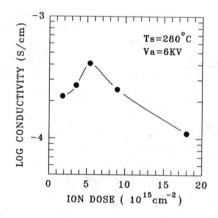

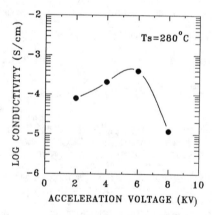

Fig.1 Room temperature conductivity of ion doped n-type a-Si:H plotted against ion dose. The substrate temperature and acceleration voltage were fixed at 280℃ and 6 kV, respectively.

Fig. 2 Room temperature conductivity of ion doped n-type a-Si:H plotted against acceleration voltage. The doping temperature and ion dose were fixed at 280℃ and 5.4 x 10^{15} cm^{-2}, respectively.

Figure 3 shows the room temperature conductivity and conductivity activation energy of PECVD a-Si:H plotted against the ion doping temperature. The acceleration voltage and the ion dose were fixed at 6 kV and 5.4×10^{15} cm^{-2}, respectively. The maximum conductivity of 10^{-3} S/cm and thus miminum activation energy of 0.28 eV was obtained at a doping temperature of 330°C. With increasing ion doping temperature, the annealing of ion damage will be enhanced, however dehydrogenation will be accelerated. The out-diffusion of hydrogen atoms bonded to Si atoms degrades the quality of a-Si:H. This is related with the fact that the optimum substrate temperature to produce PECVD a-Si:H is around 250°C [7].

The room temperature conductivity and conductivity activation energy of phosphorus doped a-Si:H deposited with 1 volume % phosphine in silane are around 10^{-2} S/cm and 0.2 eV, respectively. On the other hand, the maximum conductivity and minimum activation energy obtained for PECVD a-Si:H were 10^{-3} S/cm and 0.28 eV, respectively. This difference appears to be arisen by both ion damage and unintentional hydrogen incorporation during ion doping. The hydrogen atoms will be incorporated in the sample because the ions such as $P_2H_x^+$, PH_x^+, H_3^+, H_2^+, and H^+ are accelerated toward the sample holder during ion doping [8]. The additional incorporation of hydrogen into the PECVD sample will degrade the quality of a-Si:H. Too much hydrogen in a-Si:H can induce the gap states and neutralize the substitutional boron and phosphorus atoms.

Amorphous silicon produced by CVD contains small amount of hydrogen (lower than 5 at.% when a-Si is prepared from disilane) compared to that of PECVD a-Si:H since the deposition temperature is higher than 400°C. Therefore, post hydrogenation is needed to improve the quality of CVD a-Si. The hydrogen content in APCVD a-Si is essentially the same as that of CVD a-Si because of similar deposition temperature.

Figure 4 shows the room temperature conductivity for APCVD a-Si plotted

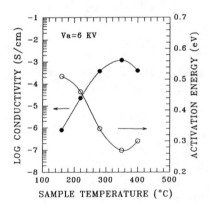

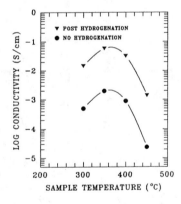

Fig. 3 Room temperature conductivity and conductivity activation energy of ion doped a-Si:H plotted against ion doping temperature. The ion dose and acceleration voltage were fixed at 5.4×10^{15} cm^{-2} and 6kV, respectively.

Fig. 4 Room temperature conductivity of ion doped APCVD a-Si plotted against ion doping temperature. The ion dose and acceleration voltage were fixed at 5.4×10^{15} cm^{-2} and 6kV, respectively.

against doping temperature. The acceleration voltage and the ion dose were fixed at 6 kV and 5.4×10^{15} cm^{-2}, respectively. Contrary to PECVD a-Si:H, the maximum conductivity and thus minimum activation energy occurs at 350°C, and the conductivity reaches above 10^{-2}S/cm after hydrogenation for 30 minutes at 250°C. Post hydrogenation enhances the conductivity by one order of magnitude. The unintentional hydrogen incorporation during ion doping can enhance the quality of CVD a-Si, however, degrades the quality of PECVD a-Si:H.

Figure 5 shows the room temperature conductivity and conductivity activation energy for ion doped p-type APCVD a-Si films plotted against ion doping temperature. The acceleration voltage and ion dose were fixed at 6 kV and 5.4×10^{15}cm^{-2}, respectively. The maximum conductivity and minimum conductivity activation energy are 1.5×10^{-4} S/cm and 0.3 eV, respectively. These values are similar to those for p-type PECVD a-Si:H prepared by the decomposition of 1 volume % diborane diluted in silane [9]. It should be noted that the conductivity decreases rapidly with increasing doping temperature above 300°C. The hydrogen in the surface region appears to be out-diffused during heating the sample before and after ion doping. The heating time was fixed at 1h in this experiment. The ion damage by boron ions appears to be small compared to that by phosphorus ions because of lighter atomic weight. The conductivity of p-type ion doped a-Si film increases with ion dose, i.e., ion doping time. Note that the conductivity of n-type ion doped a-Si decreases when the ion dose is higher than 5.4×10^{15} cm^{-2}.

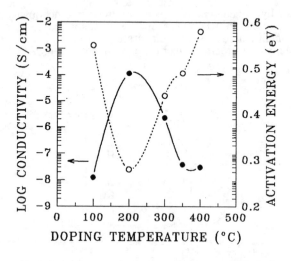

Fig. 5 Room temperature conductivity and conductivity activation energy for ion doped p-type APCVD a-Si, plotted against ion doping temperature. Ion dose and acceleration voltage were fixed at 5.4×10^{15} cm^{-2} and 6kV, respectively.

Figure 6 shows a cross sectional view of the APCVD a-Si TFT. 60 nm thick APCVD a-Si and 200 nm thick APCVD SiO$_2$ were deposited on 100 nm thick Cr gate pattern on Corning 7059 glass. The photoresistor film coated on a-Si was patterned using self-align technique, in which the UV is exposed from the back (Cr) side. And phosphorus ions were irradiated on the front surface of the sample. Al film was evaporated on the top surface and patterned to use as source/drain electrodes. Then, the sample was hydrogenated at 250℃ for 30 minutes. The ratio of the width (W) and length (L) of a TFT was 60 μm / 10 μm.

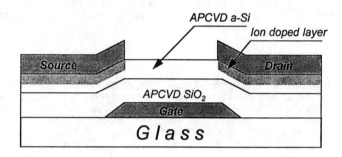

Fig. 6 Cross sectional view of APCVD a-Si TFT using ion doped n$^+$ a-Si and APCVD SiO$_2$.

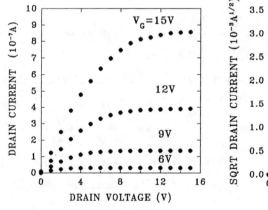

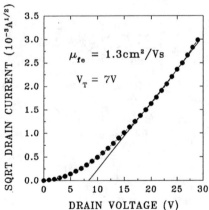

Fig. 7 Output characteristics of APCVD a-Si TFT using ion doped n$^+$ layer.

Fig. 8 I_D-V_D characteristics for APCVD a-Si TFT. The drain and gate electrodes are tied.

Figure 7 shows the output characteristics of APCVD a-Si TFT using ion doped n^+ layer. The current crowding effect caused by the resistance of source/drain region does not appear.

Figure 8 shows the drain current (I_D) - drain voltage (V_D) characteristics of APCVD a-Si TFT, measured with drain and gate electrodes tied together. The field effect mobility and threshold voltage are 1.3 cm^2/Vs and 7.0V, respectively. The ion doped n^+ layer seems to be suitable as ohmic contact layer in CVD a-Si TFT.

We found that the conductivity of ion doped APCVD a-Si can be higher than that of PECVD a-Si, which is due to the smaller hydrogen content in CVD a-Si compared to that of PECVD a-Si:H. By using APCVD SiO_2 and APCVD a-Si, we have fabricated a-Si TFTs with field effect mobility of higher than 1 cm^2/Vs. These a-Si TFTs can be used in low cost production of a-Si arrays on glass substrates.

SUMMARY

We found that the optimum doping temperatures for n-type and p-type APCVD a-Si films are 350°C and 200°C, respectively. We obtained the room temperature conductivities of $>10^{-2}$ and $>10^{-4}$ S/cm for n-type and p-type a-Si, respectively. The unintentional hydrogen incorporation in a-Si during ion doping appears to improve the quality of APCVD a-Si. We obtained the field effect mobility of > 1.0 cm^2/Vs for APCVD a-Si TFT using ion doped n^+-layer.

ACKNOWLEDGEMENT

This work was supported by the Korea Science and Engeering Foundation through Semiconductor Physics Research Center

REFERENCES

1. Y. Oana, J. Non-Cryst. Solids 115, 27 (1989).
2. M.V.C. Stroomer, M.J. Powell, B.C. Easron and J.A. Chapman, Electron. Lett. 118, 858 (1982).
3. M. Matsumura and O. Sugiura, Proc. Inter. Conf. Solid State Devices and Materials (Tsukuba, Japan, 1992), p. 46.
4. P.A. Breddels, H. Kanoh, O. Sugiura and M. Matsumura, Jpn. J. Appl. Phys. 30, 233 (1991).
5. B.C. Ahn, J.H. Kim, D. Kim, B.Y. Moon, K.N. Kim, C.W. Lee and J. Jang, Mat. Res. Soc. Symp. Proc. 297, 901 (1993).
6. A. Yoshida, M. Kitagawa, K. Setsune and T. Hirao, Jpn. J. Appl. Phys. 27, L1355 (1988).
7. H. Fritzsche, Solar Energy Mater. 3, 447 (1980).
8. A. Yoshida, M. Nukayama, Y. Andoh, M. Kitagawa and T. Hirao, Jpn. J. Appl. Phys. 30, L67 (1991).
9. D.H. Carlson, R.W. Smith, C.W. Magee and P.Z. Zanzucchi, Phil. Mag. B45, 51 (1982).

This article appears in Mat. Res. Soc. Symp. Proc. Vol. 336

40

CONSIDERATIONS FOR LARGE AREA FABRICATION OF INTEGRATED a-SI AND POLY-Si TFTs

P. Mei, G. B. Anderson, J. B. Boyce, D. K. Fork, M. Hack, R. I. Johnson, R. A. Lujan, S. E. Ready
Xerox Palo Alto Research Center, 3333 Coyote Hill Road, Palo Alto, CA 94304

ABSTRACT

The combination of a-Si low leakage pixel TFTs with poly-Si TFTs in peripheral circuits provides an excellent method for reducing the number of external connections to large-area imaging arrays and displays. To integrate the fabrication of the peripheral poly-Si TFTs with the a-Si pixel TFTs, we have developed a three-step laser process which enables selective crystallization of PECVD a-Si:H. X-ray diffraction and transmission electron microscopy show that the polycrystalline grains formed with this three-step process are similar to those crystallized by a conventional one step laser crystallization of unhydrogenated amorphous silicon. The grain size increases with increasing laser energy density up to a peak value of a few microns. The grain size decreases with further increases in laser energy density. The transistor field effect mobility is correlated with the grain size, increasing gradually with laser energy density until reaching its maximum value. Thereafter, the transistors suffer from leakage through the gate insulators. A dual dielectric gate insulator has been developed for these bottom-gate thin film transistors to provide the correct threshold voltages for both a-Si and poly-Si TFTs.

Introduction

The integration of a-Si:H large area electronics with poly-Si peripheral circuits is a promising approach for reducing the number of external connections and thereby lowering the cost of two-dimensional imagers and flat panel displays [1-4]. Since the deposition of poly-Si requires much higher temperatures compared to a-Si deposition, selective crystallization with a laser process is pursued. However, the difficulties in making both high performance a-Si:H and poly-Si TFTs on the same substrate are the following. High quality a-Si TFTs require a large amount of atomic hydrogen (H), typically 7-10 atomic %, to passivate Si dangling bonds. Whereas H passivation is essential to the electrical performance of a-Si devices, it causes film ablation during laser crystallization due to rapid H out-diffusion. In order to prevent this explosive H evolution, a 450 °C furnace anneal is normally performed for several hours to remove most of the H from the PECVD a-Si:H films prior to laser crystallization. This anneal, however, degrades the quality of a-Si TFTs. There have been several reports [1-4] on making hybrid a-Si and poly-Si TFTs with a laser process. Sera, et al., employed a top-gate device structure [1]. In this case, a low laser energy density was employed which resulted in poly-Si with large grains near the surface layer (< 50 nm) and a remaining layer with smaller grains. However, we prefer bottom-gate TFT as the pixel TFT is not compromised from its optimum structure and performance. Although hybrid, bottom-gate TFTs have been reported [2,3], the device performance of a-Si and poly-Si TFTs were not optimum. Additional difficulties arise from different requirements of gate dielectrics for a-Si and poly-Si TFTs. For large-area electronic applications, small and positive threshold voltages are usually required for both a-Si pixel switches and poly-Si peripheral TFTs. However, a-Si TFTs with an SiO_2 gate insulator have large threshold voltages, and poly-Si TFTs with SiN gate insulator have negative threshold voltages.

Mat. Res. Soc. Symp. Proc. Vol. 345. ©1994 Materials Research Society

Previously [4], we described a three step laser process with incremental increases in laser energy density to selectively remove H and crystallize PECVD a-Si:H. To obtain a small, positive threshold voltage for both a-Si and poly-Si TFTs, we have used a dual dielectric gate insulator to control the threshold voltages. In this paper, we describe the material properties and device characteristics of the three-step laser process and the dual dielectric gate insulator.

Experimental Description

In this work, the laser crystallization process was carried out with a XMR 5100 excimer laser operating at 308 nm with a 50 ns pulse duration. The beam was homogenized and focussed down to a beam spot size of about 4x20 mm. The laser crystallization was performed in a vacuum environment of 10^{-6} torr. The laser process consisted of three steps. For the first step, an irradiation at an energy density slightly above the surface melting threshold was applied. The melt was partially through the layer, which resulted in a partial H out-diffusion and microcrystalline grains distributed nonuniformly [4]. For the second step, the laser energy density was near the melt-through threshold. This laser irradiation further removed H and melted through the entire Si film. Small, columnar crystalline grains (< 20 nm) were formed. The crystallization was completed with the the third laser irradiation at a higher energy density, producing large columnar grains with average lateral grain size larger than 100 nm. The details of the laser process are described in reference 4. Transmission electron microscopy (TEM), x-ray diffraction measurement (XRD) and atomic force microscopy (AFM) were employed to characterize the films. N-channel, bottom-gate TFTs were fabricated on 4-inch glass or quartz substrates. The details of the device fabrication are described in reference 5.

Results from the Three-Step Laser Process

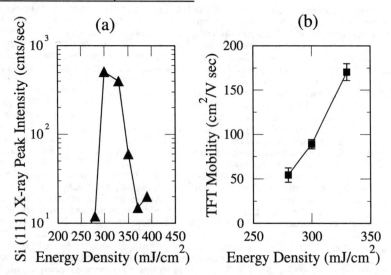

Figure 1. (a) Si (111) x-ray peak intensity as a function of the laser energy density for the final step in the three-step laser process. (b) n-channel TFT mobility as a function of the laser energy density.

The crystallinity of the Si films processed with the three-step laser dehydrogenation and crystallization process depends predominantly on the laser energy density in the final step, although the laser energy densities for the first and the second step are important to establish the proper material properties for the final processing step. Figure 1 (a) shows the Si (111) x-ray peak intensity as a function of the laser energy density for the final step of the three-step laser dehydrogenation and crystallization process. The width and intensity of the Si (111) x-ray peak relate to the average grain size, as it can be seen from TEM planar view (fig. 2). It has been found that the grain size increases gradually with increasing laser energy density of the final laser processing step until it reaches about 300 mJ/cm². The planar view TEM image for a sample irradiated at 280 mJ/cm² (fig. 3) shows an average grain size of about 100 nm. Near 300 mJ/cm², the intensity of the Si (111) x-ray peak increases rapidly and the grain size reaches a peak value which is on the order of a few µm. The x-ray intensity then decreases with further increases in laser energy density, which correlates with the smaller grain sizes observed from TEM images. Samples with various structures and substrate temperatures have been examined. We observed, in general, that the position and the width of the peak in the x-ray intensity depends on the film thickness, the composition of the dielectric, and the laser process substrate temperature and the laser pulse duration. This behavior is similar to what has been observed in conventional laser crystallization of Si films made by low pressure chemical vapor deposition [6].

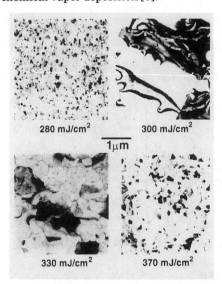

PECVD 400 mJ/cm²

Figure 2. Planar view TEM images from samples crystallized by the three-step laser process. The laser energy densities for the final step were 280, 300, 330, and 370 mJ/cm².

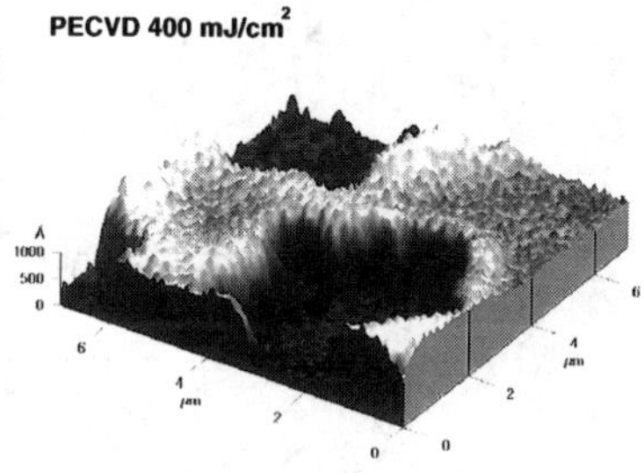

Figure 3. AFM three-dimentional image from a sample crystalized with the laser energy densities of 400 mJ/cm².

The mechanism for the increase and decrease of grain size in response to the laser energy density is not well understood. Different models have been proposed [7,8].

Further investigation is needed to understand the various phenomena related to this behavior.

Fig. 1 (b) plots the TFT field effect mobility versus laser energy density in the final processing step. The mobility increases with increasing laser energy density. Near 330 mJ/cm^2, corresponding to the peak region in x-ray intensity, the mobility is near 200 cm^2/V.sec. Beyond 330 mJ/cm^2, most devices suffer from leakage between the gate and the drain, indicateing damage to the gate insulator.

The mechanism of the leakage through the gate insulator is not fully understood. At higher laser energies (beyond the peak position in the x-ray intensity), small pin holes in the Si were observed. Fig. 3 shows a three-dimentional AFM image from a sample crystallized at 400 mJ/cm^2. Craters of a few microns wide were revealed. The depths of these caters are comparable to the Si film thickness. The bottom of the craters are rough but no cracks were observed with a AFM resolution of 30 nm. For samples crystallized at an energy near the x-ray maximum intensity, pin holes were rarely observed by AFM. We speculate that the leakage may be caused by impurity injection into the gate insulator.

Threshold Voltage with a Dual Dielectric Gate Insulator

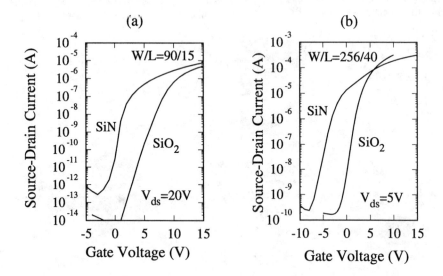

Figure 4. Transfer characteristics of the poly-Si TFT (a) and a-Si TFT (b) with SiN or SiO$_2$ as the gate insulator

Fig. 4 shows transfer characteristics for a-Si TFTs (a) and poly-Si TFTs (b) with SiN or SiO$_2$ as gate insulators. It is known that silicon nitride is an excellent dielectric gate insulator for n-channel a-Si TFTs, because it contains positive fixed charges which results in a lower defect density in the upper half of the Si bandgap [9]. However, the nitride causes negative threshold voltages on the poly-Si TFTs. While silicon oxide is suitable for poly-Si TFTs, it results in poor subthreshold slopes and large threshold voltages on a-Si TFTs because of its negative fixed charge. The poor subthreshold slope arises from a high density of defect states, created through the equilibration process, in the upper half of the a-Si bandgap.

In order to have small positive threshold voltages for both a-Si and poly-Si TFTs, while keeping the fabrication process simple, we have proposed a dual dielectric gate insulator. Figure 5 shows simulation results of the transfer characteristics for poly-Si TFTs with various film thicknesses of nitride and oxide, keeping the total dielectric film thickness at 100 nm. In this simulation we have introduced uniform densities of fixed charge into each layer of the two layer gate dielectric. We have assumed that the fixed charge density in nitride and oxide are $+4 \times 10^{17}$ and -1×10^{17} charges/cm^{-3} respectively. Our two-dimensional device simulator is based on one specifically developed for modeling amorphous silicon TFTs [10, 11], whereby the defects and grain boundaries in the poly-Si are treated as a spatially uniform density of localized states in the band gap [12]. We use Shockley-Read-Hall kinetics to account for both electron and hole capture and emission processes at these localized states or traps. To achieve convergence and ensure stability, the continuous distribution of localized states in the bandgap are modeled as a series of discrete levels. Smooth results have been obtained by placing these traps 50 meV apart, and therefore we have 22 trap levels in the bandgap of 1.12eV. Our effective density of states spectrum for poly-Si has been obtained by fitting the model to both the low drain bias transfer data as well as the activation energy of the channel conductance as a function of gate bias. This set of calculations demonstrates that the threshold voltage can be controlled by adjusting the thickness of the oxide and nitride films.

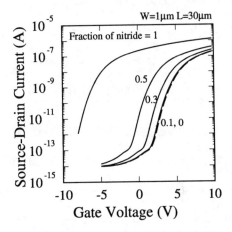

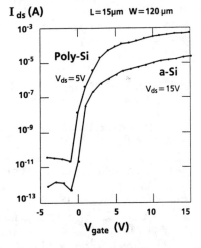

Figure 5. Simulated transfer characteristics of poly-Si TFTs with dual dielectric of nitride and oxide. The total thickness is 100 nm. The fractions of the nitride are 1, 0.5, 0.3, 0.1 and 0, and the threshold voltages are -6.4, 1.3, 3.0, 4.1, and 4.1 volts respectively.

Figure 6. Transfer characteristics of the poly-Si TFT and a-Si TFT fabricated with the three-step laser dehydrogenation and crystallization process on the same Corning 7059 glass substrate. The gate insulator consists of a dual dielectric of nitride and oxide with the oxide adjacent to the Si channel.

Hybrid Devices

Figure 6 shows the transfer characteristics for both a-Si and poly-Si TFTs fabricated on the same glass substrate. The width and length of the devices are 120 and 15 µm respectively. The gate insulator consists of a dual oxide and nitride dielectric. The threshold voltage for both devices is about 0.5 volts. The minimum leakage current for poly-Si and a-Si TFTs are 200 and 3 fA/µm under a drain bias of 5 and 15 volts respectively, which are suitable for pixel switches. The poly-Si TFT has a mobility of 21 cm^2/V·sec, and can be used in peripheral driver circuits.

We wish to thank W. B. Jackson, D. L. Smith, A. Chiang, I. W. Wu, N. Nickel of Xerox PARC and S. Chen of XMR, Inc., for valuable comments and discussions. This work was partially supported by ARPA Contract no. F33615-92-C-5811.

References

1. K. Sera, F. Okumura, H. Uchida, S. Itoh, S. Kaneko, and K. Hotta, IEEE Trans. Electron Devices, 36, 2868, (1989).

2. K. Shimizu, O. Sugiura, and M. Matsumura, Japn. J. Appl. Phys., 29, L1775, (1990).

3. T. Tanaka, H. Asuma, K. Ogawa, Y. Shinagawa, and N. Konishi, IEEE 1993 International Electron Devices Meeting Technical Digest, p389, (1993).

4. P. Mei, J. B. Boyce, M. Hack, R. Lujan, R. I. Johnson, G. B. Anderson, D. K. Fork, and S. E. Ready, Appl. Phys. Lett., 64, 1132, (1994).

5. P. Mei, J. B. Boyce, M. Hack, R. Lujan, S. E. Ready, International Semiconductor Device Research Symposium Proceedings, Vol. 1, 47, (1993).

6. R. I. Johnson, G. B. Anderson, J. B. Boyce, D. K. Fork, P. Mei, S. E. Ready, and S. Chen, Amorphous Silicon Technology-1993, Mat Res. Soc. Symp. Proc. Vol. 297, 533, (1993).

7. James S. Im and H. J. Kim, and Michael O. Thompson, Appl. Phys. Lett., 63, 1969, (1993).

8. J. B. Boyce, G. B. Anderson, D. K. Fork, R. I. Johnson, P. Mei, and S. E. Ready, to be published in Mat Res Symp Proc, (1994).

9. M. J. Powell, S. C. Deane, I. D. French, J. R. Hughes, and W. I. Milne, Philosophical Magazine B 63, No. 1, 325, (1991).

10. M. Hack and J. Shaw, "Numerical simulations of amorphous silicon thin-film transistors", Journal of Applied Physics, vol 68, No. 10 , pp. 5337-5342 (1990).

11. M. Hack and J.G. Shaw, "Transient simulations of amorphous silicon devices", Proceedings of the Materials Research Society Symposium, vol 219, pp. 315-320 (1991).

12. M. Hack, J.G. Shaw, P.G. LeComber and M. Willums, "Numerical simulations of amorphous and polycrystalline silicon thin-film transistors", Japanese Journal of Applied Physics, vol.29, No. 12, pp. L2360-2362 (1990).

This article appears in Mat. Res. Soc. Symp. Proc. Vol. 336

46

PROGRESS IN LARGE AREA SELECTIVE SILICON DEPOSITION for TFT/LCD APPLICATIONS

Jun H. Souk and Gregory N. Parsons*
IBM Research Division,
T.J.Watson Research Center,Yorktown Heights, NY 10598
*Department of Chemical Engineering,
North Carolina State University, Raleigh, NC 27695-7905

We have previously demonstrated selective area deposition of n+ microcrystalline silicon at 250°C using time modulated silane flow into a hydrogen plasma, and applied the technique to form high performance top-gate amorphous silicon TFT's with two mask sets. In this paper, we discuss issues related to process scale-up, including the effect of deposition rate on selectivity loss and non-uniformity. Uniformity can be achieved with higher growth rates by expanding the window for selectivity, and using conditions well within the process limits. We show that lower pressure and higher rf power can enlarge the window by enhancing the hydrogen-mediated silicon etching.

INTRODUCTION

Selective area silicon growth has been studied for a variety of applications for high density crystalline silicon devices[1-4]. Selective deposition could also be a powerful tool for the fabrication of advanced thin film transistor (TFT) devices[5,6] For instance, selective deposition of n-type doped microcrystalline silicon on metal allows a pre-patterned contact geometry to be used to form the critical n+ doped/intrinsic a-Si contacts in top-gate TFT's, without post-deposition patterning of the doped silicon[6]. Eliminating the need for a wet n+ etch step reduced the number of process steps, and can reduce the contamination at the n+/a-Si interface. In spite of the benefits, selective techniques are not used in manufacturing because of challenging reliability and control issues. Small variations in surface preparation or chamber conditioning, or statistical fluctuations in process variables, can lead to unexpected loss of selectivity, and ruined devices.

We are interested in a relatively new selective area silicon deposition technique compatible with low temperature processing of amorphous silicon thin film transistors. The process utilizes time modulated silane flow into a continuous hydrogen plasma, and takes advantage of substrate dependent structure of the initial monolayers of deposition. This approach differs from other selective area deposition processes, because the chemical difference in the depositing and non-depositing surfaces is refreshed in each modulation cycle. This eliminates the tenuous balance between simultaneous material deposition and removal that characterizes other selective processes, and removes a critical channel for selectivity loss. In a continuous process, the stability of nuclei, and the probability of film growth can be described statistically. There is always a finite probability for stable nuclei formation on any surface. Once a stray nucleus forms, the chemical deposition process cannot distinguish between unwanted nuclei and preferred deposition areas, leading to continued growth on the stray nuclei. Controlling stray nucleation usually involves directing the balance toward

47

increased etching, which commonly leads to slow rates and undesirable etching of exposed surfaces.

The modulated process takes advantage of the ability of hydrogen to sense differences in the bonding geometry in nuclei formed on various substrates. Strong oxidants such as fluorine and chlorine, used in most selective processes, are not required. Thin deposited silicon layers are completely removed by atomic hydrogen from the non-receptive surfaces without removing substrate material. This ability to control the structure of silicon in a layer-by-layer procedure, may give this process sufficient reliability for manufacturing. In this paper, we present an outline of critical issues we have discovered in scaling the selective process for large area fabrication. We show that some issues in uniformity and geometry dependence can be overcome by using low growth rates, and we discuss approaches to increase the growth rate while maintaining process uniformity.

ISSUES IN SCALE-UP OF SELECTIVE DEPOSITION

We have studied selective deposition of microcrystalline silicon for forming n+ silicon contact layers in thin-film transistors using a conventional parallel-plate plasma enhanced chemical vapor deposition (PECVD) configuration. Scanning electron micrographs showing selective deposition of microcrystalline silicon are shown in Figures 1 and 2. The process involves depositing thin (<100Å) silicon layers using hydrogen diluted silane, then removing the silane to expose the layers to plasma excited hydrogen. Typically, temperature is near 250°C, pressure is 1.0 Torr, the process gases (hydrogen and silane) flow at 100 and 5 sccm, respectively, and the rf power density is 100 mW/cm^2. Typical gas modulation conditions are 10 seconds of silane and hydrogen into the chamber, followed by 50 seconds of pure hydrogen. Continuing for 40 cycles results in 800-1000Å of microcrystalline silicon in receptive areas of the substrate (silicon, metal, etc.) and no growth on non-receptive areas (typically silicon dioxide or silicon nitride). During the deposition period of the cycle, growth rates can be more than 100Å/min, resulting in a net deposition rates near 25Å/min. Contact layers for some TFT's can be as thin as 100 to 200Å, and can be completed in a 10 minute deposition. However, thicker layers and shorter deposition cycles are preferred, and a factor of 10 increase in growth rate would be a significant improvement.

The following is a summary of issues we have encountered in selective deposition that are important for process implementation and scale-up.

- Low selective deposition rate. Increasing the growth rate tends to push the process toward the edge of the selectivity window. For instance, reducing the hydrogen exposure time will enhance the net growth rate, but if taken too far, will result in loss of selectivity. Net deposition rates near 25Å/min are typical for well controlled processing. We have achieved rates above 100Å/min, but values near 500Å/min are more desirable.

- Substrate loading. The conditions required to achieve selectivity depends on the fraction of substrate area that is receptive to deposition. Different device geometries and applications require individually defined and tuned process conditions.

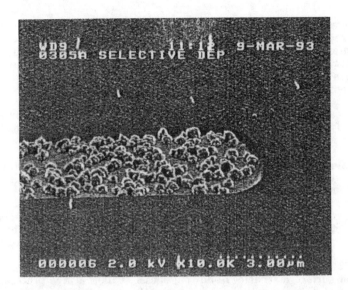

Figure 1. Scanning electron micrograph of selective deposition of microcrystalline silicon on microcrystalline silicon exposed through a silicon dioxide dielectric layer. Extended hydrogen exposure results in large dispersed crystallites.

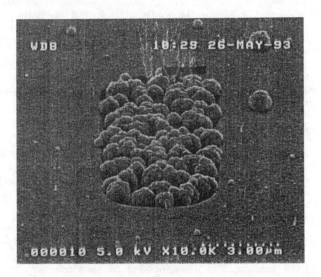

Figure 2. SEM showing complete filling of 5x10 micron via cut in silicon dioxide. Stray nuclei may result from insufficient cleaning of the surface before processing, or may be silicon crystallites broken off the main cluster after deposition.

- Proximity selective loss, and feature edge effects. Non-selective deposition can occur in regions between closely spaced receptive areas, or near the edges of more isolated receptive areas. This is believed to be related to non-homogeneous distributions of etch products in the gas phase near feature boundaries that result in re-deposition. These are more apparent working near the edge of the selectivity window.

- Feature-scale uniformity: The thickness of the deposited microcrystalline silicon may not be uniform across the receptive area, even when complete selectivity is achieved.

- Wafer-scale uniformity: The net film thickness may not be uniform across the substrate, even with complete selectivity. This is a distinct issue, typically independent of feature scale uniformity.

- Chamber conditioning requirements. The recent history of the chamber, and condition of the chamber walls can significantly affect selectivity. This can be related to surface loading (is the chamber wall a receptive or non-receptive surface?)

- Control of surface morphology and roughness. This selective process results in rough surface morphology shown in the micrographs. For contact applications in TFT's, rough surfaces may be preferred. However, the ability to modify the morphology while maintaining selectivity would give additional freedom in applications.

Non-uniformity and selectivity loss appear more often with higher growth rates near the edge of the selectivity window. A significant part of our effort, therefore, has focused on expanding the process window to achieve uniform selectivity (away from the selective edge) at reasonable deposition rates. The process window can be expanded by (1) increasing the rate of silicon removal (etching) during the non-depositing cycle period; and/or (2) coupling an increase in the deposition rate during the depositing period with an increase in the modulation frequency. In the following section, we examine the effect of rf power and gas pressure on deposition and etching rates.

EFFECT OF CONDITIONS ON PROCESS WINDOW

The effect of process conditions on film growth rates typically depends on reaction system, chamber design, etc. We focus on trends in process conditions that can make the process more viable, and/or give insight into selectivity mechanisms. For instance, increasing the rf power density can increase growth rate, and lead to an expanded process window. A non-zero intercept in thickness versus time data leads us to a model including repetitive deposition/etching processes.

Pressure can also effect growth and etch rates, and selectivity. Figure 3 shows deposition rate and film etch rate measured versus pressure. For the etch rate measurements, the thickness of pre-deposited blanket microcrystalline silicon was measured before and after exposure to the hydrogen plasma. The high etch rate at low pressures is likely due to the reduced collision frequency and recombination of hydrogen atoms in the gas phase. The growth rate data in the

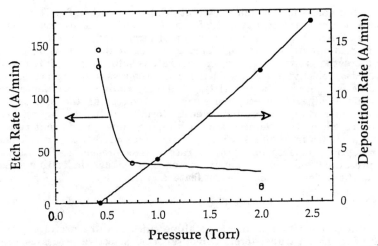

Figure 3. Effect of pressure on selective deposition rate and microcrystalline etch rate in a hydrogen plasma.

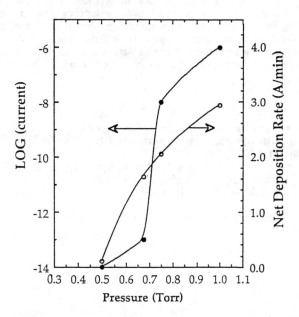

Figure 4. Current between adjacent receptive areas, and growth rate versus pressure. The high current results from loss of selectivity in the regions between contacts.

same figure that shows no net film growth at pressure less than 0.4 Torr. This is consistent with our observation that the fraction of amorphous structure, relative to microcrystalline, is increased at lower pressures, and, the etching of the deposited film is enhanced with high amorphous content. Increasing pressure lead to an increased growth rate, and the etch rate is sufficiently high to maintain selectivity. Also, selectivity is maintained because the crystallinity fraction is low, and etch rate is high, for the initial thin microcrystalline layers deposited on silicon dioxide or other non-receptive surfaces. Decreasing the pressure, and increasing the etch rate, we find improved uniformity, reduced stray nucleation around feature edges, and reduced silicon bridging between adjacent receptive areas. This is shown in Figure 4, where we have measured the current between adjacent receptive surfaces and growth rate versus pressure. We find that increased pressure results in a dramatic increase in leakage, indicating a loss of selectivity in the region between adjacent features.

CONCLUSIONS

Selective area deposition of microcrystalline silicon can be useful to simplify processing of thin film transistors. Other reported selective processes rely on balancing simultaneous deposition and removal, which makes them difficult to control in a production environment. The time modulated process separates the chemistry of deposition and removal, allowing each to be modified independently, which makes it more viable for manufacturing. In addition, this selective process is not limited to a critical thickness, nor is it limited to low growth rates. However, a number of issues particular to selective deposition, including substrate loading, chamber conditioning, and proximity effects, need further investigation. We find these issues appear less using low deposition rates, with conditions away from the boundary of the selective process window. We find that reduced pressures can improve uniformity by enhancing the hydrogen atom etching of silicon.

REFERENCES

[1] J.O.Borland, C.I.Drowley, Solid State Technology 30 (8), 141 (1987).
[2] B.J.Ginsberg, J.Burghartz, G.B.Bronner, and S.R.Mader, IBM J.Res.Develop. 34, 816 (1990).
[3] T.O.Sedgewick, M.Berkenbilt, and T.S.Kuan, Appl.Phys.Lett. 54, 2689 (1989).
[4] T.R.Yew and R.Reif, J.Appl.Phys. 65, 2500 (1989).
[5] M.Hiramatsu, A.Ishida, T.Kamimura, Y.Kawakyu Jpn.J.Appl.Phys., 6B, 3106 (1993).
[6] G.N.Parsons, Electron Device Lett. 13, 80 (1992).

This article appears in Mat. Res. Soc. Symp. Proc. Vol. 336

A LOW TEMPERATURE PLASMA-ASSISTED DEPOSITION PROCESS FOR MICROCRYSTALLINE THIN FILM TRANSISTORS, TFTS

S.S. HE and G. LUCOVSKY
Department of Physics, Materials Science and Engineering, and Electrical and Computer
Engineering, North Carolina State University, Raleigh, NC 27695-8202

ABSTRACT

The drive-current of low-temperature (~300°C) deposited TFTs has been increased by replacing the a-Si:H channel, and source and drain materials with μc-Si. Lightly B_2H_6 doped, near-intrinsic μc-Si has been used as the channel layer of the TFTs, and n^+ μc-Si was used for the source and drain contacts. The compensation of intrinsic defects in the undoped μc-Si by boron doping increases the dark conductivity activation energy from ~0.35 eV to 0.8 eV. TFTs were fabricated in a bottom gate structure, and required an H_2 plasma treatment to produce devices with effective channel mobilities of ~6.8 cm^2/V-s and threshold voltages of ~3.7 V in the saturation region.

INTRODUCTION

The rapidly expanding market for flat panel displays has driven manufacturers to look for a processing improvements to increase drive currents and hence performance of the displays. a-Si:H TFTs, which can be processed at relatively low temperatures (~300°C) and are widely used in active matrix liquid crystal displays, AMCLDs, have low effective channel mobilities, ~0.5 to 1 cm^2/V-s which place a limitation on the drive currents. Poly-Si TFTs show significantly increased effective channel mobilities, but generally must be fabricated at significantly higher temperatures of ~600 °C or more, so that they cannot be used with inexpensive glass substrates. Lower processing temperatures can be achieved by laser annealing; however, this approach is not easily adopted to large area device structures. μc-Si is an alternative material which we have considered for high performance TFTs. It has a higher Hall mobility than a-Si:H [1], and does not require high temperature deposition or post-deposition processing [2,3]. As such it represents an alternative route to improve the performance of TFTs without increasing processing temperatures. In addition, it has been shown "intrinsic" microcrystalline Si, hereafter, i-μc-Si, produced by B-atom compensation of native donor-like defects in the undoped material, shows no detectable Staebler Wronski effect and has improved majority and minority carrier transport with respect to a-Si:H [4]. These properties of the i-μc-Si make it an interesting material to explore for TFT applications that require inexpensive glass substrates.

TFT PROCESSING

μc-Si deposition

We use remote plasma-enhanced CVD to deposit μc-Si at a temperature of ~ 250°C. The remote PECVD process is driven by plasma excitation of He with the Si-source gas silane, SiH_4, being injected downstream from the plasma excitation region. The plasma power at 13.56 MHz is 50 W, and the chamber pressure is 0.3 Torr. The He flow rate through the plasma tube is 200 sccm. If no hydrogen is used in this remote PECVD process, then the deposited films are amorphous. If hydrogen is injected downstream with the SiH_4 at a flow rate ratio of H_2 to SiH_4 of 30 to 50, then the deposited films are microcrystalline provided that the deposition is on a non-crystalline substrate such as SiO_2 on Si, or glass. The addition of H_2 reduces the deposition rate and promotes the nucleation and growth of Si crystallites [5,6]. High resolution TEM imaging indicates that the μc-Si consists of ~100 Å of Si crystal grains that are encapsulated in an a-Si:H matrix. This means that this material does not contain inter-crystallite grain boundaries characteristic of poly-crystalline-Si materials. The diphasic nature of this material is also revealed in Raman scattering spectra which displays a relatively sharp peak at ~510-515 cm^{-1} which is a signature of the crystallites, and a broader peak at ~480 cm^{-1} which is due to the a-Si:H component of the material that surrounds the crystalline grains. The multichamber system used to deposit μc-Si films has on-line RHEED which was used to monitor the deposition process. Diffraction rings indicated formation of μc-Si over a thickness range from a few hundred Å to over one micron.

The undoped μc-Si deposited by remote PECVD is n-type with an activation energy of ~0.35 eV. The addition of PH_3 to the SiH_4 source gas promotes n$^+$ type doping; however, an increased flow rate of H_2 is needed to keep the deposited material μc-Si. For a 1% relative flow rate of PH_3 to SiH_4, the dark conductivity activation energy of the resulting n$^+$ μc-Si is 0.027 eV compared to 0.24 eV for n$^+$ a-Si:H, deposited under the same conditions, except for the elimination of H_2 for the reactant gas mixture. The n$^+$ μc-Si has been used as the source and drain contact material in TFTs with a-Si:H channels, where I-V characteristics of these TFTs show reduced current crowding and lower threshold voltages as compared to the use of n$^+$ a-Si:H contacts [7,8].

As noted above, the undoped μc-Si is n-type with an activation energy of ~0.35 eV. This is attributed to donor like defects that reside on, or near the surfaces of the crystallites and pin the Fermi level above midgap. Adding B_2H_6 to the downstream SiH_4 source gas mixture initially increases the activation energy by compensating the native donor-like defects, and then drives the μc-Si p-type (see Fig. 1). The maximum dark conductivity activation energy achieved in this manner is approximately 0.8 eV. Since E_{04} optical bandgap of the μc-Si is 1.9 eV (about the same as a-Si:H), this means that the Fermi level of the μc-Si has been driven to mid-gap region. We have designated the μc-Si formed in this way as "intrinsic" μc-Si or simply i-μc-Si. Figure 1 displays the dark conductivity activation energy of the μc-Si as a function of the B_2H_6 added to the gas mixture. The relative flow of B_2H_6 is in parts per million, ppm, and is *normalized* to an effective SiH_4 flow rate of 1 sccm. The activation energy, E_a, initially increases in the flow rate range from 0 to 160 ppm corresponding to native defect compensation, and then decreases as the material becomes p-type. Figure 2 displays the dark and photo-conductivities as functions of R, the ratio of the B_2H_6 to SiH_4 flow in ppm units. The photon flux for the photoconductivity measurement is 3×10^{15}/cm^2. The variation of the photoconductivity with R at this relatively low photon flux is smaller than that of the dark conductivity, so that the maximum value of the photo to dark-conductivity is achieved in the vicinity of the compensation point. The B-atom concentration at the compensation point is ~4-8x10^{17} cm^{-3} as determined by SIMS. Since only a relatively small amount of B_2H_6 must be added to the SiH_4/H_2 mixture to achieve compensation (~90 ppm), there is no need to increase the H_2 flow rate to form a μc-Si film. Table I displays the deposition conditions, and the dark conductivity and dark conductivity activation energy for undoped μc-Si, n$^+$ μc-Si, i-μc-Si, and doped and undoped a-Si:H.

μc-TFT Processing

Glass substrates were used for the TFT devices. 0.3 μm of W was sputtered onto to the glass, and then patterned by standard photo-lithographic and etch techniques to created the metal gate electrode. 450 Å of SiO_2 and 2500 Å of silicon nitride were deposited sequentially to form a dual layer gate dielectric. The SiO_2 films display no IR-detectable Si-H or Si-OH absorptions and have been used as gate electrodes in c-Si FETs, where they display fixed charged densities <10^{11} cm^{-2}. The properties of the nitride films vary considerably with the ratio of NH_3 to SiH_4. A ratio of 10 yields films with no AES-detectable Si-Si bonding, and with a relatively low concentration of IR active Si-NH bonds; nitride films deposited at this flow ratio yield optimized performance for the a-Si:H TFTs [9-11]. The double layer dielectrics show less leakage current and lower stress-induced flatband shifts compared to devices using single nitride layers [9]. 1000 Å of i-μc-Si is then deposited onto the nitride, and finally a 250 Å of n$^+$ μc-Si is deposited on the top of i-μc-Si channel layer. The active device regions are defined by etching in an SF_6/O_2 plasma and exposed to H_2 plasma at 200 °C to 2 hours in order to passivate bonding defects in the i-μc-Si layer and n+ μc-Si source and drain regions. 0.5 μm of Al is sputtered and patterned to define the source and drain contacts. The n+ μc-Si is then removed from the back of the channel by a wet chemical etch. The devices are annealed in a 200 sccm flow of He at 200 °C to 15 minutes.

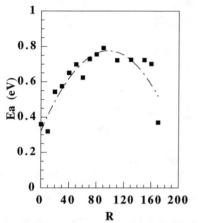

Fig. 1. Ea of μc-Si versus R, the flow ratio of B_2H_6 to SiH_4 in ppm units.

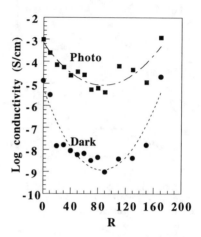

Fig. 2. Dark and photo-conductivity vs. R. The photon flux ix 3×10^{15} photons/cm²-s.

Table I Deposition Conditions and Electrical Properties of μc-Si and a-Si:H

	10 %SiH₄	Doping	E_a (eV)	H₂ flow	Dark conductivity
μc-Si	10 sccm	none	0.35	35 sccm	1×10^{-4} S/cm
n+ μc-Si	5 sccm	1% PH₃ in SiH₄	0.027	50 sccm	5 S/cm
i μc-Si	10 sccm	100 ppm of B₂H₆ to SiH₄	0.8	35 sccm	2×10^{-9} S/cm
a-Si:H	10 sccm	none	0.6-0.8	none	2×10^{-10} S/cm
n+ a-Si:H	10 sccm	1% PH₃ in SiH₄	0.24	none	8×10^{-3} S/cm

Hydrogen Plasma Treatment

To reduce defects in the i-μc-Si channel material, the processed μc-Si TFTs are exposed to a hydrogen plasma. This was done at a substrate temperature of 200°C with a He flow of 200 sccm through the plasma region at an RF power level of 15 W. 15 sccm of H_2 was introduced downstream. Since wafer is set outside of plasma region, the deposited film is not subjected to strong bombardment by charged particles. Under these conditions plasma excited H-atoms will diffuse into μc-Si and passivate defects. The plasma power must be carefully controlled since we have found that significantly higher plasma powers can promote etching the μc-Si materials.

We have fabricated a μc-Si test surface cell structure to monitor the effects of the hydrogen plasma treatment. Figure 3 displays the photo and dark-current for 0.1 μm thick test cell fabricated with undoped μc-Si before and after the plasma treatment. The dark current is relatively high for

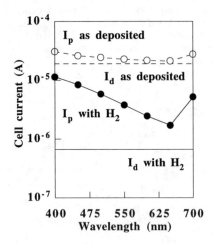

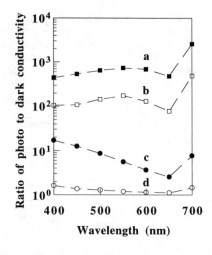

Fig. 3. Photo and dark-currents (I_p and I_d) of undoped μc-Si cell structures with and without a plasma hydrogen treatment.

Fig.4. Photo and dark conductivities of undoped μc-Si (c,d) and i-μc-Si (a,b), with (a,c) and without (b,c) the plasma hydrogen treatment.

the sample before the plasma hydrogen treatment, and the photo to dark-current ratio is small. We interpret this behavior as being indicative of Fermi level pinning by process-induced defects in the μc-Si. The plasma treatment reduces both the photo and the dark current; however, the ratio of the photo to the dark current is increased after this exposure to plasma-generated atomic-H. Similar experiments have also been performed on i-μc-Si, where the photo and dark currents are also reduced by the plasma treatment, but as for the undoped μc-Si, the ratio of photo to dark current is increased after the plasma-assisted processing.

The ratio of the photo to dark-current is displayed in Fig. 4 for undoped μc-Si and i-μc-Si, before and after the hydrogen plasma treatment. The i-μc-Si shows the highest ratio of photo to dark-current after the plasma hydrogen treatment. The lowest ratio is obtained for the undoped sample without the hydrogen treatment. From these studies we conclude that the diborane compensation which produces the i-μc-Si combined with the plasma hydrogen treatment reduces the defect states in the band gap of μc-Si. In addition, the plasma hydrogen by itself also reduces defects in the undoped μc-Si.

TFT PERFORMANCE

TFTs with μc-Si and i-μc-Si channel layers, and with and without the plasma hydrogen treatment were tested under the condition that $V_g = V_{sd}$ for a voltage range from 0 to 30 V. From plots of the square root of drain current versus V_g, the threshold voltage and field effect channel mobility in saturation range were obtained. For $V_{sd} = 0.1$ V, a plot of the drain current versus V_g gives the threshold voltage and field effect mobility in linear range. For $V_{sd} = 10$ V, a plot of the drain current versus V_g gives the On/Off states for TFT operation.

The undoped μc-Si TFT shows a relatively low channel mobilities of approximately 0.25 cm²/V-s and a threshold voltages of ~ 8V. This device also shows some hysteresis in trace and retrace tests in the 0 to 20 V range. From the direction of the hysteresis, the trapped charges are electrons. Since we have used N-rich nitride as the dielectric in contact with the channel material, by comparison with a-Si:H TFTs using the same dielectric and showing no hysteresis, we conclude that the trapped electrons are in the undoped μc-Si channel layer. Otherwise, the overall performance of the TFTs is about the same as a a-Si:H TFTs. The plasma hydrogen treatment reduces the defects in the undoped μc-Si and these TFTs shows a higher on-current than without the hydrogen treatment.

For the TFTs with an i-μc-Si channel layer receiving the hydrogen plasma treatment, the channel mobility is 6.8 cm^2/V-s and the threshold voltage is 3.7 V in the saturation range. In the linear region the mobility is ~6.4 cm^2/V-s and threshold voltage of 1.1 V. Figure 5 displays the drain current for μc-Si TFTs for $V_{sd}=10$ V for (i) undoped μc-Si, (ii) undoped μc-Si after a plasma H_2 treatment and (iii) i-μc-Si after a plasma H_2 treatment. From this figure, we find that the on-current is maximized after B-compensation creating an i-μc-Si channel layer and after that layer is subjected to the plasma hydrogen treatment. Table II gives values of the channel mobility, the threshold voltage and the On/Off drain current ratio for TFTs with the different channel materials, with and without the hydrogen plasma treatment The relative performance of the TFTs is consistent with the respective photo to dark-conductivity ratios as shown in Fig. 4. The highest on current is achieved using i-μc-Si channel layer that has been subjected the hydrogen plasma treatment. The channel mobility of this TFT is significantly higher than that of a TFT with an a-Si:H channel layer.

The TFTs described above include n$^+$ μc-Si layers for the source and drain contacts. These regions were subjected to the same plasma hydrogen treatment as the channel i-μc-Si material. We found that if the source and drain regions were overcoated with Al prior to the hydrogen plasma treatment, the TFTs with i-μc-Si channels displayed lower mobilities of ~2.4 cm^2/V-s and higher threshold voltages of 5.8 V in the saturation region. If the source and drain regions were also subjected to the plasma hydrogen treatment, then TFTs displayed higher channel mobilities of ~6.8 cm^2/V-s and lower threshold voltages of 3.7 V. Since the mobility and the threshold voltage are calculated from the drive current, these increase in mobility and decrease threshold voltage may result in part from a decreased resistance in the source and drain materials after the plasma treatment. This is consistent with the H_2 plasma treatment reducing defects in the doped μc-Si materials as well, and thereby increasing the effectiveness of the doping process. Fig. 6 presents the I-V characteristics of a TFT with an i-μc-Si channel layer that has been subjected to the plasma

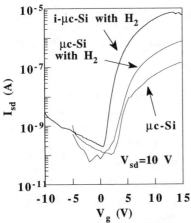

Fig. 5. I_{sd} vs. V_g for (i) i-μc-Si and (ii) undoped μc-Si after a plasma treatment and (iii) for undoped μc-Si without a plasma hydrogen treatment.

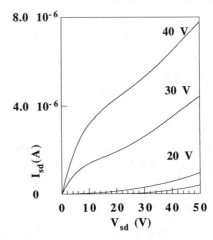

Fig. 6. Characteristics of a TFT with an i-μc-Si channel that has been subjected to the H-plasma.

hydrogen treatment after overcoated Al on source and drain regions. In previous publications we reported that using n+ μc-Si source and drain contacts with a-Si:H decreased the threshold voltage, and also resulted in an effective increase in the drive current at low applied voltages. [7,8]

Table II Properties of μc-Si TFTs

Channel Layer	Plasma H_2	μ (cm^2/V-s)	V_{th} (V)	On/Off Ratio
undoped μc-si	No	0.06	6.5	10^3
undoped μc-Si	Yes	0.26	8.0	10^4
i-μc-Si	No	0.01	5.0	10^3
i-μc-Si	Yes	6.8	3.7	10^5

SUMMARY

TFTs with B-compensated i-μc-Si channels, and n$^+$ μc-Si source and drain contacts have been fabricated using an in-situ, 250°C remote PECVD deposition process. The μc-Si layers are produced when hydrogen is used as an additional reactant gas and injected downstream along with the Si source gas SiH_4, and any necessary dopant gases in a remote PECVD process which produces a-Si:H in the absence of at least 30 sccm of downstream H_2. We have used 1 % PH_3 in SiH_4 for the n$^+$ μc-Si source and drains, and ~90 ppm B_2H_6 in SiH_4 to form i-μc-Si channel.

A post-deposition plasma hydrogen treatment is necessary to optimize the properties of the TFT devices. This is required for both the channel and source and drain materials. After the plasma hydrogen treatment, the TFTs display an effective channel mobility of 6.8 cm^2/V-s and a threshold voltage of 3.7 V for operation in saturation. This mobility is about factor six to ten higher than what is generally obtained for TFTs with a-Si:H channel regions. This comparison is based on TFTs fabricated at ~250°C.

ACKNOWLEDGMENTS

This research has been in part sponsored by ONR, NREL and the NSF Engineering Research Center for Advanced Electronic Materials Processing.

REFERENCES

[1]   W.E. Spear, G. Willeke, P.G. LeComber and A.G. Fitzerald, J. Physique **42**, C4, 257 (1981).

[2]   C. Wang and G. Lucovsky. Proc. of 21st IEEE Photovoltaic Specialists Conf., 1614 (1990)

[3]   C. Wang Ph.D. Thesis, NCSU (1991).

[4]   S.M. Cho, S.S. He and G. Lucovsky, MRS Symp. Proc. **A**, Spring (1994).

[5]   S. Veprek, F.A. Sarott and Z. Iqbal, Phys. Rev. **36**, 3344 (1987).

[6]   S. Veprek, MRS Symp. Proc. V. **164**, p.39 (1989)

[7]   S.S. He, D.J. Stephens and G. Lucovsky, MRS Symp. Proc. **297**, 871 (1993).

[8]   S.S. He, M. J. Williams, D. J. Stephens and G. Lucovsky, J. Non-Cryst. Solids, **164-166**, 731 (1993).

[9]   S.S. He, D.J. Stephens and G. Lucovsky, MRS Symp. Proc. **297**, 871, (1993).

[10]   S.S. He, D.J. Stephens, G. Lucovsky and R.W. Hamaker, MRS Symp. Proc. **282**, 505 (1992).

[11]   S.S. He and G. Lucovsky, MRS Symp. Proc. **A** Spring, (1994).

This article appears in Mat. Res. Soc. Symp. Proc. Vol. 336

IN-SITU CRYSTALLIZATION AND DOPING OF a-Si FILM
BY MEANS OF SPIN-ON-GLASS

Tomoyuki SAKODA, Chang-Dong KIM and Masakiyo MATSUMURA
Dept. of Physical Electronics, Tokyo Institute of Technology
2-12-1 Oh-okayama, Meguro-ku, Tokyo 152, Japan.

ABSTRACT

A novel technique has been proposed for selective and *in-situ* excimer-laser crystallization and doping to thin poly-Si films. Dopant atoms are supplied, during the Si laser crystallization process, to the Si film on glass from the doped SOG (spin-on-glass) film coated on the top. Conductivity of the processed film was increased to more than 10S/cm from about 10^{-8}S/cm of the starting film. This technique has been applied to the bottom gate amorphous-Si TFTs with self-aligned poly-Si source and drain. The electron field-effect mobility was 1.0cm^2/Vs and the on/off current ratio was more than 10^6. No parasitic effects were observed, and the hole conduction was effectively suppressed. This *in-situ* crystallization and doping technique can also be applied to the top gate a-Si TFT process.

INTRODUCTION

Amorphous silicon thin-film transistors (a-Si TFTs) with the high on/off current ratio have been used as switching elements in present liquid-crystal displays (LCDs). Among various efforts for next generation high quality LCDs, improvement of TFT performances by shrinking TFT size and by reducing parasitic capacitances and resistances is the most important [1,2]. We have reported a new self-alignment process using selective excimer-laser crystallization for the Si source and drain regions [3,4,5], which can satisfy above mentioned requirements for TFTs simultaneously. In this process, however, the problem arises that the a-Si film should be originally doped, resulting in the negative threshold voltage of the TFT. A doping method to the undoped film should be introduced into this new TFT process for improving the TFT on-off transition characteristics.

Various laser doping techniques have been reported using excimer lasers. Carey et al. [6] reported the Gas Immersion Laser Doping (GILD) process where Si wafer is irradiated by laser light in B_2H_6 gas ambient. Sameshima et al. [7] reported the Laser-Induced Melting of Predeposited Impurity Doping (LIMPID) technique, where a Si wafer with deposited dopant film is irradiated by a pulsed laser light. These processes have been characterized by the superficial melting of Si and liquid-phase diffusion of the dopant atoms in molten Si region. Diffusion coefficient of phosphorus atoms in molten Si is in an order of 10^{-4}cm^2/s [8], much more than that (10^{-11}cm^2/s) in solid Si [9]. Since typical duration is several 10ns for the melt-regrowth phase

59

in the excimer–laser recrystallization method, we can expect that dopant atoms can diffuse about 10nm deep from the surface, sufficient value for TFT application. Thus these techniques are promising for poly–Si TFT process [10].

We report here a simpler technique where phosphorus atoms are supplied from the pre–coated SOG film. Doping characteristics as well as the TFT characteristics are being presented.

EXPERIMENTAL

Doping Characteristics

Undoped a–Si films (50nm thick) were CVD–deposited on glass using Si_2H_6 at 460°C [11]. Then 1% phosphorus–doped SOG film was spin–coated, and the sample was baked in nitrogen ambient at 450°C for 30min. The SOG film was 150nm thick. Then the sample was irradiated by XeF excimer laser light pulses from the glass substrate side to crystallize the a–Si film. Since the top SOG film is also heated up to high temperature, phosphorus atoms diffuses into the molten Si film, resulting in the highly conductive poly–Si film. After this *in–situ* crystallization and doping, the top SOG film was removed and sample was post–hydrogenated in the atomic hydrogen ambient [12].

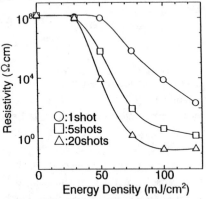

Fig.1. Resistivity of poly–Si as a function of laser energy density E.

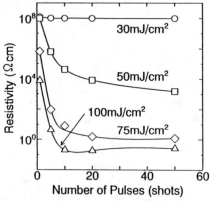

Fig.2. Resistivity of poly–Si as a function of number of laser pulses N.

Figure 1 shows the resistivity ρ as a function of the laser energy density E for various numbers N of laser pulses. For E less than 30mJ/cm^2, the film was amorphous and thus ρ was as high as $10^8\Omega$cm. ρ decreased abruptly at E around 75mJ/cm^2. However for E higher than 125mJ/cm^2, ρ took a high value again due to laser–induced reamorphization [13]. Thus, from 100mJ/cm^2 to 125mJ/cm^2, the film showed a resistivity as low as $10^{-1}\Omega$cm.

The resistivity dependence upon N is shown in Fig.2 for several E values. ρ decreased with the increase in N for N less than 10, but tended to be saturated for N more than 10. Thus we concluded that the optimum conditions for laser irradiation are 100mJ/cm^2 and 10shots.

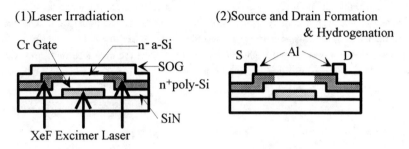

Fig.3. Process flow of the a–Si/SiN bottom gate TFT with *in–situ* doped and self–aligned poly–Si source and drain.

Table 1. Experiment conditions of laser irradiation.

Laser Source : XeF (λ=351nm)
Energy Density : 100mJ/cm^2
Number of Pulses : 10shots

Bottom Gate TFT Process

SOG doping technique has been applied to the a–Si/SiN bottom gate TFT with self–aligned poly–Si source and drain. The process flow is schematically shown in Fig.3. After the 220nm–thick SiN film was CVD–deposited as the gate insulator at 500°C using Si_2H_6 and N_2H_4 over a glass substrate with patterned 200nm–thick Cr gate–electrode [11], the 50nm–thick a–Si film was successively CVD–deposited as the active layer at 460°C using Si_2H_6. Then the 150nm–thick SOG film was spin–coated to the top, and the sample was cured at 450°C for 30min in dry N_2. And then the XeF excimer laser light pulse was irradiated from the glass substrate side. Since light wavelength is as long as 351nm, the laser light is not absorbed by the glass substrate and the SiN film. Thus the a–Si film outside the gate electrode pattern was selectively irradiated, resulting in the highly conductive n$^+$ poly–Si. Laser irradiation conditions are summarized in Table 1. After etching the unwanted Si film, source and drain electrodes of Al were formed. Finally, post–hydrogenation was carried out using atomic hydrogen to improve TFT characteristics. The channel length and width were 10μm and 100μm, respectively. Offset length between Cr gate edge and Al edge for the source and drain was as long as 10μm.

TFT Characteristics

Logarithmic drain current I_D is shown in Fig.4 as a function of gate voltage V_G for a drain voltage V_D of 1V. Threshold voltage was 6V, very near the conventional value. On current was more than 1μA. The leakage current was less than 10^{-12}A, and the hole current was effectively suppressed over a wide negative gate voltage region. Thus the on/off current ratio was greater than 10^6. The subthreshold voltage slope was about 1V/decade. This value is much better than the value previously reported [3,4,5] using the doped a–Si film.

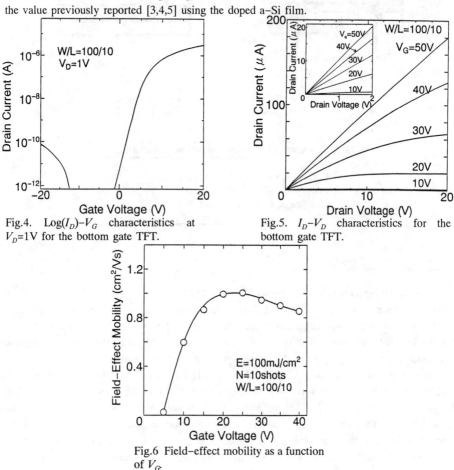

Fig.4. Log(I_D)–V_G characteristics at V_D=1V for the bottom gate TFT.

Fig.5. I_D–V_D characteristics for the bottom gate TFT.

Fig.6 Field–effect mobility as a function of V_G.

The linear I_D versus V_D characteristics is shown in fig.5. As shown in the enlarged view, I_D started linearly from the origin and increased constantly with V_G, although there was an offset poly–Si region of as long as 10μm. This is due to extremely low resistivity of poly–Si source and drain. The field–effect mobility as a function of the gate voltage V_G is shown in Fig.6. 1cm^2/Vs was obtained for a wide V_G region from 20V to 30V. Similar good characteristics were obtained for TFTs having the channel length down to 1μm.

Top Gate TFT

This selective and *in–situ* doping technique has been also applied to the top–gate a–Si TFT, where the a–Si film was CVD–deposited on the SOG coated glass. Figure 7 shows the process flow of the top–gate TFT. After patterning the Si film, the SiO$_2$ film was CVD deposited at 250°C, and then Al gate electrode was formed on it. Then XeF laser light was irradiated from the top to make doped poly–Si for source and drain. The device was successfully operated. Figures 8 and 9 show the logarithmic I_D versus V_G characteristics and the linear I_D versus V_D

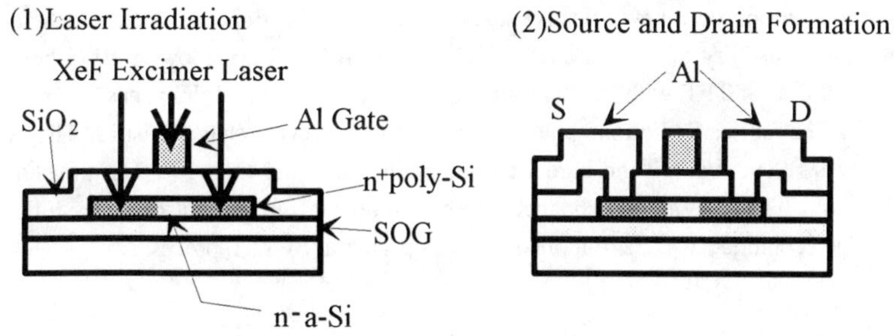

(1)Laser Irradiation   (2)Source and Drain Formation

Fig.7. Process flow of the a–Si/SiO$_2$ top gate TFT with *in–situ* doped and self–aligned poly–Si source and drain.

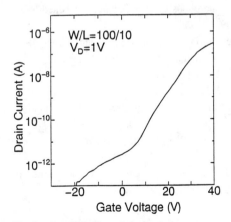

Fig.8. Log(I_D)–V_G characteristics at V_D=1V for the top gate TFT.

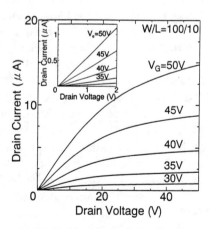

Fig.9. I_D–V_D characteristics for the top gate TFT.

characteristics, respectively. I_D started to increase from the origin, linearly with V_G and V_D, the same as in the bottom–gate TFT, by the effects of sufficiently low parasitic resistance. The detailed characteristics were not as good as those of the bottom–gate TFT. The on–current was less than $1\mu A$ and the field–effect mobility was $0.12 cm^2/Vs$. The semilogarithmic slope of I_D was as large as 7V/decade and thus the threshold voltage was around 25V. We did not study the reproducibility and the reasons for the insufficient characteristics of the top–gate TFT. But we expect that the characteristics will be improved by optimizing the post–hydrogenation conditions and SiO_2 CVD conditions, respectively.

CONCLUSION

We have proposed a new selective and *in–situ* crystallization and doping technique by use of SOG. The resistivity of the recrystallized Si (poly–Si) film was as low as $10^{-1}\Omega cm$. Using this technique, the a–Si TFT with the self–aligned poly–Si source and drain has successfully fabricated. The fabricated bottom gate TFT showed good device characteristics. The field–effect mobility was $1.0 cm^2/Vs$ and the on/off current ratio was more than 10^6. The threshold voltage was about 6V. TFTs having the channel length as short as $1\mu m$ were also successfully operated. This doping technique was also applied to the top gate a–Si TFT process.

REFERENCE

1. S. Kawai, T. Komada, et al. , Proc. Society for Information Display , **25** , 21 (1984).
2. A. Chenevas–Paule, et al. , Proc. Society for Information Display , **26** , 197 (1985).
3. O. Sugiura, C.D. Kim and M. Matsumura , Electronics Lett. , **29** , 750 (1993).
4. C.D. Kim, O. Sugiura and M. Matsumura in Amorphous Silicon Technology, edited by
   E.A. Schiff et al.(Mater.Res.Soc.Proc. **297** 1993)pp.925.
5. C.D. Kim and M. Matsumura , Display Manufacturing conf.(SID, San Francisco,Jan. 1994).
6. P.G. Carey, T.W. Sigmon, et al. , IEEE Electron Device Lett. , **6** , 291 (1985).
7. T. Sameshima, S. Usui , Jpn. J. Appl. Phys. , **26** , L1208 (1987).
8. H. Kodera , Jpn. J. Appl. Phys. , **53** , 3702 (1963).
9. S. M. Sze, Physics of Semiconductor Devices(John Wiley & Sons,New York,1981),p.68.
10. K. Shimizu , O. Sugiura and M. Matsumura , Jpn. J. Appl. Phys. , **29** , L1775 (1990).
11. H. Kanoh, et al. , IEEE Electron Device Lett. , **11** , 258 (1990).
12. Y. Uchida, H. Kanoh et al. , Jpn. J. Appl. Phys. , **29** , L2171 (1990).
13. T. Sameshima in Microcrystalline Semiconductors:Materials Science & Devices,edited by
    P.M. Fauchet, et al.(Mater. Res. Soc. Proc. **283** 1993)pp.679.

This article appears in Mat. Res. Soc. Symp. Proc. Vol. 336

INFLUENCE OF THE DEPOSITION RATE OF THE a-Si:H CHANNEL ON THE FIELD-EFFECT MOBILITY OF TFTs DEPOSITED IN A VHF GLOW DISCHARGE

H. MEILING, J.F.M. WESTENDORP, J. HAUTALA, Z.M. SALEH AND C.T. MALONE
TEL America, Inc., 123 Brimbal Avenue, Beverly, MA 01915, USA.

ABSTRACT

Inverted-staggered hydrogenated amorphous-silicon thin-film transistors (a-Si:H TFTs) were deposited in a glow discharge with an excitation frequency of 60 MHz. At 13.56 MHz it has been reported that the field-effect mobility of this type of TFT decreases with increasing deposition rate of the a-Si:H layer, due to an increase in the defect density in the channel. A successful way of increasing the deposition rate without deteriorating the material properties has turned out to be utilizing a higher excitation frequency than the conventional 13.56 MHz.

The deposition rate of the 60-MHz-deposited transistor channel was changed from 350 to 1300 Å/min by diluting the process gas silane with hydrogen and by changing the rf power. The dependence of the a-Si:H material properties on deposition parameters is described. The deposition rate dependence of the mobility in the 60-MHz deposited thin films and devices is presented and discussed in terms of hydrogen dilution in the plasma and the hydrogen content of the a-Si:H films.

INTRODUCTION

In recent years one of the key applications of hydrogenated amorphous-silicon (a-Si:H) thin-film transistors (TFTs) turned out to be the active matrix addressing of liquid-crystal displays. For this application it is essential to have a large-area, low-temperature and high panel-throughput deposition technique in order to lower production costs. In today's production equipment for this and other applications the most common technique is 13.56 MHz rf glow-discharge (Plasma Enhanced Chemical Vapour Deposition, PECVD). TFTs fabricated using these systems have shown good switching characteristics, i.e. field-effect mobilities in the saturation regime (μ_S), hereafter referred to as mobility, of around 0.5 cm^2/Vs [1], high ON/OFF current ratios (I_{ON}/I_{OFF}), and low threshold voltages for charge transport at positive gate voltages. Typically, the deposition rate (r_d) of the a-Si:H channel of these TFTs amounts to 100 Å/min and is limited mainly by the occurance of plasma polymerization when higher deposition rates are used [2]. The increase in demand for high-resolution displays, i.e. more scanning lines, feeds the search for higher-mobility TFTs, since these displays require a faster charge-up of the pixels and thus a higher current. This increase in current cannot be achieved by increasing the channel width of the TFT.

To enhance the panel throughput of PECVD production equipment high deposition rates for all the films are required. However, it has been reported [1,2] that an increase in the deposition rate of the a-Si:H channel deteriorates the TFT performance, i.e. a decrease in μ_S and less stable TFT operation upon bias voltage stress. This deterioration is probably related to the increase in the di-hydride (Si-H$_2$) content in the bulk of a-Si:H due to the use of higher rf powers that are needed to increase the deposition rates.

65

The quality of the gate dielectric/a-Si:H interface also has an influence on μ_s. One reason for this is the lattice mismatch between silicon nitride SiN_x, which is mostly used as gate dielectric and a-Si:H. This mismatch induces defect states in the interface region [3]. Also, the roughness of this interface is claimed to have an influence: the smoother the interface, the higher the value of the mobility and the more stable the TFTs are, due to a steeper tail state distribution in the a-Si:H [4,5].

In the late 80's it was reported that material deposited with a higher excitation frequency could be of the same device quality as material deposited at 13.56 MHz, except that the deposition rate was an order of magnitude higher [6]. The remaining question is whether there is also a deposition-rate dependence of the mobility of TFTs that are deposited at these higher excitation frequencies. We report on TFT performance as a function of the deposition rate of the channel in '60-MHz TFTs'.

EXPERIMENTAL

The TFTs described in our experiments were deposited using TEL America's recently developed commercially available single-panel large-area multichamber PECVD system [7]. This is the first large-area production machine that deposits SiN_x, a-Si:H and doped a-Si:H films at a higher excitation frequency than the conventional 13.56 MHz. Substrates of sizes up to 465 mm x 360 mm are handled and processed face-down. The TFTs are of the inverted-staggered type and are fabricated as follows: after sputter deposition of the gate contacts on a glass substrate the SiN_x insulator (3000 Å) is deposited, followed by 600 Å a-Si:H and an etch stoppper layer of 3000 Å SiN_x. The top SiN_x is patterned prior to the deposition of the phosphorous doped amorphous silicon (n^+a-Si:H) ohmic contact layer and the sputtered source and drain metal contacts. Finally, the n^+a-Si:H and metal on top of the etch stopper layer are patterned. This results in TFTs with a channel length $L = 35$ μm and a channel width $W = 27$ μm.

We report on four different TFTs which all have identical SiN_x gate and passivation insulators. These films were deposited from a fixed mixture of silane (SiH_4), ammonia (NH_3) and nitrogen (N_2). The power density amounts to 0.6 W/cm^2 resulting in $r_d = 1500$ Å/min. The resulting SiN_x films are nearly stoichiometric and have a breakdown electric field of more than 9 MV/cm. The index of refraction as measured with an ellipsometer is 1.88 ± 0.01. Capacitance-voltage measurements show that there is little hysteresis between the traces of the capacitance value when the insulator is brought from depletion into accumulation and back by sweeping the voltage up and down. FTIR absorption spectroscopy of these nitride films reveals that the number of N-H bonds exceeds the amount of Si-H bonds by almost a factor of 6. This low density of Si-H bonds indicates that the material is relatively stable and has a low density of carrier traps.

For the standard deposition of a-Si:H, pure SiH_4 is used. The r_d of this process amounts to 1300 Å/min at a power density of 0.27 W/cm^2. To study the effect of deposition rates lower than 1300 Å/min, we have used a hydrogen dilution of silane at a gas flow ratio SiH_4:H_2 of 1:5. Then, by changing the rf power we varied r_d from 350 to 590 and 810 Å/min.

The TFT transfer characteristics were measured in the dark. From the saturation transfer characteristics, i.e. a plot of the square root of the source-drain current ($\sqrt{I_s}$) versus the gate voltage V_g, measured with the source-drain voltage V_d equal to V_g, the field-effect mobility μ_s was determined, according to Eq. 1:

$$\sqrt{I_s} = \sqrt{\frac{W}{L}\frac{C_i}{2}}\,\mu_s(V_g - V_t),$$ (1)

in which C_i is the insulator's capacitance per unit area and V_t is the threshold voltage. The ON-current I_{ON} is the current at $V_g = V_t + 12$, and the OFF-current is determined at $V_g = V_t - 5$, both at $V_d = 10$ V.

RESULTS

In Fig. 1 the relation between the deposition rate and the rf-power density is plotted for the diluted a-Si:H film depositions (circles) along with the standard pure SiH$_4$ deposition process (square). A linear increase of r_d is observed with increasing power density, although the curve tends to level off at high power density values. There is almost a factor of two difference in deposition rate between the pure SiH$_4$ deposition and the 1:5 SiH$_4$:H$_2$ deposition.

From the FTIR absorption spectra it was determined that all hydrogen is essentially bonded as monohydride, as can be seen from Fig. 2. The stretching mode is plotted for both the pure SiH$_4$ deposition (solid line) and the 360 Å/min hydrogen diluted process (dotted line). It can be seen that the Full Width at Half Maximum (FWHM) of the peak from the pure SiH$_4$ sample is approximately 10 % smaller than that of the hydrogen-diluted deposition. The absence of any 2100 cm^{-1} absorption (Si-H$_2$ or Si-H on the surface of internal voids) indicates that the void fraction of the samples is low.

From the rocking mode absorption, centered around 650 cm^{-1}, the hydrogen content of the samples was determined. These results are plotted in Fig. 3a. For the samples from hydrogen-diluted depositions, an increase of hydrogen concentration [H] is observed with increasing deposition rate, and

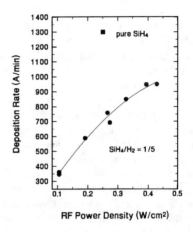

Fig. 1. Deposition rate versus rf-power density for diluted (circles) and undiluted (square) a-Si:H depositions.

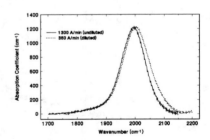

Fig. 2. FTIR stretching mode of a-Si:H films deposited from diluted (dotted line) and undiluted (solid line) SiH$_4$.

a subsequent leveling off at higher rates. However, in the pure SiH$_4$ deposition, where the deposition rate is highest, the hydrogen concentration is lower than that of most of the other (diluted process) samples.

The transfer characteristics of the TFT having the standard a-Si:H layer is shown in Fig. 4. The source-drain current I_s is plotted as a function of V_g for source-drain voltages V_d of 0.1, 1.0 and 10 V. The mobility in the saturation regime amounts to 1.14 cm^2/Vs and the ON/OFF current ratio for this TFT amounts to 3x10^7. For all the TFTs processed the mobility and the ON/OFF current ratios are plotted as a function of deposition rate in Figs. 3b and 3c, respectively.

It appears that when hydrogen dilution is used, the mobility decreases with increasing r_d (or rf power density). Also, I_{ON}/I_{OFF} tends to decrease with increasing r_d although there is a minimum at approximately 600 Å/min. It can be seen from Fig. 3b that, although μ_s decreases with r_d when H$_2$ dilution is used, the values of the mobilites remain high. Furthermore, the results of Fig. 3 indicate that the mobility reaches its highest value when the hydrogen content is lowest.

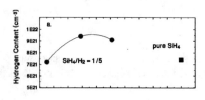

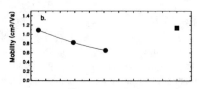

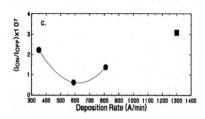

Fig. 3. Hydrogen content (a), mobility (b) and I$_{ON}$/I$_{OFF}$ (c) as a function of the deposition rate of a-Si:H.

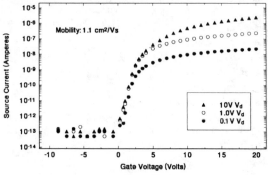

Fig. 4. Transfer characteristics of a TFT with an a-Si:H film deposited at 1300 Å/min from pure SiH$_4$.

DISCUSSION

From the experiments discussed above, it is evident that the mobility in the 60-MHz-TFTs is not solely dependent on the deposition rate of the a-Si:H channel. The chemistry in the gas phase during the discharge is of crucial importance as well. The hydrogen content in the films appears to be related to this change in the gas phase chemistry.

Finger et al. have found that the hydrogen concentration of a-Si:H films deposited at an excitation frequency of 70 MHz is substantially lower than the hydrogen concentration of 13.56 MHz material [8]. The hydrogen concentration in our 60 MHz films show excellent agreement with those reported by Finger. Let us compare the 360 Å/min film from diluted SiH_4 and the 1300 Å/min film from pure SiH_4. Even though the deposition rates differ greatly the hydrogen concentration of these two films is the same. That is remarkable and shows the attractiveness of VHF deposition: the high low-energy ion flux during VHF deposition reported by Heintze [9] efficiently removes hydrogen and enhances the mobility of adsorbed radicals allowing for the deposition of a-Si:H at high rates and low hydrogen concentration. The performance of the high deposition rate TFT is as good as the one with the 360 Å/min film. This is to be compared with the situation at 13.56 MHz where in order to obtain deposition rates of 1300 Å/min the rf power would have to be increased which results in an *increase* of ion energy and is known to lead to build-in of more hydrogen and $Si-H_2$ and a concomitant decrease of TFT performance [1].

Although both films have the same hydrogen concentration and although all hydrogen is essentially bonded as monohydride, there is a difference in the FWHM of the stretching mode peak of the two films. This result indicates that there is a more homogeneous structural order and less bond angle distortions in the sample made from pure SiH_4 despite the higher deposition rate. One of the parameters that changes with hydrogen dilution is the ion flux towards the growing surface of the film. This may result in a different microstructure. However, both films have virtually identical electrical behaviour in terms of mobility and the ON/OFF current ratio.

Comparing the three films made from diluted SiH_4 we see that the hydrogen concentration initially increases and then levels off with increasing power density. With the increase in power density the electrical performance of the TFTs degrades, although the performance at 850 Å/min is still good. Comparison of the stretching mode of the FTIR spectra of these three films does not reveal a significant difference. This shows that for the optimization of deposition processes for TFT production electrical measurements are a necessity. Further research is in progress to investigate the effects of surface morphology, the density of states and the Urbach edge in these a-Si:H films. Also additional structural analysis with X-ray diffraction and Raman scattering is underway.

CONCLUSIONS

The use of a 60 MHz rf glow discharge allows for the deposition of a-Si:H at high rates while maintaining low hydrogen concentrations. This yields TFTs of high quality at deposition rates much higher than those at 13.56 MHz. The a-Si:H films deposited with and without H_2 dilution over the range of deposition rates from 350 to 1300 Å/min show virtually no evidence of $Si-H_2$

bonding. Deposition from undiluted SiH_4 results in material with higher structural order than the material deposited from hydrogen diluted SiH_4. However, for both type of materials high mobility TFTs can be made. The mobility as well as the ON/OFF current ratio appears to be related to the total hydrogen concentration. In this production PECVD system, TFTs with a saturation mobility of 1.14 cm^2/Vs and an ON/OFF current ratio of $3x10^7$ were obtained where the channel a-Si:H layer was deposited at a rate of 1300 Å/min.

ACKNOWLEDGEMENTS

We gratefully acknowledge the contribution of the TFT processing group at IBM Research.

REFERENCES

1. N. Ibaraki, K. Matsumura, K. Fukuda, N. Hirata, S. Kawamura, and T. Kashiro, in *1994 Display Manufacturing Technology Conference* (Society for Information Display, Playa del Rey, CA, 1994), pp. 121-122; Y. Watabe, *ibid.*, pp. 61-62.

2. P. Roca i Cabarrocas, J. Non-Cryst. Solids **164-166**, 37 (1993).

3. J. Jang, M.Y. Jung, S.S. Yoo, H.K. Song, and J.M. Jun, in *Amorphous Silicon Technology 1992*, edited by M.J. Thompson, Y. Hamakawa, P.G. LeComber, A. Madan, and E. Schiff (Mater. Res. Soc. Proc. **258**, Pittsburgh, PA, 1992) pp. 973-978.

4. H. Uchida, K. Takechi, S. Nishida, and S. Kaneko, Jpn. J. Appl. Phys. **30** (12B), 3691-3694 (1991).

5. K. Taketchi, H. Uchida, and S. Kaneko, in *Amorphous Silicon Technology-1992*, edited by M.J. Thompson, Y. Hamakawa, P.G. LeComber, A. Madan, and E. Schiff (Mater. Res. Soc. roc. **258**, Pittsburgh, PA, 1992) pp. 955-960.

6. H. Curtins, N. Wyrsch, M. Favre, and A.V. Shah, Plasma Chem. Plasma Process. **7** (3), 267 (1987).

7. J.F.M. Westendorp, H. Meiling, J.D. Pollock, D.W. Berrian, A.H. Laflamme Jr., J. Hautala, and J. Vanderpot, in these proceedings (1994).

8. F. Finger, U. Kroll, V. Voret, A. Shah, W. Beyer, X.M. Fang, J. Weber, A. Howling and C. Hollenstein, J. Appl. Phys. **71** (11), (1992).

9. M. Heintze, R. Zedlitz and Y.H. Bauer, in *Amorphous Silicon Technology 1993*, edited by E.A. Schiff, M.J. Thompson, A. Madan, K. Tanaka P.G. LeComber (Mater. Res. Soc. Proc. **297**, Pittsburgh, PA, 1993) pp. 49-54.

THE LOW TEMPERATURE POLYSILICON TFT TECHNOLOGY FOR MANUFACTURING OF ACTIVE MATRIX LIQUID CRYSTAL DISPLAYS

TATSUO MORITA, SHUHEI TSUCHIMOTO AND NOBUO HASHIZUME
Central Research Laboratories Sharp Corp.,Tenri Nara,Japan

ABSTRACT

The amorphous silicon thin transistor (a-Si TFT) has successfully industrialized the active matrix liquid crystal displays (AMLCDs), which would get a vast market on the basis of their wide potential use for displays. Whereas, the polysilicon TFT (p-Si TFT) also has been intensely investigated and intended to realize smarter AMLCDs,   with monolithic peripheral circuits.

In this paper, we will discuss the applicable range of low temperature p-Si TFTs compared with high temperature p-Si TFTs. After reviewing the materials which comprise low temperature p-Si TFTs, we will introduce our self aligned aluminum gate process which could allow fast addressing even in enlarged AMLCDs in the future.

INTRODUCTION

The successful industrialization of active matrix liquid crystal displays (AMLCDs) with amorphous silicon (a-Si) has brought about the demand of the advanced monolithic peripheral circuits AMLCDs comprised of low temperature process polysilicon TFTs. The low temperature process polysilicon TFTs are expected to lower the cost of AMLCDs and also to meet a wide range of applications from high resolution view finders to the large size of direct view displays. The integration of peripheral drivers has also a potential to electrically check pixel elements.

Polysilicon TFTs must possess high speed driving capability, low leakage current performance, and durability under high voltage operation (e.g.20 V).

The good uniformity of TFTs' properties in giant area is also demanded, because a large size of glass substrate is preferred from the mass production point of view. Currently, the low temperature means less than 600°C because the glass substrate which is endurable up to 600°C is the best option economically. This is a sort of compromise with the present level of developed substrates and the   effort of lowering the TFTs process temperature.

We will show the potential application range of this technology in AMLCDs and review the materials which compose AMLCDs. Then we would like to introduce the aluminum self aligned gate polysilicon TFTs process.

71

APPLICATIONS

A variety of AMLCDs have already appeared on the market including a view finder with high temperature polysilicon TFTs. A larger number of display dots bring a finer picture. This will however make the connections between the pixel addressing lines and its driving circuits difficult. The monolithic driver circuits AMLCDs using polysilicon TFTs could solve this problem. The current driving capability of TFTs, on the other hand, would be required to be higher in order to meet a variety of LCDs. Table 1 shows the applicability of two ranks of low temperature polysilicon TFTs of which the field mobility(μ_{eff}) and the threshold voltage are 50 cm^2/v•s, 5 volts and 100 cm^2/v•s, 1 volts respectively.

Table 1: The applicable field of monolithic AMLCDs with polysilicon TFTs.

	Panel size(inch)	0.97	2.8	3	6	11.8
Modules	Display dots(V×H)	480×576	1024×1280	480×1280	480×640×3	768×1024×3
	Dot pitch(μm)	25×37	34×48	77×77	190×63	234×78
	Color arrangement	RGB 3panels	RGB 3panels	RGB Delta	RGB Stripe	RGB Stripe
	Circuit parameters	4 divided source driver, VDD=20v, R=0.027Ω/μm C=1.85×10^{2}pF/pixel, L/W=5/600μm(buffer TFTs)				
Low temp. TFTs	TFT I μ :50cm^2/v•s Vth:5v		⇐--------⇒			
	TFT II μ :100cm^2/v•s Vth:1v		⇐------------⇒ a p p l i c a b l e			
High temp. TFTs	TFT μ :150cm^2/v•s Vth:1v	⇐-----⇒		quartz substrates are unrealistic		

ELEMENTAL MATERIALS AND PROCESSES

(1) Glass Substrates

Glass substrate is the key material in this development, because the upper limit of the process temperature is restricted by its strain point. Several types of glass whose strain points are around 600°C have been developed so far. Therefore the TFTs' process temperature should be kept under 600°C to utilize them. The endurance of these glasses to heating refers to a small enough change of their sizes to perform fine lithography. Meanwhile, a large size is imperative for the substrate to meet the enlarged displays. This will make the allowance for the deformation severe. Moreover, shrinkage is one of the most serious problems causing change in the shape of the glass plates. The amount of the shrinkage depends deeply on the strain points of glass plates, as shown in Fig.1. Thus, the higher the strain point, the better the glass is for the TFT process. However the shrinkage of the glass plates is also related to the history of heat treatments applied on them. For example we can see a correlation between shrinkage and pre-annealing term in Fig.2. Less shrinkage can be expected through pre-annealing. Anyway, taking account of the microelectronics with giant substrates, we have to look for as low shrinkage glasses as possible.

The behavior of the glass in the TFT process affects not only lithography performance as mentioned above but TFTs properties. Fig.3 shows the correlation between subthreshold swing S of TFTs and thermal expansion coefficients in which the ways of hydrogenation are taken as a experimental parameter. In the case of plasma hydrogenation, as the thermal expansion coefficient of a glass plate increases, the subthreshold swing S increases. On the other hand, any dependency is not clear in the cases of the hydrogenation from a silicon-nitride (SiN:H) layer and by Al sintering. It is supposed that the inner-stress distributions in TFTs caused by the glass substrate during the TFT process would govern the hydrogenation performance.

(2) POLYSILICON

Several kinds of methods for the polysilicon formation have been developed which are accompanied by glass substrates. The solid phase crystallization (SPC), among them, is one of the most promising ways to realize well qualified and leveled TFTs in a large area. SPC takes, however, fairly long term (almost 1 day) to bring polysilicon from amorphous. In order to reduce the crystallization time, it has been indicated that the purification of source materials is effective[1]. We are using disilane (Si_2H_6) as the source of silicon, and a 100 nm thick silicon is deposited at 450 °C in amorphous form by low-pressure chemical vapor deposition (LPCVD). In our case, the crystallization period was shortened by reducing the deposition pressure. LPCVD at 0.2 Torr and 12 hours crystallization are currently taken, in which there is no remarkable sacrifice of TFT performances compared to the other conditions: 0.4 Torr and 0.8 Torr LPCVDs.

SPC brings fairly large grains (1μm~5μm), which include a lot of twins though. The high symmetric twins like {211}$\sum$=3 and {122}$\sum$=9 are considered to leave no state in the energy band gap of silicon [2][3]. However, A large number of low symmetric twins also supposed to be involved in SPCed grains [4], and of which details have not been unveiled yet. Anyway it would be better for TFTs to reduce not only grain boundaries but also the twin's density.

One way to reduce the number of twins is to control the direction of SPC. It was found that the facet preferred grain growth could suppress the twin generation in grains [5]. Another way is to employ additional heating for example excimer laser irradiation

73

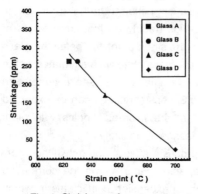

Fig. 1. Shrinkage after annealing at 600°C for 24h versus strain point of glass substrates.

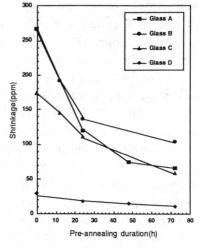

Fig. 2. Shrinkage of glass substrates versus 600°C pre-annealing duration.

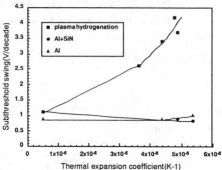

Fig. 3. Subthreshold swing of TFTs versus thermal expansion coefficient of glass substrates

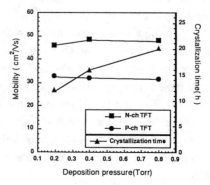

Fig. 4. Field effect mobility and crystallization time vesus deposition pressure.

after SPC [6]. It will be necessary to lower the defect density and control the types of them based on their characters.

Excimer laser annealing is an excellent way to obtain the high performance of TFTs. In this case, however, how to keep the good uniformity of TFT properties over the large area and also high throughput is important. An alternative to the laser annealing (LA) might be the rapid thermal annealing (RTA) with an infrared lamp. RTA is potentially superior to LA in terms of throughput and uniformity by utilizing a large size of lamp [7].

(3) Gate Dielectric

There have been several kinds of gate dielectric formation methods which can be applied to the low temperature polysilicon TFTs. They include not only chemical vapor deposition (CVD) but liquid phase one (LPD) for SiO_2 [8].

It has been shown that conventional atmospheric chemical vapor deposition (APCVD) and also low pressure chemical vapor deposition (LPCVD) have been applicable [9][10]. Plasma enhanced CVD (PECVD) and sputtering are also suitable [11][12]. The pre-conditioning process of the polysilicon surface by using plasma treatments might be beneficial to the performance of TFTs just as for MOSFETs of single crystalline silicon [13].

(4) Source and Drain (S/D)

Self aligned ion doping would be desirable for the TFT processes, because it can primarily avoid the stray capacitance from gate and source electrodes overlapping, which causes flicker in a display, and also make the process simpler than that of stagger TFTs. However, the activation following the ion doping should be achieved beneath 600°C. It takes at least several hours.

We have already reported that the incorporation of hydrogen can bring simultanious activation with the doping (self-activation: SA) [14]. From the data for P and B ion-doping in Fig. 5 and Fig. 6, respectively, it can be seen that source and drain can be formed automatically with incorporation of hydrogen above a threshold.

Another effective way for fast S/D formation is laser annealing. However in this case, the gate electrode must be composed of high melting point metals like doped polysilicon. It is very difficult to use aluminum here.

(5) Gate Metal

It is favorable to avoid contacts between the bus lines and the electrodes of TFTs in order to increase aperture ratio of LCDs and to alleviate fabrication difficulties of circuits. Taking into account the great lengths of both the data and scan bus lines, the resistivity of the wiring metal should be as low as possible. SA technique allows the use of aluminum, which could meet such demands.

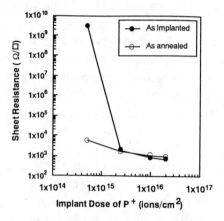

Fig. 5. Dependence of polysilicon film sheet resistance on the phosphorus implant dose.

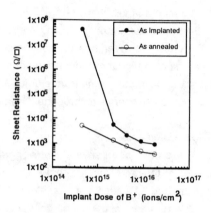

Fig. 6. Dependence of polysilicon film sheet resistance on the boron implant dose.

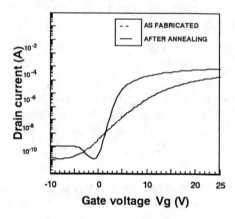

Fig. 7. Drain current vesus gate voltage characteristics of Al gate TFT.

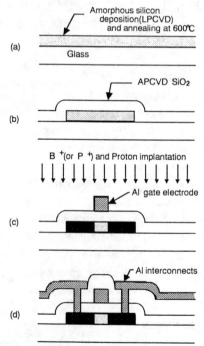

Fig. 8. Fabrication process flow of fully-selfaligned Al gate polysilicon TFT

When aluminum is employed as the gate metal, we can also expect remarkable improvements of TFT properties after an annealing at 400°C for 30 min. in N_2 ambient (Fig.7). This supposes that the catalytic effect of Al decomposes moisture [15]. That eventually gives hydrogenation to the polysilicon.

Self-Aligned Aluminum Gate TFTs

We have developed a self-aligned aluminum gate process for TFTs with the SA technique [16]. The fabrication process is described in Fig.8. Silicon films (100 nm) were deposited in a conventional LPCVD reactor using pure disilane as the source gas. Several kinds of glass substrate were used for the comparison in terms of TFT performance. Despite this, there was no difference in the results. SPC was achieved by 600 °C annealing for 12hours in N_2 ambient. SiO_2 layers were deposited by APCVD at 430° C over polysilicon islands which were defined by lithography and dry-etching. Then, a 600°C annealing for 12 hours was employed to densify the SiO_2 layer. Pure aluminum was deposited by sputtering in 300 nm thickness and shaped into gate electrodes and bus lines.

Dopants were implanted into the S/D regions by using the ion doping instrument described in a previous report [14]. The implant doses of phosphorus and boron were $6 \times 10^{15}/cm^2$ each, and hydrogen was simultaneously implanted at the dose of 1.4×10^{16} /cm2 in both cases. The accelerating energy was 90 kev for phosphorous and 33 kev for boron. Prior to the source and drain electrode formation, a SiO_2 interlayer was deposited at 350 ° C by a plasma-enhanced chemical vapor deposition (PECVD), utilizing tetraethoxysilane as the source gas. After the contact openings, the aluminum electrodes for source and drain were formed and annealed at 400 °C for 0.5 hours.

TFT properties obtained through this process are shown in table 2. Fig.9 shows the performance of the driver circuits using these TFTs. The configuration of a CMOS driver circuit is illustrated in Fig.10.

Table 2. TFT properties with L=15 μm, W=50 μm

	N-ch	P-ch
Effect Mobility (cm²/V•s)	46	27
Threshold Voltage (V)	6.0	-9.7
Subthreshold swing(V/dec.)	1.5	0.7

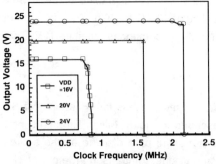

Fig. 9. Output voltage versus clock frequency characteristics of the CMOS scanning driver circuit.

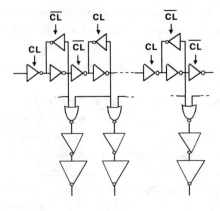

Fig. 10. Configuration of CMOS driver circuit

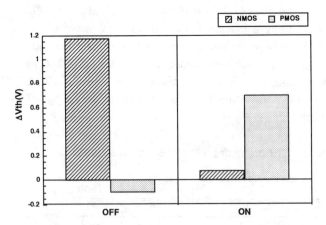

Fig. 11. Threshold voltage shift under ON and OFF states D. C. vias stress.

OFF STATE CURRENT AND RELIABILITY

The off state current of an addressing TFT must be less than a few pico amperes in order to maintain the good quality of LCDs. Unfortunately, however, it has been indicated that the polysilicon TFTs have an enormous leakage current compared to the single crystalline silicon MOSFETs. That would make it difficult to realize AMLCDs. Carrier trap state models related to the leakage current have been employed [17]. Trap states mainly originate from the crystalline defects and the polysilicon/SiO_2 inter-faces. The hydrogen passivation can surely reduce the leakage current as seen in Fig.7, but still not enough for the application to the addressing TFTs. Some configurational modifications such as lightly doped drain (LDD) or off set gate (OSG) have been shown effective in alleviating the electrical field of drain edge [18][19]. Nevertheless, it would be preferable to use the same process for all TFTs in the monolithic AMLCDs from the manufacturing point of view.

Reliability of the TFT devices and circuits is crucial for the robust opertaion of AMLCD products. Polysilicon TFTs are known to degrade under to d.c. and a.c. bias stress. TFTs threshold voltage shifts after both on and off states biasing stress are shown in Fig.11. Drain voltages (Vd) were 17V for n channels, and -17V for p channels respectively in both cases. Gate voltages (Vg) to the n channels were 17V for on state and -17V for off state respectively, while to the p channels they were -17V for on and 17V for off. The stress duration was 30 min. The threshold voltage shift of the n-ch TFTs after the off state stress was worst among them and next was that of the p-ch TFTs after the on state stress. According to [20][21], this behavior is thought to be referring to the damage caused to the hydrogenated polysilicon by the holes. The on stressed n-ch and the off stressed p-ch TFTs did not suffer so severely as the n-ch off and p-ch on stressed TFTs. However, there are some instabilities still existing which might be related to the gap states linked behaviors.

SUMMARY

The low temperature polysilicon TFTs have been thoroughly investigated to realize the monolithic AMLCDs, which can meet the commercial based production. A remarkably big advancement has been made so far. However, it is necessary to concentrate on managing the defect chemistry including polysilicon surface in order to get better and robust properties of TFTs and their good uniformities.

ACKNOWLEDGMENT

We wish to acknowledge helpful discussions with staff of dept. 2. of Central Research Labs. and dep.1 of Liquid Crystal Labs. in Sharp Corporation.

REFERENCES

[1] E. F. Kennedy et al, J. Appl. Phy., 48 (1977)

[2] M. Koyama et al, J. Phys. C21 (1988) L695

[3] R.E. Thompson et al, Phys, Rev. B29 (1985) 889

[4] S. Maekawa et al, to be published

[5] S. Maekawa et al, to be published

[6] T. Noguchi et al, MRS. Sym. Proc. 146 (1989) 35

[7] J. Mehlhaff et al, AMLCD '93 Sym. Proc. (1993) 158

[8] D.W. Greve et al, AMLCD '93 Sym. Proc. (1993) 68

[9] A. Mimura et al, IEEE Trans. Electron Devices ED-36 (1989) 351

[10] A.G. Lewis et al, IEDM Technical Digest (1990) 843

[11] H. Ohsima et al, IEDM Technical Digest (1989) 157

[12] T. Serikawa, IEDM Technical Digest (1988) 222

[13] G. G. Fountain et al, J. Appl. Phys. 63 (1988) 4744

[14] A. Yoshinouchi et al, MRS. Symp. Proc. 268 (1992) 363

[15] F. Montillo et al, J. Electrochem. Soc. 118 (1971) 1463

[16] E. Ohno et al, SSDM. Ext. Abs. (1993) 425

[17] J. G. Fossum et al, IEEE Trans. Elect. Dev. ED-32 (1985) 1878

[18] K. Nakazawa et al, SID 90 Digest 311

[19] S. Morozumi et al, SID 83 Digest 156

[20] W. B. Jackson, Phys. Rev. B 41 (1990) 1059

[21] A.G. Lewis et al, IEDM Technical Digest (1991) 575

A COMPREHENSIVE STUDY OF PLASMA ENHANCED CRYSTALLIZATION OF a-SI:H FILMS ON GLASS

Aiguo Yin, Stephen J. Fonash, D. M. Reber, Y. M. Li*, and M. Bennett*.
Electronic Materials and Processing Research Laboratory, The Pennsylvania State University, University Park, PA 16802.
* Solarax Corporation, Thin-Film Division, Newtown, PA 18940

ABSTRACT

An extensive study is reported here on plasma enhanced crystallization of a-Si:H films on glass. Both electron cyclotron resonance (ECR) helium plasma exposures and ECR oxygen plasma exposures were investigated to obtain enhanced crystallization of a-Si:H films. We have found that the ECR helium plasma exposure can render more crystallization enhancement than the ECR oxygen plasma exposure. This is because ECR helium plasma exposures can produce more dangling Si bonds, voids, and "interstitial" Si atoms in a-Si:H films than ECR oxygen plasma exposures. These dangling Si bonds, voids, and "interstitial" Si atoms are believed to be the cause of the observed reduced incubation time as well as enhanced grain growth of the plasma exposed a-Si:H films in subsequent crystallization processes. This model is supported by the effects of plasma exposure time on the enhanced crystallization process of a-Si:H films.

INTRODUCTION

One of the most important and widely studied materials in microelectronics technology is polycrystalline silicon (poly-Si). It has been established that the amorphous phase of silicon (a-Si) is an excellent precursor material for forming polysilicon films that can be far superior to as-deposited polysilicon for the application in poly-Si thin film transistors (TFTs). This has been shown for both low pressure chemical vapor deposited (LPCVD) precursor films deposited at T ~ 550 °C [1] [2] and plasma enhanced chemical vapor deposited (PECVD) precursor films deposited at T ~ 250 °C [3]. In order to fabricate poly-Si TFTs on inexpensive glass substrates, low thermal budget processes have to be investigated for the polycrystallization of these precursor amorphous silicon films. It has been reported that PECVD precursor a-Si:H films deposited on Corning 7059 glass at 250 °C can be crystallized at thermal budgets as low as 700 °C/4 minute using rapid thermal annealing [4] and this low crystallization thermal budget can be reduced further to 650 °C/4 minute with the aid of an ultra-thin Pd surface treatment [5]. In very recent reports, we have demonstrated that an oxygen plasma exposure of PECVD a-Si:H films can cause these films to crystallize with a much lower thermal-budget than that required for the same a-Si:H films without this plasma exposure [6], and this oxygen plasma enhanced crystallization process has been used to successfully fabricate poly-Si TFTs on glass substrates[7].

In this report, we present a comprehensive study of the plasma enhanced crystallization of PECVD a-Si:H films. Both electron cyclotron resonance (ECR) oxygen plasma exposures and helium plasma exposures were used to reduce the crystallization thermal budget of a-Si:H films. We have found that the ECR helium plasma treatment can even more efficiently enhance the crystallization process of a-Si:H films than the ECR oxygen plasma treatment. The ECR helium plasma is much more efficient than the ECR oxygen plasma at causing the generation of dangling Si bonds, voids, and interstitial Si atoms in a thin top layer of the precursor a-Si:H films. These changes are believed to cause the observed reduction in the incubation time as well as the enhanced grain growth of a-Si:H films in the subsequent crystallization process.

EXPERIMENTAL PROCEDURE

Two different types of hydrogenated amorphous silicon deposited by plasma-enhanced chemical vapor deposition were used in this study. One was a 1000 Å a-Si:H film on Corning 7059 glass substrates (type I) deposited at T ~ 215 °C with a 20:1 hydrogen dilution; another was a 1500 Å a-Si:H film on Si_3N_4 coated 7059 glass substrates (type II) deposited at T ~ 250 °C. After deposition, both type I and type II a-Si:H films were first exposed to our ECR oxygen plasma or ECR helium plasma treatment prior to the furnace thermal annealing for crystallization.

All type I samples, those used as controls (without the plasma exposure treatment) and those exposed to ECR O_2 or He plasma treatment, were then crystallized by furnace annealing at 575 °C for times ranging from 6 hours to 20 hours in an N_2 ambient. All type II samples (controls and those exposed to plasma treatment) were crystallized by furnace annealing at 600 °C for times ranging from 4 hours to 36 hours. UV reflectance measurements were taken on all samples to monitor the conventional crystallization process and the plasma enhanced crystallization process of both type I and type II a-Si:H films. Transmission electron microcopy (TEM) was also used to characterize the polysilicon films obtained from the different crystallization processes.

EXPERIMENTAL RESULTS AND DISCUSSIONS

It is established that the UV reflectance spectrum of a single crystal Si shows two reflectance peaks at 276 nm and 365 nm which are due to optical transitions at the X point and along the Γ-L axis of the Brillouin zone [8]. These characteristic reflectance peaks were also observed to first appear as the a-Si precursor film begin to crystallize, then to increase during grain growth and finally to saturate when the crystallization was completed [6]. The reflectance peak height (ΔR), defined as from the minimum reflectance at around 240 nm to the maximum reflectance at around 276 nm as in previous reports [6] [7], was used to monitor the crystallization process and determine the crystallization thermal budget as a function of plasma exposure in this study.

Comparison of ECR Oxygen Plasma Exposure and ECR Helium Plasma Exposure

In this experiment, both the ECR oxygen plasma treatment and the ECR helium plasma treatment were performed for 60 minutes with the microwave power at 700 watts and the substrate temperature at 400 °C. For oxygen the pressure was at 0.5 mTorr and for helium the pressure was at 1.0 mTorr. In Figure 1, the UV reflectance peak heights at 276 nm of the ECR plasma (oxygen and helium) treated samples as well as control samples without any plasma treatment are plotted as a function of annealing time.

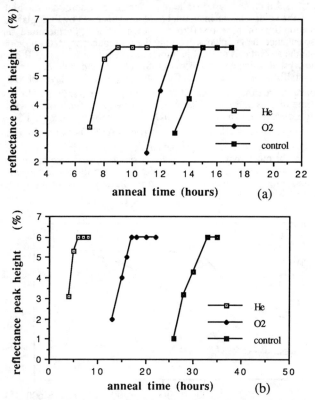

FIG. 1. UV reflectance peak height ΔR at 276 nm (4.5 ev) as a function of furnace annealing time: (a) type I samples, annealed at 575 °C; (b) type II samples, annealed at 600 °C.

For type I a-Si:H films, as shown in Fig. 1(a), control samples need 15 hours furnace annealing at 575 °C to become polysilicon, while the ECR oxygen plasma exposed samples need 13 hours and the ECR helium plasma exposed samples need only 9 hours. For type II a-Si:H films, as shown in Fig. 1(b), control samples need more than 32 hours furnace annealing at 600 °C to become polycrystalline silicon, while ECR oxygen plasma exposed samples need 17 hours and ECR helium plasma exposed samples need only 6 hours. It is seen that for both type I and type II a-Si:H films, ECR helium plasma exposures can cause more crystallization enhancement than ECR oxygen plasma exposures.

It is well known that an ECR plasma can produce a high density of ions with long ion lifetimes ensured by maintaining a low pressure plasma [9]. Therefore, the samples in our ECR plasmas were exposed to a very high density ion fluence. This ion fluence can produce a high density of dangling Si bonds, voids, and extra (ie, "interstitial") Si atoms in a thin top layer of our films [10]. Dangling Si bonds, especially charged ones, have been reported in another context to facilitate solid phase crystallization [1]. We suggest here that the high density of dangling Si bonds, the voids, and the interstitial Si atoms generated by ECR plasma can greatly reduce the incubation time of these a-Si films as shown in Fig. 1. Furthermore, the interstitial Si atoms can also enhance the grain growth during the subsequent crystallization process [11].

To investigate the advantages of ECR helium plasma exposures over ECR oxygen plasma exposures for the crystallization enhancement of a-Si:H films (and to point out the potential for selective area crystallization), some type II films were covered by a layer of SiO_2 during the ECR oxygen plasma treatment or the ECR helium plasma treatment. In Figure 2, the crystallization time of plasma exposed samples is plotted as a function of the thickness of masking SiO_2. It is clearly shown that 200 Å SiO_2 can effectively mask the a-Si:H films from the oxygen plasma exposure, while much thicker (>400 Å) SiO_2 is required in case of the helium plasma exposure due to much deeper penetration of helium ions. Therefore, the helium plasma exposure can be much more efficient than the oxygen plasma exposure in modifying a surface layer of the precursor a-Si:H films. The picture is that it does so by generating more dangling Si bonds, voids, and interstitial Si atoms thereby causing more crystallization enhancement of the a-Si:H films.

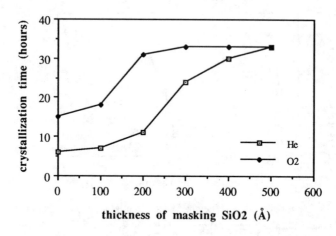

FIG. 2. Crystallization time of type II a-Si:H films as a function of the thickness of mask SiO2 covering the a-Si:H films during the plasma treatment. Oxygen plasma treatment was taken for 80 minutes with oxygen pressure at 0.5 mTorr; helium plasma treatment was taken for 40 minutes with helium pressure at 1.5 mTorr.

Effect of ECR Plasma Exposure Time

In order to investigate the effect of ECR plasma exposure time on the plasma enhanced crystallization process, type II a-Si:H films were also exposed to the ECR helium plasma treatments for different periods of time. In Figure 3, the crystallization time is plotted as a function of plasma exposure time. As shown, the ECR helium plasma is so efficient that it can advantageously modify the a-Si:H films even in a short 20 minute plasma exposure. Even such a short exposure is seen to dramatically reduce the crystallization thermal budget of type II a-Si:H films. In addition, more crystallization enhancement is obtained for longer plasma exposure times, but this crystallization enhancement is seen to tend to saturate for plasma exposure times.

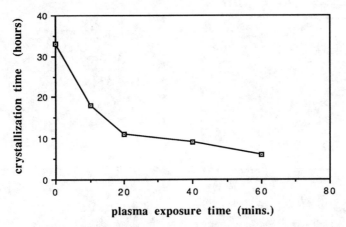

FIG. 3. Crystallization time of type II a-Si:H films as a function of helium plasma exposure time. The plasma treatment was taken with He pressure at 1.0 mTorr, temperature at 400 °C and microwave power at 700 W.

Characterization of Crystallized Silicon

We note here that all crystallized films, controls and plasma exposed ones, show the same grain orientation of (110) using X-ray diffraction, although no quantitative comparison was taken in this study. A Phillips EM-420ST scanning transmission electron microscope (TEM) was also used for the TEM investigation of crystallized type I silicon films. Figure 4 (a) and (b) show the bright field TEM micrograph and the selection area diffraction pattern (SADP) of a control sample, which was crystallized using 16 hours furnace annealing at 575 oC. Figure 4 (c) and (d) show the corresponding TEM micrograph and SADP of a helium plasma treated sample, which was crystallized using 9 hours furnace annealing at 575 °C. These TEM pictures further demonstrate a-Si:H films exposed to a high density plasma can be crystallized at a much lower thermal budget than unexposed a-Si:H films.

CONCLUSION

We have demonstrated in this study of plasma enhanced crystallization of a-Si:H films that exposure to high density plasma, such as the ECR oxygen plasma or the ECR helium plasma used here, can dramatically reduce the crystallization thermal budget of a-Si:H films. We show here for the first time that ECR helium plasma exposures can cause more crystallization enhancement than ECR oxygen plasma exposures. We believe that this is because ECR helium plasma exposures of a-Si:H films can produce much more dangling Si bonds, voids, and interstitial Si atoms. These changes in the top layer of our a-Si:H precursor films are believed to greatly reduce the incubation time as well as enhance the grain growth of these plasma exposed a-Si:H films in subsequent crystallization processing.

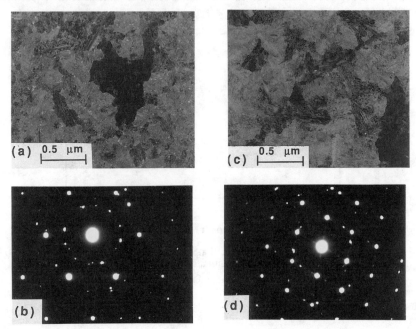

FIG. 4. TEM of the type I crystallized silicon films: (a) (b) TEM image and TEM SADP of a control sample which was annealed for 16 hours at 575 °C; (c) (d) TEM image and TEM SADP of a helium plasma treated sample which was annealed for 9 hours at 575 °C

REFERENCES

1. T. Aoyama, N. Konishi, T. Suzuki, and K. Miyata, MRS Symp. Proc. Vol. 106, PP 347-352, (1988).
2. M. Hatalis and D. Greve, J. Appl. Phys. 63, 2260 (1988).
3. R. Kakkad, J. Smith, W. S. Lau, and S. J. Fonash, J. Appl. Phys. 65(5), 2069(1988)
4. Gang Liu and S. J. Fonash, Jpn. J. Appl. Phys. 30(2B), L269(1991)
5. Gang Liu and S. J. Fonash, Appl. Phys. Lett. 62(20), 2554(1993)
6. Aiguo Yin and S. J. Fonash, to be published on JVST, Jul-Aug(1994)
7. Aiguo Yin and S. J. Fonash, Technical Digest, IEDM, pp397-400(1993)
8. C. Harbeke, Polycrystalline Semiconductors. Physical Properties and Applications. (Spinger, Berlin,1985)
9. M. E. Day, M. Delfino, and W. Tsai, J. Appl. Phys. 74(8), 15, pp 5217-5224(1993).
10. R. W. Collins and C. J. Tuckerman, J. Vac. Sci. Technol.A 4(5), pp 2343-2349(1986).
11. C. V. Tompson, MRS Symp. Proc. vol. 106, pp115-125(1988)

HIGH MOBILITY NON-HYDROGENATED
LOW TEMPERATURE POLYSILICON TFTs

F.PLAIS, P.LEGAGNEUX, T.KRETZ, R.STROH, O.HUET AND D.PRIBAT
Thomson-CSF LCR, 91404 Orsay cedex, France

ABSTRACT

We have fabricated polysilicon (poly-Si) thin film transistors (TFTs) using a standard 4-mask sequence, with self-aligned ion implantation for source and drain doping. The active layer was obtained by solid phase crystallisation of high purity Si_2H_6-deposited amorphous Si, whereas the gate oxide was synthesised by a novel plasma deposition technique, namely distributed electron cyclotron resonance plasma enhanced chemical vapour deposition (DECR PECVD). We have obtained high carrier mobilities (70 $cm^2V^{-1}s^{-1}$ for electrons and 40 $cm^2V^{-1}s^{-1}$ for holes) with an excellent uniformity and without the need for a post-hydrogenation treatment. Moreover, we show that the TFT characteristics are practically insensitive to hot carrier effects.

INTRODUCTION

The current interest in polysilicon (poly-Si) technology for active matrix liquid crystal displays (AMLCDs) stems from the prospect of integrating the addressing and clocking circuitry at the periphery of the active plate, without additional cost. Moreover, for dedicated applications, such as video projectors, the reduced size of the display (2 to 6 inch for the projector cell) makes it difficult to mount the peripheral circuitry with an acceptable yield, in particular when high definition cells are of concern [1].

Depending on whether the polysilicon TFT is used in the driving circuitry or as a switch in the matrix, different properties are requested. The TFTs used in the driving circuitry should present a high mobility and a very high stability even at high drain-to-source voltages (up to 25V) whereas those used in the matrix should exhibit a very low leakage current and on- to off-current ratios higher than 6 decades. These last properties, which are easily obtained with amorphous silicon TFTs, are only attained with polysilicon material after a thorough passivation of the grain boundary defects by post-hydrogenation [2,3] and with the use of lightly doped drain (LDD) structures [4]. However, when a final hydrogenation step is implemented, the stability of the TFTs suffers from the weakness of Si-H bonds [5] and their use in driving circuitry could turn out to be problematic. Actually, recent studies have shown that the drain-to-source voltages involved in the driver circuitry induce various degradations in the TFT characteristics [6,7].

We will show in the following of this paper that by using specific deposition techniques for active layer and gate oxide fabrication, we have obtained high mobility TFTs which are weakly affected by hot carrier effects.

TFT FABRICATION

The active layer was deposited by low pressure chemical vapour deposition (LPCVD) in an ultra clean reactor (UHV- grade background atmosphere) using point-of-use-purified Si_2H_6 diluted in H_2 carrier gas [8]. More precisely, the deposition pressure was held at 2 Torr whereas the temperature was maintained at 480°C. The H_2 and Si_2H_6 flow rates were respectively 1960 and 40 sccm.

We took much care of the cleanliness of this process, since impurities (oxygen or carbon) introduced into the active layer during its deposition and subsequent processing, can occupy dangling bonds at the grain boundaries. Once they are introduced, they create stable extrinsic defects (eventually complexed with metallic impurities) which may affect mobility and stability.

The carbon and oxygen levels in our layers are of the same order of magnitude as those measured in floating zone monocrystalline silicon substrates, i.e. a few 10^{16} cm^{-3} for each [9]. These values are between three to four orders of magnitude lower than the ones found in films deposited in "classical" LPCVD systems [10].

The initially amorphous material was solid phase crystallised (SPC) in a furnace at 580°C under flowing nitrogen for 90 hours. As clearly evidenced by the TEM plan views of Figure 1, the material is completely crystallised after this treatment. We have obtained grain sizes of about 3 μm for layers of thicknesses around 120 nm.

1μm

Figure 1 : TEM plan views of a polysilicon thin film obtained by SPC at 580°C.
(a) bright field micrograph and (b) dark field micrograph of the same area.

These layers were then patterned and etched by reactive ion etching (RIE). The channel width is thereafter designated by W.

Next, the gate oxide was deposited to a thickness of 120 nm by distributed electron cyclotron resonance plasma enhanced chemical vapor deposition (DECR PECVD). This method allows us to deposit a device-grade oxide which exhibits properties similar to those of high temperature thermal oxides [11]. The high quality of the Si/SiO$_2$ interface is routinely checked using simultaneous high and low frequency capacitance measurements with a Keithley system 82 on MOS diodes fabricated on (100) silicon substrates (Fig. 2a). In this case, the density of interface states is below 2 10^{10} cm^{-2}eV^{-1} at mid-gap (Fig. 2b).

· The gate conductor is an amorphous silicon layer deposited by APCVD at 580°C. The doping of the gate layer is obtained either by implantation or during deposition using a mixture of SiH$_4$ and PH$_3$ in H$_2$ carrier gas. The gate finger is defined by a RIE etch; the gate length is thereafter designated by L. For n-channel TFTs, the self-aligned source and drain contacts were formed by a phosphorus implant through the gate oxide, at 120 KeV and to a dose of 2×10^{15} cm^{-2}. For p-channel devices, boron was used at 40 KeV and also to a dose of 2×10^{15} cm^{-2}. These implantations were activated by a furnace anneal at 580°C for 20 hours. This treatment also converted the amorphous gate material to degenerated polycrystalline silicon. Following the aluminium deposition and patterning by lift-off, the contacts were annealed at 450°C in flowing forming gas (10% of H_2 in N_2).

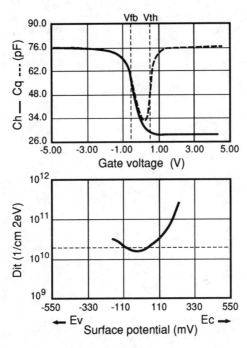

Figure 2 : a- High and low frequency C-V characteristics for a DECR SiO$_2$ film deposited at floating temperature and potential.
b- D_{it} spectrum corresponding to the C-V characteristics of (a).

Finally, the samples were covered with a SiO$_2$ passivation layer which was opened on the contacts in order to permit tip probing and the transfer characteristics of the transistors (Ids = f(Vgs)) were measured for different Vds.

TFT CHARACTERISTICS

Figure 3 presents the transfer characteristics of non-hydrogenated single gate (continuous line) and double gate (dashed line) n-channel TFTs (W = 40 μm and L = 10 μm or 2 x 5 μm). The on-state characteristics are strictly the same for either type of device. The carrier mobility (μ),deduced from the linear plot at Vds = 0.1 V, is as high as 70 ± 5 cm^{2}V^{-1}s^{-1}, averaged over 20 measurements. This value is comparable to the ones obtained by multi-shot excimer laser annealing, without heating the substrate [12]. Moreover, it should be emphasised that our values are obtained without hydrogenation which is not the case in the work of Chen et al [12] and that the uniformity is much better using SPC rather than laser annealing. The threshold voltage and subthreshold slope are respectively 10 V and 1.6 V/dec. The off-current exhibits a well-known shape, showing an exponential variation with increasing negative values of the gate voltage. The off-current is slightly reduced by the double gate structure which decreases the electrical field at the channel-drain junction. The off-current level is not compatible with the pixel TFT requirements as no hydrogenation step nor LDD structure were implemented on these devices.

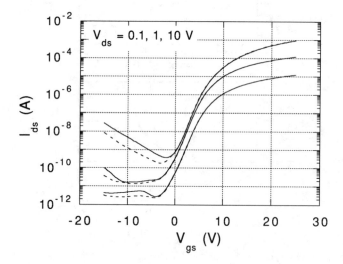

Figure 3 : Transfer characteristics of single gate (continuous line) and double gate (dashed line) non-hydrogenated TFTs, with W = 40 μm and L = 10 μm or 2 x 5 μm.

Figure 4 presents Ids = f(Vds) characteristics at Vgs = 25 V, for three different channel lengths, namely 5, 10 and 20 μm. The Ids current does not saturate at high Vds for gate length below 10 μm. This behaviour (Kink effect) is commonly observed in polysilicon TFTs and is known to induce a degradation of the on-current as well as an increase in the off-current [6]. Therefore, we have examined the evolution of the transfer characteristics of 5 μm-length TFTs stressed during two hours at Vgs = Vds = 25V. In these conditions, a constant current of 3.5 mA flows through the device (see Figure 4).

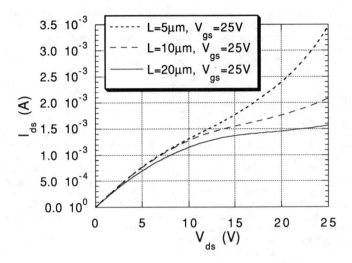

Figure 4 : Ids = f(Vds) characteristics at Vgs = 25 V,
for three different channel lengths, 5, 10 and 20 μm.

Figure 5 presents the transfer characteristics before and after stress (2 hours at Vgs = Vds = +25 V). Obviously, the off-current slightly increases after stress but the remarkable result is the stability of the on-current. The threshold voltage remains virtually unchanged and the relative decrease of the on-current measured at Vgs = 20 V and Vds = 10 V is less than 5 %.

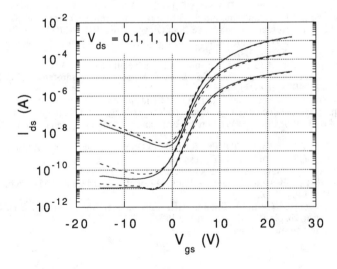

Figure 5 : Transfer characteristics measured on a TFT with W / L = 40 μm / 5 μm, before
(continuous line) and after (dashed line) stress at Vgs = Vds = 25 V for 2 hours.

Hot carriers are believed to generate interface acceptor states near the conduction band edge which are responsible for the on-current degradation as well as mid-gap centers which are responsible for the off-current degradation [6,13]. Considering that we do notice the kink effect (Figure 4) and that consequently hot carriers are generated at the drain, we believe that the good stability that we observe is the result of the absence of hydrogenation.

CONCLUSIONS

We have shown that the combined use of high purity silicon films and high quality deposited oxide allowed the fabrication of thin film transistors exhibiting large mobilities (70 cm^2 V^{-1} s^{-1} for electrons, which is probably the highest value reported to date for solid phase crystallised, non-hydrogenated devices) and practically no degradations after severe stressing in the "kink region". We emphasise that these characteristics have been obtained with a maximum processing temperature of 580°C and without hydrogenation treatment. We believe that the very good stability that we observe is directly related to the fact that the devices are not hydrogenated and that no weak Si-H bonds are present at the grain boundaries. Such devices are certainly adequate for use in peripheral circuitry in active matrix displays. We are currently implementing lightly doped source and drain structures, in order to reduce the leakage currents and be able to use the TFTs for pixel switching as well.

REFERENCES

1. K.Adachi, Solid State Technology, January 1993, p. 63.
2. I.W.Wu, A.Lewis, T.Huang and A.Chiang, IEEE Electron Device Lett. **EDL-10**, 123 (1989).
3. S.D.Brotherton, J.R.Ayres and N.D.Young, Solid State Electronics **34**, 671 (1991).
4. U.Mitra, B.Khan, M.Venkatesan and E.H.Stupp, Conference Record of The 1991 International Display Research Conference (San Diego), IEEE 91CH-3071-8, 207.
5. S.Bhattacharya, R. Kovelamudi, S.Batra, S.Banerjee, B.Y.Nguyen and P.Tobin, IEEE Electron Device Lett. **EDL-13**, 491 (1992).
6. N.D.Young, A.Gill and M.J.Edwards, Semicond. Sci. Technol. **7**, 1183 (1992).
7. G.Fortunato, A.Pecora, G.Tallarida, L.Mariucci, C.Reita and P.Migliorato, IEEE Trans. Electron Devices, 1994, in press.
8. T.Kretz, R.Stroh, P.Legagneux, O.Huet, M.Magis and D.Pribat, to appear in Polycrystalline semiconductors III - Physics and Technology, Solid State Phenomena Vol. XXX, edited by H.P.Strunk, J.H.Werner, B.Fortin and O.Bonnaud (Trans. Tech., Zürich, 1994).
9. D.Pribat, F.Plais, P.Legagneux, T.Kretz, R.Stroh, O.Huet, C.Walaine and M.Magis, Rev. Techn. Thomson-CSF, March 1994, in press.
10. A.T.Voutsas and M.K.Hatalis, J. Electrochem. Soc. **140**, 871 (1993).
11. N.Jiang, M.C.Hugon, B.Agius, T.Kretz, F.Plais, D.Pribat, T.Carriere and M.Puech, Jpn. J. Appl. Phys. **31**, L1404 (1992).
12. S.Chen, J.B.Boyce, I.W.Wu, A.Chiang, R.I.Johnson, G.B.Anderson and S.E.Ready, proceedings of Eurodisplay'93 (Strasbourg), p.195.
13. N.Young, private communication.

RAPID THERMAL CRYSTALLIZATION OF LPCVD AMORPHOUS SILICON FILMS

A.T. VOUTSAS[1], M.K. HATALIS[1], K.R. OLASUPO[2], A.K. NANDA[2] and D. ALUGBIN[2]

[1]Lehigh University, Display Research Laboratory, Bethlehem, PA. 18015

[2]AT&T Bell Laboratories, Allentown, PA. 18103

ABSTRACT

The crystallization of LPCVD a-Si by Rapid Thermal Anneal was investigated. RTA polysilicon films can find application in the fabrication of TFTs for AMLCDs, due to the lower thermal budget associated with fast crystallization at high temperatures. It was found that the grain size of the crystallized films decreases with the temperature, in the range of 700°C to 1100°C, while for higher temperatures the opposite trend is observed. The latter observation was attributed to the high thermal vibration of sub-critical clusters, that was assumed responsible for the decline in the nuclei population at high annealing temperatures, combined with the faster crystalline growth rate at high temperatures. RTA silicon films were found to have lower intra-grain defect density, that may result in the improvement of the electrical characteristics of the polysilicon films.

INTRODUCTION

Polycrystalline silicon is emerging as a key material for the fabrication of thin film transistors (TFTs) for active matrix liquid crystal displays (AMLCDs) [1]. Due to their higher effective carrier mobility, poly-Si TFTs can be used to increase the aperture ratio of the pixels and to integrate the peripheral circuit drivers on the same display. To improve the performance of the TFTs, control of process related material properties, such as grain size, intra-grain defect density and poly-Si film roughness is very important. In addition, AMLCDs fabricated on glass substrates require a low thermal-budget process to avoid degradation of the glass substrate due to thermal damage. Moreover, the fabrication technology has to take into consideration the current trends towards higher throughput and process automation and control.

Crystallized amorphous silicon films can yield good quality poly-Si films. Crystallization can be accomplished by several methods. Furnace anneal at temperatures in the range of 550°C to 600°C is the simplest and most widespread technique. However, this crystallization step can be a limiting factor in the processing of glass substrates due to its long duration [2], especially at low annealing temperatures. Multi-step furnace anneal of amorphous silicon films [3], that has been shown to improve the uniformity of the grain size, also suffers from high thermal budget for glass substrate processing. In contrast to furnace anneal, laser anneal has also been investigated for the crystallization of amorphous silicon films [4]; with this technique, polysilicon films with very large grains can be achieved.

As an alternative to these methods, RTA can be employed for the crystallization of

93

Mat. Res. Soc. Symp. Proc. Vol. 345. ©1994 Materials Research Society

a-Si films. Previous studies have shown encouraging results for the implementation of this method in the fabrication of TFTs [5] and the cost-effective processing of glass plates [6]. However, no extensive characterization of the polysilicon film characteristics has been performed. In this study we present and discuss results pertinent to the grain size in rapid thermal annealed silicon films. Particularly, we show the nature of the dependence of the grain size upon the annealing temperature and the crystallization time.

EXPERIMENTAL DETAILS

Amorphous silicon was deposited on 5" silicon wafers. Prior to the deposition of the silicon film the wafers were cleaned in a H_2SO_4/H_2O_2 solution with a final BHF step, followed by the deposition of 100 nm of LPCVD SiO_2 by TEOS pyrolysis at 720°C. The amorphous silicon was deposited in an LPCVD reactor by the pyrolysis of silane at 550°C. The process pressure was kept at 0.5 Torr.

The rapid thermal anneal was performed in a Heat-Pulse 4108 RTA system, made by AG Associates. The anneal temperature ranged between 700°C and 1250°C. Typically, 2-3 seconds were required for the RTA system to reach the target temperature.

Transmission electron microscopy was employed to investigate the structural characteristics of the crystallized films. TEM samples were prepared by utilizing a method reported elsewhere [7] and were examined in a Philips 400T electron microscope at 120 kV.

RESULTS and DISCUSSION

Figure 1 shows the average grain size of crystallized amorphous silicon films as a function of the RTA temperature. The crystallization time is also shown on this plot. In general, increase of the annealing temperature results in a reduction of the crystallization time. This reduction, however, is much more pronounced for annealing temperatures in the vicinity of 900-1000°C than for higher annealing temperatures. This observation is the direct consequence of the type of the dependence of the nucleation rate and growth rate on the annealing temperature during crystallization. It is known that, at higher temperatures both quantities increase with exponential rates [8]. Therefore, the rate by which the transformation of amorphous material to polycrystalline occurs, demonstrates an overall exponential dependence upon the annealing temperature. As a result, the crystallization time decreases exponentially as the annealing temperature increases, initially at a fast rate and subsequently slowing down. Such dependence is consistent with the observed pattern of crystallization time with respect to annealing temperature, shown in figure 1.

Focusing on the dependence of the grain size on the annealing temperature, a non-monotonic pattern is observed. The grain size is shown to initially decrease as the anneal temperature increases in the range of 600°C to 1100°C, pass through a minimum at approximately 1100°C and subsequently increase at higher anneal temperatures. This pattern is not consistent with the traditional nucleation theory approach that mandates a monotonic decrease for the grain size, as the annealing temperature increases, due to the associated exponential increase of the nucleation rate. Even though this statement is true for a range of annealing temperatures, it cannot explain the overall behavior of the grain size.

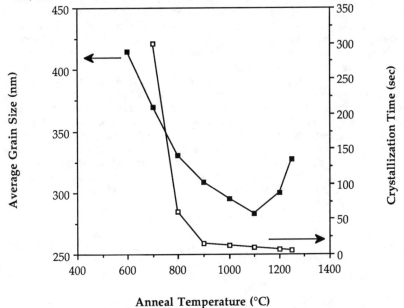

Anneal Temperature (°C)

Figure 1: Average grain size and crystallization time as a function of the annealing temperature for RTA polysilicon films

There has been a previous work where a maximum in the nucleation rate was predicted, for evaporated silicon films, to occur at temperatures around 800°C [9]. This maximum translates to a minimum in the grain size of the crystallized silicon films, located at about the same temperature (800°C). Even though the location of the observed minimum in the grain size is different in our case, the physical mechanism should be the same. Thus, it is possible that effects relative to the method of preparation (evaporation *versus* LPCVD) may be responsible for the shift in the location.

It is of interest, however, to establish a plausible interpretation for this dependence, since it may dictate a way to increase the grain size. To this extent, we propose two possibilities. The first possibility arises through the competition in magnitude between nucleation rate and growth rate. If the annealing conditions are such that the grain growth can occur much faster than the generation of new grains, then larger grains will develop. As the previous work has projected [9], such a possibility is much more likely to occur at high annealing temperatures. The second possibility is related to secondary grain growth. This type of growth occurs more readily at high annealing temperatures and results in the increase of the grain size through additional grain growth.

In order to discriminate between the two hypotheses we tried to establish whether secondary grain growth was an important issue within our experimental conditions. To this extent, the duration of the anneal was extended beyond the necessary time for complete crystallization, to evaluate the contribution of secondary grain growth in the measured grain size. Figure 2 shows a plot of the grain size as a function of the annealing time for three annealing temperatures. The grain size in each case was determined by averaging over the size of the fifty largest grains of the silicon film. The trend in figure 2 is that the grain size increases as the annealing time increases at any given temperature. In addition, the rate of increase becomes steeper as the annealing temperature increases. Even though, the grain size is observed to increase with time, this increase is not as pronounced as it may have been expected to be during secondary grain growth conditions. Moreover, the constructed grain size distributions do not illustrate a bimodal pattern, typical of secondary grain growth [10], as the time increases. Finally, the possibility of a saturation in the grain size, extrapolated from the data of figure 2, suggests that the small enlargement of the grain size should be attributed rather to normal grain growth than to abnormal (secondary) grain growth [11].

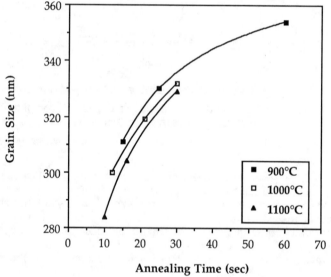

Figure 2: Average grain size of RTA polysilicon films as a function of the annealing time at: 900°C, 1000°C and 1100°C.

Due to the relatively weak effect of the additional annealing time on the grain size of the films, we will turn our attention to the other possibility that we proposed as a plausible explanation for the non-monotonic dependence of the grain size upon the annealing temperature. Our interpretation of this phenomenon can be summarized as follows. According to the model proposed by Johnson-Mehl [8], the increase of the nucleation rate associated with higher annealing temperatures is responsible for the observed decrease of the grain size at higher annealing temperatures. This argument is consistent with the first part of the curve shown in figure 1, which roughly corresponds to the temperature range of 600-1100°C. As the annealing temperature increases further, however, a decline in the population of stable nuclei should be expected as a result of the higher thermal vibration of subcritical clusters at high temperatures. In addition, due to the continuously decreasing average separation between generated stable nuclei, the probability of a silicon atom or silicon sub-cluster to rather join a stable nucleus than form a new one becomes larger. Thus, above a certain temperature threshold, fewer nuclei will be finally formed within the amorphous volume. This expected maximum in the nucleation rate corresponds to a minimum in the average grain size, as the one observed in figure 1. Thus, on the basis of these two complementing mechanisms it is possible to explain the observed non-monotonic dependence of the average grain size on the annealing temperature.

Another feature of the RTA polysilicon films is the lower intra-grain defect density as a result of the higher processing temperatures involved. As figure 3(a,b) indicates, the RTA polysilicon film has a higher structural perfection within the grains (fig. 3a) than the furnace annealed polysilicon film (fig. 3b). It has been reported before that this higher intra-grain perfection in RTA films may explain the observed improvement in the electrical characteristics of poly-Si TFTs, even though the grain size of these films is smaller than that of furnace annealed poly-Si films [6].

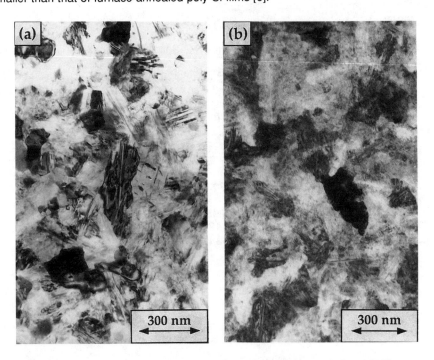

Figure 3: (a) RTA poly-Si at 1200°C, (b) furnace annealed at 600°C.

SUMMARY

In this work we investigated the crystallization of LPCVD amorphous silicon films by Rapid Thermal Anneal (RTA). We found that the grain size of the crystallized films demonstrates a non-monotonic behavior with respect to the annealing temperature. At low temperatures it decreases with the annealing temperature, while at high temperatures (> 1100°C) the opposite trend is observed. The latter trend was attributed to the high thermal vibration of sub-critical clusters at high temperatures that leads to the formation of fewer stable nuclei, complemented by the higher growth rates at high annealing temperatures. As a consequence, the grain size of the films increases at temperatures above 1100°C. RTA annealed silicon films were found to have lower intra-grain defect density, due to the higher temperatures involved. RTA polysilicon films can find application in the fabrication of TFTs for AMLCDs, either on glass or quartz substrates.

ACKNOWLEDGMENTS

Two of the authors (A.T.V. and M.K.H.) would like to acknowledge financial support from ARPA under contract MDA 972-92-J-1037.

REFERENCES

1. A.G. Lewis, D.D. Lee and R.H. Bruce, IEEE J. Solid-State Circuits, 27, 1833 (1992).
2. M.K. Hatalis and D.W. Greve, J. Appl. Phys., 63, 2260 (1988).
3. E. Korin, R. Reif and B. Mikic, Thin Solid Films, 167, 101 (1988).
4. S. Chen, J.B. Boyce, I.-W. Wu, A. Chiang, R.I. Johnson, G.B. Anderson and S.E. Ready, SID Eurodisplay'93 Proc., 195 (1993).
5. M. Bonnel, N. Duhamel, M. Guendouz, L. Haji, B. Loisel and P. Ruault, Jap. J. Appl. Phys., 30, L1924 (1991).
6. J. Mehlhaff and J. Fair, AMLCDs'93 Symp. Proc., Lehigh University, Oct. 21-22, 158 (1993).
7. A.T. Voutsas and M.K. Hatalis, J. Electrochem. Soc., 139, 2659 (1992).
8. W.A. Johnson and R.F. Mehl, Trans. AIME, 135, 416 (1939).
9. U. Koster, Phys. Stat. Sol. A, 48, 313 (1978).
10. C.V. Thompson, J. Appl. Phys., 58, 763 (1985).
11. C.V. Thompson, Annu. Rev. Mater. Sci., 20, 245 (1990).

EFFECT OF O_2 PLASMA EXPOSURE ON THE PERFORMANCE OF POLYCRYSTALLINE SILICON THIN FILM TRANSISTORS

CHUL HA KIM, IL LEE*, Ki SOO SOHN**, SU CHUL CHUN and JIN JANG***
*Orion Electrics, Gumi-shi, Kyungpook 730-030, Korea
**Kyungpook National University, Taegu 702-701, Korea
***Kyung Hee University, Dongdaemoon-ku, Seoul 130-701, Korea

ABSTRACT

We have studied the effect of O_2 plasma exposure on the performance of polycrystalline silicon (poly-Si) thin film transistor (TFTs). The field effect mobility is increased and the drain currents at negative gate voltages are reduced by O_2 plasma exposure on the surface of the TFT. These improvements in the performance of the poly-Si TFTs are larger in offset structure compared to overlap one. We obtained the on/off current ratio of ~ 10^8 after O_2 plasma exposure for the poly-Si TFTs with 3 or 4 µm offset length.

INTRODUCTION

Polycrystalline silicon (poly-Si) thin film transistor (TFT) can be used as switching device and to implement peripheral circuits in active matrix liquid crystal display (AMLCD) [1]. Major issues relating poly-Si TFT are to make TFT on hard glass, for example Corning 7059, and to reduce the drain currents at negative gate voltages, i.e., off currents. The off current is related with the structure of the TFT as well as with the material properties of poly-Si such as the trap state density at grain boundary [2]. Lightly doped drain (LDD) [3], multi-gate [4], and offset [5] structures are conventional methods to reduce the off currents, and post hydrogenation is used to reduce the trap density at grain boundary.

In the present work we have made the offset type poly-Si TFTs with various offset lengths. The on/off current ratio, which is an important quantity to use as a switching device in AMLCD, was ~10^6 when the offset length is 3 µm. The effect of O_2 plasma exposure on the performance of the poly-Si TFT has been studied. With increasing exposure time to 10 hrs, the off current drops significantly and the field effect mobility increases slightly. As a result, the on/off current ratio for the poly-Si TFT with offset length of 3 or 4 µm is increased to ~10^8 after O_2 plasma exposure.

EXPERIMENTAL

Figure 1 depicts a cross sectional view of the poly-Si TFT studied in the present work. The 100 nm thick amorphous silicon (a-Si) film on quartz glass was deposited at 550°C using silane by low pressure chemical vapor deposition and then solid-phase crystallized at 610°C for 72 hrs in a furnace. Thermal SiO_2 in 20 nm thickness was grown at 950°C and then 100 nm thick SiO_2 was deposited by atmospheric pressure chemical vapor deposition (APCVD). The oxide film was patterned and then phosphorus ions were implanted to make source/drain ohmic contacts. The ion dose was fixed at 10^{14} cm^{-2}. Then Al film was deposited and then patterned to make

99

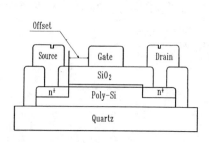

Fig. 1 Cross sectional view of the poly-Si TFT fabricated in the present work.

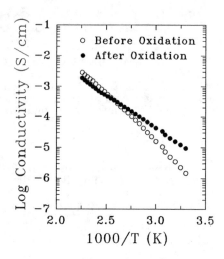

Fig. 2 Temperature dependence of conductivity for the poly-Si films before and after oxidation.

source/drain and gate electrodes. The offset region was defined as the distance between gate and source/drain electrodes. We have made both offset and overlap structures of poly-Si TFTs. The width and length of a TFT for overlap structure was 60μm/12μm with 1 μm overlap. The width of all TFTs was 60μm and the length of a gate electrode was fixed at 10μm with variable equal offset length at right and left sides of a gate.

Oxygen radicals were generated by O_2 plasma in a conventional plasma enhanced CVD system. The oxidation was carried out at 300°C on the poly-Si TFT. The RF power and O_2 pressure were fixed at 0.5 W/cm^2 and 0.5 Torr, respectively.

RESULTS AND DISCUSSION

The grain size of the poly-Si film studied in this work was about 100nm which was observed by a scanning electron microscope (SEM). The peak position and the full width at half maximum of the Raman transverse optical (TO) lines of this poly-Si film were 520 cm^{-1} and 5 cm^{-1}, respectively.

Figure 2 shows the temperature dependence of dark conductivity for 100 nm thick poly-Si film measured before and after oxidation. The O_2 plasma was exposed on the surface of poly-Si for 20 hrs. Both films show an activated conductivity with a single activation energy. The room temperature conductivity increases from 1.4×10^{-6} to 7.9×10^{-6}S/cm, and the activation energy decreases from 0.52 eV to 0.42 eV after oxidation. On the other hand, the photoconductivity under 100 mW/cm^2 increases from 9.3×10^{-7} to 3.6×10^{-5}S/cm after oxidation. This increase appears to be due to the reduction in the density of states at the energies lower than midgap, results in shifting the Fermi-level upward and increasing photoconductivity [6].

Figure 3 shows the effect of O_2 plasma exposure on the drain current (I_D)

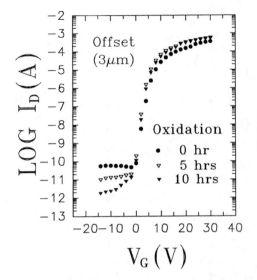

Fig. 3 Effect of O_2 plasma exposure on the I_D – V_G characteristics for the poly-Si TFT with offset length of 3μm.

– gate voltage (V_G) characteristics of the poly-Si TFT with offset length of 3 μm. The drain currents at $V_G > 10V$ increase slightly after oxidation, while the currents at $V_G < -10V$ decrease significantly. And the subthreshold slope, defined as $dV_G/d(\log I_D)$, decreases from 1.2 to 0.85 V/dec.

The field effect mobility of poly-Si TFT was obtained using the following equation which is valid in the saturated region of metal oxide silicon field effect transistor (MOSFET). The I_D – V_G relation was measured with gate and drain electrodes tied together [7].

$$I_{D,sat} = \frac{\mu_b C_{ox} W}{2L}(V_G - V_{th})^2 .$$

Where μ_b, C_{ox}, V_{th}, W, and L are effective field effect mobility, the capacitance of gate insulator, threshold voltage, the width and length of a TFT, respectively. The as-fabricated poly-Si TFTs with offset lengths of -1 μm (overlap structure) and 4 μm show the mobilities of 94 and 4 cm²/Vs, respectively. On the other hand, the TFT with offset length of 3 μm shows a field effect mobility of 43 cm²/Vs.

The trap state density in poly-Si TFT was obtained using the relation derived by Levinson et al. [8],

$$I_D = W \mu_b C_{ox} \frac{V_D}{L} V_G \exp(\frac{-q^2 N_t^2 t}{8\varepsilon_{si} V_G kT}),$$

where N_t, t, ε_{Si}, k, q, and T are trap density, thickness of poly-Si, electric permittivity, Boltzmann constant, electronic charge, and absolute temperature, respectively.

Figure 4 shows the field effect mobility and the trap density plotted against the oxidation time. The mobility increases from 43 to 60 cm²/Vs and the trap density decreases from 8×10^{11} to ~5×10^{11} cm⁻². The trap states

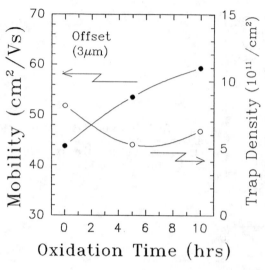

Fig. 4 Field effect mobility and trap density for the poly-Si TFT plotted against oxidation time.

at the grain boundaries can be saturated by exposing O₂ plasma on the poly-Si TFT. And the field effect mobility is enhanced after oxidation because the potential barrier between the grains in poly-Si appears to be decreased by the reduction of charges in the grain boundary states. Oxygen atoms or ions can diffuse into poly-Si through the oxide layer.

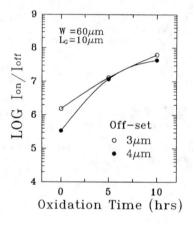

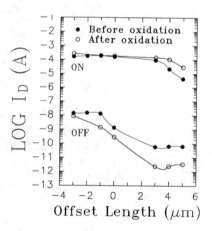

Fig. 5 Effect of O₂ plasma exposure on the on/off drain current ratios for the poly-Si TFTs.

Fig. 6 On and off drain currents of the poly-Si TFTs plotted against the offset length. The on and off currents were measured with V_D = 10V & V_G = 15V and V_D = 10V & V_G = -10V, respectively.

Figure 5 shows the on/off drain current ratios for the poly–Si TFTs with offset lengths of 3 and 4 μm, plotted against the oxidation time. The ratios for 3 and 4 μm offset are increased from 1.6×10^6 to 7×10^7 and from 3×10^5 to 5×10^7, respectively.

Figure 6 shows the on and off drain currents of the poly–Si TFTs with various offset lengths, plotted against oxidation time. The on current does not change significantly for the TFTs with offset length of lower than 3 μm, however, the on current increases by 7 times for the TFTs with offset lengths of 4 and 5 μm. This is due to the increase in the mobility of poly–Si. The transport of carriers through the intrinsic (offset) region becomes easier by both the reduction of potential barriers in poly–Si and the shift of the Fermi level upward. The off currents of poly–Si TFTs are decreased after oxidation, however, the amount of the decrease is higher for the TFTs with offset structure.

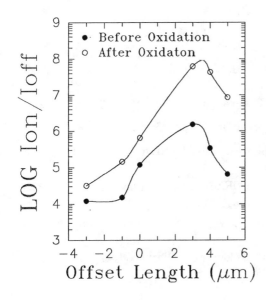

Fig. 7 On/off drain current ratio of the poly–Si TFT measured before and after oxidation, plotted against offset length of poly–Si TFT.

Figure 7 shows the on/off current ratio of the poly–Si TFT, plotted against the offset length of a TFT. The ratio increases by $\sim 10^2$ for the offset type poly–Si TFT, but the improvement in the ratio for the poly–Si TFT with overlap structure is lower than 10.

The flat drain currents at negative gate voltages for offset type poly–Si TFTs are due to the existence of intrinsic poly–Si layers between gate and source/drain electrodes. This intrinsic layer separates the induced holes beneath the gate electrode and the electrons in the n^+ layers, resulting in the decrease of electron–hole recombination/generation currents through the gap states. The off-currents in overlap structure are mainly caused by these recombination/generation currents. The saturation of grain boundary traps by oxidation decreases the off-currents further. The analysis of these off-currents are now carried out and will be published later.

SUMMARY

We have studied the O_2 plasma exposure effect on the performance of the poly-Si TFTs with various offset lengths. The field effect mobility increases and trap density decreases slightly after oxidation, but the drain currents at negative gate voltages are reduced significantly, resulting that the on/off current ratio increases by $\sim 10^2$ times after 10 hr O_2 plasma exposure on the poly-Si TFT with offset length of 3 or 4 μm. We obtained the leakage current of 2×10^{-14} A/μm for the poly-Si TFT with 3 μm offset length.

ACKNOWLEDGMENT

This work was supported by the HDTV program of Korea.

REFERENCES

1. Y. Matsueda, T. Ozawa, J. Nakamura, S. Takei, H. Kamakura, N. Okamoto, Japan Display'92, 561 (1992).

2. C.F. Yeh, T.Z. Yang, C.L. Chen, T.J. Chen and Y.C. Yang, Jpn. J. Appl. Phys. **32**, 4472 (1993).

3. M. Yazaki, S. Takenaka and H. Oshima, Jpn. J. Appl. Phys. **31**, 206 (1992).

4. I.W. Wu, A. Lewis, A. Chiang, Japan Display'92, 455 (1992).

5. S. Seki, O. Kogure and B. Tsujiyama, IEEE Electron Device Lett. EDL-**8**, 434 (1987).

6. H.N. Chern, C.L. Lee and T.F. Lei, IEEE Tran. Electron Devices **40**, 2301 (1993).

7. S.M. Sze, Physics of Semiconductor Devices (John Wiley & Sons Inc., New York, 1981), p. 442.

8. J. Levinson, F.R. Shepherd, P.J. Scanlon, W.D. Westwood, G. Este and M. Rider, J. Appl. Phys. **53**, 1193 (1982).

IMPROVED ABRUPTNESS OF Si/SiN INTERFACE BY ArF EXCIMER-LASER PRE-ANNEALING TO SiN

Yasutaka UCHIDA[*] and Masakiyo MATSUMURA[**]
[*]Department of Electronics and Information Sciences, Nishi-Tokyo University, Uenohara-machi, Kitatsuru-gun, Yamanashi 409-01, JAPAN.
[**]Department of Physical Electronics, Tokyo Institute of Technology, Oh-okayama, Meguro-ku, Tokyo 152, JAPAN.

Abstract

XPS measurement showed that undesirable SiNH component was reduced drastically from the low-temperature deposited SiN surface by intense ArF excimer-laser irradiation. Although the improved layer was as thin as 15nm, it was very effective to stop diffusion of N atoms from the bottom SiN layer to the top Si layer during the excimer-laser recrystallization step. N-diffused Si layer at the Si/SiN interface was less than the XPS resolution limit for the pre-annealed SiN structure, but about 5nm thick. As a result, the field-effect mobility of the poly-Si/SiN TFT was increased drastically by laser-irradiation to SiN film. Annealing characteristics are also presented for the various SiN film thicknesses and for both the ArF and KrF excimer-laser lights.

Introduction

Recently, high performance thin-film transistors (TFTs) have received much attention for their use in high-quality active-matrix liquid-crystal displays [1,2]. It is essential for high performance TFTs that electrical characteristics not only of the Si film as the active layer, but also of the SiO_2 or silicon-nitride (SiN) film as the gate insulator, can be improved compared to those of the low-temperature deposited films commonly used in present amorphous-silicon (a-Si) TFTs.

In the case of the Si film, it is well known that the poor-quality film, such as the a-Si or the low-temperature-deposited polycrystalline silicon (poly-Si) film, on the glass substrate can be improved drastically by excimer-laser annealing [3,4], because the film can be heated to its melting temperature and recrystallized without introducing damage into the non-heat-tolerant glass substrate. Several papers have already reported on excimer-laser recrystallized poly-Si TFTs with mobility as high as 300 cm^2/Vs [5,6,7].

In the case of insulating films no results had been reported on laser annealing before we showed the desirable effects of ArF excimer-laser annealing on the SiN film and applied to the gate insulator of high-performance bottom-gate TFTs with laser-recrystallized poly-Si films [8]. Based on the results of infrared absorption spectra and of buffered-HF etching rates, we proposed a two-layer model of the excimer-laser annealed SiN film where the improved thin layer is positioned at the top of the unchanged thick layer. However, we did not have direct evidence of the two-layer model and detailed information on the annealing mechanism. The reason is also not clear why poly-Si TFT using excimer-laser pre-annealed SiN film as a gate insulator showed good characteristics.

In this paper we report various experimental data on the excimer-laser annealing of

Mat. Res. Soc. Symp. Proc. Vol. 345. ©1994 Materials Research Society

the SiN film, on chemical bonds in the SiN film and on the abruptness of the poly-Si/SiN interface to clear the reason of improvement of poly-Si TFTs using excimer-laser pre-annealed SiN film as a gate insulator.

2. Experimental

2.1 Annealing characteristics

The SiN films were deposited on the quartz substrate from a N_2H_4 and Si_2H_6 gas mixture by the low-pressure CVD method at 500°C. The details of deposition conditions are listed in Table I. Absorption characteristics were evaluated as shown schematically in Fig. 1(a). Absorbed light energy I_{ab} per unit sample area was calculated from

$$I_{ab} = I_{in} - I_{out} - I_{ref} \qquad (1)$$

Table I. The deposition conditions for the SiN film

Si_2H_6 gas-flow rate	1sccm
N_2H_4 gas-flow rate	5sccm
Pressure	0.5Torr
Temperature	500°C

where I_{in}, I_{out} and I_{ref} are incident light energy density, transmitted light energy density and reflected light energy density, respectively. Experimental set-up for the measurement of I_{in}, I_{out} and I_{ref} were shown in Fig. 1(b). I_{in} or/and I_{ref} were measured separately by rotating the beam splitter. Before the experiment, we confirmed that absorption coefficient of quartz substrate α is almost zero to ArF and KrF excimer-laser lights. We did not take into account the reflection at the SiN/quartz interface and multi-reflection in the SiN film. This is because that absorption coefficient α of SiN is extremely large for ArF excimer-laser light. For KrF excimer-laser light this assumption will not be accepted satisfactorily due to small α. But, since absorbance increased linearly with the SiN film thickness, the effect of the reflection and multi-reflection will have no serious influence to the results.

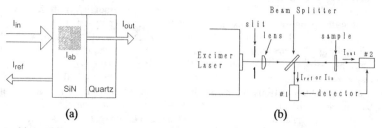

(a)   (b)

Fig. 1. (a) Definition of the parameters used in caluculation. (b) The experimental set-up for the measurement.

Figure 2 shows I_{ab} as a function of I_{in} for ArF and KrF excimer-laser lights. The film thickness d was 40nm. For weak light intensity, I_{ab} increased linearly with I_{in} and thus it can be written by

$$I_{ab} = I_{in} - I_{out} - I_{ref} = (I_{in} - I_{ref})(1 - e^{-\alpha d}) \qquad (2)$$

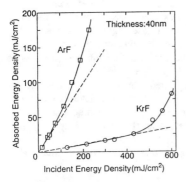

Fig. 2. The absorbed energy density as a function of incident energy density for ArF and KrF excimer-laser lights.

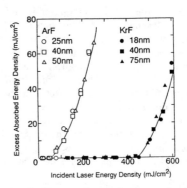

Fig. 3. Excess absorbed energy density as a function of incident laser energy density for various values of the SiN film thickness.

From the logarithmic slope, absorption coefficient α was calculated as $5 \times 10^5 \text{cm}^{-1}$ for the ArF excimer-laser light and $2 \times 10^4 \text{cm}^{-1}$ for the KrF excimer-laser light. There were, however, the threshold I_{in} values of 75mJ/cm^2 for the ArF excimer-laser light and 420mJ/cm^2 for the KrF excimer-laser light, above which I_{ab} increased superlinearly with I_{in}. Thus we defined excess absorbed energy density I_{ex} as follows:

$$I_{ex} = (I_{in} - I_{out} - I_{ref}) - (I_{in} - I_{ref})(1 - e^{-\alpha d}) \qquad (3)$$

In the first parentheses is the total absorbed energy and the product of the second and the third parentheses represents normally absorbed light energy density extrapolated from the low intensity region, respectively. We thought that the I_{ex} resulted from "molten" SiN.

The details of this phenomenon will be discussed in section 3. Thus I_{ex} contributes predominantly to the improvement of the SiN film and is triggered by the background absorption of 20mJ/cm^2. The threshold I_{in} value of the excess absorption for theexcimer-laser light coincided with that of the reduction of the buffered-HF etching rate. It is worth noting that I_{ab} at the threshold was 20mJ/cm^2 for both lights although the α value is more than an order in magnitude smaller for the KrF excimer-laser light than for the ArF excimer-laser light.

Figure 3 shows I_{ex} as a function of I_{in} for various film thicknesses, d. The excess absorption characteristics were the same for various 'd values, and also for the ArF and KrF excimer-laser lights

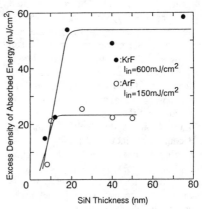

Fig. 4. The excess density of absorbed energy as a function of the SiN film thickness.

when I_{in} for the KrF excimer–laser is shifted to the left by about 350mJ/cm^2.

Figure 4 shows I_{ex} as a function of SiN thickness d. I_{in} was 150mJ/cm^2 for the ArF excimer–laser light and 600mJ/cm^2 for the KrF excimer–laser light. I_{ex} did not depend on the thickness d for more than 15nm as shown in the previous figure, but reduced drastically for films less than 15nm thick. Thus the excess absorption was absorbed only in the top SiN layer within a 15nm depth from the surface.

Figure 5 shows the XPS spectra of the as–deposited film surface (a) and the laser–annealed film surface (b), respectively. The chemical composition is determined by curve–resolving the Si2p peak spectrum into the representative three components shown by dashed curves of the stoichiometric SiN bond (at about 102eV), incompletely bonded chemical state of silicon–nitrogen–hydrogen bond SiNH (at about 100eV) [9] and SiO$_2$ (at about 104eV). There was a clear SiO$_2$ component due to oxidation of the surface

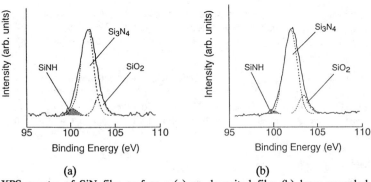

(a)   (b)

Fig. 5. XPS spectra of SiN film surface : (a) as–deposited film (b) laser annealed film.

during storage. There was also a small peak caused by SiNH. The as–deposited sample was concluded to have a SiNH component of about 6%. For the annealed sample, the SiNH component was reduced to as low as 1.3%. Unwanted SiNH bonds incorporated in the as–deposited film vanished from the SiN surface by the ArF excimer–laser irradiation, resulting in stoichiometric SiN.

Figure 6 shows the depth profile. The SiNH component increased rapidly with Ar ion etching time and reached its original value of about 6%. The improved region was as thin as 15nm. These results coincided with the two–layer model based on the buffered–HF etching rate.

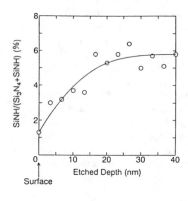

Fig.6. Chemical bond profile of the annealed SiN film as a function of etched depth.

2.2 Poly–Si/SiN interface characteristics

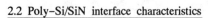

The 50nm thick a–Si film was deposited by the CVD method at 460°C on the SiN film [10]. Then the top Si film was recrystallized by ArF excimer–laser light at an energy density of 450mJ/cm^2, and atomic composition N/Si was evaluated from the N1s (at about 397eV) and Si2p (at about 102eV) XPS spectra. The ratio N/Si is shown in Fig. 7 as a function of sputter–etching time. The ratio increased sharply from zero to 1.33, indicating that the left half of the figure is of the Si region and the right half is of the stoichiometric SiN region. The profile shown by squares is of the as–deposited a–Si/SiN structure. The width of the transition region between the Si region and the SiN region was about 5nm, which can be thought of as the resolution limit of our XPS analyzer. The profile shown by closed circles is of the excimer–laser crystallized Si/SiN structure. Since the transition region was more than 10nm wide, a more than 5nm–thick transition region was newly formed during the excimer–laser crystallization step of Si. The profiles shown by open circles is of the excimer–laser crystallized Si film on the ArF excimer–laser pre–annealed SiN film. The pre–annealing was done by 5 shots of the ArF excimer–laser light pulse at an energy density of 150mJ/cm^2. Since the transition was as steep as the resolution limit of the system (i.e., as steep as that of the reference a–Si/SiN sample), we have concluded that, by the effects of the excimer–laser pre–annealing of the SiN film, the abruptness of the Si/SiN interface was not deteriorated by the excimer–laser crystallization step of Si. This is the reason for the superior performance of the poly–Si/pre–annealed SiN thin–film transistors [8].

In order to confirm the improvement of SiN film quality, we evaluated O/Si depth profile of poly–Si/thermally grown SiO$_2$ at 1100°C in dry O$_2$ ambient. The SiO$_2$ and Si film thicknesses and polycrystallized conditions were same. Figure 8 shows ratio N/Si or O/Si normalized by stoichiometry evaluated by XPS. The profile shown by triangles is of poly–Si/SiO$_2$ structure. The transition of poly–Si/SiO$_2$ was as steep as that of poly–Si/pre–annealed SiN. From this results, the pre–annealed SiN top layer has good film quality same as that of thermally grown SiO$_2$.

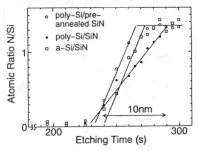

Fig. 7. Depth profile of N and Si atoms near the Si/SiN interface evaluated by

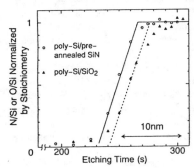

Fig. 8. Depth profile of N/Si or O/Si normalized by stoichiometry.

3. Discussion

From the experimental results, the following four characteristics became clear:
(1)There is a threshold absorbed energy of about 20mJ/cm^2 for the improvement of the SiN film.
(2)There is an excess absorption above the threshold, and the excess absorbed energy increases superlinearly with the incident light energy.

(3)The excess energy is absorbed within a 15nm-depth from the SiN surface.
(4)The excess absorption characteristics do not depend on SiN film thickness for more than 15nm nor on excimer-laser light wavelength.

Since the excess absorption occurs within 15nm-depth from the surface, we can roughly estimate that the surface temperature increases to the melting temperature of SiN of about 1900°C at the threshold absorbed energy. The "molten" SiN region of a few nm in thickness drastically changes the optical characteristics from those of the solid SiN film, and thus excess light energy is absorbed in the "molten" SiN region, which accelerates the temperature rise and width of the "molten" SiN region. Then the positive feedback mechanism is triggered, resulting in the improved SiN film characteristics.

4. Conclusion

We have investigated the excimer-laser annealing of SiN film. ArF excimer-laser annealing was found effective not only for the semiconductor films but also for insulating SiN films, since the undesirable SiNH component was removed from the top SiN layer. The annealing mechanism of SiN film seems to be the same as that of Si film. Though the improved layer is as thin as 15nm, it satisfactorily provides an abrupt poly-Si/SiN interface by preventing nitrogen diffusion into the poly-Si overlayer from the SiN underlayer during laser-recrystallization of Si film.

References

[1] M. Takabatake, J. Ohwada, Y. A. Ono, A. Mimura and N. Konishi, IEEE Trans. Electron Devices ED-38 (1991) 1303.
[2] T. Kaneko, Y. Hosokawa, M. Tadauchi, Y. Kita and H. Andoh, IEEE Trans. Electron Devices ED-38 (1991) 1086.
[3] T. Serikawa, S. Shirai, A. Okamoto and S. Suyama, IEEE Trans. Electron Devices ED-36 (1989) 1929.
[4] K. Sera, F. Okumura, H. Uchida, S. Itoh, S. Kaneko and K. Hotta, IEEE Trans. Electron Devices ED-36 (1989) 2868.
[5] H. Kuriyama, S. Kiyama, S. Noguchi, T. Kuwahara, S. Ishida, T.Nohda, K.Sano, H. Iwata, S. Tsuda and S. Nakano, Extended Abstract of Int'l. Electron Devices Meet. 1991 (1991) 563.
[6] H. Zhang, N. Kusumoto, T. Inushima and S. Yamazaki, IEEE Electron Device Lett. EDL-13 (1992) 297.
[7] K. Shimizu, O. Sugiura and M. Matsumura, IEEE Trans. Electron Devices ED-40 (1993) 112.
[8] K. Shimizu, K. Nakamura, M. Higashimoto, O. Sugiura and M. Matsumura, Jpn. J. Appl. Phys. 32 (1993) 452.
[9] I. Kobayashi, T. Ogawa and S. Hotta, Jpn. J. Appl. Phys. 31 (1992) 336.
[10] B. C. Ahn, H. Kanoh, O. Sugiura and M. Matsumura, Conf. Record of the 1991 Int'l. Display Research Conference, (1991) 85.

IMPROVEMENT OF GRAIN SIZE BY CRYSTALLIZATION OF DOUBLE-LAYER AMORPHOUS SILICON FILMS

DAE GYU MOON[*], JEONG NO LEE[*], HO BIN IM[*], BYUNG TAE AHN[*], KEE SOO NAM[**] AND SANG WON KANG[**]
[*]Department of Electronic Materials Engineering, Korea Advanced Institute of Science and Technology, 373-1 Kusong-dong, Yusong-gu, Taejon, 305-701 Korea
[**]Electronics and Telecommunications Research Institute, P. O. Box 8, Daeduk Science Town, Taejon, 305-606 Korea

ABSTRACT

We investigated the solid phase crystallization (SPC) behavior of 1000 Å amorphous Si (a-Si) films deposited by plasma enhanced chemical vapor deposition (PECVD) at various temperatures and were able to enhance the grain size of the crystallized polysilicon films using double layers of a-Si films. The deposition temperature of monolayer a-Si films varied from 200 to 400 °C and the films were recrystallized at 600 °C in nitrogen. As the deposition temperature increased, the incubation time was decreased and both the nucleation rate and growth rate were increased. Especially, the nucleation rate strongly depended on the deposition temperature.

Since the Si-SiO₂ interface provides a large number of nucleation sites, it is desirable to suppress nucleation at the interface. As an idea we employed a structure with double layer a-Si films. The bottom a-Si layer deposited at lower temperature could suppress the nucleation at the Si-SiO₂ interface while the top a-Si layer deposited at higher temperature could nucleate with a smaller number of nucleation sites. The incubation time and transformation behavior were determined by the deposition temperature of the top layer. As an example, the grain size of the double layer film deposited sequentially at 150 °C and 200 °C enhanced to 1.8 μm while that of the monolayer film deposited at 200 °C was 1.4 μm.

INTRODUCTION

Polycrystalline Si(poly-Si) thin film transistors (TFTs) are promising for high resolution liquid crystal displays (LCDs) because poly-Si has a higher mobility compared to a-Si. To obtain high mobility poly-Si films, grain enlargement has been investigated by several methods such as laser annealing [1], rapid thermal annealing [2], and solid phase crystallization (SPC) [3]. Among them, SPC processing might be attractive because the process is simple and least capital intensive. Also, SPC might produce films with better uniformity and reproducibility at low annealing temperature (< 600 °C), where glass can be utilized as a substrate.

A-Si films for SPC processing can be prepared by LPCVD [4], PECVD [5], and preamorphization of poly-Si [6]. The grain size of SPC Si films with a thickness of 1500 Å ranges from 1 to 2 μm except that of Si film prepared by LPCVD with SiH_4 gas is about 0.4 μm.

Generally, a-Si crystallizes at low annealing temperatures by a nucleation and growth mechanism. Therefore, nucleation rate and growth rate mainly determine the grain size of poly-Si. The rates depend on the bulk and interface structures of a-Si, which might be affected by deposition conditions such as deposition temperature, gas flow rate, and chamber pressure.

111

In this paper, the effect of deposition temperature on the crystallization behaviors of a-Si films was investigated because the PECVD method provides a wide range of deposition temperature for a-Si films. The annealing time dependence of crystallinity was also investigated. The crystallization behaviors were studied from the crystallization parameters and grain sizes, using transmission electron microscope (TEM) and Raman spectroscopy. And then we suggest double-layer Si films to control nucleation rate and growth rate independently.

EXPERIMENTAL PROCEDURE

Intrinsic a-Si films were deposited on Corning 7059 glass substrates by a conventional PECVD method. The rf power and rf frequency were 10 W and 13.56 MHz respectively. The operation pressure was 0.4 torr. The SiH_4 gas diluted in Ar was used as a source gas and the total flow rate was 150 sccm. The deposition temperature was varied from 200 to 400 °C. The thickness of the a-Si films was 1000 Å. These amorphous Si films were annealed at 600 °C in nitrogen. For the double-layer Si films, the bottom layer were deposited at 150 °C and top layer was deposited at various temperature from 200 °C to 400 °C. And the thickness of these films were 200 Å and 800 Å respectively. The annealing time was also varied to study the nucleation and growth process. The grain size and the number of nuclei were observed by transmission electron microscopy (TEM). The crystallinity of the Si films was examined by TEM and Raman spectroscopy. The samples for TEM observation were made by lift-off technique: the underlying glass substrate was removed by HF.

RESULTS AND DISCUSSION

Figure 1 shows the measured grain size in the crystallized films as a function of deposition temperature. The measured grain size is expressed as the average size of large grains observed in TEM dark-field images. As the deposition temperature increases from 200 to 400 °C, the grain size is decreased from 1.1 to 0.5 μm.

Figure 2 shows the crystalline fraction of the Si films as a function of annealing time. The a-Si films were deposited at 200, 300 and 400 °C. All the films need incubation times to generate the crystalline nuclei. During incubation time no nuclei formed. The film deposited at 400 °C requires an incubation time of about 3 hr. But the film at 200 °C requires a longer incubation time of about 12 hr. The films deposited at lower deposition temperature requires a longer incubation time. In addition, the films deposited at lower deposition temperature have a longer transformation time. The transformation time of the films deposited at 400 and 200 °C are about 6 hr and about 36 hr, respectively. Therefore, the total annealing time for completely crystallization increases from 9 to 48 hr as the deposition temperature decreases from 400 to 200 °C.

Both the grain size and the transformation fraction are related to the nucleation rate and growth rate. The time dependence of the crystalline fraction, X(t), can be expressed by the following equation [6].

$$X(t) = 1 - \exp\left[-\left(t - t_o\right)^3 / t_c\right] \qquad (1)$$

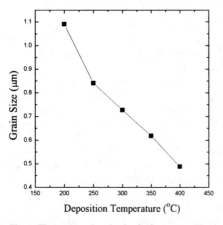

Fig. 1. The measured grain size in the recrystallized films as a function of deposition temperature.

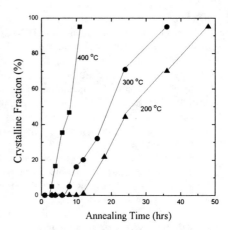

Fig. 2. Crystalline fraction of the silicon films deposited at various deposition temperatures as a function of annealing time. The annealing was performed at 600 °C

Where, t_c is the characteristic transformation time after incubation t_o and has the following relation

$$t_c = (p / 3) g^2 hI \qquad (2)$$

where h is the thickness of the films and g the grain growth rate and I the nucleation rate. The transformation fraction follows a typical Avrami equation with the time exponent of 3 and the t_c depends on the nucleation rate and the square of the growth rate.

And the final grain size is expressed as

$$d = K (g / hI)^{1/3} \qquad (3)$$

where, d is the grain size. Equation (3) suggests that the slow nucleation rate and fast growth result in larger grains. We determined the nucleation rate and growth rate using TEM micrograph.

Figure 3 shows the nucleation rate and growth rate of crystalline as a function of deposition temperature. The nucleation rate was determined from the gradient of the annealing time dependence of the nuclei density at the early stage of transformation. The nucleation rate strongly increases with increasing deposition temperature. The nucleation rates of films deposited at 200 and

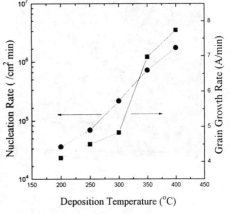

Fig. 3. Nucleation rate and grain growth rate as a function of deposition temperature.

400 °C are ~3 x 10^4 and ~ 2 x 10^6 cm^{-2} min^{-1}, respectively.

The grain growth rate was estimated from the gradient of the annealing time dependence of the maximum grain size observed in the TEM dark-field images. The grain growth rate increases with increasing the deposition temperature. The grain growth rates of films deposited at 200, 300 and 400 °C are 4, 5 and 8 Å/min respectively. Note that the change of the growth rate is not so strong as that of the nucleation rate as the deposition temperature varies.

In conclusion, both the nucleation and grain growth rates decrease as the deposition temperature decreases. The grain enlargement and the increase of the incubation time of the films deposited at lower deposition temperature resulted from the retardation of the nucleation. On the other hand, the transformation time increases by the decrease of both the nucleation and the grain growth rate.

From equation (3), reducing of nucleation rate and enhancing growth rate are required to gain Si films of larger grain. It was reported that nuclei are forming at Si-SiO$_2$ interface mainly and at free surface. Since the Si-SiO$_2$ interface provides a large number of nucleation sites, it is desirable to suppress nucleation at the interface[7].

As an idea we suggest a structure with double-layer a-Si thin films. The bottom layer deposited at lower temperature suppresses nucleation at Si-SiO$_2$ interface and the top layer deposited at higher temperature maintains high growth rate. As an example figure 4 shows

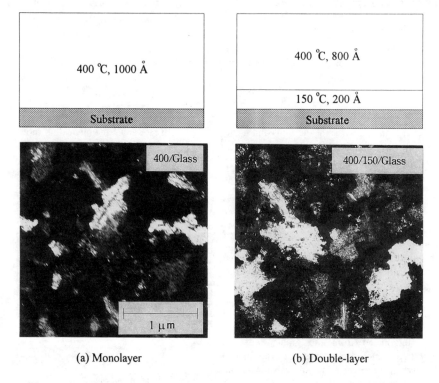

(a) Monolayer   (b) Double-layer

Fig. 4. Shematic diagrams of the monolayer and the double-layer Si films and TEM dark field images of the crystallized films.

schematic diagrams of monolayer and double-layer a-Si films and TEM dark field images of crystallized Si films. Thickness of bottom and top layer were 200 Å and 800 Å, respectively. As shown in the figure 4 the grain of the double-layer Si film was larger than that of the monolayer film. Figure 5 shows the grain size of the monolayer and double-layer Si films as a function of deposition temperature. For the double-layer Si films, the deposition temperature of the bottom layer was fixed at 150 °C. Note that the grain size is clearly enhanced by the double-layer Si films, especially at lower deposition temperature. As an example, the grain size of the double-layer film deposited 200 °C enhanced to 1.8 μm, while that of the monolayer film deposited at 200 °C was 1.4 μm. Figure 6 shows the crystalline fraction of the double-layer amorphous Si films. The incubation time of the double-layer Si films increase slightly but growth behavior of crystalline was similar to that of the monolayer Si films. As shown in figure 6, more than 20 % of films remain amorphous state because the bottom layer deposited at 150 °C is not fully crystallized. So this residual amorphous layer would be controlled by the thickness of the bottom layer.

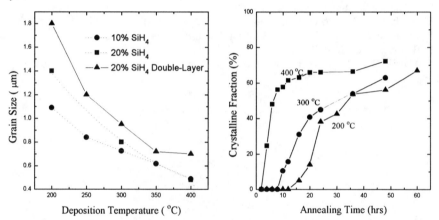

Fig. 5. Grain size as a function of deposition temperature. The deposition temperature of the bottom layer in double-layer structure is fixed at 150 °C

Fig. 6. Crystalline Fraction of the double-layer Si films as a function of annealing time at 600 °C. Marked temperatures on the figure are the deposition temperature of top layers.

It is expected that the lower the deposition temperature of bottom layer was, the larger the grain of double-layer Si film would be. Actually a double-layer specimen which was deposited at 65 °C and 200 °C sequentially, has a grain size of 2.1 μm. But even though it is possible to suppress nucleation at the Si-SiO$_2$ interface there are many nucleation sites like surface. So the further improvement of grain size using double-layer a-Si films may be limited by the fact.

CONCLUSIONS.

The effect of deposition temperature on the crystallization of a-Si films deposited by PECVD in the deposition temperature range of 200 to 400 °C has been investigated. As the deposition temperature decreases, the annealing time for crystallization of a-Si increased because the incubation time before nucleation increased and the transformation time after nucleation increased. As the deposition temperature increased from 200 to 400 °C, the nucleation rate increased from ~3 x 10^9 cm^{-3} min^{-1} to ~ 2 x 10^{11} cm^{-3} min^{-1} and the growth rate increased from ~ 4 Å/min to ~ 8 Å/min.

To reduce the nucleation rate at the Si-SiO$_2$ interface, we introduce a structure of double-layer a-Si films of which the bottom layer was deposited at lower temperature and the top layer was deposited at higher temperature. The SPC of the double-layer structure clearly enhanced the grain size of the crystallized film. The nucleation behavior in the double-layer structure needs to be further studied.

REFERENCES

1. T. Serikawa, S. Shirai, A. Okamoto, S. Suyama, Jpn. J. Appl. Phys. **28**, L1871 (1989).
2. M. Bonnel, N. Duhamel, T. Henrion, B. Loisel, J. Electrochem. Soc. **140**, 3484 (1993)
3. K. Nakazawa, J. Appl. Phys. **69**, 1703 (1991).
4. M. K. Hatalis and D. W. Greve, J. Appl. Phys. **63**, 2260 (1988).
5. S. Takenaka, M. Kunii, H. Oka, H. Kurihara, Jpn. J. Appl. Phys. **29**, L2380 (1990).
6. R. B. Inverson and R. Reif, J. Appl. Phys. **57**, 5169 (1985).
7. J. W. Park, D. G. Moon, B. T. Ahn, H. B. Im, K. Lee, Thin Solid Films, in press (1994)

DEPOSITION OF HYDROGENATED Si FILMS
BY HYDROGENATION OF THE SiO$_2$ SURFACE AND HYDROGEN DILUTION
WITH PE-CVD AND ECR-CVD

Kun-Chih Wang*, Tri-Rung Yew** and, Huey-Liang Hwang*
*Department of Electrical Engineering, National Tsing-Hua University, Hsinchu, Taiwan, 30043, ROC.
**Materials Science Center, National Tsing-Hua University, Hsinchu, Taiwan, 30043, ROC.

ABSTRACT

This paper presents the results of low temperature deposition of poly-Si films deposited on SiO$_2$ layers. Hydrogen dilution, hydrogen atom treatment, and hydrogenation of the SiO$_2$ surface steps were applied to deposit the Si films. The above treatment steps were usually used in the plasma enhanced chemical vapor deposition and they were extended to be used in the electron cyclotron resonance chemical vapor deposition to identify the grain growth effects. The nucleation and microstructure of the silicon films were observed by cross-section transmission electron microscopy (XTEM).

I. INTRODUCTION

Hydrogenated amorphous silicon (a-Si:H) films are indispensable for many large area devices such as solar cells, contact image sensors, and thin film transistors. The factors limiting their applications are the low electron mobilities and light induced degradation of electrical conductivity of a-Si:H [1], which are generally related to the intrinsic network structure. Hydrogen dilution method and hydrogen atom treatment method were found to be effective in the low temperature (250°C) deposition of microcrystalline silicon (μc-Si), deposited on insulators (e.g. SiO$_2$ or SiN$_x$) in a plasma enhanced chemical vapor deposition system (PE-CVD) [2-5]. The μc-Si films deposited by hydrogen dilution and hydrogen atom treatment has been attempted to be used as the active layer of thin film transistors (TFT's), the electron mobilities of the TFT's made from them were higher than those made by the conventional methods [6]. Applying the sulfurization treatment to compensate voids and dangling bonds of the SiO$_2$ surface, the nucleation of silicon on SiO$_2$ could be further improved [7-8].

Hydrogen dilution, hydrogen atom treatment, and hydrogenation of the SiO$_2$ surface steps were applied to deposit the silicon films at a temperature of 250°C using PE-CVD. Hydrogen dilution and hydrogenation of the SiO$_2$ surface steps were also utilized in the electron cyclotron resonance chemical vapor deposition (ECR-CVD). In this paper, we will show the results of low temperature film deposition made from PE-CVD and ECR-CVD.

II. EXPERIMENTAL

In the PE-CVD experiments, steps like hydrogen dilution, hydrogen atom treatment, and hydrogenation of the SiO$_2$ surface were employed, the substrate temperatures were kept at 250°C. Hydrogenation of the SiO$_2$ surface was applied prior to the Si film

Mat. Res. Soc. Symp. Proc. Vol. 345. ©1994 Materials Research Society

deposition. The experiment procedures were reported previously [2-6], and the conditions are summarized in Tables I to III.

Table I. Growth conditions of hydrogenation of the SiO_2 surface.

Substrate Tempera	250^{0}C
Plasma P	10-50 W (0.32-016 W/cm^2)
H$_2$ Flow	150-380 sccm
Total Pres	180-440 mTorr
Period	15 min

Table II. Growth conditions of hydrogen dilution.

Substrate Tempera	250^{0}C
Plasma P	10-50 W (0.32-016 W/cm^2)
H$_2$/(H$_2$+SiH$_4$) Flow	90-95%
Total Pres	450 mTorr
Period	30-45 min

Table III. Growth conditions of hydrogen atom treatment.

Substrate Tempera	250^{0}C
Plasma P	10 W (0.32 W/cm^2)
H$_2$/(H$_2$+SiH$_4$) Flow	90%
Total Pres	430-450 mTorr
Deposition time/Treating	20s/50s, 10s/50s, 10s/100s

In the ECR-CVD experiments, hydrogenation of the SiO_2 surface and hydrogen dilution were employed at a substrate temperature of 300^{0}C. The gases used for hydrogenation of the SiO_2 surface were H$_2$ and Ar. The gases used for hydrogen dilution were SiH$_4$ and H$_2$. The other conditions were kept the same as described in Table. IV.

Table IV. Growth conditions of hydrogenation of the SiO_2 surface and hydrogen dilution used in an ECR-CVD system.

Substrate Tempera	30 0^{0}C
ECR P	300 W
H	100 sccm/100sccm
H$_2$/(H$_2$+SiH$_4$) Flow	80-95%
Total Pres	30 mTorr
Period	25-35 min

III. RESULTS AND DISCUSSION

The utilization of 95% hydrogen dilution in a PE-CVD system, with or without hydrogenation of the SiO_2 surface, produced silicon films all in the polycrystalline phase. The results indicated that the Si film deposited with a low plasma power and a high H_2 flow rate for hydrogenation of the SiO_2 surface was the best one. Fig. 1 shows the result of sample deposited with hydrogenation of the SiO_2 surface, hydrogen atom treatment, and 95% hydrogen dilution. But for a 90% hydrogen dilution, despite hydrogenation of the SiO_2 surface step was employed or not, the films only presented the amorphous phase.

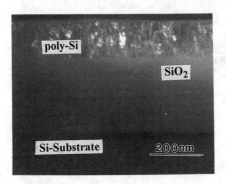

Fig. 1 XTEM dark field image of sample deposited with hydrogenation of the SiO_2 surface, hydrogen atom treatment, and 95% hydrogen dilution.

The hydrogen dilution has been proved to be the most effective step for the low temperature poly-Si film deposition. As the hydrogen flow ratio of the reactive gases exceeds 92%, it would then be easy to grow a poly-Si film at a low substrate temperature as 250°C [2-6]. Hydrogenation of the SiO_2 surface tends to apply a H_2 plasma to passivate the surface of SiO_2. The H_2 plasma bombards the SiO_2 surface and reacts with the SiO_2 surface atoms. The H_2 plasma could smooth out the SiO_2 surface and compensate voids and dangling bonds of the SiO_2 surface. Low plasma power might reduce the damage caused by surface bombardment and a high H_2 flow rate might provide a hydrogen-rich SiO_2 surface. By far, the effects of hydrogenation of the SiO_2 surface has not been quite reproducible.

After hydrogenation of the SiO_2 surface, a 5-period hydrogen atom treatment was adopted and then the 90% hydrogen dilution step was applied to deposit the Si films. The results were different from those without a hydrogen atom treatment. When hydrogen atom treated samples had a deposition time/treating time ratio of 10s/50s, the Si film was still in the amorphous phase. When hydrogen atom treatment was done at a deposition time/treating time ratio of 20s/50s and 10s/100s, the Si films were all polycrystalline phase. The results are shown in Fig. 2.

Hydrogen atom treatment is effective to grow a poly-Si film at 250°C, hoewever, the experiments typically consumed a lot of time. We combined the hydrogen atom treatment with hydrogenation of the SiO_2 surface and hydrogen dilution steps, the Si film was amorphous when the deposition time/treating time ratio is 10s/50s. Increasing (or decreasing) the time ratio to 20s/50s (or 10s/100s), the Si film became polycrystalline. The reason is still not known.

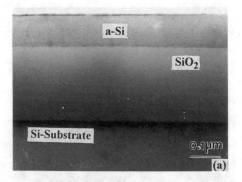

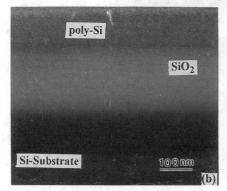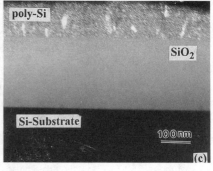

Fig. 2 XTEM images of samples deposited with hydrogen atom treatment with a deposition time/treating time ratio of (a) 10s/50s, (b) 20s/50s, and (c) 10s/100s.

The thermally oxidized Si wafer was used as the substrate in the low temperature poly-Si deposition with 95% hydrogen dilution in an ECR-CVD system. Fig. 3 (a) shows the result deposited without hydrogenation of the SiO_2 surface and Fig. 3 (b) shows the result deposited with hydrogenation of the SiO_2 surface. Both results show that they are polycrystalline. The microstructure of the silicon films are distinctly columnar poly grains. The poly grains extend from the bottom to the top of the film. They are superior to those of the Si films deposited by PE-CVD. This indicates that ECR-CVD could be useful for the low temperature poly-Si deposition.

Fig. 4 shows the result of the Si film deposited by hydrogenation of the SiO_2 surface at two hydrogen dilution conditions (5 min 95% and 30 min 80%). There are two silicon layers successively deposited on SiO_2. The first layer was deposited by a 95% hydrogen dilution and its phase was polycrystalline. When the dilution level was changed to 80%, the subsequent silicon film became amorphous. As viewed from the window of the patterned wafer, the silicon deposited on (100)-oriented Si wafer was similar to that deposited on SiO_2. The "seeding" effect of the (100)-oriented Si wafer

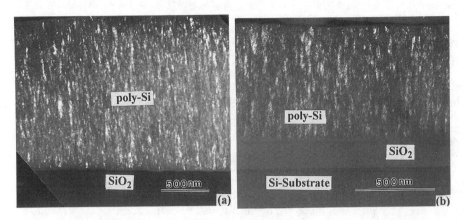

Fig. 3 XTEM dark field images of samples deposited with 95% hydrogen dilution by ECR-CVD (a) without a hydrogenation of the SiO$_2$ surface and (b) with a hydrogenation of SiO$_2$ surface.

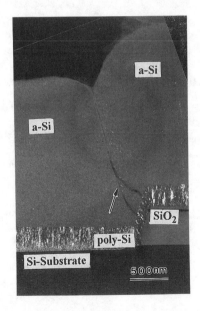

Fig. 4 XTEM dark field image of sample deposited with hydrogenation of the SiO$_2$ surface at two hydrogen dilution levels (5 min 95% and 30 min 80%)

was not evident when hydrogen dilution was applied. There are some small grains in the region of the interface between the Si film deposited on the Si surface and the Si film deposited on the SiO_2 surface. The reason for the presence of these small gains need further study.

IV. CONCLUSION

Hydrogenation of the SiO_2 surface might change the morphology of the SiO_2 surface and the bonding configurations of the surface atoms. The effect of hydrogenation of the SiO_2 surface step was still not stable. The effect of hydrogen dilution was quite distinct, either in the PE-CVD or in the ECR-CVD, the latter produced distinct columnar grain structures. This is the first attempt of the hydrogen dilution experiment using ECR-CVD.

ACKNOWLEDGMENT

Dr. K. C. Hsu, Mr. M. C. Hong, and Y. C. Hsian are appreciated for their technical assistance. This work was supported by the National Science Council of the Republic of China under contract number NSC82-0404-E007-183 and NSC83-0208-M007-089. All of the experiments were carried out at the Materials Science Center of National Tsing-Hua University.

REFERENCES

1. D. L. Staebler and C. R. Wronski, J. Appl. Phys., **51**, 3262 (1980).
2. K. C. Hsu, H. Chang, C. S. Hong, and H. L. Hwang, MRS Symp. Proc. **258**, 69 (1992).
3. K. C. Hsu and H. L. Hwang, Appl. Phys. Lett., **61**, 2075 (1992).
4. K. C. Hsu and H. L. Hwang, MRS Symp. Proc. **259**, 67 (1993).
5. K. C. Hsu, H. Chang, and H. L. Hwang, J. Appl. Phys., **73**, 4841 (1993).
6. K. C. Hsu, B. Y. Chen, H. T. Hsu, K. C. Wang, T. R. Yew, and H. L. Hwang,, Jap. J. Appl. Phys. (1994) (in press).
7. K.C. Wang, H.L. Hwang, C.Y. Kung, and T.R. Yew, Mat. Res. Soc. Symp. Proc., **259**, 137 (1992).
8. K.C. Wang, H.L. Hwang, C.Y. Kung, and T.R. Yew, Appl. Phys. Lett. (1994) (in press).

DEPOSITION AND CRYSTALLISATION BEHAVIOUR OF AMORPHOUS SILICON THIN FILMS OBTAINED BY PYROLYSIS OF DISILANE GAS AT VERY LOW PRESSURE

T. KRETZ, D. PRIBAT, P. LEGAGNEUX, F. PLAIS, O. HUET AND M. MAGIS
Thomson-CSF LCR, 91404 Orsay Cedex, France

ABSTRACT

High purity amorphous silicon layers were obtained by ultrahigh vacuum (millitorr range) chemical vapor deposition (UHVCVD) from disilane gas. The crystalline fraction of the films was monitored by *in situ* electrical conductance measurements performed during isothermal annealings. The experimental conductance curves were fitted with an analytical expression, from which the characteristic crystallisation time, t_c, was extracted. Using the activation energy for the growth rate extracted from our previous work, we were able to determine the activation energy for the nucleation rate for the analysed-films. For the films including small crystallites we have obtained $E_n \sim 2.8$ eV, compared to $E_n \sim 3.7$ eV for the completely amorphous ones.

INTRODUCTION

In so far as thin film transistor (TFT) fabrication is concerned, polysilicon (poly-Si) films are usually obtained by solid phase crystallisation (SPC) of an amorphous precursor (a-Si) deposited by low pressure chemical vapour deposition (LPCVD). This particular way of processing stems from the facts that (i) a material with larger grains is obtained after SPC compared to directly deposited poly-Si and (ii) the surface of the films after SPC remains smooth and uneven, whereas films deposited directly in the polycrystalline state (direct-poly) tend to exhibit an important surface roughness. This roughness is detrimental to carrier transport, given the fact that accumulation or inversion layers in TFTs never exceed a thickness of 20 to 30 nm beneath the surface of the active material.

Consequently, the deposition of silicon films in LPCVD conditions has been thoroughly studied, in order to precisely determine the operating parameters leading to the obtaining of amorphous material [1-8]. Schematically, decreasing the pressure or increasing the temperature tends to favour the deposition of direct-poly, because the surface diffusion coefficient is enhanced. When SiH_4 is used as parent gas and the pressure is around 1 Torr (say between 0.5 and several torrs) the transition from amorphous material to direct-poly is around 570°C. This transition temperature decreases as the pressure is lowered, but at the expense of the deposition rate. So, for practical reasons SiH_4 pyrolysis is preferably performed in the torr pressure range and at a temperature around 550°C, i.e. slightly below the transition temperature. In such conditions, grain sizes of 0.3 to 0.5 µm are obtained after SPC at 600°C [9, 10].

Recently, the use of disilane (Si_2H_6) as gas precursor in replacement of SiH_4 has attracted much attention, because very large grains (up to several microns) have been obtained after SPC [10-15]. Most of the work published to date on the deposition of amorphous Si from Si_2H_6 has stressed the fact that the deposition temperature could be lowered below 500°C while still maintaining an appreciable deposition rate. However, the deposition pressure has been kept in the torr range (again say between 0.3 and several torrs) [10, 12-17] with the exception of Scheid and co-workers [11, 18] and Guillemet *et al.* [19] who investigated the kinetics of deposition and subsequent SPC for films deposited down to 35 mTorr.

In this paper, we investigate the millitorr pressure regime for a-Si deposition from Si_2H_6. In addition, we present some results concerning the kinetics of crystallisation, in particular estimates of the activation energies for the nucleation and growth rates.

SILICON DEPOSITION

The depositions were carried out in an UHVCVD-like reactor [20, 21]. Briefly, this system is composed of a load-lock chamber and a quartz tube (150mm in diameter) evacuated by a high pressure turbo-pump equipped with magnetic bearings and backed by a dry roughing pump. The

123

process gas is purified by a point-of-use mineral getter which limit the content of oxygen-bearing molecules (O_2, H_2O, CO, CO_2) to around 10 ppb. The total residual pressure in the LPCVD chamber, measured by a cold Penning gauge after several deposition runs, is 2.10^{-9} Torr for a furnace temperature of 550°C. The residual gas phase is composed of 90% of H_2 and the partial pressure of the impurities (O_2, H_2O, CO, CO_2) is of the order of 2.10^{-10} Torr [22].

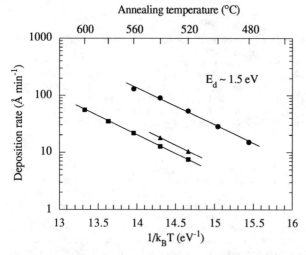

	Si_2H_6 (sccm)	p_d (Torr)
●	40	40.10^{-3}
▲	32	4.10^{-3}
■	13.5	2.10^{-3}

Figure 1 : Deposition rate versus reciprocal deposition temperature for Si_2H_6 gas for various pressures.

The silicon films were deposited to a thickness of 100 nm on 4-inch Si wafers coated with 200 nm of thermally grown oxide. The variations of the deposition rate observed in the reactor at very low pressures (2 and 4 mTorr) are reported on Fig. 1 versus the inverse of the deposition temperature. At constant pressure, the deposition rate follows an Arrhenius law with an activation energy of the order of 1.5 eV. The deposition rate at 40 mTorr is also plotted on Fig. 1, and the same value of activation energy is found for this pressure, roughly in agreement with the results of Scheid *et al.* [18] at 35 mTorr. For the films obtained at 2 and 4 mTorr, plan view TEM observations performed on as-deposited material indicate an amorphous state at 520°C. When the temperature is raised to 540°C, small silicon crystallites begin to appear in the amorphous matrix. Fig. 2.a shows such a crystallite found in a film deposited at 2 mTorr. At 560°C we have found a mixture of a-Si and poly-Si (Fig. 2.b). At 600°C, the films are completely crystalline, with a grain size of the order of 20 nm as shown on Fig. 2.c.

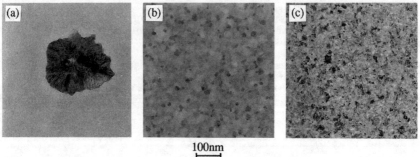

100nm

Figure 2 : TEM micrographs of silicon films deposited at 2 mTorr for different deposition temperatures ; (a) 540°C, (b) 560°C and (c) 600°C.

Concerning the impurity concentrations (essentially carbon and oxygen), our former measurements performed on films deposited in the same reactor but at a pressure of 2 Torr had shown that they were very low (a few 10^{16} cm^{-3} for O) and comparable to the ones found in float-zone single-crystal Si [10, 22]. In the present work, the deposition pressure is decreased by three orders of magnitude compared to the above mentioned experiments. We therefore expect an even better purity, with O and C concentrations well below the detection limits of SIMS apparatus.

Finally, we would like to point out that, as the depositions are performed practically in the molecular regime (mean free path ~ 2cm), the thickness uniformity on the 4-inch wafers is excellent, of the order of 4%.

CRYSTALLISATION

After deposition, the films were unloaded from the UHVCVD reactor and the crystallisation experiments were carried out at atmospheric pressure, under flowing nitrogen, in a standard quartz tube at various temperatures. The two sets of deposition conditions used for the crystallisation study are summarised in Table I.

Si$_2$H$_6$ [sccm]	Pressure [mTorr]	Temperature [°C]	Rate [Å.min^{-1}]
32	4	520	10.4
13.5	2	540	12.8

Table I : Deposition conditions of the a-Si films.

After several hours of furnace crystallisation at 580°C, both type of films were fully crystallised and the maximum grain size was about 1 µm and 0.5 µm for the films deposited respectively at 520 and 540°C (Fig. 3). The grain shape and sizes are very similar to the ones obtained when the a-Si films are deposited by pyrolysis of silane gas at 550°C and a pressure of 2 Torr [10]. Moreover, the TEM images of the two type of layers show a fine structure inside the grains indicating the presence of microtwins [23-25].

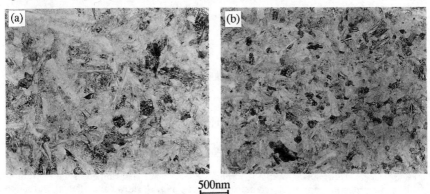

500nm

Figure 3 : TEM micrographs of 100nm-thick films annealed at 580°C ; (a) film deposited at 520°C and (b) film deposited at 540°C.

In order to study the kinetics of crystallisation, we have performed *in situ* electrical conductance measurements during the isothermal furnace crystallisation of the amorphous films. The precise experimental conditions are the same as previously reported [10]. Typical electrical conductance curves are plotted as a function of crystallisation time in Fig. 4 and 5.

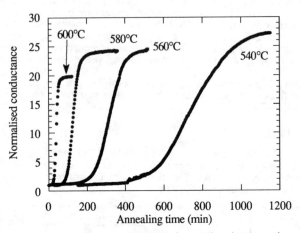

Figure 4 : Normalised conductance as a function of annealing time at various crystallisation temperatures for films deposited at 520°C.

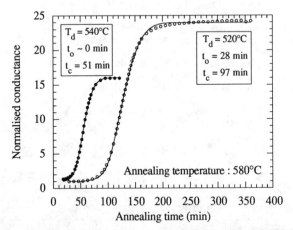

Figure 5 : Normalised conductance as a function of annealing time at 580°C for 100nm-thick films deposited according to Table I. Solid lines are analytical fits to the experimental data.

The conductance is normalised by the amorphous conductance determined at the beginning of annealing, in order to eliminate geometrical effects. Fig. 4 shows that the polycrystalline conductance, G_c, determined in the saturation region of the curves increases as the annealing temperature decreases. This is probably due to the increase of the grain size as the annealing temperature decreases [9, 10]. Moreover, G_c is higher for the 520°C-deposited films than for the 540°C-ones (see Fig. 5), which again, is probably due to the larger grain size of the former (see Fig. 3).

We were able to obtain a fit to the experimental data by combining the theory of conductance of a binary system, developed by Landauer [26], with the expression of the crystallised volume fraction, given by Avrami [27], Johnson and Mehl [28] for the two-dimensional growth of crystallites. This procedure has been explained in some details in ref. 10. Note that we only use two adjustable parameters to obtain the fits : the characteristic crystallisation time, t_c, and the incubation time, t_0, after which the first crystallites with a critical size are formed. The fits are shown as solid lines in Fig. 5.

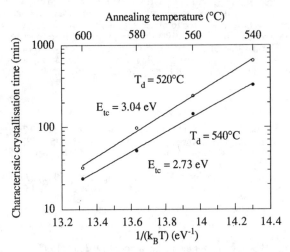

Figure 6 : Characteristic crystallisation time versus reciprocal temperature for films deposited according to Table I.

The incubation time is very small for the 540°C-deposited film. This is in good agreement with the presence of crystallites (Fig. 2.a) and probably clusters which are just subcritical in the as-deposited film. By contrast, the films deposited at 520°C exhibit an incubation time of about 30 min. In Fig. 6, we have plotted t_c, obtained by fitting conductance curves measured at various temperatures, versus $1/k_BT$; a least square fit gives a characteristic energy E_{tc} of about 2.73 eV for the 540°C-deposited film compared to 3.04 eV for the 520°C case. For the analysed films, we were able to calculate the activation energy for the nucleation rate, E_n, by using the activation energy for the growth rate, E_g = 2.7 eV, extracted from our previous work [10] for the silane-deposited films. We have used the following expression : $3E_{tc} = E_n + 2E_g$ given by the Avrami-Mehl-Johnson equation for two-dimensional growth. We decided to use E_g = 2.7 eV (which is the value that we had previously obtained for SiH_4-originated films) instead of E_g = 2.3 eV (obtained for Si_2H_6-originated films) [10] because of the similarity of the the grain size and shape in the present work compared to the grain size and shape observed for the SiH_4-originated films in ref. 10. Actually, we believe that the value of E_n and E_g are intimately related to the microscopic structure of the amorphous phase, which not only depends on the chemistry of the gas precursor used for deposition, but also on the deposition parameters (temperature, pressure, deposition rate...). The results are summarised in Table II.

T_d [°C]	E_{tc} [eV]	E_n [eV]	ΔH^* [eV]
540	2.73	2.79	0.09
520	3.04	3.72	1.02

Table II. Comparison of the crystallisation parameters of the two layers deposited in the Table I conditions. ΔH^* represents the maximum enthalpy of the formation of a cluster ($E_n - E_g$).

CONCLUSION

The kinetics of crystallisation of high purity amorphous silicon films deposited from disilane gas by UHVCVD were studied. The layers had been deposited at pressures around 2 and 4 mTorr and temperatures of 540°C and 520°C, respectively. The deposition rate was about 11 Å.min^{-1} in both cases. From fits to *in situ* electrical conductance measurements, performed at various temperatures, we have been able to obtain the "activation" energy of the characteristic crystallisation time and estimate the activation energy of nucleation rates for both films analysed, by supposing a value of 2.7 eV for the activation energy for the growth rate. The larger E_n for 520°C-deposited film, corresponding to slower nucleation, is the reason for the larger grains observed after SPC compared to the layers deposited at 540°C and including small crystallites.

REFERENCES

1. T.I.Kamins, M.M.Mandurah and K.C.Saraswat, J. Electrochem. Soc. **125**, 927 (1978).
2. E.Kinsbron, M.Sternheim and R.Knoell, Appl. Phys. Lett. **42**, 835 (1983).
3. G.Harbeke, L.Krausbauer, E.F.Steigmeier, A.E.Widmer, H.F.Kappert and Neugebauer, J. Electrochem. Soc. **131**, 675 (1984).
4. R.Bisaro, J.Magariño, N.Proust and K.Zellama, J. Appl. Phys. **59**, 1167 (1986).
5. D.B.Meakins, N.A.Economou, P.A.Coxon, J.Stoemenos, A.Lowe and P.Migliorato, Appl. Surf. Sci. **30**, 372 (1987).
6. P.Joubert, B.Loisel, Y.Chouan and L.Haji, J. Electrochem. Soc. **134**, 2541 (1987).
7. T.Aoyama, G.Kawachi, N.Konishi, T.Suzuki, Y.Okajima and Miyata, J. Electrochem. Soc. **136**, 1169 (1989).
8. A.T.Voutsas and M.K.Hatalis, J. Electrochem. Soc. **139**, 2659 (1992).
9. M.K.Hatalis and D.W.Greve, J. Appl. Phys. **63**, 2260 (1988).
10. T.Kretz, R.Stroh, P.Legagneux, O.Huet, M.Magis and D.Pribat, to appear in Polycrystalline semiconductors III - Physics and Technology, Solid State Phenomena Vol. XXX, edited by H.P.Strunk, J.H.Werner, B.Fortin and O.Bonnaud (Trans. Tech., Zürich, 1994).
11. E.Scheid, B.De Mauduit, P.Taurines and D.Bielle-Daspet, Jpn. J. Appl. Phys. **29**, L2105 (1990).
12. K.Nakazawa, J. Appl. Phys. **69**, 1703 (1991).
13. C.H.Hong, C.Y.Park and H.J.Kim, J. Appl. Phys. **71**, 5427 (1992).
14. A.T.Voutsas and M.K.Hatalis, J. Electrochem. Soc. **140**, 871 (1993).
15. S.Hasegawa, S.Sakamoto, T.Inokuma and Y.Kurata, Appl. Phys. Lett. **62**, 1218 (1993).
16. M.Akhtar, V.L.Dalal, K.R.Ramaprasad, S.Gau and J.A.Cambridge, Appl. Phys. Lett. **41**, 1146 (1982).H.Kanoii, O.Sugiura and M.Matsumura, Jpn. J. Appl. Phys. **32**, 2613 (1993).
17. H.Kanoii, O.Sugiura and M.Matsumura, Jpn. J. Appl. Phys. **32**, 2613 (1993).
18. E.Scheid, J.J.Pedroviejo, P.Duverneuil, M.Gueye, J.Samitier, A.El Hassani et D.Bielle-Daspet, Mater. Sci. Eng. **B17**, 72 (1993).
19. J.P.Guillemet, B.Pieraggi, B.de Mauduit and A.Claverie, to appear in Polycrystalline semiconductor III - Solid State Phenomena (see reference 10).
20. B.S.Meyerson, Appl. Phys. Lett. **48**, 797 (1986).
21. D.W.Greve and M.Racanelli, J. Vac. Sci. & Technol. **B8**, 511 (1990).
22. D.Pribat, F.Plais, P.Legagneux, T.Kretz, R.Stroh, O.Huet, C.Walaine, M.Magis, N.Jiang, M.C.Hugon and B.Agius, to appear in Rev. Techn. Thomson-CSF, March 1994, in press.
23. A.Nakamura, F.Emoto, E.Fujii, A.Yamamoto, Y.Uemoto, K.Senda and G.Kano, J. Appl. Phys. **66**, 4248 (1989).
24. T.Noma, T. Yonehara and H. Kumomi, Appl. Phys. Lett. **59**, 653 (1991).
25. J.L.Batstone, Phil. Mag. **A67**, 51 (1993).
26. R.Landauer, J. Appl. Phys. **23**, 779 (1952).
27. M.Avrami, J. Chem. Phys. **7**, 1103 (1939).
28. W.A.Johnson and R.F.Mehl, Trans. Am. Inst. Min. Metall. Pet. Eng. **135**, 416 (1939).

Characteristics of Sub-micron Polysilicon Thin Film Transistors

Kola R. Olasupo
AT&T Bell Laboratories, Allentown, PA 18103, Tel: (215)439-7348

Professor M. K. Hatalis
EECS Department, Display Research Laboratory, Lehigh University,
Bethlehem, PA 18105, Tel:(215)758-3944

ABSTRACT

The polysilicon thin film transistor has been actively studied for the large area display applications like active matrix liquid crystal displays and for load cell in static random access memories. Due to low effective carrier mobility in polysilicon, the circuit speed is limited. Since the circuit delay time is directly proportional to the square of the channel length, short channel TFTs will be advantageous for high speed applications. In this work, we have studied the current voltage characteristics of an inverted sub-micron P-channel polysilicon thin-film transistor with self-aligned LDD structure to obtain a well-controlled channel and drain offset lengths. The particular features we examined are the leakage current and mobility. The leakage current and the ON current were found to be in the pico-amp and micro-amp range respectively for devices having channel length in the range of 1.0μm to 0.35μm. Even very small devices having L&W = 0.35μm x 0.35μm exhibited characteristics similar to wider devices. The on/off current ratio was in the order of 10^5 before hydrogenation.

INTRODUCTION

Polysilicon thin-film transistor (TFTs) has been widely investigated for active matrix liquid crystal display (AMLCDs). In addition to its higher current drive capability[1] compared to the amorphous devices, polysilicon TFT devices offers the flexibility of being used to build peripheral drive circuitry on the same substrates to interface with AMLCD.
Current research activities largely focused on longer ($\geq$ 2.0 μm) channel length devices. However, as packing density and the complexity of peripheral circuitry increases, better understanding of fabrication issues and characteristics of submicron polysilicon TFT's will be important.

Mat. Res. Soc. Symp. Proc. Vol. 345. ©1994 Materials Research Society

In this paper we present result of sub-micron polysilicon TFT fabricated with a self-aligned LDD technique to achieve a controlled channel length, and a reliable smaller geometry devices (0.35μmx0.35μm) with minimum short channel effect.

DEVICE FABRICATION

The inverted P-channel polysilicon TFT was fabrication on a 5" diameter silicon wafer. The fabrication process starts with a sequential H_2SO_4/H_2O_2 and BHF cleans. This is followed by the deposition of 400-nm of LPCVD SiO_2 by TEOS pyrolysis at 720° C. A 120-nm heavily doped n-type polysilicon gate electrode was deposited and defined. The gate definition was followed by the deposition of 50-nm gate oxide and the deposition of 50-nm α-Si in an LPCVD reactor by pyrolysis of SiH_4 at 550°C and 0.5 Torr. The α -Si is used for the TFT channel. Subsequent processing steps included, low temperature (≤ 600°C) re-crystallization furnace anneal for 15 hours, doping of the source and drain region by ion implantation of $1x10^{15}$ BF_2, followed by implant activation anneal at 850° C; the offset regions were not implanted. The process is completed with the deposition of dielectric layers for isolating metal contacts from device terminals and metallization for making contacts as depicted in figure 1. The TFT devices were fabricated with coded channel length ranging from 1.0 μm to 0.35 μm and channel with ranging from 1.4 μm to 0.35 μm.

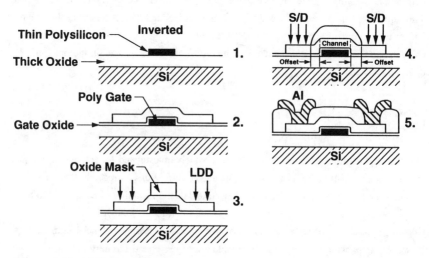

Figure 1. The TFT process sequence

RESULT & DISCUSSION

Figure 2 and 3 show the current-voltage characteristics of devices having channel width and length equal 0.35μm x 0.35μm. At a drain bias of -5 V, in figure 2, the "OFF" (I_{off}) current of a device having channel and width dimensions in the order 0f 0.35μm x 0.35μm is 5pA and the "ON" (I_{on}) current is 2.7μA resulting in I_{on} /I_{off} current ratio of 5.4×10^5. As shown on the figure, the I_{off} increases as the drain bias was increased from -0.1 V to -5.1 V. This effect can be explained by carrier emission from trap centers located in the drain depletion region. The emitted carriers readily contributed to the drain current in the "OFF" state because the potential barrier has been reduced by the drain field. The switching characteristics are broad. The subthreshold slope (S) ranges from 660 mV/decade to 800 mV/decade of current. Because the on-currents (I_{on}) are low, the effective mobility (μ_{eff}) obtained from I-V expression

$$\frac{\partial I_D}{\partial V_G} = \frac{W}{L} C_{ox} \mu_{eff} V_D \qquad (1)$$

at low drain voltage (-0.1 V) are very low. The values are summarized in table I. It has been reported[2] that further reduction of I_{off} is achievable after the passivation of the dangling bonds at polysilicon grain boundaries with atomic hydrogen. As such, further improvement in I_{on} and subthreshold characteristic is expected after hydrogenation.

Table I. Poly-Si TFT characteristics as a function of channel length (W=0.6μm)

Coded Channel Length (μm)	I_{on}/I_{off}	S (mV/decade)	μ_{off} (cm^2/V.s)
1.0	4.1×10^5	762	0.193
0.9	8.1×10^5	763	0.196
0.8	6.8×10^5	662	0.300
0.7	6.4×10^5	734	0.540
0.6	4.9×10^5	737	0.183
0.5	4.4×10^5	763	0.023
0.4	3.3×10^5	792	0.049
0.35	5.4×10^5	800	0.086

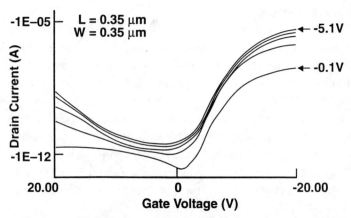

Figure 2. ID-VG characteristics for 0.35 μm poly-Si TFT's for several drain biases

In figure 3, the ID-VD characteristics for different gate voltage are shown for a device having channel length and channel width of 0.35μm and 0.35μm respectively. No significant short channel effect was observable for drain bias less than -10 V. However, above -10 V on the drain, an increase in drain current was observed. This increase can be attributed to drain-induced barrier lowering effect. Further increase of drain bias above -15 V will result in punch-through. This is not surprising, at VD = -12 V, the drain depletion width was estimated to be 0.293 μm which is more than 80% of the source to drain separation.

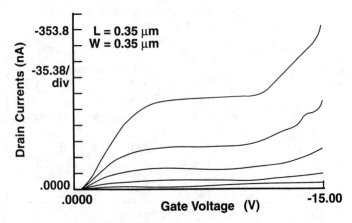

Figure 3. ID-VD characteristics for 0.35 μm x 0.35 μm poly-Si TFT's with several gate biases.

132

The minimum leakage current (see figure 4 (a) & (b)) at VD = -5V showed no unique dependency on the channel dimensions. This is contrary to earlier report[3] where a unique dependency was observed for devices with larger polysilicon grain size. In our result, we examined channel length ≤ 1.0 μm and channel width ≤ 1.4 μm, and average polysilicon grain size was 0.4 μm. The result shown on figure 4(a) is for 0.6 μm channel width. Contrary to the result of figure 4(a), the minimum leakage current shown in figure 4(b) exhibited dependency on channel width. Although minimal, the leakage current was rising as the channel width increases from 0.4 μm to 1.4 μm. In both instances, the leakage current was less than 11 pA.

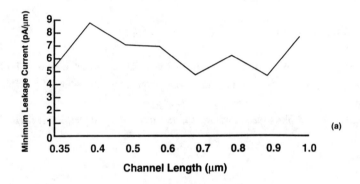

(a)

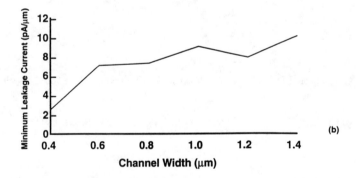

(b)

Figure 4. (a) Minimum leakage (I_{off}) current as a function of Channel length and
(b) Minimum leakage (I_{off}) current as a function of Channel width

CONCLUSION

We have presented preliminary result on polysilicon TFT's having submicron channel dimensions. The devices exhibited normal characteristics down to 0.35μm x 0.35μm channel length and width dimensions. The devices exhibited off current less than 11 pA, a broad switching characteristic, and a moderate (10^5) on/off current ratio. Due to the broad switching characteristics and low on-current, the effective mobility was low. However, we believe further improvement in the switching characteristics and in effective mobility are achievable after hydrogenation.

ACKNOWLEDGMENT

Kola Olasupo would like to thank the staff of Device Development Line of AT&T Bell Laboratory in Allentown for their help and cooperation in the fabrication of the Thin-Film Transistors.
M. K. Hatalis would like to acknowledge support from ARPA under contract MDA972-92-J-1037

REFERENCES

[1] Alan G. Lewis et al, IEDM Technical Digest. pp. 575-578 (1991).
[2] M. K. Hatalis and D. W. Greve, IEEE Elect. Dev. Lett. vol. EDL-8, pp. 361-364 (1987).
[3] Noriyoshi et al., IEEE Trans. Elect Dev. vol. 38 NO 1 pp. 55-60 (1991).

HYDROGENATION MECHANISM OF TOP-GATED POLYSILICON THIN FILM TRANSISTORS

YONG-MIN HA, JUNG-IN HAN, CHUL-HI HAN, CHOONG-KI KIM
Dept. of Electrical Engineering, Korea Advanced Institute of Science and Technology, 373-1 Kusong-Dong Yusong-Gu, Taejon, 305-701 Korea.

ABSTRACT

Hydrogen diffusion paths in top-gated polysilicon thin-film transistors have been investigated by measuring the current-voltage characteristics of the transistors with various sizes after hydrogenation. Hydrogenation has been performed in ECR plasma sysytem. It is noted that hydrogen is introduced through three main paths instead of one predominant path. The hydrogen from different paths affects the device parameters differently.

INTRODUCTION

The electrical characteristics of poly-Si TFT's such as mobility, subthreshold slope, threshold voltage, and leakage current are believed to be degraded by the defects in the active layer due to the strained bonds as well as the dangling bonds[1]. Thus, hydrogenation is essential to passivate the defect states in order to improve the electrical performance of poly-Si TFT's[2]. Although hydrogenation can be performed using hydrogen ion implantation[3] or diffusion from plasma silicon nitride film[4], the most popular method seems to be exposing poly-Si TFT to hydrogen plasma source[5,6]. Considering the importance of hydrogenation, it is essential to understand diffusion paths of hydrogen and hydrogenation mechanism. Mitra[7] has proposed four possible paths for the introduction of hydrogen into the channel region: A) through the gate polysilicon and gate oxide B) through the channel polysilicon C) through the gate oxide, then by lateral diffusion in the gate oxide, and into the poly-Si film D)through the quartz substrate (or buried oxide), then into the poly-Si channel. Although Mitra reported that path D) is most probable, recently Jackson[8] reported that hydrogen diffuses predominantly through path C).

It seems that the best method to understand the mechanism of hydrogenation is to measure the hydrogen concentration and the trap state density in the active poly-Si films after hydrogenation. However, since it is impossible or very difficult to measure them directly, we can use only indirect method. In this paper, we report on the measurements of I-V charateristics of poly-Si TFT's with various device sizes after hydrogenation and discuss the various hydrogen diffusion mechanisms reported and their effects on the device characteristics.

EXPERIMENTAL

The process sequence for obtaining the poly-Si TFT's to be hydrogenated is as follows: First, a 500nm SiO_2 is grown on silicon wafers and a 70nm amorphous silicon film is deposited using LPCVD. Solid phase crystallization (SPC) of the amorphous silicon film is performed in an N_2 ambient at 600°C for 72 hours. Active island is patterned using a dry etching and a 10nm SiO_2 is formed by oxidation and 70nm LTO is deposited as a gate insulator. Polysilicon is deposited and doped using $POCl_3$ source and then, gate electrodes are formed by lithography and dry etching. Source/drain regions are formed by phosphorus ion implantation for NMOS and BF_2 ion implantation for PMOS, followed by subsequent annealing at 600 °C for 12 hours. Interlayer LTO is deposited and contact holes are formed. After aluminum metallization, metal alloy is performed in an N_2/H_2 forming gas ambient at 450°C for 30 minutes.

ECR plasma is used to hydrogenate the fabricated poly-Si TFT efficiently[9]. The substrate temperature is 300°C, the microwave power is 600W, and the process pressure is 2 mtorr.

RESULTS AND DISCUSSION

Fig. 1 shows the typical I_D - V_{GS} characteristics of poly-Si TFT's at V_{DS} = 4V, with different

135

device sizes (W/L = 15μm/15μm, 4μm/15 μm, and 15μm/4μm) after 100 minutes hydrogenation. Our data is silimilar to that of Mitra[7] in that the devices with smaller feature size can be hydrogenated more efficiently and in shorter time. However, comparing the result of the short device(W/L = 15μm/4μm) with that of the narrow device(W/L = 4μm/15μm), some interesting results can be observed. The short device shows smaller subthreshold slope and lower threshold voltage than the narrow device, but the narrower device shows the higher normalized transconductance, Gm·(L/W).

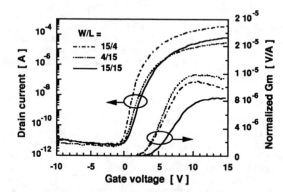

Fig. 1 Drain currents and normalized transconductances (Gm L/W) of n-type poly-Si TFT's vs. gate voltage after 100 minutes hydrogenation.

The degree of hydrogenation and consequent improvement of the device characteristics are shown in Fig. 2 and Fig. 3 for various device dimensions. Fig. 2 shows the variation of the device parameters: subthreshold slope, threshold voltage, field effect mobility, and leakage current, with the channel length for the fixed channel width of 50μm, where the threshold voltage is the gate voltage at a fixed current(100nA) scaled by the device geometry and the leakage current is the minimum drain current in the I_{DS}-V_{GS} curve at V_{DS} = 7V. From this figure it can be seen that all the parameters are improved as the channel length decreases except for the leakage current, for which the improvement stays constant for all channel lengths. Fig. 3 shows the variation of the device parameters with the channel width while the channel length is fixed to 15 μm. While the mobility has been improved much more in a narrower channel device, little channel width dependence has been found for the subthreshold slope.

With hydrogenation, the performance of a device with a smaller feature size is improved much more than the characteristics of a large device. It has been reported in the literature[10] that the diffusion coefficient of hydrogen atoms in single-crystal silicon at 300°C is about 10^{-10} cm²/sec. However, the diffusion of hydrogen is impeded in heavily n+ doped silicon[10] and the diffusion in polysilicon film is also retarded by trapping at grainboundaries[8]. Moore et al[11] found the diffusion coefficients in polysilicon by electrical method to be about 1×10^{-13} cm²/sec at 250°C and about 5×10^{-13} cm²/sec at 350°C. From our results and low diffusivity of hydrogen in n+ doped polysilicon, path A shown in Fig.4 (a) can be ruled out as the predominant diffusion path. The strong channel length dependence of the parameters in Fig. 2 shows that hydrogen atoms are diffused laterally through gate oxide (path C), channel polysilicon (path B), or gate oxide-channel interface to improve threshold voltage, mobility, and subthreshold slope. Thus, the subthreshold slope of Ids-Vgs curve may be determined by the trap state density of the center region of channel. Since the trap states in the channel polysilicon can be estimated from the relationship[12]

$$Q_T = [(S/\ln 10) q/kT - 1] (C_{ox}/q)$$ (1)

where, S is the subthreshold slope, the distribution of trap states in the channel can be obtained from the subthreshold slopes of the devices with various channel length. The values obtained by

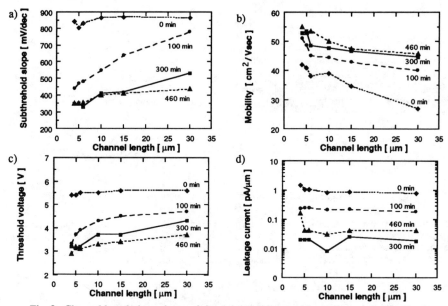

Fig. 2   Channel length dependence of a) subthreshold slope, b) mobility, c) threshold voltage
and d) leakage current density with hydrogenation. Channel width is 50μm.

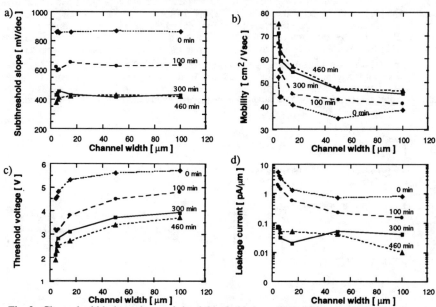

Fig. 3   Channel width dependence of a) subthreshold slope, b) mobility, c) threshold voltage
and d) leakage current density with hydrogenation. Channel length is 15μm.

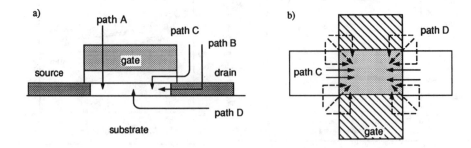

Fig. 4   Possible hydrogen diffusion paths a) cross-sectional view b) plan view

subtracting the trap states after hydrogenation from those before hydrogenation are the passivated trap state densities with hydrogenation. Fig. 5 represents the passivated trap states distribution in the channel after 100 minutes hydrogenation and 300 minutes hydrogenation, respectively. And these distributions can be fitted very well using general diffusion equation

$$C(x) = C_0 \, \text{erfc} \, [\, x \, / \, (\, 2\sqrt{Dt} \,) \,] \tag{2}$$

where, D is diffusion coefficient, t is diffusion time, and x is the distance from the source or drain junction. Diffusion coefficients calculated after 100 minutes hydrogenation and after 300 minutes are $9.4 \times 10^{-11} \text{cm}^2/\text{sec}$ and $2.7 \times 10^{-10} \text{cm}^2/\text{sec}$. These values are about 1000 times larger than Moore's value[11]. Thus, it seems that hydrogen atoms diffuse laterally through the gate oxide or the gate oxide-channel polysilicon interface rather than the whole channel polysilicon (path B). In addition, if path B is the predominant diffusion path, the reported channel thickness dependence[7], where poly-Si TFT's with thinner active films are hydrogenated in shorter time can not be explained. Considering the large hydrogen diffusion coefficient of $10^{-7} \sim 10^{-8} \text{ cm}^2/\text{sec}$ in oxide film[8], it is a reasonable conclusion that hydrogen can diffuse laterally through both path C and path D. The lower diffusion coefficients of our data than those in oxide films tell us that the oxide-polysilicon interface and(or) the channel polysilicon may affect the hydrogen diffusion.

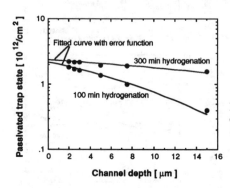

Fig. 5   Passivated trap state density which is calculated from subthreshold slope of the poly-Si TFT's with several different channel lengths.

If we suppose that hydrogen diffuses laterally only through the gate oxide according to the report of Jackson[8], the strong channel length dependence of device parameters such as subthreshold slope, threshold voltage, and mobility would be observed. However, since the two outer regions in the channel width direction (hatched region in Fig. 4 b)) are covered with poly-Si gate, device characteristics would not show the channel width dependence. Considering the fact that the diffusion cross-section of the substrates is larger than the gate oxide, it is not difficult to imagine that the hydrogen can be introduced through the substrates under the poly-Si gate electrode and also under the active island (path D).

Till now, the hydrogenation characteristics of NMOS poly-Si TFT's have been discussed since most of the results of PMOS devices are similar to those of NMOS devices with hydrogenation. However, there is some difference in subthreshold slope between PMOS device and NMOS device. The subthreshold slopes of PMOS devices are larger than those of NMOS devices and while the channel width dependence of the subthreshold slope of NMOS device is not observed , the subthreshold slope of narrower PMOS device is improved much more with hydrogenation as shown in Fig. 6. These differences are due to the structure of PMOS, the gate electrode is n+

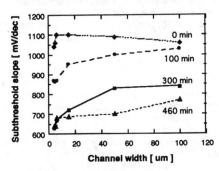

Fig.6 Channel width dependence of subthreshold slope of PMOS devices after hydrogenation.

doped polysilicon and the substrate which acts as a back gate is p-type silicon. With this structure, PMOS device is an accumulation-mode device. When the gate voltage is positive, the active film is depleted. With increasing gate bias toward negative voltage, hole concentration increases and finally, the front side of film is accumulated due to the work function difference between the front gate and the p-type substrate[13]. Thus, the trap states at the back side of film as well as at the front side of the film affect the subthreshold slope of devices while the subthreshold slope of the NMOS devices which are an enhancement-mode device is affected mainly by the traps at the front side film. Fig.7 (a) and (b) shows the Ids-Vgs curve of narrow PMOS device ($5\mu m/15\mu m$) and wide PMOS device ($100\mu m/15\mu m$), respectively. All the parameters of the narrow devices are improved much more than those of the wide devices with hydrogenation. It seems that since the

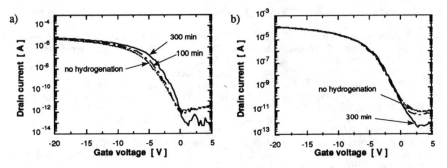

Fig. 7   Drain currents of a) narrow p-type TFT(W/L = $5\mu m/15\mu m$) and b) wide p-type TFT (W/L = $100\mu m/15\mu m$) vs. gate voltage before and after hydrogenation.

trap states of devices are passivated effectively also by the hydrogen introduced through path D, the subthreshold slope of a narrow PMOS device is smaller than that of a wide device.

From our results, it is difficult to explain the mechanism of the hydrogenation of top-gated poly-Si TFT's with one predominant diffusion path. Instead, it appears that the hydrogen is introduced through different paths as shown in Fig. 4 and affects the parameters of poly-Si TFT's differently. The off state leakage current is mainly due to the trap states in a small region near the drain junction region[14], and it can be reduced due to the hydrogen coming from the S/D region to the junction through the poly-Si films or the gate oxide (path B or path C). Since hydrogen can diffuse laterally through the gate oxide easily (path C), it appears that the improvement of threshold voltage, mobility, and especially subthreshold slope shows strong dependence on the channel length. It may be deduced that the hydrogen through path C has passivated the interface states between the gate oxide and the channel polysilicon and the trap states of the poly-Si film near the gate oxide. Hydrogen may also have been introduced through the back oxide(or the quartz substrate), and finally into the back interface of active poly-Si films. Thus, the mobility and the threshold voltage of narrower devices are improved much more but the improvement of the subthreshold slope is less dependent on the channel width for NMOS device. However, the subthreshold slope of an accumulation-mode PMOS device show the strong channel width dependence.

CONCLUSION

Even though more study is required to understand the mechanism of the hydrogenation of top gate poly-Si TFT exactly, it can be concluded from our experiments that hydrogen atoms are introduced into poly-Si films through different paths and affect the device parameters differently: First, hydrogen atoms enter the junction from the S/D region and reduce the off-state leakage current. Second, hydrogen atoms move laterally through the gate oxide and enter poly-Si channel, thus improving mobility, threshold voltage, and especially subthreshold slope. In addition, hydrogen atoms can also be introduced through the substrates and improve threshold voltage and mobility for NMOS.

ACKNOWLEDGMENT

We would like to thank Mr. Won-Kyu park in Goldstar Co. for the preparation of devices.

REFERENCES

1. J. Levinson, F. R. Shepherd, P. J. Scanlon, W. D. Wesrwood, G. Este, and M. Rider, J. Appl. Phys. 53, 1193 (1982).
2. I.-W. Wu, T. Y. Huang, W. B. Jackson, A. G. Lewis, A.Chiang, IEEE Elec. Dev. Lett. 12,181 (1991).
3. M. Rodder, D. A. Antoniadis, F. Scholg, and A. Kalnitsky, IEEE Elec. Dev. Lett. 8, 27 (1987).
4. G. P.Pollack, W. F. Richardson, S. D. S. Malhi, T. Bonifield, H. Shichijo, S. Banerjee, M. Elaby, A. H. Shab, R. Womack, and P. K. Chatterjee, IEEE Elec. Dev. Lett. 5, 468 (1984).
5. T. I. Kamins and Marcoux, IEEE Elec. Dev. Lett. 1, 150 (1980).
6. K.Nakazawa, H.Arai, and S. Kohda, Appl. Phys. Lett. 51, 1623 (1987).
7. U. Mitra, B. Rossi, and B. Khan, J. Electrochem. Soc. 138, 3420 (1991).
8. W. B. Jackson, N. M. Johnson, C. C. Tsai, I. -W. Wu, A. Chiang, and D. Smith, Appl. Phys. Lett. 61, 1670 (1992).
9. R. A. Ditizio, G.Liu, and S. J. Fonash, Appl. Phys. Lett. 56, 1140 (1990).
10. S. J. Pearton, J.W. Corbett, and T. S. Shi, Appl. Phys. A 43,153 (1987).
11. Chad B. Moore, Dieter G. Ast, MRS Symp. Proc. vol.182, 341 (1990).
12. C.A. Dimitriadis, P. A. Coxon, Laszlo Dozsa, Leonidas Papadimitrion and Nicolas Economou, IEEE Elec.Dev. 39, 598 (1992).
13. Jean-Pierre Colinge, in Silicon-on Insulator Technology: Materials to VLSI (Kluwer Academic Publishers, Massachusetts, 1991), pp. 149-157.
14. A. O. -Conde and J. G. Fossum, IEEE Elec. Dev. 33, 1563 (1986).

A NEW OFFSET GATED POLY-SI TFT USING A WET OXIDATION

B.H. MIN, J.M. OH AND M.K. HAN

Department of Electrical Engineering, Seoul National University, San 56-1, Shinrim-dong, Kwanak-ku, Seoul 151-742, Korea

ABSTRACT

Several off-set gated TFTs have been proposed to reduce the off current. However, those structures may require an additional mask and photolithography process step. We propose a novel off-set gated poly-Si TFT which reduces the off current considerably without any additional mask.

We have simulated the device characteristics by a numerical simulator in order to verify the proposed TFT. The simulation results show that the off current of the new device has been reduced to 0.1pA. The reduction of on current is much less than the off current reduction and the on/off current ratios exceeding 10^7 have been accomplished.

INTRODUCTION

In recent years, polycrystalline silicon thin film transistors (poly-Si TFTs) have been attracted a considerable attention for large-area and high-resolution active matrix liquid crystal displays (AMLCD). [1] In AMLCD, the poly-Si TFTs can be used for both the switching elements of the active matrix and the peripheral drive circuits on the glass substrate because of their potentially high mobility and current drive capability.

However, conventional poly-Si TFTs with large off current are not suitable for switching elements in AMLCD. It has been known that the dominant leakage current mechanism is the field emission via grain-boundary traps in the drain depletion region.[2] This suggests that decreasing the grain-boundary trap density in the depletion region may reduce the off current. Hydrogenation passivation, which decreases the grain-boundary trap density effectively, is widely used to reduce the off current of the poly-Si TFT.[3,4] However, hydrogenation of poly-Si TFT's may not be satisfactory to reduce the leakage current with large gate voltage V_g and drain voltage V_d. Therefore, the electric field in the drain depletion region is alleviated to suppress the increase in the off current. In order to decrease the electric field in the drain depletion region, several TFT structures such as off-set gated TFTs,[5] field-induced-drain (FID) TFTs [6] have been proposed. Although off-set gated TFT and FID TFT have been reported to improve the off current, these structures may require an additional photolithographic step and additional electric connections which may be rather difficult to fabricate.

The purpose of our work is to propose a novel off-set gated TFT which may reduce the off current considerably. The new structure employs a widely used conventional TFTs fabrication process without an additional mask. Also, we have simulated the device geometry by silicon process simulator (SSUPREM-4) and device characteristics by polysilicon TFT simulator (SPISCES-2B) in order to verify the proposed TFT. The simulation results show that the off current of the new device has been reduced to 0.1pA while that of conventional structure exceeded 0.5pA. The reduction of on current is much less than the off current reduction and the on/off current ratios exceeding 10^7 have been accomplished.

PROCESS SIMULATION

We have performed the process simulation in order to verify whether the proposed structure may be implemented accurately by employing the process as shown in Fig. 1. The process simulation steps are as follows. The undoped polysilicon 100nm thick layer is deposited on buffered oxide. All processes prior to the gate patterning are identical to those of conventional poly-Si TFTs. Namely, after definition of silicon islands, 100nm thick gate oxide and 100nm n^+ doped polysilicon gate electrode are deposited and patterned. The key process sequence different from a conventional poly-Si TFT fabrication may be described as follows. After gate electrodes are patterned, the gate oxide below gate edge is etched away by a wet etch process. The wet etched oxide length varies from 500nm to 1500nm. Phosphorous and boron ions are implanted into the source and drain regions respectively. Then, a thermal oxidation in wet ambient, of which oxide thickness is 100nm and 150nm, is performed. During the wet oxidation, the poly-Si gate on the wet etched oxide is oxidized and the length of gate electrode is reduced. The offset region in the undoped poly-Si, which acts as a channel region, is extended to the degree of etched oxide adjacent to the gate edge so that an off-set gated TFT is realized. Then, phosphosilicate glass (PSG) is deposited and annealed at 900°C for 30 min in nitrogen. The PSG is removed, gate and source/drain contact windows are opened, and Al was deposited and patterned.

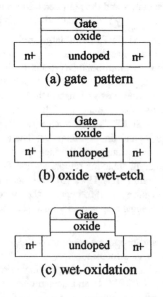

(a) gate pattern

(b) oxide wet-etch

(c) wet-oxidation

Fig.1 Schematic process sequences of our proposed poly-Si TFT structure

DEVICE SIMULATION

We have simulated the device characteristics such as I-V characteristic and electric field distribution by SPISCES-2B simulator. In the simulator, the densities of defect states (DOS) within the bandgap are incorporated in order to accurately evaluate the influences of grain boundary on the poly-Si TFT. The DOS model is composed of a combination of exponentially decaying localized defect densities of band tail states and Gaussian distributions of mid-gap states. Fig. 2 shows typical density of gap defect states in polysilicon and a schematic diagram of the proposed TFT structure.

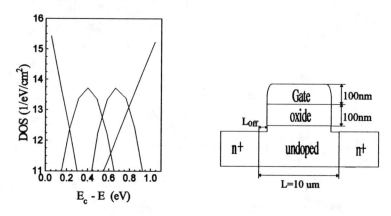

Fig. 2 Typical density of gap defect states in polysilicon and a schematic diagram of the proposed TFT structure

RESULTS AND DISCUSSION

The simulated transfer characteristics of the proposed poly-Si TFT of which wet oxide thickness is 100nm and 150nm respectively are shown in Fig. 3. The wet etched oxide below gate edge (L_{off}) is varied from 0.0um to 1.5um. In the proposed off-set structure TFT, the off current is suppressed at the negative gate bias, compared with that of the conventional one. As an offset length (L_{off}) increases, both on and off current decrease although the reduction of on current is much less than the off current reduction. However, a remarkable reduction in off current is observed when the offset length increases from 1.0um to 1.5um. This indicates that the offset structure is more effective to decrease the anomalous leakage current than the conventional one.

The on current is also decreased with increasing offset length (L_{off}) due to the increase of parasitic resistance. As shown in Fig. 3(a), The on current at V_g=20V and V_d=5V decreases from 8E-5 A to 5E-5 A as L_{off} increases from 0.0um to 1.5um. And also, the trend of the off-set structure with wet oxide thickness 150nm (Fig. 3(b)) is similar to that of the device with wet oxide thickness 100nm.

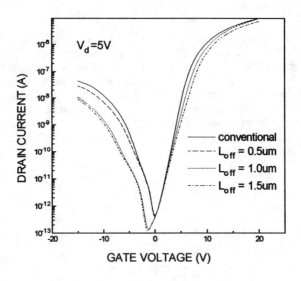

(a) wet oxidation thickness of 100nm

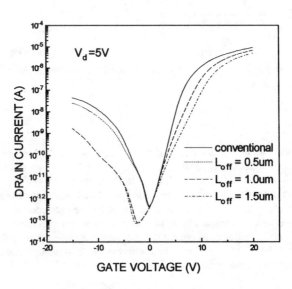

(b) wet oxidation thickness of 150nm

Fig. 3 Typical I_g-V_g characteristics of poly-Si TFTs with a conventional structure and a new off-set structure at V_d=5V

In order to clarify the major factors dictating the off current in poly-Si TFTs, the total electric field strength (E_T) in the drain depletion region, which consists of the lateral electric field (E_l) normal to the metallurgical junction between the channel and S/D region and vertical electric field (E_v) parallel from gate to channel region, was calculated. Fig. 4(a) indicates that the conventional structure has larger total electric field in the drain depletion region than that of the new structure. However, the lateral electric field strength has no difference while the vertical electric field strength is higher in the conventional one. These results show that the maximum vertical electric field strength plays a significant role to reduce the off current in the proposed offset structure poly-Si TFT.

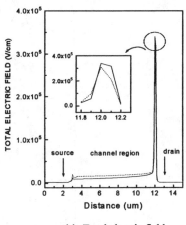

(a) Total electric field

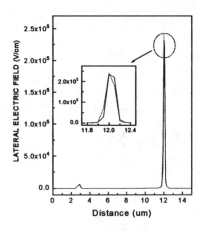

(b) Vertical electric field

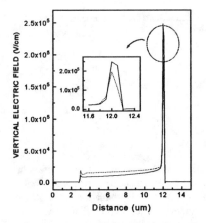

(c) Vertical electric field

Fig. 4 Electrical field strength along the channel region at V_{ds}=5V and V_{gs}=-20V.

145

We have already shown that the off current in the proposed off-set gated TFT is reduced considerably and the on current is also decreased slightly. It is well known that the on/off current ratio is an important device problem. The on/off current ratio with various offset lengths is evaluated and shown in Fig. 5. The maximum on/off current ratio occurs at the offset length (L_{off}) of 1.0um and the on/off ratio is 7E7. The on/off ratio of 7E7 is sufficient for a practicable device application to AMLCD.

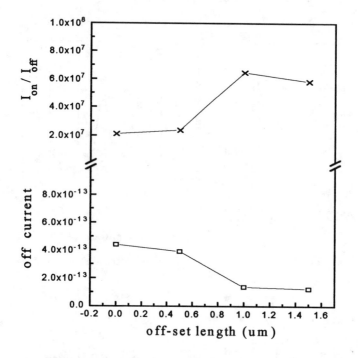

Fig. 5 Off current and I_{on}/I_{off} as a function of the offset length (L_{off})

CONCLUSION

We have proposed a novel offset gated poly-Si TFT which may reduce an off current by employing wet oxidation process without any additional mask. The characteristics of a poly-Si TFTs with this structure have been investigated by a numerical simulation. This off-set structure has been proved effective in reducing the anomalous leakage current. Moreover, the optimization of the offset length has been proven to increase the on/off current ratio. The off current reduce from 5E-12 A to 1E-13 A with increasing offset length from 0.0um (conventional structure) to 1.5um. A maximum on/off current ratio of 7E7 is obtained at $L_{off}=1.0$um.

We have found that the reduction of off current in the proposed TFT may be attributed to the peak vertical electric field strength in the drain depletion region.

REFERENCES

[1] M.G. Clark, IEE Proc. -Circuit Devices Syst., **141**, 3 (1994)

[2] J.G. Fossum, A. Oritz, H. Shichijo and S.K. Baneriee, IEEE Tras. on Electron Devices, **32**, 1878 (1985)

[3] S.D.S. Malhi, Electron Lett., **19**, 993 (1983)

[4] Y.S. Kim, K.Y. Choi, S.K. Lee, B.H. Min and M.K. Han, Jpn. J. Appl. Phys. **33**, 649 (1994)

[5] S. Seki, IEEE Electron Device Lett., **8**, 434 (1987)

[6] K. Kobayashi, H. Murai, T. Sakamoto and K. Baert, Jpn. J. Appl. Phys., **32**, 469 (1993)

CRYSTALLIZATION BEHAVIOR OF THE AMORPHOUS $Si_{1-x}Ge_x$ FILMS DEPOSITED ON SiO_2 BY MOLECULAR BEAM EPITAXY(MBE)

CHANG-WON HWANG[*],MYUNG-KWAN RYU[*], KI-BUM KIM[*], SEUNG-CHANG LEE[**], AND CHANG-SOO KIM[***]

[*] Department of Metallurgical Engineering, Seoul National Universitv, Seoul, Korea, 151-742
[**] Unit Process Research Section, Electronics and Telecommunications Research Institute, Chungnam, Korea, 305-606
[***] Materials Evaluation Center, Korea Research Institute of Standards Science, Chungnam, Korea, 305-606

ABSTRACT

We have investigated solid phase crystallization behavior of the MBE grown amorphous $Si_{1-x}Ge_x$ (x=0 to 0.53) layers using x-ray diffractometry and transmission electron microscopy (TEM). It is found that the thermal budget of the solid phase crystallization of the film is significantly reduced as the Ge concentration in the film is increased. In addition, we find that the amorphous Si film crystallizes with a strong (111) texture while the $Si_{1-x}Ge_x$ alloy film crystallizes with a (311) texture suggesting that the solid-phase crystallization mechanism is changed by the incorporation of Ge. TEM analysis of the crystallized film shows that the grain morphology of the pure Si is an elliptical or a dendrite shape with a high density of microtwins in the grains while that of the $Si_{0.47}Ge_{0.53}$ alloy is more or less equiaxed shape with a much low density of crystalline defects in them.

INTRODUCTION

It is recently proposed that the poly-$Si_{1-x}Ge_x$ film can be used as an active layer of the thin film transistor(TFT) due to such advantages of not only reducing the thermal budget of the solid phase crystallization but also having the potential to increase the field effect mobility.[1,2] Although reasonable device characteristics has been demonstrated at a maximum processing temperature of 550 °C with a 20 % Ge active layer, a systematic study of the crystallization mechanism of the $Si_{1-x}Ge_x$ alloy film and the resulting microstructure has not been performed. The purpose of this paper is to investigate the solid state crystallization mechanism of $Si_{1-x}Ge_x$ alloy film in relation to the evolution of microstructure and compare that with those of pure Si film.

EXPERIMENTAL METHODS

Amorphous $Si_{1-x}Ge_x$ films of which the Ge concentration x = 0, 0.14, 0.34, and 0.53 were deposited by MBE on thermally oxidized Si <100> wafers. The nominal thickness of the film was 1000 Å and the deposition temperature was 300 °C. The base pressure and the deposition pressure were 1×10^{-10} Torr, and 1×10^{-9} Torr, respectively, and the deposition rate was about 30 Å/min. The composition of the film was identified by Rutherford Backscattering Spectrometry (RBS). The as-deposited amorphous film was annealed at 500 °C, 550 °C, and 600 °C in the tube furnace using the high purity nitrogen gas as an ambient. Finally, the amount of crystallization and the resulting microstructure were investigated by using both x-ray diffractometry and transmission electron microscopy (TEM).

Mat. Res. Soc. Symp. Proc. Vol. 345. ©1994 Materials Research Society

EXPERIMENTAL RESULTS

X-ray Diffractiometry Results

Figure 1 shows the results of the x-ray diffractometry of the $Si_{1-x}Ge_x$ ((a) x = 0, (b) x = 0.14, (c) x = 0.34, and (d) x = 0.53) alloy films annealed at 600 °C. The samples of each concentrations were annealed at different times to investigate the progress of the crystallization. The diffraction peaks appearing at around $2\theta = 28°$, 47°, and 55° represent the diffraction peaks from the (111), (220) and (311) planes, respectively.

We first note that the pure Si, $Si_{0.86}Ge_{0.14}$, and $Si_{0.66}Ge_{0.34}$ films were deposited as an amorphous state since the x-ray results do not show any peaks. However, for the case of as-deposited $Si_{0.47}Ge_{0.53}$ film, a weak and broad peak occurs at around $2\theta = 28°$ indicating that crystalline phase is already formed during deposition. The x-ray results also show that the crystallization started in between 5 to 10 hours of annealing time for the pure Si film since no diffraction peak occurs for the samples annealed for 5 hours and only weak diffraction peaks occur for the samples annealed for 10 hours. Similarly, the results show that the $Si_{0.86}Ge_{0.14}$ film started to crystallize in between 5 and 10 hours and the $Si_{0.47}Ge_{0.53}$ film started to crystallized after about an hour of annealing. Clearly, we note that the incubation time of the crystallization is gradually reduced by the Ge incorporation in the film. Similar trend appears for the samples annealed at 550 °C and 500 °C. Figure 2 shows the variation of crystallization fraction at each annealing conditions obtained from the measurement of the (111) peak intensities. Here, we define the time for full crystallization of the film when the diffraction peak

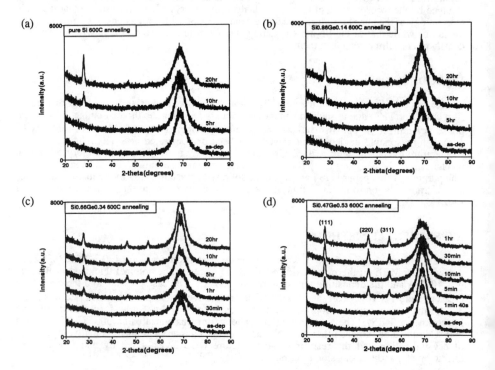

Fig. 1 X-ray diffraction pattern of the Si1-xGe alloy films annealed at 600 °C ((a) Pure Si, (b) $Si_{0.14}Ge_{0.86}$, (c) $Si_{0.66}Ge_{0.34}$, and (d) $Si_{0.47}Ge_{0.53}$) at different annealing times.

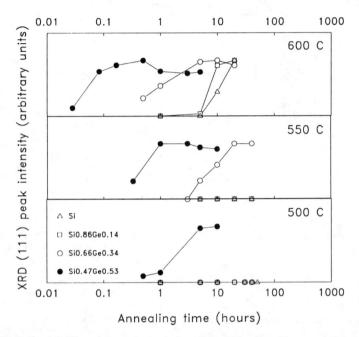

Fig.2 Normalized (111) peak intensity variation of the SiGe-alloy films annealed at 600 °C, 550 °C, and 500 °C.

intensity does not increase by further annealing. Once the saturation intensity is determined for each samples, all the other peak intensities were calibrated by that intensity value. Our result thus confirms the previous results of Maenaa et al.[3] and Edelman et al.[4] which shows that the thermal budget of the crystallization is reduced by using Si_xGe_{1-x} alloys.

In addition, by the careful investigation of the x-ray results, we found that the texture of the film is also changed by the incorporation of Ge. For instance, the x-ray diffraction results of the pure-Si film annealed at 600 °C (Fig. 1(a)) clearly show that the (111) peak intensity is much larger than that of any other crystalline Si peaks meaning that the film crystallized with a strong (111) texture. However, as the Ge is incorporated in the film, the relative intensity of the (111) peak is becoming smaller (Figs 1(b) ~ (d)) compared to other peak intensities such as (220) and (311). It thus appears that the texture of the film is changed with the Ge incorporation. In order to clearly identify the variation of the texture of the films, we have compared the intensity of each peaks after calibrating each diffraction intensities with the following equation;[5]

$$G_x = 1 - \exp(-2\mu t / \sin \theta)$$ (1)

where G_x is the calibration factor, μ is the absorption coefficient, t is the thickness of the film, and θ is the diffraction angle of each peaks. Absorption coefficient of the film is obtained by averaging that of the Si and Ge by the composition of each films. Figure 3 shows the results of normalize intensity of each peaks with respect to that of (111). Again, it can be clearly shown that the pure Si forms a (111) texture while the other films forms a (311) texture. It has been well known that the solid phase crystallized Si forms a strong (111) texture[5,6] However, as far as we are aware of, the changes of texture with the Ge incorporation has not been reported. While

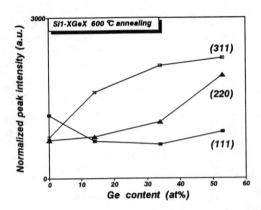

Fig. 3 Normalized XRD intensity variation of the film annealed at 600 °C with the Ge
concentration in the film.

the orgin of texture formation in the solid phase crystallized Si films is not well established, our
results suggest that the solid phase crystallization mechanism is somewhat different in these two
cases.

<u>TEM Results</u>

Figure 4 shows a sequence of plan-view TEM micrographs of the pure Si film annealed at
600 °C with annealing time. As is shown in the figure, at the initial stage of crystallization, an
elongated type of grains is formed in the amorphous Si matrix and, as the crystallization is
progressed, a dendritic shape grains with many arms are formed. In addition, we note that
microtwins and stacking faults are existed along the long axis of the elliptical grains and in the
middle of the arms of the denritic shape grains. On the other hand, the evolution of
microstructure of the $Si_{0.47}Ge_{0.53}$ alloy films annealed at 550 °C is quite different than that of
the pure Si film as is shown in a series of plan-view TEM micrographs (Fig. 5). We note that the
grains formed at the initial stage of crystallization are more or less circular and this circular shape
is maintained during the whole crystallization process. Also, we note that the defect density in
the grains is much lower than that of pure Si films.

DISCUSSION

It has been well documented that the thermal budget of the $Si_{1-x}Ge_x$ alloy is much reduced
than that of the pure Si film.[9,10] Indeed, this has been one of the major motivation for using the
$Si_{1-x}Ge_x$ alloy layer as an active layer for an AMLCD.[1,2] Our results thus quite well agree with
the previous results in that we can indeed decrease the thermal budget of the solid phase
crystallization.

Moreover, what we have identified in this work is that the evoultion of texture is different in
between pure Si films and $Si_{1-x}Ge_x$ alloy films and the evolution of grain microstructure is also
striking different in these two cases. In the case of pure Si film, it has been well documented that
the solid phase crystallized film forms a (111) texture and the grain microstructure is an elliptical
and a dendritic shape with a high density of microtwins in them.[5,7-11] For intance, Koster[7]
reported that the pure amorphous Si film crystallizes to form a dendritic grain shape in the
temperature ranges from 550 °C to 750 °C and that the grain growth occurs predominantly by the
formation of stacking fault bundles and/or microtwins in parallel to the fastest growing direction
[211]. They also identified that Si shows a much more pronounced crystallization morphology

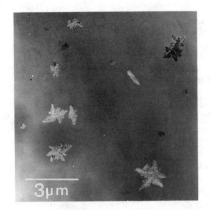

Fig. 4 A sequence of plan-view TEM micrographs of the pure Si film annealed at 600 °C.

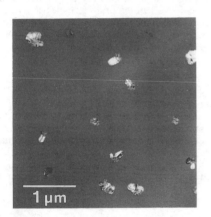

Fig. 5 A sequence of plan-view TEM micrographs of the $Si_{0.47}Ge_{0.53}$ film annealed at 550 °C.

with growth in [211] direction than Ge. The model proposed by Hamilton and Seidensticker[8] to explain the formation of long lathlike dendrites of Ge from undercooled melts can also be used to explain the formation of dendrites during solid phase crystallization. Namely, the formation of more than two microtwins at the initial stages of crystallization makes the grain growth easier by supplying the ledge or steps at the growth front. Recently, Nakamura et al.[9] also explained that the formation of crystals at relatively low crystallization temperature is promoted by the formation of microtwins. All these results support that the grain growth of Si and Ge, either from amorphous or from liquid state, is assited by the formation of microtwins, and for this reason, the microstructure of the grains appears as an elliptical or a dendritic shape. However, it should also be noted that the grain microstructure is changed as the solid phase crystallization temperature is increased. For instance, Kamins et al.[5] observed the formation of dendrite grains at the solid phase crystallization temperature of 800 °C and equiaxed grains at 1200 °C.

Nagashima et al.[10] also noted the similar trend that they observed the needle-like grains at 700 °C and the equiaxed grains at 1100 °C. In addition, Anderson[11] also noted the formation of dendrite structure at the annealing temperature of 600 °C and the equiaxed microstructure at 1040 °C. These results, thus, indicate that the solid phase crystallization mechanism of amorphous Si is changed by the annealing temperature.

In this respect, we can explain the difference of the grain structure in between pure Si and $Si_{1-x}Ge_x$ alloys. The fact that we observed the formation of equiaxed grains in the $Si_{0.47}Ge_{0.53}$ alloy indicates that the thermal vibration energy is high enough for the random growth mode even though the annealing temperature is the same as Si. It is well known from the equilibrium binary phase diagram of the Si-Ge system that the melting temperature of the alloy is gradually decreased as the Ge concentration in the film is increased.[12] Thus, if we assume that the melting temperature(T_m) of each film can be determined by the solidus line, then the melting temperature of the $Si_{0.47}Ge_{0.53}$ alloy film is 1368 K. Therefore, the 600 °C annealing temperature is about $0.76 T_m$. Considering that the crystallization mechanism changes at about 1000 °C for Si, which is about $0.75 T_m$,[5,10,11] we can easily conclude that the formation of equiaxed grain structure in the $Si_{0.47}Ge_{0.53}$ alloy film is due to the low melting temperature of the film.

Finally, it is interesting to note the relationship between the evolution of microstructure and the texture of the film. For instance, Kamins et al.[9] reported that the texture changes from (111) for the films annealed at 600 °C to (311) for the films annealed higher than 800 °C. There results, therefore, suggest that the texture change is also closely related to the grain growth mode of the film. It appears that when the grain growth occurs predominantly by the twin-assited mechanism the film typically forms a (111) texture and, when the grain growth occurs by the random mode, the film typically forms a (311) texture. Although the relationship between the formation of texture of the film and the grain growth mode is not clear at this moment, it certainly appears that there is a close correlation between them.

CONCLUSION

In conclusion, we have studied the crystallization mechanism of the as-deposited amorphous $Si_{1-x}Ge_x$ alloy films. We not only identified that the incorporation of Ge significantly reduces both the crystallization temperature and annealing time but also identified that the crystallization mechanism is also changed. By the TEM analysis of the grain microstructure, we have identified that pure Si forms an elliptical and a dendritic type of grains with high density of microtwins in the grain when annealed at 600 °C. However, the $Si_{0.47}Ge_{0.53}$ alloy forms an equiaxed type of grains with much reduced defects in them. We suggest that the lowering of melting temperature by the incorporation of Ge does a role in changing the crystallization mechanism. In addition, we identified that the texture of the film is also changed from (111) for pure Si to (311) for the $Si_{1-x}Ge_x$ alloys.

REFERENCES

1. T.-J. King and K.C. Saraswat, **IEDM 91**, 567 (1991)
2. T.-J. King, K.C. Saraswat, and J. R. Pfiester, IEEE Elect. Dev. Lett. **12**, 584 (1991)
3. M. Maenaa and S.S. Lau, Thin Solid Films **82**, 343 (1981)
4. F. Edelman, Y. Komem, M. Bendayan, and R. Beserman, J. Appl. Phys. **72**, 5153 (1992)
5. T.I. Kamins, M.M. Mandurah, and K.C. Saraswat, J. Electrochem. Soc. **125**, 927 (1978)
6. K. Kobayashi, J. Nijs, and R. Mertens, J. Appl. Phys. **65**, 254 (1988)
7. U. Koster, Phy. Stat. Sol. **48**, 313 (1978)
8. D.R. Hamilton and R.G. Seidensticker, J. Appl. Phys. **34**, 1165 (1960)
9. A. Nakamura, F. Emoto, E. Fujii, A. Yamamoto, Y. Uemoto, K. Senda, and G. Kano, J. Appl. Phys. **66**, 4248 (1989)
10. N. Nagashima and N. Kubota, J. Vac. Sci. and Technol. **14**, 54 (1977)
11. R.M. Anderson, J. Electrochem. Soc. **120**, 1540 (1973)
12. *"Binary Alloy Phase Diagrams"* edited by T.B. Massalski, 2nd Edition.

DEGRADATION PHENOMENA OF LOW-TEMP. POLY-Si TFT's
UNDER ELECTRICAL STRESS BEFORE AND AFTER HYDROGENATION

Y.S. KIM, K.Y. CHOI, M.C. JUN, and M.K. HAN

Department of Electrical Engineering, Seoul National University, Seoul 151-742, KOREA

ABSTRACT

The degradation mechanism in hydrogen passivated and as-fabricated poly-Si TFT's are investigated under the various electrical stress conditions. It is observed that the charge trapping in the gate dielectric is the dominant degradation mechanism in poly-Si TFT's which was stressed by the gate bias alone while the creation of defects in the poly-Si film is prevalent in gate and drain bias stressed devices. The degradation due to the gate bias stress is dramatically reduced with hydrogenation time while the degradation due to the gate and drain bias stress is increased a little. From the experimental results, it is considered that hydrogenation suppress the charge trapping at gate dielectrics as well as improve the characteristics of poly-Si TFT's.

INTRODUCTION

Polycrystalline-silicon (poly-Si) thin film transistors (TFT's) have attracted much attention recently. Especially, poly-Si TFT's fabricated by a low-temperature ($\leq$ 600 °C) process are considered to be promising device in realizing future LCD's on large glass substrates.[1] However, in poly-Si TFT's, grain boundaries exert a profound influence on the device characteristics and degrade carrier transport. The hydrogen passivation of grain boundaries may be an important process to improve the performance of poly-Si TFT's.[2,3] We have previously reported that active layer thickness and channel length play an important role in hydrogen passivation process.[4]

In addition to optimization of hydrogenation process, the stability issue of poly-Si TFT's is important as a long-term reliability concern.[5,6] Although the instability of poly-Si TFT's may not be serious problems unlike widely used a-Si:H TFT's, the degradation of device characteristics can not be ignored. There are few reports with respect to the reliability problems, furthermore, the effects of hydrogen passivation on the degradation phenomena in poly-Si TFT's has not been investigated yet.

The purpose of our work is to report the relationships between hydrogen passivation and degradation mechanism. The degradation phenomena in poly-Si TFT's, which are as-fabricated and hydrogen passivated, is investigated by employing various electrical stress conditions.

EXPERIMENTAL

N-channel polysilicon TFT's were fabricated on oxidized silicon wafers below the temperature of 600 °C. The amorphous silicon (a-Si) for active layer, of which thickness was 1000 Å, was deposited by low-pressure chemical vapor deposition (LPCVD) at 550 °C. These a-Si films were

Mat. Res. Soc. Symp. Proc. Vol. 345. ©1994 Materials Research Society

crystallized by thermal annealing at 600 °C for 48 h in N_2 ambient. After definition of silicon islands, 1000-Å-thick silicon dioxide film deposited by atmospheric-pressure chemical vapor deposition (APCVD) was used as a gate dielectric layer. The thickness of poly-Si gate, which was deposited in the amorphous phase by LPCVD at 550 °C and crystallized by thermal annealing at 600 °C, was 1000 Å. The polysilicon for gate and source/drain electrodes was heavily doped by self-aligned P^+ implantation at an energy of 30 keV and dose of 5×10^{15} ions/cm^2. The implant was annealed at 600 °C for 12 h. A 7000-Å-thick interlayer oxide film was deposited by APCVD. Contact holes were opened and 10000-Å-thick AlSi film was deposited and defined. The devices were then sintered at 450 °C for 30 min in H_2.

Plasma hydrogenation was performed with various periods. The hydrogen plasma treatment conditions were 300 °C and 0.5 Torr. The power density was 7×10^{-2} W/cm^2 at the frequency of 13.56 MHz. Other hydrogenation procedures are similar to earlier report.[4] After measuring the initial device characteristics, two types of electrical stress, which consist of 30 V of gate bias and drain bias and 30 V of gate bias alone, were applied to r.f. plasma hydrogenated and as-fabricated (before hydrogenation) low-temperature poly-Si TFT's up to 6 hrs.

RESULTS AND DISCUSSION

Fig. 1 shows the transfer characteristics (I_{ds} vs V_g) of poly-Si TFT's with W/L=10/20 (μm/μm) at V_{ds} = 5 V as a function of hydrogenation time, which was varied from 0 min (as-fabricated) to 300 min. There are significant improvement of device characteristics, which include the increase of on current (I_{on}) and field effect mobility (μ_{fet}) and the decrease of threshold voltage (V_{th}) and

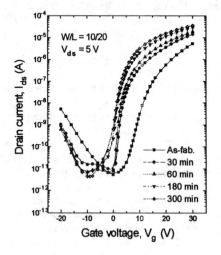
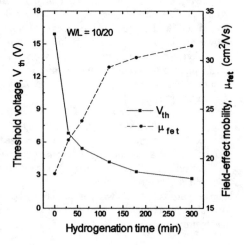

Fig.1 Transfer characteristics (I_{ds} vs V_g) of poly-Si TFT's (W=10 μm, L=20 μm) measured at V_{ds} = 5 V as a function of hydrogenation time.

Fig.2 Improvement of device parameters with hydrogenation time. The increase of field-effect mobility and the decrease of threshold voltage.

subthreshold slope (S).   The variation of device parameters, such as threshold voltage and subthreshold slope, is represented in Fig. 2.   The threshold voltage is reduced predominantly within 60 min and reaches a saturated value of about 2.5 V after 300 min hydrogenation.   The field-effect mobility increases monotonically with hydrogenation time up to 120 min, above which μ_{fet} slowly saturates to a value of about 31 cm^2/V·s.   In our experimental conditions, saturated passivation is achieved after about 180 min hydrogen passivation.

Two types of electrical stress, which consist of 30 V of gate bias and drain bias and 30 V of gate bias alone, was applied to poly-Si TFT's which were hydrogen passivated with various periods.   Fig. 3 shows $I_{ds}^{1/2}$ vs. V_g characteristics of poly-Si TFT's before and after 6 hrs electrical stress.   The 60 min hydrogenated poly-Si TFT was subjected to a gate bias stress of V_g = 30 V and the 300 min hydrogenated device to gate and drain bias stress of $V_g = V_{ds} = 30$ V, respectively.   As can be seen in Fig 3(a), there is an increase of threshold voltage and a parallel shift of these characteristics to higher gate voltages by the electrical stress of $V_g = 30$ V alone, which indicates that the dominant degradation mechanism is a electron trapping in gate insulators. On the other hand, the decrease of the slope in $I_{ds}^{1/2}$ vs. V_g plot and the increase of threshold voltage were occurred together as shown in Fig. 3(b).   It indicates that the gate and drain bias stress brings the increase of threshold voltage and the decrease of field-effect mobility.   These effects can not be explained only by the electron trapping mechanism.   The above results may imply that the electron trapping in the gate dielectric is the dominant degradation mechanism under the gate bias stress alone while the creation of defects in the poly-Si film is prevalent under the gate and drain bias stress.

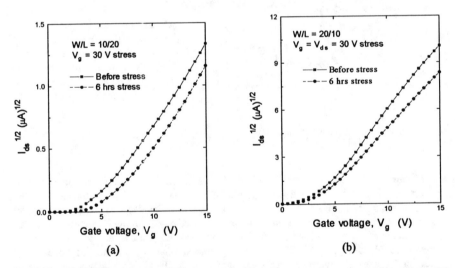

Fig. 3 $I_{ds}^{1/2}$ vs. V_g characteristics of poly-Si TFT's before and after 6 hrs electrical stressing.   The stress conditions and hydrogenation time are (a) $V_g = 30$ V and 60 min, (b) $V_g = V_{ds} = 30$ V and 300 min.

In order to verify the above results, the transfer characteristics were measured both in forward-mode and in reverse-mode (source and drain reversed) before and after the application of a stress voltage.   The device characteristics of the gate bias stressed poly-Si TFT, were almost identical both in forward-mode and in reverse-mode as expected. However, much difference between forward-mode and reverse-mode was occurred in the gate and drain bias stressed device. Fig. 4 shows the variation of transfer characteristics measured in forward-mode and in reverse-mode after the 6 hrs gate and drain bias stress. In forward-mode, a leakage current increased significantly but a little degradation of subthreshold characteristics was observed after the application of electrical stress. However, the characteristics measured in reverse-mode show much degradation of subthreshold characteristics and almost identical leakage current as can be seen in Fig. 4. This asymmetric degradation informs us that defects have been created mainly in the drain depletion region because the characteristics of leakage current in poly-Si TFT depends on defect density in drain depletion region while subthreshold characteristics on source junction.[7,8]

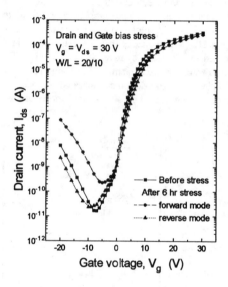

Fig. 4 Variation of transfer characteristics measured both in forward-mode and in reverse-mode (source and drain reversed) before and after the application of a stress voltage for 300 min hydrogenated poly-Si TFT.

Fig. 5 shows the threshold voltage shift (ΔV_{th}) as functions of hydrogenation time and electrical stress time. The threshold voltage shifts of Figs. 5(a) and 5(b) are extracted from the transfer characteristics of poly-Si TFT's under the different types of electrical stress which are 30 V of gate bias alone and 30 V of gate and drain bias, respectively. As can be seen in Fig. 5, the threshold voltage increase significantly by both cases of gate bias stress alone and gate and drain bias stress in as-fabricated poly-Si TFT's. On the contrary, when we have applied the gate and drain bias of 30 V to 300 min hydrogen passivated poly-Si TFT's, threshold voltage increases while there is not any considerable degradation due to the gate bias stress as expected.

Fig. 6 is a plot of threshold voltage shift as a function of hydrogenation time under the different bias conditions. It can be seen in this figure that the amount of threshold voltage shift due to gate bias stress is dramatically reduced with hydrogenation time whereas that due to gate and drain bias stress increases a little. It may be summarized that degradation due to gate bias stress is much more than that due to gate and drain bias stress in as-fabricated poly-Si TFT's (before hydrogenation) while this tendency turns over in hydrogenated devices more than 180 min.

These results may be explained as follows ; Hydrogen passivates the interface trap states at poly-Si/SiO$_2$ as well as grain boundary trap states in poly-Si. Thus, the effects of charge trapping in gate oxide is reduced owing to the decrease of interface trap states while that of defect creation is slightly increased due to the existence of weak Si-H bond after hydrogen passivation.

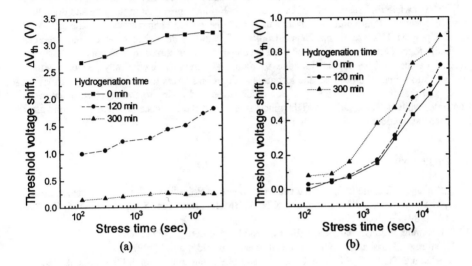

Fig. 5 Threshold voltage shift as functions of stress time and hydrogenation time.   The stress conditions are (a) V$_g$ = 30 V and (b) V$_g$ = V$_{ds}$ = 30 V.

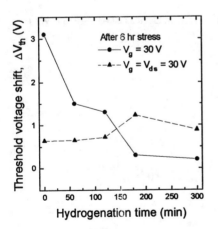

Fig. 6 Variation of threshold voltage shift as a function of hydrogenation time. The shift of threshold voltage is measured after 6 hrs stress.

159

CONCLUSION

We have investigated the degradation phenomena in poly-Si TFT's under the various electrical stress conditions, especially with respect to the relations with hydrogen passivation. The charge trapping in the gate dielectric is the dominant degradation mechanism in the gate bias stressed poly-Si TFT while the creation of defects in the poly-Si film is prevalent in the gate and drain bias stressed device. It is confirmed by the facts that the device characteristics of the gate bias stressed poly-Si TFT are almost identical both in forward-mode and in reverse-mode whereas much difference between forward-mode and reverse-mode is occurred in the gate and drain bias stressed device. The degradation due to gate bias stress is dramatically reduced with a hydrogenation time whereas that due to gate and drain bias stress increases a little. It may be considered that the charge trapping in gate oxide is reduced owing to the decrease of interface trap states while defect creation is slightly increased due to the existence of weak Si-H bond after hydrogen passivation.

REFERENCES

1. A. Chiang, T.Y. Huang, I.-W. Wu and M. Zarzycki in Polysilicon Films and Interfaces, edited by C.Y. Wong, C.V.Thompson, and K.N. Tu (Mater. Res. Soc. Symp. Proc., **106**, Boston, MA, 1987) pp. 305-310.
2. T.I. Kamins and P.J. Marcoux, IEEE Electron Device Lett. **1**, 159 (1980).
3. U. Mitra, B. Rossi and B. Khan, J. Electrochem. Soc. **138**, 3420 (1991).
4. Y.S. Kim, K.Y. Choi, S.K. Lee, B.H. Min, and M.K. Han, Jpn. J. Appl. Phys. **33**, 649 (1994).
5. I.-W. Wu, W.B. Jackson, T.Y. Huang, A.G. Lewis, and A. Chiang, IEEE Electron Device Lett. **11**, 167 (1990).
6. N. Kato, T. Yamada, S. Yamada, T. Nakamura, and T. Hamano, in IEDM Tech. Dig., 677 (1992).
7. J.G. Fossum, A. Ortiz-Conde, H. Shichijo, and S.K. Banerjee, IEEE Trans. Electron Devices **ED-32**, 1878 (1985).
8. S.K. Madan and D.A. Antoniadis, IEEE Trans. Electron Devices **ED-33**, 1518 (1986).

PART III

Emissive Displays

FLAT PANEL DISPLAY SUBSTRATES

DAWNE M. MOFFATT
Corning Incorporated, Research and Development, SP-FR-5-1, Corning, New York 14831

ABSTRACT

The performance of advanced flat panel displays is intrinsically linked to critical properties of the substrate material. In the manufacture of active-matrix liquid crystal displays (AMLCDs) and some emissive displays, there are certain process steps that require extreme conditions such as strong chemical washes and temperatures in excess of 600°C. As a result, the glass substrate used in these displays must be able to withstand these environments without degradation of its properties. It has become apparent that the flat panel display (FPD) manufacturers will benefit from substrates with improved acid durability, higher temperature capability, and thermal expansion coefficients consistent with other display materials.

This paper focuses on one of the less-understood features of the glass substrate: the expansion characteristics as a function of temperature. Thermal expansion is important as it affects the compatibility of the glass with display materials, which, in the case of AMLCDs and some silicon-microtip field emission displays (FED), require an expansion close to that of silicon. In addition, thermal breakage during processing is directly proportional to the expansion coefficient.

This study focused on the thermal expansion characteristics of two different FPD substrate glasses. The first one is code 7059, manufactured by Corning Incorporated and currently the standard in AMLCDs. A new substrate composition, Corning code 1737, with enhanced durability, temperature capability, and expansion tuned to the AMLCD applications will also be discussed.

INTRODUCTION

Glass is an essential part of flat panel displays (FPDs), whether it be in liquid crystal displays, plasma displays, or electroluminescent displays, to name a few. Flat panel displays require certain properties of glass such as its transparency, rigidity, and thermal stability. The requirements for flat glass in these applications are rather stringent in that they are completely determined by the process for making the entire display. The most severe requirements are associated with the active matrix liquid crystal display (AMLCD), which at this time is the most highly commercialized of the high-information FPD technologies [1-3]. This is the application of interest in the discussion that follows.

There are two predominant types of AMLCDs: ones based on thin film transistors (TFTs) of amorphous silicon and ones based on polycrystalline silicon TFTs. From the processing standpoint, one way that these two types of AMLCDs differ is by their maximum processing temperature. Amorphous silicon (a-Si) displays are processed no higher than 450°C, and for brief (< 1 hour) process times. Silicon deposition, for example, is done at a substrate temperature of 300°C or less. For polycrystalline silicon (poly-Si) displays, the actual maximum temperature is a function of the specific process. In the case of poly-Si with deposited-gate dielectrics, often called the low-temperature poly-Si process, processing temperatures can exceed 600°C and process times may exceed tens of hours. In the thermal oxide gate process, or IC-type poly-Si process, the maximum temperature can be higher than 800°C [1-5].

The substrate requirements for AMLCDs are as follows: very low alkali content, no surface defects at the micron level, no internal defects at the tens of microns level, the ability to withstand temperature cycles to greater than 350°C (for a-Si, higher for poly-Si) without dimensional changes or thermally-induced stress build-up, high dimensional precision and flatness, a thermal expansion coefficient in the range of $30\text{-}50 \times 10^{-7}/°C$, and good resistance to the etchant chemicals used throughout the process [1-3].

ROLE OF THERMAL EXPANSION IN ACTIVE MATRIX LCD SUBSTRATES

Much of the published work on FDP substrates is focused on certain glass requirements including thermal and dimensional stability and temperature capability [1-3]. However, one of the least discussed, and yet quite important, characteristics of the glass is the thermal expansion and the change in expansion with temperature. This glass property is important for reasons described below.

First, thermal stress build-up during panel processing is proportional to the thermal expansion coefficient [6]. The stresses that develop during the customer process may cause breakage due to thermal shock and, in general, the greater the thermal expansion of the glass, the more stress and the higher the probability of breakage.

Second, thermal expansion plays a role in the matching of the two glass substrates that make up the LCD: color filter (or passive plate) and TFT plate (or active plate). These two pieces of glass undergo different heat treatment cycles during processing. In particular, the color filter substrate is not subjected to the same high temperatures as those of the active plate. As a result, if the thermal expansion coefficients are too different, there will be a mismatch in features when the display is assembled, and problems with the reliability of cell sealing materials and lead connections to driver chips, etc. may arise.

Finally, thermal shrinkage with respect to semiconductor films and silicon driver chips mounted on the glass (chip-on-glass) is an issue. Chip-on-glass techniques give a more reliable and higher resolution capability for driver chip integration to displays than the conventional TAB process. The greater the mismatch between the glass and the gate materials, the greater the chance for reliability problems during the temperature cycles of the process.

The thermal expansion characteristics of glass are unusual when compared to other materials such as metals and ceramics and may be better understood with the help of a specific volume versus temperature curve such as that shown in Figure 1. When glass is cooled, it undergoes a combination of two effects: an instantaneous change in temperature coefficient and a change in the system itself. Both effects are reversible, but the latter is time dependent. This time dependence is also related to viscosity and, in turn, temperature: the relaxation time increases as the viscosity decreases (corresponding to a decrease in temperature). The range of temperatures in which the cooling rate of the glass may affect the structure-sensitive properties of the glass is called the transformation range. Such properties include density, refractive index, and volume resistivity. In addition, this temperature range generally contains both the anneal and strain temperatures [7-8].

As a glass cools at a given rate, the specific volume change can be represented by the slope of the line AB. At the low temperature end of this range, the glass follows the path indicated by CD and is composed of a structure in its non-equilibrium state. At a faster cooling rate, the structure is frozen in at a higher temperature (EF). Slowly reheating the glass from point F will cause the specific volume to follow the dashed line and the glass will compact at temperatures near the transformation range. Here the temperature has increased enough to cause a decrease in viscosity and allowed the structure to collapse. The non-equilibrium state can be characterized by the fictive temperature, which is defined as the temperature at which the glass structure would be in equilibrium if the glass was brought infinitely rapidly to that temperature [7-8].

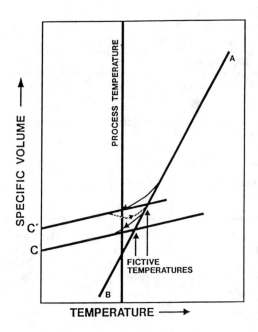

Figure 1: Specific volume versus temperature behavior of glasses in the transformation range.

There are two ways to overcome the potential problem of glass densification in the transformation range. The first way is to anneal the glass through this temperature regime, therefore "preshrinking" the substrate before further processing. The other way to avoid the problem is to use a glass that has a high temperature transformation range, well above the processing temperature. This manifests itself in a higher strain point glass.

CODE 7059 SUBSTRATE CHARACTERISTICS

The preferred substrate material for AMLCDs is code 7059, a barium aluminoborosilicate glass presently manufactured by Corning Incorporated. This glass is formed by the Fusion process, in which a stream of homogeneous molten glass is delivered into a tapered trough at the top of a refractory form also known as the Fusion pipe. As the glass fills the trough, it flows down around the sides of the Fusion pipe and meets at the bottom. The sheet is pulled downward (or drawn) from the bottom of the pipe, and cooled rapidly. The key to this technology is that the final glass sheet's two surfaces never contact any surface during the process, i.e. the glass has turned "inside out". For this reason, this process is extremely important in producing nearly defect-free surface glass that requires no additional finishing. In addition, the dimensional control is precise down to thicknesses near 0.5 mm [1-3].

Other forming operations for the manufacture of flat panel substrates are the float process, redraw process, and slot draw process [1-3]. All of these forming methods apparently need substantial surface refinishing to qualify them for the AMLCD application. The properties of code 7059 are shown in Table I. Its strain point of 593°C is sufficiently high for a-Si AMLCD (i.e. the AMLCD processing temperatures are sufficiently lower than the transformation range of the glass), but not poly-Si. The thermal expansion coefficient of code code 7059 is 46.0 x 10^{-7}/°C, somewhat higher than that of silicon.

There are three potential issues related to the forming and finishing of the glass substrate that could have an effect on the thermal expansion characteristics. First, since the Fusion-formed

Table I: Physical properties of some Fusion-formed AMLCD substrate glasses developed by Corning Incorporated.

Physical Properties	Code 7059	Code 1733	Code 1735	Code 1737
Strain Point (°C)	593	640	665	666
Anneal Point (°C)	639	689	713	721
Softening Point (°C)	844	928	924	975
Thermal Expansion (x10^{-7}/°C)	46.0	37.0	48.7	37.8
Density (g/cc)	2.76	3.70	2.70	2.54

glass is exposed to a directional stress during the short forming process, there is the possibility that glass properties such as thermal expansion may reflect this directional component. Second, since the physical properties of the glasses will depend upon previous thermal history, the effect of annealing on the thermal expansion characteristics of the glass is important. Finally, glass finishing steps such as polishing could have an effect on the thermal expansion properties of the resulting glass. In order to determine the impact of these issues on the expansion characteristics of AMLCD substrate glasses made by the Fusion process, studies have been carried out on a variety of samples. These include samples that are parallel or perpendicular to the draw direction, ones with either as-drawn or polished surfaces, ones with different heat treatments (i.e. as-drawn or annealed), and combinations of these. Thermal expansion versus temperature curves were determined using dilatometric experiments performed in the Physical Properties Laboratory at Corning's Sullivan Park. Both heating and cooling curves were recorded over a temperature range of 50-600°C.

Figure 2 shows the expansion behavior as a function of temperature measured on heating for code 7059 both parallel and perpendicular to the direction of the draw for both the as-drawn and annealed conditions. In this case, it is evident that up to 400°C, the glass thermal expansion is the same whether or not it is annealed. It also appears that there is a difference in the expansion curves between the parallel and perpendicular to draw directions: the expansion in the perpendicular direction is slightly higher than the parallel direction. Although the difference is very slight, the fact that expansion is lower in the direction of the draw is consistent with simple arguments based on glass structure.

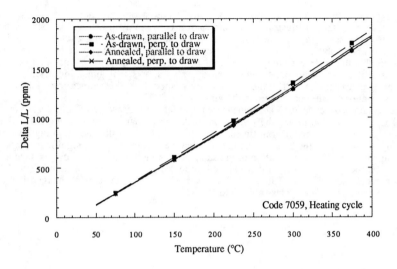

Figure 2: Expansion versus temperature for code 7059 glass measured on heating, comparing the as-drawn and annealed samples both parallel and perpendicular to the direction of the draw.

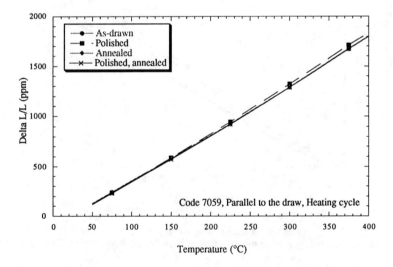

Figure 3: Expansion versus temperature for code 7059 glass measured on heating, parallel to the direction of the draw, for four cases: as-drawn, polished, annealed and polished, annealed.

As expected, polishing the glass does not have strong impact on the expansion characteristics. Figure 3 illustrates the comparison between as-drawn and polished samples which were measured in the direction of the draw during the heating cycle. The polished sample appears to have a very slightly higher expansion, especially at elevated temperatures. It is possible that this difference may be due to the change in composition of the outer surface of the glass that occurs with polishing. Figure 3 also shows that annealing after polishing removes this expansion difference. One may speculate that annealing removes the compositional or density differences in the glass surface.

When a sample of code 7059 sheet measured parallel to the draw direction is cycled from 50 to 600°C, it is possible to see the relaxation in the glass that occurs as it goes through the transformation range a total of four times. After the first cycle, as illustrated in Figure 4, there is less of a hysteresis in the data. This indicates that the first cycle does a significant amount of annealing and therefore densification of the sample, making the subsequent cycles have less of an effect on the glass. This is further verified by looking at the change in sample length over the four cycles, as shown in Table II. For code 7059 glass, the sample changed length by 0.06% over four complete cycles from 50 to 600°C.

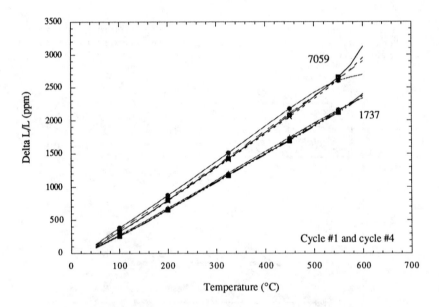

Figure 4: Expansion versus temperature for as-drawn samples of codes 7059 and 1737 glass measured parallel to the direction of draw on the first and fourth cycle from 50 to 600°C.

Table II: Glass shrinkage data for codes 7059 and 1737 from thermal cycling.

Thermal Cycle	Sample Shrinkage (ppm)	
	Code 7059	Code 1737
1	763	155
2	213	55
3	141	39
4	93	35
Total length change (ppm)	1210	284
Percent Shrinkage after 4 cycles	0.06%	0.01%

NEW ACTIVE MATRIX LCD SUBSTRATE GLASS COMPOSITION

In order to reduce shrinkage in the a-Si process and have a substrate capable of use for poly-Si AMLCDs, the temperature resistance (strain point) needs to be increased beyond the code 7059 level. Internal Corning experimentation has shown that a strain point greater than 660°C is capable of the current poly-Si requirements [9]. It is also desirable to decrease the thermal expansion of the glass in order to more closely match silicon and to reduce thermal stress issues. Figure 5 illustrates the trend in commercial LCD substrates over the past 14 years. There has obviously been a trend toward higher strain point. Two such glasses developed at Corning Incorporated for the Fusion process are codes 1733 and 1735 (see properties in Table 1). Code 1733 has a somewhat higher strain with the desirable low expansion, however indications are that the strain point is not sufficiently high for poly-Si. Code 1735, while having a strain point high enough for poly-Si, has an expansion even higher (and less desirable) than code 7059. Figure 6 illustrates these differences in expansion.

There are two potential ways to develop a glass with an expansion closer to that of silicon. One way to do this is to modify the glass composition to decrease the thermal expansion coefficient without compromising the other properties that are important to the glass in this application. In the case of code 7059, a barium boroaluminosilicate glass, decreasing the BaO in the glass will cause a decrease in the thermal expansion coefficient, although it causes other significant properties of the glass to change as well, including strain point, viscosity, and softening point. In order to decrease the thermal expansion without having a deleterious effect on strain, etc., substitutions of other oxides for BaO must be made. Such substitutions could be other alkaline earth oxides such as CaO, MgO, and SrO, intermediates such as B_2O_3 and Al_2O_3, or combinations thereof.

Since a higher strain point and a lower thermal expansion coefficient than code 7059 are required for poly-Si AMLCDs and chip on glass applications, modification of code 7059 may not be the best approach. At Corning Incorporated, a new glass composition has been developed that meets these requirements. Code 1737, as described in Table 1, has a strain point of 666°C and a thermal expansion of 38.7 x 10^{-7}/°C, much closer to that of silicon than code 7059. The glass is an alkaline earth aluminosilicate glass formed in a similar manner to code 7059. In comparison with the other high strain glasses and code 7059, code 1737 is much closer to silicon than codes 7059 and 1735 and comparable to code 1733, as shown in Figure 6.

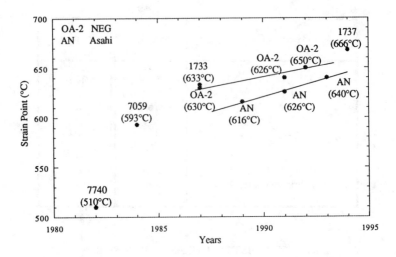

Figure 5: Trends in commercial LCD glass substrates over the past 14 years.

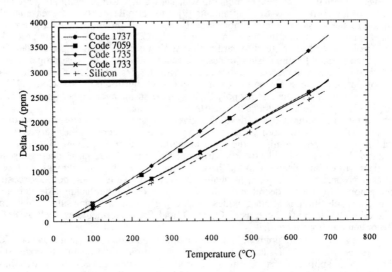

Figure 6: Expansion versus temperature for several Fusion-formed LCD substrate glasses and silicon.

For a closer look at the expansion versus temperature behavior of code 1737, Figure 7 illustrates the behavior of code 1737 measured on heating parallel to the direction of the draw in several different situations: as-drawn, polished, annealed, and polished and annealed. The curves are very close, showing that this glass can be utilized in the as-formed state for applications which have processing temperatures in this range. Only the polished, as-drawn sample is different at higher temperatures. Figure 8 illustrates the two cases of parallel and perpendicular to the draw direction in both the as-drawn and the annealed conditions. The parallel, as-drawn sample has an expansion curve that is slightly different from the perpendicular, as-drawn, but the same as the annealed case for either direction. In terms of polishing, it has been observed that the as-drawn glass is slightly different for the parallel and perpendicular to draw, but once they have both been annealed, all the curves are essentially identical.

The temperature-dependent expansion behavior of code 1737 is different from code 7059 in two respects: the magnitude of the expansion and the effect of annealing on the glass. Code 1737 has a smaller thermal expansion coefficient than code 7059, so the curves for code 1737 repeatedly fall below code 7059 as shown in Figure 9, which illustrates a comparison between as-drawn codes 7059 and 1737. Figure 10 shows the difference in expansion between the as-drawn and annealed glass for each case, measured in heating. The difference between the two increases as the temperature increases. Code 7059 shows a large difference in expansion between the as-drawn and annealed near 480°C, while the as-drawn sample of code 1737 has an expansion relatively close to the annealed sample until near 550°C. This shows that not only is code 1737 more stable than code 7059 at elevated temperatures, but also that the expansion behavior of the as-drawn glass is very similar to the annealed up to temperatures well above that of code 7059.

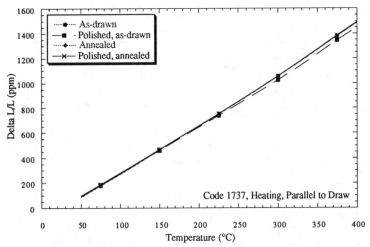

Figure 7: Expansion versus temperature for code 1737 measured on heating parallel to the direction of the draw for four cases: as-drawn, polished, annealed, and polished, annealed.

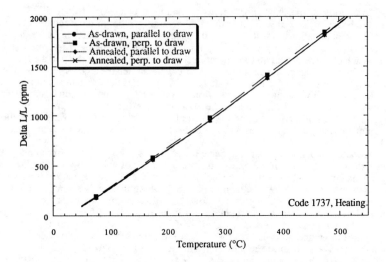

Figure 8: Expansion versus temperature for code 1737 measured on heating both parallel and perpendicular to the direction of the draw for both the as-drawn and annealed cases.

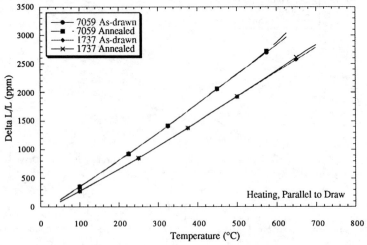

Figure 9: Expansion versus temperature for codes 7059 and 1737 measured on heating parallel to the direction of the draw for two cases: as-drawn and annealed.

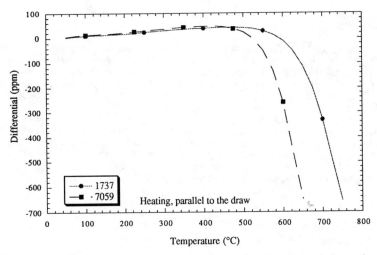

Figure 10: Difference in expansion between the as-drawn and annealed samples of both codes 7059 and 1737 as a function of temperature, measured on heating, parallel to the direction of the draw.

The results of cycling code 1737 from 50 to 600°C are somewhat different from code 7059 in two ways. First, as stated earlier, the magnitude of the expansion in code 1737 is smaller, so the curves for the two glasses differ appreciably, as seen in Figure 4. Second, the hysteresis in the measurement is smaller for code 1737, another illustration of the higher thermal stability of code 1737. This point is further clarified by examining data on the change in length of the sample used for the cycling experiment, shown in Table II. The initial shrinkage for code 1737 was significantly different from code 7059 and the subsequent changes are then smaller. Furthermore, the total shrinkage over four complete cycles was 0.014%, significantly lower than code 7059. Table III shows a comparison of thermal shrinkage during annealing for codes 7059 and 1737 [10]. It is clear that code 1737 has a notably smaller shrinkage as-formed and practically zero after annealing for one hour at various temperatures.

Table III: Thermal shrinkage data for codes 7059 and 1737 at various thermal cycles [10].

Thermal Cycle	Thermal Shrinkage (ppm)			
	Code 7059 Annealed	Code 7059 As-formed	Code 1737 Annealed	Code 1737 As-formed
350°C/1 hr	1	6	0	1
400°C/1 hr	--	15	0	4
450°C/1 hr	2	41	0	9
450°C/8 hr	20	128	4	29

CONCLUSIONS

It is evident from this discussion that the thermal expansion behavior of an AMLCD substrate glass can be critical to not only the reliability of the substrate, but also the shrinkage characteristics and the maximum temperature in processing. In the case of glasses that are formed by the Fusion process, there are subtle differences in the expansion as function of draw direction and polishing. In addition, the effect of annealing the glass can easily be seen, particularly at elevated temperatures.

The new high strain glass developed for non-anneal a-Si and low temperature poly-Si AMLCDs has superior thermal expansion characteristics for several reasons. First, its thermal expansion coefficient is closer to silicon than code 7059. Second, the amount of shrinkage that occurs over successive thermal cycles is significantly better than code 7059. Finally, its higher strain point allows for higher processing temperatures, helping to create opportunities for further progress in the area of both a-Si and poly-Si AMLCD technology.

ACKNOWLEDGMENTS

The author would like to acknowledge B. Tyndell and the Thermal Lab in the Physical Properties Department for their help in preparing and measuring samples, and B. Dumbaugh and P. Bocko for their insight over the past year.

REFERENCES

1. W.H. Dumbaugh and P.L. Bocko, SID Proceedings, **31** (4) 269-272 (1990).

2. W.H. Dumbaugh, P.L. Bocko, and F.P Fehlner, in High Performance Glasses, edited by M. Cable and M. Parker (Chapman and Hall, New York, 1992) pp. 86-101.

3. P.L. Bocko and R.K. Whitney, in Engineered Materials Handbook, Volume 4: Ceramics and Glasses (ASM International, USA, 1991), p. 1045.

4. L.E. Tannas, Flat Panel Displays and CRTs (Van Nostrand Reinhold, New York, 1992).

5. J.A. Castellano, Handbook of Display Technology (Academic Press, Inc., San Diego, 1992).

6. H.R. Lillie, in The Handbook of Physics, edited by E.U. Condon and H. Odishaw (McGraw-Hill, New York, 1958) p. 8-38.

7. W.D. Kingery, H.K. Bowen, and D.R. Uhlmann, Introduction to Ceramics, 2nd ed. (John Wiley and Sons, New York, 1976), p. 583.

8. D.G. Holloway, The Physical Properties of Glass (Wykeham Publications, London, 1973).

9. P.L. Bocko (private communication).

10. M. Anma (internal Corning Incorporated memorandum).

HIGH DEPOSITION RATE PECVD PROCESSES FOR NEXT GENERATION TFT-LCDs

J.F.M. WESTENDORP, H. MEILING, J.D. POLLOCK, D.W. BERRIAN,
A.H. LAFLAMME Jr., J. HAUTALA and J. VANDERPOT
TEL America, Inc., 123 Brimbal Avenue, Beverly, MA 01915, USA.

ABSTRACT

The demand for lower cost per panel in TFT-LCD production is driving the PECVD market to deposition systems that combine high throughput and uptime with high yield. Today it is generally believed that a multichamber system that combines a number of single-panel deposition chambers is the best way to achieve these goals.

For these PECVD systems to be economical, the deposition rate of a-Si:H, SiN_x and SiO_2 has to be in the 1200-1500 Å/min range. In 13.56 MHz parallel-plate glow discharge systems SiN_x and SiO_2 deposition rates exceeding 1500 Å/min are commonly achieved, whereas the deposition rate of a-Si:H is limited to 100-200 Å/min due to powder formation. Over the last 5 years significant progress has been made to increase the deposition rate of a-Si:H. Methods include the use of very-high-frequency glow discharge (VHF-GD) and pulsing of the rf discharge. However, substrate sizes never exceeded 100mmx100mm.

We have developed a multichamber PECVD system for TFT-LCD production where VHF-GD is used to obtain uniform high deposition rates for (doped) semiconductors and insulators, such as a-Si:H, n^+ a-Si:H, SiN_x and SiO_2 over areas as large as 470mmx370mm. Even at deposition rates well above 1200 Å/min hydrogen in a-Si:H is exclusively bound as monohydride. The optoelectronic properties of the films are at least as good as those of their 13.56 MHz counterparts and thus good-quality TFTs can be obtained. At the same time the number of added particles is low allowing for high production yields.

1. INTRODUCTION

The requirement for low cost-per-panel in thin-film transistor liquid-crystal display (TFT-LCD) manufacturing is driving the market for Plasma Enhanced Chemical Vapour Deposition (PECVD) production systems to single-panel processing. The basic components that constitute cost-per-panel are PECVD system throughput, yield, uptime and operational cost. The throughput of conventional batch systems is steadily decreasing with the increase in panel size since the number of panels that can be loaded in one process chamber is decreasing. As a result the low hydrogenated amorphous silicon, a-Si:H, deposition rates of 100-200 Å/min that are used in today's production lines have become a limiting factor for throughput. Also, conventional batch type systems suffer from low yield and uptime for a variety of reasons: (i) microcracking of films accumulated on the carriers that are used to hold the panels cause the particle count to go up with an adverse effect on the yield and will force system shutdown (ii) cleaning of the system is complicated and time consuming which, with the required re-qualification after each mechanical clean, results in a system uptime of not more than fifty percent.

Single panel PECVD systems allow for carrierless transport of panels and therefore the concomitant particle problem is eliminated. Process chambers are simpler and therefore

Mat. Res. Soc. Symp. Proc. Vol. 345. ©1994 Materials Research Society

mechanical cleaning, if required, is easier. Uniformities can be optimized over the area of one single panel without having to compromise in favour of uniformity over the whole batch load.

For single panel PECVD systems to be economical the deposition rate of the TFT films has to be in the 1200-1500 Å/min range. While for silicon nitride (SiN$_x$) films these deposition rates are commonly achieved in 13.56 MHz deposition systems, deposition rates for (doped or undoped) a-Si:H are limited by a deterioration of film quality [1] and plasma polymerization [2] whenever the pressure and/or power is increased to increase the deposition rate. The deterioration of film quality is ascribed to an enhanced incorporation of Si-H$_2$ type bonding in the material. Si-H$_2$ bonds cause electron traps close to the conduction band and will result in a decrease of the field-effect mobility, μ_{FE}. Plasma polymerization leads to particle formation and consequently to yield loss. Attempts to shift the onset of plasma polymerization to higher deposition rates by pulsing the rf discharge have been successful to around 400 Å/min [3]. However, still a concomitant increase of Si-H$_2$ type bonding in the a-Si:H film and a decrease of the field-effect mobility from 0.7 cm^2/Vs at 100 Å/min to 0.3 cm^2/Vs at 400 Å/min was observed, making the method undesirable for XGA and EWS class displays, where mobilities of at least 0.6 cm^2/Vs are required.

More recently, a single panel PECVD system for TFT-LCD manufacturing was introduced, employing 13.56 MHz as the excitation frequency [4]. The deposition rates reported are higher than in conventional batch type systems, however, the mobility drops from 0.89 cm^2/Vs at 700 Å/min to 0.67 cm^2/Vs at 1300 Å/min. So even though deposition rates are higher, one is still forced to compromise on mobility when deposition rates of 1200-1500 Å/min are required. No data on Si-H$_2$ type bonding or particles were given.

It appears that at 13.56 MHz there is a *fundamental limit* of the deposition rate of good quality a-Si:H which lies *below* that what is required for high throughput single panel TFT-LCD manufacturing, i.e. 1200-1500 Å/min. Therefore other deposition techniques will have to be pursued.

Very-high-frequency glow discharge deposition of a-Si:H

In recent years a lot of attention has been devoted to a-Si:H deposition using frequencies other than the conventional 13.56 MHz. The so-called very-high-frequency glow discharge, in which the plasma excitation frequency is in the range of 13-150 MHz, was introduced in 1987 [5]. It was shown that deposition rates up to 1200 Å/min could be obtained while maintaining good optoelectronic properties. Soon other groups followed [6]. Even though initial measurements indicated that there was an optimum in the frequency dependence of the deposition rate [5], it is presently believed that the deposition rate increases monotonically with frequency for constant plasma power. This is illustrated in figure 1, which gives the a-Si:H deposition rate as a function of frequency while all process parameters relevant for deposition were kept constant [7].

Since then, Finger et al. [8] carried out an extensive comparison of a-Si:H material deposited at 13.56 and 70 MHz. Figure 2 shows the variation of the hydrogen content (as determined by infra-red absorption spectroscopy, FTIR) as a function of the deposition temperature for depositions at 13.56 and 70 MHz. It was found that the hydrogen content of the 70-MHz films remained well under that of the 13.56-MHz material in the temperature range of 50 to 280 °C. The authors also found that for films made at 70 MHz an increase in deposition rate did not significantly influence the structure and the electronic properties. This is consistent with the

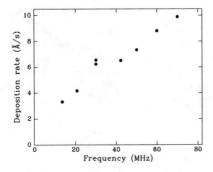

Fig. 1. Deposition rate as a function of plasma excitation frequency. Plasma power is kept constant; gas source is undiluted silane [7].

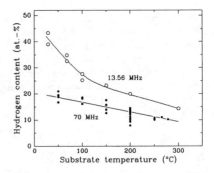

Fig. 2. Total hydrogen content measured with FTIR for a-Si:H films prepared at 13.56 and 70 MHz as a function of temperature [8].

results of an earlier study [9] where it was reported that the hydrogen content of a-Si:H films deposited at 70 MHz remains virtually constant as a function of deposition rate up to at least 1300 Å/min. This is depicted in figure 3. The variation of deposition rate was brought about by changes in silane flow rate, pressure and rf power.

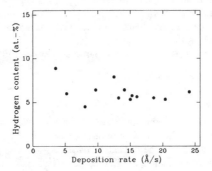

Fig. 3. Hydrogen content as measured with FTIR as a function of deposition rate for a-Si:H layers deposited at 70 MHz [9].

Figures 1 through 3 show the attractiveness of VHF-GD a-Si:H deposition. While the deposition rate increases with frequency (Figure 1) the hydrogen content of the a-Si:H film does not increase (Figure 2). Compared with 13.56 MHz, VHF-GD a-Si:H deposition allows for lower deposition temperatures while maintaining low hydrogen concentrations (Figure 2). In addition to that, at a given frequency (70 MHz, Figure 3) the deposition rate can be varied by means of power and pressure without changing the hydrogen content. Therefore good optoelectronic properties can be maintained at deposition rates even above 1200 Å/min. This is in contrast with the situation at 13.56 MHz where the hydrogen content increases when power and/or pressure are used to increase the deposition rate [1]. Therefore, when 13.56 MHz is used as excitation frequency the deposition rate of the highest quality a-Si:H is limited to values a factor of two to three lower than at 70 MHz.

It is presently believed, based on work of Heintze et al. [10] that in VHF-GD a-Si:H deposition the increase of the deposition rate with frequency is not a result of enhanced silane dissociation, resulting in an increase of the amount of precursors, but of an increase of the ion flux towards the growing surface. At the same time the maximum ion energy decreases with frequency. The effect of these two phenomena working together is that the surface is exposed to a higher flux of ions with an average energy lower than at 13.56 MHz. This is believed to enhance the desorption of hydrogen from the surface of the film (the rate limiting step) thus allowing for deposition of a-Si:H at high rates and low hydrogen concentration.

Outline of this paper

All work on VHF-GD deposition of a-Si:H reported above was done on small substrate sizes, i.e. typically 100mmx100mm. Obviously in TFT-LCD production much larger substrate sizes are used. This paper presents the first multichamber production system where VHF plasma deposition is performed on substrates as large as 470mmx370mm. Not only (doped and undoped) a-Si:H but also SiN_x films are deposited using VHF. In the following we will first discuss the layout of the multichamber system with its basic components. Then we will discuss the quality of a-Si:H and SiN_x films deposited in this system and TFT characteristics will be shown.

In TFT-LCD production high deposition rates of good quality a-Si:H and SiN_x are only meaningfull if the number of particles added to the substrate during processing is low. We will discuss some features of the process chamber design that are aimed at achieving low particle counts. Also, we will highlight the advantage that VHF-GD a-Si:H deposition offers over 13.56 MHz deposition as far as gas phase nucleation of particles is concerned.

2. SYSTEM LAYOUT

Figure 4 gives the layout of a production system for a back-channel-etch type TFT. Since in this type of TFT the intrinsic a-Si:H film is several thousands of Angstrom thick the system requires two a-Si:H deposition chambers, next to two SiN_x and one doped a-Si:H deposition chamber to optimize chamber utilization and throughput. The number of SiN_x process chambers for the etch-stopper type TFT will be two or three, versus one a-Si:H chamber since in this type of TFT the a-Si:H film thickness is very thin, i.e. around 500 Å. Since the design is modular the system can be configured with any number of process chambers that is required to optimize throughput for a specific film stack.

In the system depicted in figure 4 panel storage is provided by two cassettes in atmosphere. Before each panel is introduced in the vacuum loadlock it is flipped upside down to allow for face-down processing. Face-down processing is a key aspect to ensure low particle counts, we will elaborate more on this in Section 4. After introduction in the vacuum system each panel is preheated in a dedicated heat/cool chamber to the temperature required for the first deposition. The heat/cool chamber contains a rack with slots for heating the panels before deposition and cooling before unloading into the vacuum loadlock. After the first film is deposited, depending on the deposition temperature of the next film, the panel is either transferred directly to the next process chamber or it is placed in a heat slot in the heat/cool chamber for an intermediate panel temperature adjustment up or down. After the final film has been deposited the panel is placed in a cool slot to cool down before it is unloaded.

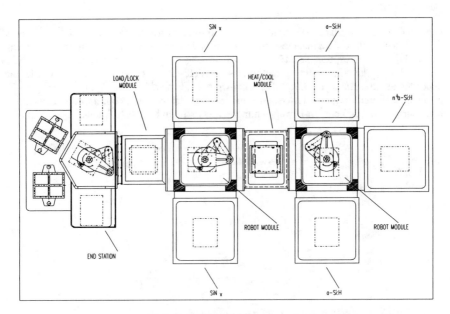

Fig. 4. Layout of a TEL PECVD production system for TFT manufacturing. The configuration
presented is optimized for a back-channel-etch type TFT.

3. FILM DEPOSITION

Process chamber design

The design of the process chamber is driven by obtaining high deposition rates of good
quality material with low particle counts. High deposition rates are achieved using 60 MHz as
the excitation frequency. The quality of the a-Si:H and SiN_x films deposited at this frequency is
discussed in the next section.

Several measures were taken to obtain low particle counts. First, as mentioned before, the
panel is oriented face-down during deposition. This will cause larger particles to move away
from the film substrate rather than towards it as is the case in systems where panels are
processed face-up. Second, proces gas is admitted on one side of the panel and pumped away on
the opposing side of the panel. This allows the panel during deposition to face a flat and
featureless rf electrode. This avoids the particle generation that may occur from a showerhead
gas delivery system. Furthermore, the plasma is confined in such a way that the film deposited in
the plasma fringing area is of good quality, i.e. is of high density and adheres well to the surface
it is deposited on. This prevents peeling and subsequent release of particles.

Film characterization

In our system a-Si:H films are deposited at rates of typically 1200 Å/min and a substrate
temperature of 250 °C. Figure 5 represents the FTIR stretching mode of a typical a-Si:H film

deposited from pure silane. The solid circles denote the measured spectrum, while the dashed line represents a fit to determine the relative contributions of Si-H type absorption at 2000 cm^{-1} and Si-H$_2$ type absorption at 2100 cm^{-1}. All hydrogen apears to be bound exclusively as monohydride. This shows the attractiveness of VHF-GD deposition since an a-Si:H film deposited at 1200 Å/min at 13.56 MHz is known to show significant Si-H$_2$ type bonding with a concomitant deterioration of device performance. The total hydrogen concentration as measured by integrating the 640 cm^{-1} Si-H wagging mode was found to be 7.4x10^{21} at/cm^3.

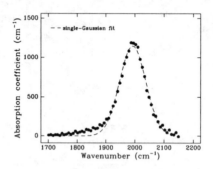

Fig. 5. The Si-H stretching mode of an a-Si:H film deposited at 1200 Å/min using 60 MHz as excitation frequency. Solid circles represent the measured spectrum. The dashed line is a Gaussian fit.

As in the case of 13.56 MHz, SiN$_x$ films at 60 MHz are deposited from a gas mixture of SiH$_4$, NH$_3$ and N$_2$. Deposition rates of good quality gate dielectric, i.e. low trap density SiN$_x$ films amount to 1200-1500 Å/min. These nitrides are nearly stoichiometric with a refractive index of 1.88+/-0.01 and have a breakdown electric field of 9 MV/cm. Also, FTIR reveals that the number of N-H bonds exceeds the amount of Si-H bonds by a factor of 5 or more. Typically, the hydrogen content of these films amounts to 3.5x10^{22} at/cm^3.

TFT characterization

Figure 6 gives a schematic representation of the bottom-gate etch-stopper type TFT structure that was used as test device for our 60 MHz a-Si:H and SiN$_x$ films. The films were deposited in a system with three process chambers but with an otherwise identical loadlock and heat/cool chamber arrangement as the system depicted in figure 4. The first (gate dielectric) and second (etch stopper) SiN$_x$ film were deposited in one chamber using the same process conditions. After the first SiN$_x$ was deposited the panels were transported to a dedicated a-Si:H chamber for deposition of the a-Si:H film. The deposition rate of the SiN$_x$ films was 1500 Å/min whereas that of the a-Si:H film amounted to 1300 Å/min.

Figure 7 shows a typical set of transfer characteristics of these TFTs for source-drain voltages V$_d$ of 0.1, 1.0, and 10 V, respectively and the ON/OFF current ratio for this TFT amounted to 3x10^7 at V$_d$=10 V. More detailed information on the deposition of these TFTs, the analyses of the characteristics and the single-film properties can be found in [11].

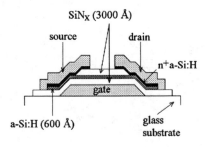

Fig. 6. Schematic representation of the TFT device used to test the quality of a-Si:H and SiN$_x$ films deposited at 60 MHz.

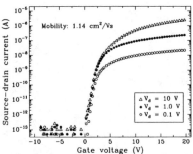

Fig. 7. Transfer characteristics of a TFT made with SiN$_x$ and a-Si:H films deposited with 60 MHz as excitation frequency [11].

The high saturation mobility and high ON/OFF current ratio show that good quality TFTs can be made with high deposition rate 60 MHz a-Si:H and SiN$_x$ films.

4. PARTICLE PERFORMANCE

As mentioned before high deposition rates of good quality a-Si:H and SiN$_x$ films are of no practical use if the number of added particles during processing is high. Particles in PECVD TFT processing have two distinct sources: (i) microcracking and peeling of films adherent to chamber walls and electrodes and (ii) gas phase nucleation in the plasma. Both sources are partly determined by process chamber design, whereas gas phase nucleation of particles is also influenced by plasma conditions.

We have already mentioned that the design of our process chamber is driven by achieving low particle counts. As far as gas phase nucleation of particles is concerned, Dorier et al. [12] did an elaborate study of gas phase nucleation ('powder formation') in VHF-GD silane plasmas. The authors studied the threshold power below which the plasma is powder-free and above which powder forms. The threshold power is determined as the power at which the plasma impedance, the rf voltage, and reflected power change as a result of powder formation. Figure 8 shows the plasma power threshold as a function of rf excitation frequency. It was found that as the rf frequency increases a higher power is permitted in the plasma before powder formation sets in.

The authors also measured spatial profiles of powder in VHF-GD silane plasmas. For that purpose, the plasma volume was illuminated with white light and the scattered intensity, which is a measure of the total volume of particulates in the plasma, was monitored. Figure 9 shows the scattered intensity as a function of distance from the heated (ground) electrode for three different rf excitation frequencies. The plasma power is identical for the three frequencies. It is found that the total scattered intensity as well as the width of the region in which the powder is suspended decrease with increasing frequency. While the authors only speculate about the origins of the effects shown in figures 8 and 9, the observations illustrate an inherent advantage of VHF-GD a-Si:H deposition, in that as the rf frequency is increased higher power levels can be tolerated before powder is formed. This means that higher deposition rates can be achieved.

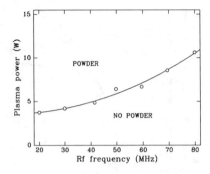

Fig. 8. Plasma power threshold for powder formation as a function of rf frequency [12].

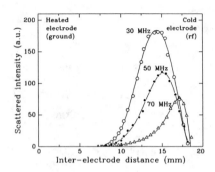

Fig. 9. Scattered intensity as a function of distance from the heated (ground) electrode for various rf excitation frequencies [12].

The actual number of particles added during film deposition, being the sum of particles released from the rf electrode and chamber walls and particles nucleated in the plasma, is dependent on the process conditions employed and therefore dependent on the requirements of a specific film or film stack. Furthermore, the maximum number of added particles of a given size allowed varies with the type of display that is being processed. It is therefore difficult to give a general specification of the particle performance of our system that includes film deposition. However, as far as panel transport alone in a clean system is concerned we can state that the number of added particles of $0.5\mu m$ or larger is less than 0.04 cm^{-2}. When film deposition is included, we can safely say that face-down processing and the application of VHF-GD film deposition allows for the number of panels being processed before NF_3 in-situ cleaning is required to be significanlty higher than in face-up 13.56 MHz deposition systems.

5. CONCLUSIONS

A single-panel PECVD system for the TFT-LCD production market has been presented. The system employs VHF-GD (doped) a-Si:H and SiN_x deposition at an excitation frequency of 60 MHz to obtain deposition rates over 1200 Å/min. Good quality TFTs have been demonstrated. The application of face-down processing allows the number of panels being processed before NF_3 cleaning is required to be substantially higher than in face-up deposition systems.

ACKNOWLEDGMENTS

The authors wish to acknowledge the TFT processing group at IBM Research, Yorktown Heights.

REFERENCES

1. Y. Hishikawa, N. Nakamura and S. Tsuda, Proc. Jpn. Symp. Plasma Chem., Vol. 4 (1991) pp. 221-226.
2. P. Roca i Cabarrocas, J. Non-Cryst. Solids **164-166**, 37 (1993).
3. K. Takechi, H. Uchida and H. Hayama, in Ext. Abs. 1993 Int. Conf. Solid State Dev. And Mat., Makuhari, Japan (1993), pp. 970-971.
4. N. Ibaraki, K. Matsumura, K. Fukuda, N. Hirata, S. Kawamura, and T. Kashiro, in *1994 Display Manufacturing Technology Conference* (Society for Information Display, Playa del Rey, CA, 1994), pp. 121-122; Y. Watabe, *ibid.*, pp. 61-62.
5. H. Curtins, N. Wyrsch, M. Favre, and A.V. Shah, Plasma Chem. Plasma Process. **7** (3), 267 (1987).
6. S. Oda, J. Noda and M. Matsumura, in *Amorphous Silicon Technology*, edited by A. Madan, M.J. Thompson, P.C. Taylor, P.G. Lecomber and Y. Hamakawa (Mater. Res. Soc. Proc. **118**, Pittsburgh, PA, 1988) pp. 117-122.
7. A.A. Howling, J.-L. Dorier, Ch. Hollenstein, U.Kroll and F. Finger, J. Vac. Sci. Technol. A **10** (4), 1080 (1992).
8. F. Finger, U. Kroll, V. Viret, A. Shah, W. Beyer, X.-M. Tang, J. Weber, A. Howling and Ch. Hollenstein, J. Appl. Phys. **71** (11), 5665 (1992).
9. H. Curtins, N. Wyrsch, M. Favre, K. Prasad, M. Brechet and A.V. Shah, in *Amorphous Silicon Semiconductors-Pure and Hydrogenated*, edited by A. Madan, M.J. Thompson, D. Adler and Y. Hamakawa (Mater. Res. Soc. Proc. **95**, Anaheim, CA, 1987), pp. 249-253.
10. M. Heintze, R. Zedlitz and Y.H. Bauer, in *Amorphous Silicon Technology-1993*, edited by E.A. Schiff, M.J. Thompson, A. Madan, K. Tanaka and P.G. LeComber (Mater. Res. Soc. Proc. **297**, Pittsburgh, PA, 1993) pp. 49-54.
11. H. Meiling, J.F.M. Westendorp, J. Hautala, Z.M. Saleh and C.T. Malone, in these proceedings (1994).
12. J.-L. Dorier, Ch. Hollenstein, A.A. Howling and U. Kroll, J. Vac. Sci. Technol. A **10** (4), 1048 (1992).

NEW MATERIALS FOR LASER REPAIR OF
ACTIVE MATRIX LIQUID CRYSTAL DISPLAYS

PAUL B. COMITA AND CARL E. LARSON
IBM Research Division, Almaden Research Center, 650 Harry Road, San Jose, California
95120-6099

ABSTRACT

New materials have been developed for the repair of electrical open defects in AMLCD panel circuitry The metal-containing precursors are volatile, easily pyrolyzed to high purity conducting metal, and are decomposed at temperatures which will not damage the glass substrate or thin film circuitry. New materials have been developed for additive metal repair as well as additive passivation repair. The repair of data line metallurgy on prototype arrays has been achieved, resulting in electrical resistances of the repaired interconnects which were comparable to those of unrepaired interconnects of identical geometry.

INTRODUCTION

Many microelectronics companies have invested heavily in manufacturing facilities for color active matrix liquid crystal displays (AMLCD), including IBM.[1] AMLCD production has been scaled-up and yield is one of the major problems associated with their manufacture. At present, color thin film transistor (TFT) technology has been restricted to small size applications, due to manufacturing difficulties and production costs. Large display panels in particular are extremely difficult to manufacture in mass quantities because of the labor intensive microelectronics fabrication process and low production yields. In general, the primary yield problems for the AMLCD backplane are opens and shorts in the interconnect circuitry which comprise the active matrix, although the liquid crystal fill process has had equivalent yield problems. For example, a 10 inch diagonal 640- X 480- pixel three color display will consist of a total of 921,600 subpixels. Each subpixel is driven by a transistor, which must be fabricated, along with the interconnecting electrodes, by thin-film manufacturing techniques. Any defect in the transistor metallurgy can cause a non-functioning pixel, and defects in the interconnection metallurgy may cause a row or column of pixels to not function. In order to have a defect-free panel, the thin film transistor and interconnect metallurgy must be defect-free.

A laser additive technique[2] which can be used to repair defects in metallurgy of the interconnect circuitry which comprise the row or column electrode of the TFT active matrix will be a useful technology for yield improvement. The repair process described here can be inserted at any point in the build-up of the multilayer TFT to repair defects in the metallurgy. It is expected that the process will be most useful near the end of the fabrication procedure because of the increased value of the display at this point. In an additive open repair process, a conducting metal is deposited in an open defect on the display metallurgy in such a manner as to connect the existing metal, making a continuous circuit. To join the two sections of metal, a laser beam is focussed onto the substrate surface within the region to be electrically connected. The irradiating laser may be pulsed or continuous. Photolytic or thermal decomposition of the vapor of a reactant occurs in the heated and/or irradiated region, resulting in localized deposition of high purity material. Because additive laser repair is a dry process, contamination problems associated with wet processes are avoided. The precursors, are volatile, easily pyrolyzed to high purity, conducting material, and are decomposed at temperatures which will not damage the glass substrate surface.

185

REPAIR OF OPEN DEFECTS

For localized thermal deposition, a Spectra Physics Model 220-05 argon ion laser was operated at 514 nm. The beam was expanded (3X), collimated, and focused through a 0.2 NA microscope objective. The measured beam diameter was approximately 10 $\pm$1.0 μm at the 1/e intensity points and was approximately Gaussian. TFT display prototypes were supplied by IBM Yorktown Research or DTI Inc. Open defects were fabricated into the metallurgy by ablating gaps with an excimer laser. The metallurgy on prototype display consisted of 1000 angstroms of molybdenum. The defects were generally single line defects with and without adjacent metallurgy by the laser-deposited metal. Repaired circuits were examined by four-point electrical resistance measurements on a probe station equipped with a digital voltmeter. The repaired electrical circuits were compared to unrepaired interconnects of identical geometry. The repair metal generally overlaps the metallurgy side of the open gaps, in order to provide a large area of contact.

Additive Metal Repair

The utility of laser direct-writing of metals for microcircuitry applications such as repair depends on the ability of the laser-written metal line to conduct current with low electrical resistance. The current conducting capability can be influenced by many properties, which can be divided into two classes: those intrinsic to the added metal, i.e. associated with the resistivity of the metal, and those intrinsic to the interface between the added metal and the existing metallurgy. The resistance associated with this junction is referred to as the contact resistance. The total resistance of the repaired line can be treated as a series of resistors consisting of the resistance of the laser-deposited repair, the interface contact resistance, and the contact resistance of the probes to the metallurgy. Experimentally measured repair resistances without any treatment of the contact site are typically the expected contribution from the deposited repair metal, and indicate that contact resistance has little effect resistance for repairs made on the metallurgy of the prototype display.

The prototype display panel to be repaired was placed in a vacuum chamber and the ambient air was pumped out. The panel was exposed to a measured vapor pressure of a metal containing compound. To deposit aluminum, a 1:1 association complex of triethylamine with aluminum hydride was used. The material is a volatile, air- sensitive liquid with an ambient vapor pressure in the torr range. To deposit gold, a dimethyl gold (trifluoroacetylacetonate) complex, $Me_2Au(tfac)$, was used. This material is a white, volatile solid, has a melting point of 40 °C and an ambient vapor pressure of 40 mT. The thermal decomposition of the solid begins at 160 °C and results in reductive elimination of ethane and trifluoroacetylacetone, with the production of high-purity gold metal.[3] To deposit platinum, $Pt(PF_3)_4$ was used.[4] This material is a liquid at room temperature, and is highly volatile, with an ambient vapor pressure over 10 Torr. The thermal decomposition takes place between 200 °and 300 °C.

The deposition of Al resulted in repairs which were at or below the measured resitance of the gate interconnect. The resitance of the Al repaired gate interconnects were 3.8 ohms +/- 0.8 (see Table 1). The calculated resistivity of Al in the repair patch is 1 to 2 X bulk resistivity, based on this set of repairs. The purity of the Al has been estimated at greater than 97 At % by Auger electron spectroscopy. Two passes at different powers and scan speeds were used (see Table 1) resulting in a total repair time of approximately 8 seconds. The deposition of gold results in a repair which is at or below the resistance of a gate interconnect. The resitance of an Au repaired interconnect was 4.55 +/- 0.9 ohms (see Table 1). The calculated resitivity of Au in the repair patch is 1 to 4X bulk based on this set of repairs. Conventional surface analytical techniques have demonstrated that the laser-deposited gold from dimethyl gold β-diketonates is > 95% atomic purity.[3] Previous four-point electrical resistance measurements have placed the resistivities between 3 and 10 times bulk gold over a wide range of laser deposition conditions. The scan sequence consisted of two scans at 60 microns/sec, resulting in a total repair time of approximately 1.33 seconds. The deposition of platinum resulted in repairs which were at or above the measured resitance of the gate interconnect. The resitance of the Pt repaired gate interconnects were 19.2 ohms +/- 9.3 (see Table 1). The calculated resistivity of Pt in the repair film is 2 to 10X bulk resistivity. The resistivity of Pt deposited from this reactant has been found to be 5 to 10X bulk Pt. The purity of the Pt has been estimated at greater than 97 At % by Auger electron spectroscopy. Two passes at different powers and scan speeds were used (see Table 1) resulting in a total repair time of approximately 16.8 seconds.

Table 1. Direct Write Conditions for Repair Sites on Prototype Displays

Metal	Pressure (torr)	Power (mw)	Scan Speed (uc/sec)	Scans	Time (sec)	Number of Sites	Resistance (ohms)
Al	0.15	100	150	2	0.53	14	3.81
	0.15	40	20	4	8.0		
Au	0.04	42	60	2	1.33	10	4.55
Pt	0.275	90	50	1	0.8	5	19.2
	0.275	70	20	8	16		
control						100	6.527

The use of any of the precursors results in good, electrically conducting repairs of the interconnect or TFT metallurgy. It is expected that derivatives of these materials will also result in excellent repairs if the metal produced is of high quality. The 514 nm line of an argon ion laser was scanned between the ends of the existing metallurgy, such that metal was deposited on top of the existing metal, as well as in between the end points. The process conditions were tailored so as to give an interconnected circuit which has approximately the same thickness and width as the lines of the existing circuit, as depicted in Figure 1. For 20 micron open defects in the display metallurgy, the repair process took approximately 1 second for Au interconnects, 8 seconds for Al interconnects, and 17 seconds for Pt interconnects. Resistance measurements of the repaired structures resulted in resistances which were at or less than the control resistances for both Au (8 out of 8 repaired sites) and Al (14 out of 14 repaired sites). In a typical repair of open line defects, no electrical shorting to the adjacent lines was evident either optically or by electrical probing.

Additive Passivation by Excimer Laser Deposition of Dielectric Films

In order to laser repair open defects on AMLCD's in an efficient way for high volume manufacturing, we have established a technique for making repairs after the passivation of the entire backplane circuitry and transistors. In order to accomplish this effectively for defects of a random size and location it is necessary to be able to open up the dielectric used for passivation, deposition of a conducting metal at the open defect, and deposition of passivation over the exposed metal repair. For repairing open defects on panels, this involves deposition of a dielectric in order to passivate the exposed contact regions on the data line metallurgy. The technique must cleanly deposit a passivation layer and not remove, damage, or corrode the underlying metallurgy which will be in contact with the repair metallurgy. Using excimer laser light at 248 nm we have found a number of oxides can be cleanly added to the data line metallurgy, including chromium oxide and silicon oxide. Laser light (Lambda-Physik 205i) was coupled into a gas cell with a quartz window. The depositions

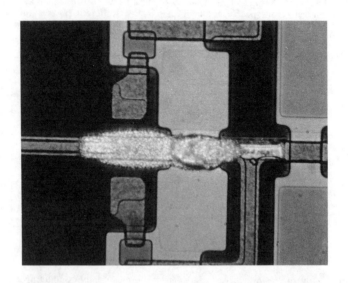

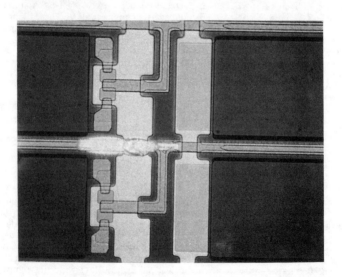

Figure 1. SEM photomicrograph of aluminum repaired interconnect.

were generally carried out with a continuous flow of the precursors, adjusted by a variable leak valve inlet and an variable aperture outlet valve to the vacuum system. The exposures were generally carried out at constant energy from the laser and typically for 2 minutes exposure time.

In all of the previously reported studies of deposition of SiO_2 films, radiation of 193 nm or less had been used or photosensitizer had been applied.[5-8] The use of these wavelengths was necessary since the investigated silicon compounds and coreactants had weak absorption cross sections above 200 nm. These processes have drawbacks for many applications since they require the use of expensive optical elements, compatible with this wavelength. Silanes which exhibit some absorbance at higher wavelength due to one or more light adsorbing functional groups may be used as SiO_2 precursors for photolytic deposition at 248 nm.

We have found that three reactants, triethoxyvinylsilane (TEVS), tetraallyloxysilane (TAOS), and di-t-butoxydiacetoxysilane (TBSA) produce uniform films of SiO_2 with a reasonable rate of growth for practical laser exposures. The optical parameters of the deposits were characterized by small spot ellipsometry (628 nm). Up to 300 mJ/cm^2 laser fluence the deposition resulted in visually transparent deposits. The ellipsometry data showed that the SiO_2 films have very good quality with $n = 1.47-1.50$ and $k < 0.006$ below a laser fluence of 325 mJ/cm2. A deposition rate as high as 0.25 angstrom/pulse was obtained at 200 mJ/cm2 flux and 10 Hz. SEM photographs showed densely packed layer with the grain size of less than approximately 150 nm. Elemental composition of the deposits were obtained by XPS, and showed an Si:O ratio of close to 1:2. We have also produced uniform films of Cr_2O_3 with a 248 nm pulsed deposition process. The SEM of chromium oxide films on AMLCD circuitry is shown in Figure 2.

Laser Repair of Open Defects on TFT/LCD Backplanes

All panels had substrate passivation applied which required the open repair sites to be opened up at the contact sites. The open defects were repaired by using AlH3-NEt3. The repair process consisted of 80 to 100 mw of cw laser power, and 6 to 8 scans at approximately 200 microns/sec. The linewidths achieved matched the data line widths of approximately 8-10 microns. For repair after passivation, excimer laser ablation of the SiNx was used. The excimer laser beam was imaged to approximatelly 10X40 microns with a variable xy aperture, and two regions along the data lines were ablated to expose contact regions for the repair metallurgy. Followup testing consisted of performance recovery, problems with hillocks of repaired metal, thermal cycle test after cell process, and reliability after cell process.

In summary, we have described some new materials for a laser-based repair technique for liquid crystal display panels, which involves the use of laser- induced deposition. The technique as described can be used to repair the thin film transistor interconnect metallurgy and replace the passivation. It is expected that this technique will be generally applicable at any point in the build-up process of the multilayer structure of the TFT display. As display panels become larger in area, the ability to repair open defects on the thin-film display panel will be critical for high yields in the display manufacturing process.

Acknowledgments

We would like to acknowledge the encouragement of John Batey, Steve Depp, and Webster Howard for this work.

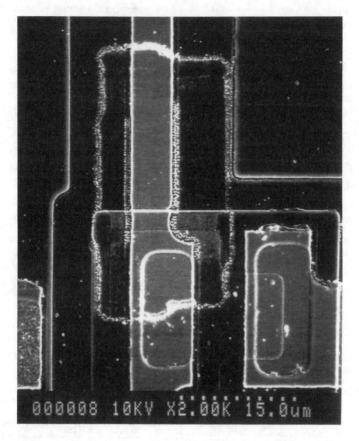

Figure 2. Existing metallurgy of AMLCD with added passivation of CrOx in a localized region.

REFERENCES

1. D. Lieberman, article in Electronic Engineering Times, March 12, 1990, p 1.
2. P. B. Comita, *Advanced Materials*, **2**, 82 (1990).
3. T. H. Baum and C. R. Jones, *J. Vac. Sci. Tech. B*, **4**, 1187 (1986); T. T. Kodas, T. H. Baum and P. B. Comita, *J. Appl. Phys.*, **62**, 281 (1987).
4. M. J. Rand, *J. Electrochemical Soc.*, **120**, 686 (1973).
5. See for example, the Proceedings of the Laser Surface Processing and Characterization Symposium, 1991 E-MRS Conference, in Applied Surface Science, Vol. 54, 1992.
6. C. Licoppe, C. Meriadec, Y.I. Nissim, J.M. Moison, *Appl. Surf. Sci.*, **54**, 445 (1992)
7. R. Ashokan, R. Singh, V. Gopal, M. Anandan, *J. Appl. Phys.* **73**, 1943 (1993).
8. D. Rieger, F. Bachmann, *Appl. Surf. Sci.* **54**, 99 (1992).

INTERFACIAL SOLID-STATE OXIDATION REACTIONS IN THE Sn-DOPED In_2O_3 ON Si AND $Si_{0.85}Ge_{0.15}$ ALLOY SYSTEMS

CLEVA W. OW-YANG, YUZO SHIGESATO*, RITA MOHANTY, AND DAVID C. PAINE
Division of Engineering, Brown University, Providence, RI 02912
*Advanced Glass R&D Center, Asahi Glass Co. Ltd., Yokohama, 221, Japan

ABSTRACT

We have experimentally demonstrated that the interface between ITO and Si or $Si_{0.85}Ge_{0.15}$ is metastable, with silicon reducing ITO to form an amorphous oxide layer and In metal. A 400nm-thick ITO layer was deposited on two types of substrates: p-type, <100> silicon wafers and a silicon wafer with a 400nm-thick layer of $Si_{0.85}Ge_{0.15}$ grown by CVD. Annealing of the ITO/Si system resulted in the growth of a 5nm-thick planar, interfacial SiO_2 layer and the formation of In metal in the ITO above the SiO_2 layer. In contrast, annealing of the ITO/$Si_{0.85}Ge_{0.15}$ system produced an interfacial $Si_{0.85}Ge_{0.15}O_2$ layer that was non-uniform in thickness and which had a non-planar surface morphology. As-deposited and annealed samples were characterized by HREM, EDS, and C-V measurements. Thermodynamic and kinetic arguments predicted both of the different reaction paths that were observed in the two systems.

INTRODUCTION

The stability of the ITO/Si interface has a significant impact on active matrix addressed LCD technology[1,2,3] where, as a transparent conductor, Sn-doped In_2O_3 (ITO) is a used as an electrode material in thin film transistors. In such applications, ITO makes direct contact with Si. The stability of the resulting interface becomes a concern for processing and device applications and offers an interesting example of solid-state interfacial reaction. Earlier observations of interfacial reactions in the ITO/Si system[4] were further explored, and the interfacial stability of ITO deposited on $Si_{0.85}Ge_{0.15}$, was investigated. Two very different reaction paths were observed and are discussed here.

EXPERIMENTAL

Two types of substrates were used. P-type, <100>-oriented silicon wafers with and without a 400nm-thick layer of $Si_{0.85}Ge_{0.15}$ grown by CVD. Both types of substrates were subjected to a modified RCA clean, concluding with an HF-dip immediately prior to deposition.

The 400nm-thick layer of ITO was deposited by rf-magnetron sputtering, using a 400V bias with respect to the plasma.

RESULTS AND DISCUSSION

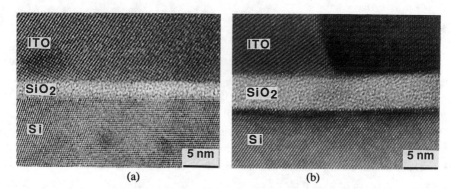

(a)   (b)

Figure 1: High-resolution electron micrographs showing the cross-section lattice image of (a) an as-deposited ITO/Si interface; (b) an ITO/Si interface annealed at 800°C in flowing UHP N_2 for 33min.

The high-resolution electron micrograph in Fig. 1a shows a cross-section lattice image of ITO as deposited on single crystal silicon. The bright band of contrast across the middle corresponds to an amorphous oxide layer measured to be 2nm in thickness. This interfacial oxide is rather thick for a native oxide, which typically grows to a thickness of 0.2-0.6nm[5]. We speculate that the increase in oxide thickness occurs during the sputter deposition, which is a relatively energetic process, that produces a flux of energetic oxygen ions, some with sufficient energy to penetrate the Si wafer to form an intermixed layer of Si and O at the substrate surface. An ion implantation profile calculated using the TRIM software package predicts penetration to a depth of 3nm for 400eV O^- ions, which is reasonably consistent with the observed as-deposited interfacial oxide thickness.

In order to predict the phases in equilibrium at the ITO/Si interface, we examined the thermody-

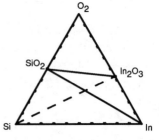

Figure 2: Gibbs triangle representation of the standard In-Si-O_2 phase diagram at 800°C.

namics of the In-Si-O_2 system. In our analysis, we neglected the presence of the 6wt% Sn. Equilibrium phase analysis was carried out using a Gibbs triangle representation of the standard ternary phase diagram (see Fig. 2). To complete the phase diagram for the In-Si-O_2 system at

800°C , two factors need to be considered. First, Gibbs phase rule demands that no more than three phases may be in equilibrium at a fixed pressure and temperature. Also, ΔG_{rxn}, the free energy of reaction for Eqn. 1:

$$3Si + 2In_2O_3 = 3SiO_2 + 4In \quad , \Delta G_{rxn} = -744.40 kJ/mole \quad (1)$$

was calculated to be negative, establishing the thermodynamically stable tie-lines to be SiO_2-In_2O_3 and SiO_2-In. This predicts that the original diffusion couple of In_2O_3-Si is metastable with a tendency towards the formation of SiO_2 and In metal at the interface.

These thermodynamic predictions were examined by annealing a sample of ITO/Si at 800°C in flowing ultra-high purity (UHP) nitrogen for 33 minutes. The cross-section lattice image of the annealed interface in Fig. 1b demonstrates an increase in the oxide layer thickness to 5nm. This interfacial oxide is planar on a 2-4 monolayer scale over hundreds of nm's. X-ray diffraction analysis of this sample revealed the presence of an In metal product phase.

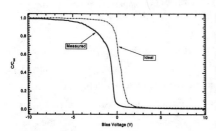

Figure 3: Comparison plot of a measured and an ideal high-frequency C-V curve.

The interfacial reaction produces a metal-insulator-semiconductor (MIS) structure, which can potentially be useful if the quality of both the oxide and the oxide/Si interface are known. To evaluate these two parameters, we formed ITO capacitor dots on a silicon wafer, which was subsequently annealed as described above. The 1MHz capacitance was measured as a function of gate bias voltage on these MIS capacitors to produce the p-type high-frequency C-V curve shown in Fig.3. Comparison of this measured curve with an ideal curve calculated for a substrate of the same doping level provides insight into two issues. First, the slope of the depletion region does not change with annealing. This establishes that the In product phase does not dope the Si substrate[6]. Second, the interface trap density level at mid-gap can be approximated by using the Terman Method, which compares the stretch-out of a measured high-frequency C-V curve along the gate voltage axis with an ideal curve. Although the interface traps cannot move quickly enough to follow the 1MHz ac signal, they still follow slow changes in gate bias as the capacitor is swept from accummulation to inversion. The presence of interface traps produces a stretch-out of the C-V curve along the bias voltage axis, consequently affecting the band-bending from which the density of interface traps can be obtained[7]. For our structures, the estimated interface trap density level at midgap was high ($5 \times 10^{13} cm^{-2} eV^{-1}$) compared to the $10^{10} cm^{-2} eV^{-1}$ level demanded for modern MOS technology. The interfacial properties of ITO/$Si_{0.85}Ge_{0.15}$ were too poor to enable the use of the C-V technique.

Surprisingly, we observed a different interfacial morphology when we annealed the ITO/$Si_{0.85}Ge_{0.15}$ sample at 800°C in flowing UHP nitrogen for 30minutes. The electron micrograph in Fig. 4a shows the formation of an interfacial oxide of rougher morphology compared to the planar ITO/Si case. Energy dispersive spectroscopy (EDS) was used to establish

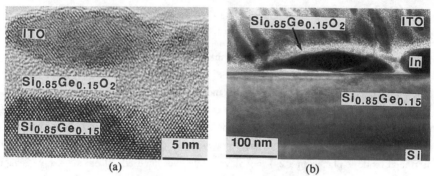

Figure 4: High-resolution electron micrographs showing the cross-section lattice image of an ITO/$Si_{0.85}Ge_{0.15}$ interface annealed at 800°C in flowing UHP N_2 for 33min.: (a) note the rougher interfacial morphology and (b) appearance of In clusters at the oxide/substrate interface.

that the amorphous oxide composition is consistent with $Si_{0.85}Ge_{0.15}O_2$. Thermodynamic analysis of the Si-Ge-O_2 system predicts the selective removal of Si from the alloy to form SiO_2 leaving a build-up of Ge at the oxide/substrate interface[8]. The relatively low temperature at which the interface is annealed, however, minimizes the interdiffusion of Si and Ge, and, as a consequence, prevents the selective oxidation of Si. The formation of $Si_{0.85}Ge_{0.15}O_2$ thus occurs as a result of the kinetics of the annealing conditions. Other methods for the formation of $Si_{0.85}Ge_{0.15}O_2$ have been reported, such as the low temperature, high pressure oxidation method[8].

The thickness of the oxide is not uniform, and the ITO/oxide and oxide/substrate interfaces contain dips and bumps which we are as yet unable to explain. The In reduction product appeared as randomly distributed clusters at the oxide/substrate interface, as revealed in Fig. 4b. EDS identified these clusters to be predominantly In, but containing both Si and Ge. Note that this is in contrast to the ITO/Si case where In appeared above the SiO_2 layer.

The addition of Ge to the In-Si-O_2 system requires a new phase diagram representation to accommodate a quaternary system. Fig. 5 shows the

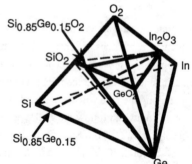

Figure 5: Roozeboom-Feydorov tetrahedron of the quaternary In-Si-Ge-O_2 system at 800°C.

Roozeboom-Feydorov tetrahedron representation of the system at 800°C. The thermodynamically stable tie-lines are $Si_{0.85}Ge_{0.15}O_2$-In, $Si_{0.85}Ge_{0.15}O_2$-Ge, and Ge-In_2O_3. The metastable original diffusion couple, In_2O_3-$Si_{0.85}Ge_{0.15}$, is indicated by the dashed line. Because the Ge content in the amorphous oxide is relatively small, we approximated the amorphous oxide to be pure, stoichiometric SiO_2 for purposes of discussion. This allows us to restrict analysis of the reaction paths to the back face of the tetrahedron, which corresponds to the In-Si-O_2 ternary phase diagram in Fig. 2.

There are two thermodynamically possible reaction paths in the In-Si-O_2 system at 800°C. The first involves oxygen as the sole diffusing species (see Fig. 6). Oxygen diffuses from the In_2O_3 layer and through the In and SiO_2 layers to react with Si at the oxide/Si interface. This corresponds to the reaction path taken when the ITO/Si system is annealed. C-V measurement demonstrated that the In product phase does not dope the Si substrate. While trace amounts of In may be incorporated into the oxide, the bulk of the In product phase appears on the ITO side of the SiO_2 layer.

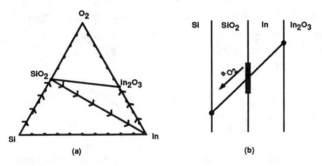

Figure 6: (a) Reaction path taken during annealing of the ITO/Si system; (b) corresponding product layer sequence.

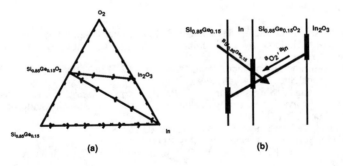

Figure 7: (a)Reaction path taken during annealing of the ITO/$Si_{0.85}Ge_{0.15}$ system; (b) corresponding product layer sequence.

On the other hand, the annealed ITO/$Si_{0.85}Ge_{0.15}$ system exhibits a different product layer sequence, as shown in Fig. 4b: ITO/amorphous oxide/In/$Si_{0.85}Ge_{0.15}$ substrate. The key difference between this product layer sequence and the ITO/Si system one is where the In product phase appears. In the ITO/$Si_{0.85}Ge_{0.15}$ case, the In phase appears on the opposite side of the amorphous oxide layer, i.e. at the oxide/substrate interface. This result indicates that another reaction path is taken during annealing of the ITO/$Si_{0.85}Ge_{0.15}$ system (see Fig.7). The second reaction path involves two diffusing species, In and O_2. The presence of the 15wt% Ge in the amorphous oxide layer apparently enhances the diffusivity of In metal through the oxide thus allowing the formation of clusters of In metal at the $Si_{0.85}Ge_{0.15}O_2/Si_{0.85}Ge_{0.15}$ interface.

CONCLUSION

We have developed a model that describes the evolution of the interface microstructure in the ITO/Si and ITO/$Si_{1-x}Ge_x$ systems. The annealed ITO/Si system showed the reduction of ITO by Si to form an SiO_2 interlayer, with the In product phase appearing on the ITO side of the SiO_2. In the case of the ITO/$Si_{0.85}Ge_{0.15}$, ITO is reduced to form an interlayer of $Si_{0.85}Ge_{0.15}O_2$, but the In product phase appears on the opposite side of the oxide layer at the $Si_{0.85}Ge_{0.15}O_2/Si_{0.85}Ge_{0.15}$ interface.

ACKNOWLEDGEMENTS

The authors are grateful to Alan F. Schwartzman for his helpful discussions. This work was funded by the Office of Naval Research under Grant No. N00014-91-J-1837 and the National Science Foundation under Grant No. DMR-9115054.

REFERENCES

1. H. Kobayashi, T. Ishida, Y. Nakato, and H. Tsubomura, J. Appl. Phys. **69**, 1736 (1991).
2. M. Hagerott, H. Jeon, A. V. Nurmikko, W. Xie, D. C. Grillo, M. Kobayashi, and R. L. Gunshor, Appl. Phys. Lett. **60**, 2825 (1992).
3. Y. Shigesato and D. C. Paine, Appl. Phys. Lett. **62**, 1268 (1993); ibid., S. Takaki, and T. Haranoh, Appl. Surf. Sci. **48/49**, 269 (1991).
4. C. W. Ow-Yang, Y. Shigesato, and D. C. Paine, *Interface Control of Electrical, Chemical, and Mechanical Properties*, edited by S. Murarka, T. Ohmi, K. Rose, T. Seidel (Mater. Res. Soc. **318**, Pittsburgh, PA, 1994).
5. E. A. Irene, J. Electrochem. Soc. **125** (10), 1708 (1978).
6. T. J. Mego, Solid State Technology (May 1990).
7. E. H. Nicollian and J.R. Brews, *MOS Physics and Technology* (John Wiley & Sons, New York, 1982).
8. D. C. Paine, C. Caragianis, A. Schwartzman, J. Appl. Phys. **70**, 5081 (1991).

SURFACE ANALYSIS OF LCD MATERIALS IN VARIOUS STAGES OF PRODUCTION BY TIME-OF-FLIGHT SECONDARY ION MASS SPECTROSCOPY (TOF-SIMS)

J.J. Lee, P.M. Lindley and R.W. Odom
Charles Evans & Associates, Redwood City, CA 94063

INTRODUCTION

Time-of-flight secondary ion mass spectrometry (TOF-SIMS) is a surface analysis technique which provides a sensitive characterization of the elemental and molecular composition of the near-surface region (top few monolayers) of solid materials[1]. This mass spectrometry technique can also localize the distribution of specific elements, molecules or molecular fragments at sub-micrometer (μm) lateral resolutions[2].

This paper presents the results of TOF-SIMS analyses of LCD material surfaces during various stages of production of the color filter side of Thin Film Transistor (TFT) LCDs. Specific surfaces analyzed included the Cr mask, Cr patterned surface, color filter (RGB) regions, topcoat polymer and Indium Tin Oxide (ITO) layer. Both elemental and molecular contaminants were detected on the surfaces of these samples at several of the processing stages. Typical organic contaminants included polydimethylsiloxane (a common mold release agent and/or machine lubricant), polyethylene glycols (PEG), various fatty acids and glycerides. Inorganic contaminants included Na, K, Ca, Cl, Br, sulfates and phosphates. Positive or negative ion images showed distinctive patterns for most of these contaminants. Molecular ions of Cu phthalocyanine used as the blue dye in the RGB deposition step were also detected and localized. Although TOF-SIMS provides both elemental and molecular or chemical structure analysis, Paper M6.8 in these proceeding discusses the quantitative analysis of elemental contamination on these surfaces using the Total Reflection X-ray Fluorescence (TXRF) technique.

EXPERIMENTAL

Specimens from each of the 5 phases mentioned above were pulled from the production process and placed in clean polyethylene containers. Each of these specimens was analyzed using a Charles Evans & Associates time-of-flight secondary ion mass spectrometer (TFS™) equipped with $^{69}Ga^+$ primary ion beam, a low energy electron neutralization system and triple electrostatic energy analyzers (ESAs) for accurate ion flight time measurements[3]. Positive and negative ion mass spectra were acquired over a mass-to-charge (m/z) range from 0 to 1000 and the mass resolution (M/ΔM) was ~2000 at mass 41. Primary ion doses for these analyses were on the order of 10^{12} ions/cm^2, thus insuring minimal chemical damage of the molecular constituents of the surfaces. The $^{69}Ga^+$ primary ion beam was focused to a 0.5 μm spot size in this work and secondary ion images were acquired over 260 X 260 μm^2 image field.

197

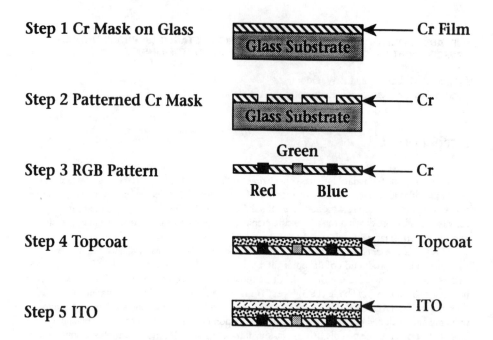

Step 1 Cr Mask on Glass ◄──── Cr Film

Glass Substrate

Step 2 Patterned Cr Mask ◄──── Cr

Glass Substrate

Green

Step 3 RGB Pattern ◄──── Cr

Red   Blue

Step 4 Topcoat ◄──── Topcoat

Step 5 ITO ◄──── ITO

Figure 1.   LCD materials in various production stages.

A schematic diagram of the 5 sample types analyzed in this study are illustrated in Figure 1. All substrates were glass. The Cr Pattern on Sample #2 was analyzed in both the Cr and glass substrate regions. The RGB patterned sample was analyzed in the blue dye region only.

RESULTS and DISCUSSION

Figure 2 illustrates typical positive and negative ion TOF-SIMS mass spectra acquired from the surface of the Cr black mask. The low mass region of the positive ion spectrum (top plot) is dominated by Na^+ and Cr^+ ions. The intense sodium signal indicates probable handling contamination while the formation of Si^+ (m/z 28) from this surface indicates either inorganic or organic silicon contamination. The peaks observed at m/z 43, 73 and 147 are identified as organic silicones having the structures $Si(CH_3)^+$, $Si(CH_3)_3^+$, and $(CH_3)_3\text{-}Si\text{-}O\text{-}Si\text{-}(CH_3)_2^+$, respectively. These peaks are commonly observed in TOF-SIMS analysis of surfaces contaminated with polydimethylsiloxanes (PDMS). This type of contaminant is ubiquitous in many manufacturing and chemical environments because siloxanes are commonly used as machine lubricants and mold release agents in the manufacture of many types of polymer products.

The middle spectrum in Figure 2 illustrates the higher mass region of the positive ion spectrum for the Cr black mask surface. The series of peaks from m/z 507 to 683 are most likely formed from polyethylene oxide (PEO) or polyethylene glycol (PEG) contaminants on the sample surface. The series of peaks, 507-551, 551-595, 595-639 and 639-683, are separated by 44 mass units corresponding to the $-C_2H_4O-$ species which forms the back-bone of PEO and PEG. These types of polymeric contaminants could be surfactants or plasticizers in polymers exposed to the Cr mask.

A typical negative ion mass spectrum of the Cr black mask is illustrated in the lower spectrum in Figure 2. This spectrum is displayed over m/z range from 200 to 400 in order to illustrate the organic contaminants detected in negative ion analysis. These contaminants include negative siloxane ions $(CH_3)_3-Si_3O_4^-$ along with a series of peaks having the formula $C_nH_{2n-1}O_2^-$. These peaks correspond to anions of fatty acid contamination on the surface. Specific peaks indicating fatty acid contamination are detected at several m/z values including 227 ($C_{14}H_{27}O_2^-$), 255 ($C_{16}H_{31}O_2^-$), 283 ($C_{18}H_{35}O_2^-$) and 339 ($C_{22}H_{43}O_2^-$). This type of contamination is very commonly observed in manufacturing environments because fatty acids are contained in finger oils and are constituents of lubricants and polymer additives.

A typical positive ion spectrum of the Cr mask region after patterning (Step 2 in Figure 1) is shown in Figure 3. The top plot in this figure illustrates the spectrum over m/z values from 0 to 650 in which the positive ion intensity is displayed on a logarithmic scale. This type of display is often very useful for identifying low intensity signals in the presence of high intensity ions produced from the major and minor constituents on the surface. This particular spectrum contains intense low mass signals dominated by the $^{52}Cr^+$ ion along with lower mass aliphatic and aromatic hydrocarbon signals. This spectrum does not contain distinctive peaks for the various siloxane ions observed in the unpatterned sample (cf. Figure 2). However, the patterned sample does contain prevalent ions for higher mass esters and glycerides. For example, the peak at mass 237 has the empirical formula $C_{16}H_{29}O^+$ and is probably a fragment of a C16 acid ($C_{16}H_{29}O_2H$) or ester ($C_{16}H_{29}O_2R$) where R is an alkyl group.

Glycerides peaks are readily produced about m/z 550 from this sample surface. The lower spectrum in Figure 3 has been expanded about this mass range and illustrates approximately 8 distinctive peaks between m/z 500 and 600. The nearly uniform intensities of most of these peaks suggests a mixture of glycerides containing different alkyl groups. Positive ions of glycerides are frequently detected by TOF-SIMS in this mass range. Fragment ions from higher glycerides peaks are also detected in this spectrum. For example, the series of peaks at m/z 369, 341 and 313 probably have the empirical formula, $C_xH_yO_3^+$, which could form by loss of the R_1CO- moiety from the glyceride structure illustrated in Figure 3. The 28 mass unit difference between these three fragments correspond to a difference of $-C_2H_4-$ units. Since water-based cleaning agents often contain glyceride compounds, the glyceride peaks detected in this analysis probably indicate incomplete cleaning of the surface after the patterning process.

The analysis of the glass regions produces elemental ion peaks for Al^+, Si^+, Sr^+, Ba^+, Ce^+ and Pb^+.

A third example of TOF-SIMS analysis of LCD surfaces is illustrated in Figure 4. The positive spectrum in this figure was produced from the blue-dye well in the patterned device. The dye molecule in this well was organometallic phthalocyanine having a molecular weight of 575 daltons (Da). The empirical formula for this compound is $CuC_{32}N_8H_{16}$. The top spectrum in this figure indicates the presence of significant siloxane contamination strongly suggesting that the surface was exposed to a siloxane rich environment during this step of the processing. It is also possible that the siloxane contamination was introduced during handling and/or storage of the samples. However, since all of the 5 samples did not exhibit similar levels of siloxanes, we postulate that the majority of the siloxane was introduced during specific processing steps. The

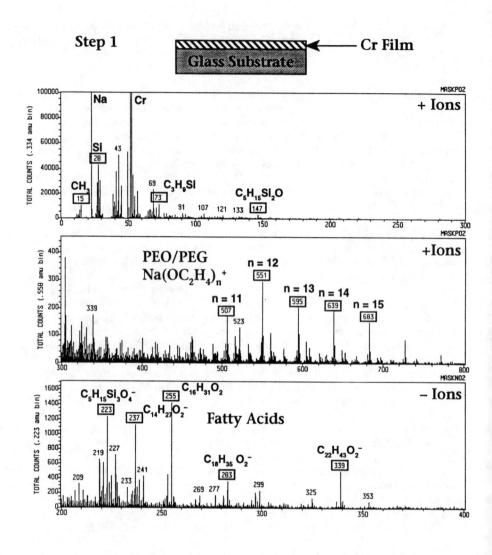

Figure 2. Positive (top and middle panels) and negative (bottom) ion spectra from Cr black mask, Step 1 of Figure 1.

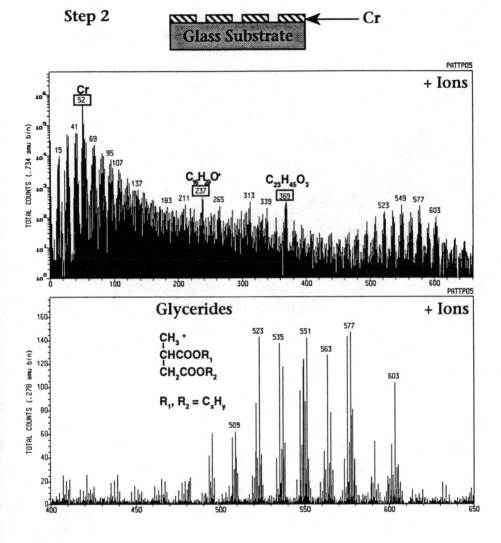

Step 2

Cr

Glass Substrate

PATTP05

+ Ions

Cr
52

41

69

15

95
107

137

$C_{16}H_{29}O^+$
237

183   211   265

313

339   $C_{23}H_{45}O_3$ 369

523   549   577

603

TOTAL COUNTS (.734 amu bin)

PATTP05

Glycerides   **+ Ions**

CH_3^+
|
$CHCOOR_1$
|
CH_2COOR_2

$R_1, R_2 = C_xH_y$

523   535   551   577

563

509   603

TOTAL COUNTS (.278 amu bin)

Figure 3.   Positive ion spectrum of the Cr surfaces after patterning, Step 2 of Figure 1.

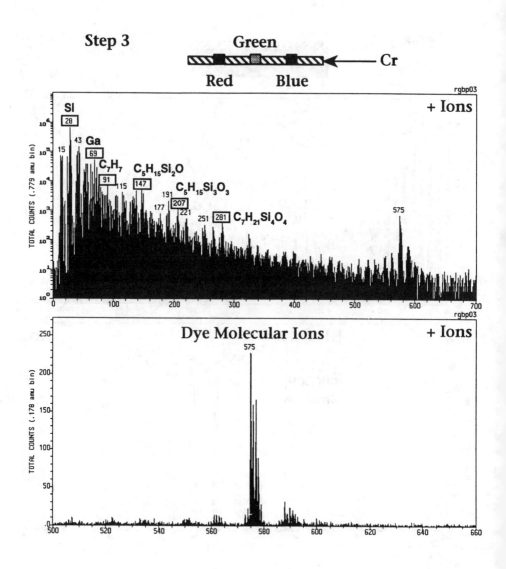

Figure 4. Positive ion spectrum from the blue region of the RGB pattern, Step 3 of Figure 1.

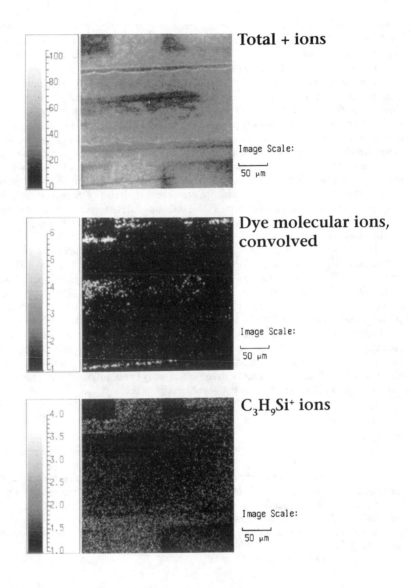

Total + ions

Image Scale:
50 μm

Dye molecular ions, convolved

Image Scale:
50 μm

C₃H₉Si⁺ ions

Image Scale:
50 μm

Figure 5.   Ion images from the RGB pattern sample, Step 3 of Figure 1.

higher mass region of the dye-well spectrum contains a very distinctive molecular ion peak of the dye molecule. The lower spectrum in this figure illustrates this higher mass peak detected at m/z 575. The satellite peaks above mass 575 mass correspond to ^{13}C and the ^{65}Cu adduct of the molecular ion. Elemental Cu is also detected from this sample surface.

Three examples of TOF-SIMS ion imaging are displayed in Figure 5. These images were acquired from the blue dye sample using an image field of 260 X 260 μm^2. The top image illustrates the total ion image which is the sum of the secondary ions from a m/z range of 0 to 1000. The total ion image typically provides an overview of the sample topography and defines regions of high, intermediate and low ion emission. The middle image was produced from the molecular ion of the dye molecule and this image demonstrates that the dye molecule was exposed in the central region of the well. In addition, dye molecules are detected along the sides of the well suggesting either that the dye has diffused from the central region or that the deposition technique poorly localized the dye within the center region. Either of these proposed mechanisms could result in poor LCD performance. TOF-SIMS imaging is an ideal method for detecting such molecular diffusion or localization since it can detect and image these types of higher molecular weight molecules under static SIMS conditions.

The bottom image in Figure 5 illustrates the distribution of one of the PDMS peaks on the dye well surface. This image was produced from (CH$_3$)$_3$-Si$^+$ which is detected at m/z 73. This contaminant ion is distributed across most of the analytical surface suggesting that siloxane contamination was introduced either during or after the dye deposition. The surface spectra of the sample from Step 4 of Figure 1 are dominated by PDMS peaks. The PDMS ions are also present on the sample from Step 5. It is not known whether the appearance of siloxane contaminants on the surfaces of many of these samples will cause potential yield problems in LCD manufacture. It is known that siloxanes reduce surface adhesion and promote adhesive failures. Siloxane on conductor surfaces may also cause intermittent electrical discontinuity. The observation that 4 out of 5 samples analyzed in this study contain siloxane contamination suggests that siloxanes could be a problem in this manufacturing process.

CONCLUSIONS

This study has demonstrated the capabilities of TOF-SIMS in analyzing the surface of LCD materials for organic and inorganic contamination at various stages of processing. TOF-SIMS provides high sensitivity, specificity and detection of molecular or fragment ions on the top surfaces. The detection of both elemental and molecular contamination on processed surfaces will provide essential information for improving manufacturing yields and product qualities of LCD materials.

REFERENCES

1. Schueler, P. Sander and D.A. Reed, *Vacuum*, **41**, 1661(1990).
2. Odom in *Microscopic and Spectroscopic Imaging of the Chemical State*, Ed. M.D. Morris, Marcel Dekker, New York (1993), Ch.10.
3. Schueler, *Microsc. Microanal. Microstruct.* **3**, 1(1992)

ALIGNMENT OF SMECTIC LIQUID CRYSTAL MOLECULES BY GRATED GLASS AND SILICON SUBSTRATES

L. J. Martínez-Miranda, E. Smela and H. Liu
University of Pennsylvania, Department of Electrical Engineering, Philadelphia, PA 19104

ABSTRACT

We present the results of a study of the effect of photolithographed gratings on glass and silicon wafers on the alignment of smectic liquid crystal molecules. The gratings have periods in the range of 200nm - 200µm, and depths of up to 2µm. We found that smectic liquid crystals align *sharply* along the gratings, depending on the temperature cycling method used in loading the sample. This result applies both to silicon gratings as well as glass gratings, despite the increased roughness observed in glass gratings. The quality of the alignment is uniform in the range 664nm - 24µm, and breaks down outside this region, setting lower and upper boundaries for grating preparation.

INTRODUCTION

The understanding of how liquid crystal (LC) molecules interact and align when in contact with diverse surfaces is important both fundamentally as well as for the development and improvement of LC display and sensing devices. This research is concerned with the interactions of liquid crystals with solid substrates, such as those used in liquid crystal displays (LCD's). LCD's require encasing LC's in thin films, between appropriately prepared substrates. The LC molecules align at right angles with respect to the surface of substrates such as air or clean, uniform glass surfaces. The molecules align parallel or at a small angle with respect to the surface of grooved or grated substrates. The need to confine LC materials inside low dimensional geometries requires an understanding of how LC's interact with different substrate materials, as well as the different methods used to prepare these substrates. Substrate preparation affects the quality of liquid crystal alignment in a film, which in turn affects the optical quality and reproducibility of a sensing or display device. Other factors that affect the quality smectic liquid crystal alignment are the speed of the temperature cycling process, which allows the liquid crystal molecules to respond to the presence of a prepared substrate. Changes in the ambient temperature can affect further the ability of the substrate to maintain a uniform, long-range alignment of the liquid crystal films.

We have used x-ray scattering in the study of small aligned regions in films of 8CB in the smectic phase, and to examine the effect of substrate topology on the alignment of this phase[1]. A LC droplet deposited onto a grooved substrate experiences a competition between the aligning forces at the LC-air interface, which force the molecules to align normal to the surface, and the aligning forces at the LC-substrate interface, which forces the molecules to align parallel to the plane of the substrate. For a smectic LC, the ordered layers must rotate in order to satisfy both boundary conditions. We found[1] that for 8CB in the smectic A phase deposited on gratings with periods of 9, 15 and 24 µm, surface tension was the dominant aligning force, followed by surface topology. The presence of a grating produces an excess in the Frank elastic energy of the liquid crystal. In addition, we observed an absence of LC alignment along the gratings in films thinner than 15-20µm. Films thicker than 20µm show the presence of regions of molecular alignment parallel to the gratings, which increase nearly linearly with increasing film thickness. Finally, we observed that grated silicon or glass substrates are equally effective in aligning the liquid crystal films, in spite of differences in the smoothness and morphology of the grooves produced on each substrate.

In this paper, we summarize the results of a our structural studies of smectic LC films deposited on photolithographed gratings with periods ranging from 664nm - 200µm and depths of up to 2µm. We also summarize the results of an optical microscopy experiment which confirms our x-ray observations. Finally, we present preliminary results on the evolution of the ordered

205

layers as a function of temperature. A detailed discussion of our results appears elsewhere in the literature[2-4].

EXPERIMENTAL

This project combines the use of well characterized substrates with a detailed structural and orientational study of the LC layers within the films. The most efficient and economic way of preparing substrates for LC alignment is the "rubbing" method[5]. In order to control better the topography and cleanliness of our substrates, we have used conventional photolithography, using a chemical etch of buffered HF, to prepare gratings both on soda lime glass and silicon of uniform period and depth. The gratings studied have periods of 9,15, 24 and 200μm, a maximum depth of 2μm and a surface area of 1cm[2].

The gratings were etched photolithographically. The preparation methods are described else-where[1,2]. Soda lime glass microscope slides 1mm thick, which were cut into 1x1" pieces, were used as substrates because of their availability, isotropy, and good etching properties. P-type (100) silicon wafers were used to prepare the silicon-based substrates. The resulting glass sub-strates had uniform periods and were characterized by rough grating grooves. As mentioned above, both the glass and silicon substrates were equally effective in aligning the LC samples, in spite of higher roughness of the glass gratings. In our discussion we will refer to the samples indistiguishably.

The 664nm period gratings were prepared by laser holography[2]. Light from a He-Cd laser with a wavelength of 325nm, 10mW of output power, and a 1.2mm beam diameter was used to expose a photoresist coated glass slide. In the interference exposure system a 10mm focal length lens and a 5 micrometer diameter pinhole were used as spatial filters. A 28°, 20 second cross angle gave a 664nm grating pitch. The exposure stage was 28 cm from the spatial filters for each arm. After developing, the slides were etched in a solution of buffered hydrofluoric acid, and the remaining photoresist was removed. Examination of SEM photographs of the resulting gratings showed them to be shallow, approximately 100nm in depth.

The compound 8CB was chosen for our studies because of its chemical stability, availability and because it is a room temperature smectic A. The smectic phase is a bilayer $A_{2'}$ phase, with a spacing of approximately 31.6Å. The films were prepared as follows. The thickness of the films was varied systematically with the use of a high precision 0.5μl resolution pipette set to dispense 5μl of material at a time. The samples were weighed before and after the addition of liquid crystal, using a 0.1mg resolution analytical balance; 1μl is equal to 1mg of material. The addition of 5μl of material results in an increase of approximately 5μm in the thickness of the films. The sample is carefully distributed over the grating area (1cm^2) using a warm wire or a piece of Teflon tubing. The 8CB is heated into the isotropic phase after each addition and with the use of a hot air blower. Other cycling methods include heating the slide from the side, or applying a hot finger to the bottom of the slide. We use this process to change the thickness of the films in-situ at the experimental site. The final slide is weighed at the end of the experiment to determine the final film thicknesses.

X-ray scattering is a particularly appropriate tool for characterizing the structure of thin films. We use the grazing angle x-ray scattering technique[6] to analyze the structure of the liquid crystal layers close to the LC-substrate interface. We summarize the diffraction geometry as follows: The x-ray scattering experiments were performed at the National Synchrotron Light Source, beamline X22B, using 9keV (1.403Å) x-rays, focused on a spot of 2mm^2 at the sample position. The detector slits were kept at a 10(vertical)x4(horizontal)mm^2 opening. The samples were mounted on a four circle Huber goniometer. The experiments on beamline X22B used 1.403Å, 1.182Å or 1.305Å x-rays, focused on a spot of 2mm^2 at the sample position. The detector slits were kept at a 10(vertical)x4(horizontal)mm^2 opening. The samples were mounted on a four circle Huber goniometer. In order to study the orientation of the smectic layers in the films, we perform both out-of-plane (00*l*) as well as in-plane ((h00) and (0k0)) Bragg scans. The grating direction is chosen to coincide with the k direction on the plane. In addition, we performed a series of χ scans on the films to observe the evolution of the inplane peaks in the film. One can study the regions of varying smectic layer orientation by changing the value of the angle χ: this scan is equivalent to changing the value of the out of plane component of *l* in reciprocal space continuously. We performed these scans at angles corresponding to directions along the gratings ([01*l*] direction) as well as directions perpendicular to the gratings ([10*l*] direction). The diffraction angles $\theta, 2\theta$ were held constant at the Bragg value for 8CB. Finally, we performed azimuthal ϕ-scans at $\chi = 0°$ and $\chi = 10°$ in order to observe the degree of in-plane disorder. For these scans, $\phi = 0°$ corresponds to the [01*l*] direction.

To perform the optical measurements, the samples were examined by using a Leitz optical microscope in transmission mode with crossed polarizers. The magnification of the microscope was x400, and its resolution for depth measurement was 2μm. Because it is difficult to find the defects at the boundary of two layers for slowly cooled samples of any thickness, the samples analyzed optically were prepared using a fast cooling rate of approximately 10 seconds[3]. This has the effect of producing a domain layer near the substrate surface, the height of which can be easily measured. To make the thickness measurement, we first focused on the substrate and then moved the focus on the defects at the boundary between the homogeneous and the homeotropic layers of the LC film. We determined thus the thickness of the homogeneous layer as a function of film thickness.

Substrates used to analyze the effect of temperature variation on liquid crystal alignment consisted of gratings prepared as described above, with a chromel-alumel thermocouple deposited along the perimeter and the center of the grating, and a nickel heater deposited on the bottom of the grating. The thermocouple response was linear in the range 22°-100°C and the heater was able to control the temperature within 0.1°C[4,7].

RESULTS AND DISCUSSION

8CB films of different thickness were prepared at different cooling rates following the procedures summarized above. We show in Figure 1 the results obtained for the thickness of different aligned layers within these films. To determine the number and thickness of these layers, we used χ scans on both slow and fast cooled samples to determine the thickness of the aligned layers within the films. Figure 2 shows such a scan taken on a 51μm thick film on a 9μm period grating. The χ scan results were fit to a multilayer model, consisting of a series of slabs which may have different thicknesses, orientations and mosaic (angular) spreads. The scattering is proportional to

$$I = A \exp\left[\frac{-2x\mu}{(\sin\alpha\cos\chi)}\right], \tag{1}$$

where α is the angle of incidence of the x-ray beam, μ is the average absorption length at the chosen x-ray wavelengths[14], and 2x is the pathlength of the x-rays inside the sample. Details of this analysis appear elsewhere in the literature. The result of the fit to this model for the 51μm film χ scan appears as a dotted line on Figure 2.

The layer thicknesses of fast cooled samples deposited on both 9 and 15μm period gratings were obtained by directly measuring the layer height as described in Section 2, using the optical microscope. We observed similar measured layer thicknesses for both the 9μm and 15μm period grating. We included in Figure 1 the results of the direct optical microscope observation. We note that the cooling rate does not affect the measured layer thickness. In addition, the results obtained using optical and x-ray methods agree with each other within experimental uncertainty.

For a grated substrate, the air-LC interface dominates the aligning forces for small thicknesses, and all films smaller than 20μm exhibit homeotropic alignment of the LC molecules. In thicker films, the gratings induce a degree of uniform homogeneous alignment in the direction of the grating grooves. These regions are concentrated near the surface of the substrate for films up to 70μm thick[3,6]. The thickness region 30-40μm appears to be an unstable region. The analysis of quickly cooled samples showed that films as thick as 30μm could still consist of only a homeotropic layer[8]. Films thicker than 31μm have a stable homeotropic layer that can be as large as 10-12μm or as small as 3μm in the very thick films. This sets an upper limit to the influence of the air-LC interface in these systems. Beyond the critical region, the grating imposed orientation of the LC molecules affects the ordering of the bulk film; the homogeneously aligned region constitutes up to 80% of the film thickness.

In contrast to the above results, no in-plane peak was observed on the 664nm grating for films up to 40μm thick. However, the azimuthal orientation of the in-plane layers in thicker films did not correspond to the direction along the gratings. Films thicker than 50μm exhibited a larger degree of rotation. Shallow 200μm gratings exhibit a very small in-plane layer peak. Grating depth seems to play a role in molecular alignment both in the 664nm and, to a lesser extent, in the 200μm period grating. The 100nm depth of the 664nm grating may be in the region where the air-LC interface dominates the film alignment, thus representing a lower limit in depth. On the other hand, the 200μm grating aligns the film in the shallow depth region. It is not clear if the air-LC interface dominates the molecular alignment in this case, or if the grating cross section exceeds a critical area beyond which the LC molecules do not reorient. Both the 664nm and 200μm gratings represent lower and upper limits to achieve uniform LC alignment. Reference 2 contains a more detailed discussion on these limits.

We note that in most films studies, only two layers were needed to fit the χ scan data to the multilayer model given by equation 1. A third layer was required on a 34μm slow-cooled sample, which lies in the unstable region described above[2]. This result suggests that the transition layer between the homeotropic and homogeneous layers is a very sharp one. However, the result does not rule out the possibility that this transition layer is a disordered one, nor that a third (dis)oriented layer may exist in the region in between the gratings, which is not accessible with our experimental probes[2].

The cooling rate, and the cooling procedure, which allow the molecules to respond to the influence of both the air and the substrate surfaces, plays an important role in the alignment of the LC molecules, and influences the degree of disorder of the homogeneous layers[9]. Figure 3 shows the results of a ϕ scan taken on a 51μm film deposited on a 9μm grating, and cooled using the three cycling methods described in Section 2. In this figure, $\phi = 90°$ designates the direction along the gratings. The azimuthal ordering of fast cooled films was very broad, exhibiting low reproducibility. These fast cooled films showed a highly defected region that extended the thickness of the homogeneously aligned region when observed under a microscope with crossed polarizers[6]. Films that were cooled using a slow cycling method, such as that obtained when heating the sample from the side, showed a high degree of orientation along the grating direction. The films appeared very uniform when observed under a microscope; only those defects associated with the rotation of the LC molecules at the edge of the gratings could be observed clearly. The sharp single peak observed in the azimuthal scan of the slowly cooled samples[2], and the uniform domain free layer on similar samples observed under the microscope with cross polarizers[3] suggest that there must be only a single homogeneous region in the film. Within this region, all molecules interact to have the same relative tilt angle with respect to the grating, rather than exhibiting a continuous variation in tilt angle through the thickness of the layer. This evidence further supports the existence of a sharp homogeneous-homoetropic layer interface.

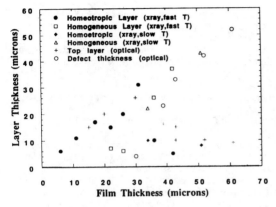

Figure 1: Summary graph of experimental layer thickness as a function of deposited liquid crystal film thickness.

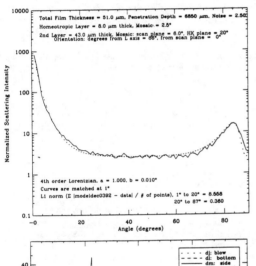

Figure 2: χ scan on a slowly cooled 51μm thick film on a 9μm period grating. The dotted line is a fit to equation 1. In this figure, $\chi = 90°$ Angle.

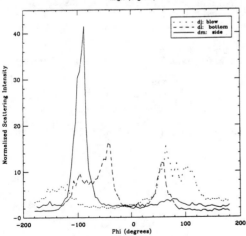

Figure 3: Phi scans obtained on a 51μm film, using three cooling cycling methods. Solid line: long (2 min.) cooling cycle. Cut and dotted line: fast cooling cycle (approx. 10 seconds.)

We have recently completed a study of the effect of temperature change on the alignment of the LC films. Preliminary results indicate that the gratings preserve structural order well above the smecticA -nematic transition for 8CB, which occurs at 33.5°C. However, the size of both ordered layer is reduced about 3°C below this transition, which may suggest that a disordered layers develops in the middle of the film. The azimuthal ordering of the film is preserved as a function of temperature over the 15°C range studied[10].

The results of this work are directly applicable in the study and development of sensing devices that depend both on an aligning surface as well as a flexible contact membrane[1]. The strength of the surface anchoring can be controlled by varying the grating dimensions between 10 and 100µm, based on the results shown above of the effect of grating size on LC molecular orientation[2]. The temperature cooling cycle can affect the optical uniformity, and the reproducibility of a device based on smectic liquid crystals. This information can be used in the design of substrates for ferro-electric LC cells that operate in the smectic phase. A second issue raised by our results which is applicable to symmetrical smectic cells is the study of the effect on LC layer alignment by mis-aligned or rotated cell plates. Rotated plates compete with each other since they induce alignment along two different directions[1]. They induce a twist in the LC layers, which produces an excess in elastic energy and may result in the formation of defects in the film. These defects, while decreasing the free energy of the LC film, may decrease the effectiveness of the device. Studies on the effect of plate rotation on LC alignment and layer uniformity are in progress currently[11].

We extend our thanks to Takashi Isoshima and Nong Chen of Dr. Yoshiaki Nakano's group under Professor Kunio Tada, Department of Electronic Engineering, University of Tokyo, for making the 664nm gratings. We also thank Prof. T. Swagger and his group for kindly allowing us to use their optical microscope facility.

This work was supported by an NSF Grant No. ECS-9201986. The work at Brookhaven National Laboratory was made possible through an NSLS Faculty-Student Research Support Program Grant.

REFERENCES

1. E. Smela and L.J. Martínez-Miranda, J. Appl. Phys, 73, 3299-3304 (1993); E. Smela and L.J. Martínez-Miranda, Liq. Cryst., 14, 1877-1883 (1993).
2. E. Smela and L.J. Martínez-Miranda, "The Effect of Substrate Preparation on Smectic Liquid Crystal Alignment: a Structural Study II", submitted to J. Appl. Phys., 1994.
3. H. Liu and L.J. Martínez-Miranda, "An Optical Study of Effect of Grated Substrates on Smectic Liquid Crystal Alignment", to be submitted to Liq. Cryst., 1994.
4. H. Liu and L.J. Martínez-Miranda, in progress, 1994.
5. .J. Kahn, Physics Today, 35, 66 (1982).
6. W.C. Marra, P. Eisenberger, and A.Y. Cho, J. Appl. Phys., 50, 6927 (1979).
7. B. Collings, report on the NSF-REU Summer Program, Dept. of Electrical Eng., University of Pennsylvania, 1993.
8. E. Smela, Ph. D. Thesis, University of Pennsylvania, 1992.
9. E. Smela and L.J. Martínez-Miranda, submitted to J. Appl. Phys., 1994.
10.   For a discussion on sharp boundaries in other LC systems, see, for example, Z. Li, W. R. Folks and O.D. Laurentovich, SPIE, Vol. 2175, in press (1994).
11.   K. Ko, report on the NSF-REU Summer Program, Dept. of Electrical Eng., University of Pennsylvania, 1993.

OPTICALLY CONTROLLED ALIGNMENT OF LIQUID CRYSTALS

WAYNE M. GIBBONS, PAUL J. SHANNON, AND SHAO-TANG SUN
Hercules Incorporated, Hercules Research Center, 500 Hercules Road, Wilmington, DE 19808

ABSTRACT

Optically controlled homogeneous-to-homogeneous alignment of liquid crystals using polarized light is reviewed. Application of this technology to liquid crystal display manufacturing is discussed. Important processing parameters such as tilt angle and optical energy density will be addressed.

INTRODUCTION

In 1991, we published the results of our efforts on the homogeneous-to-homogeneous alignment of liquid crystal molecules using polarized light and specially designed optically controlled alignment polymers.[1] Since then similar work has been published by other researchers using different optically controlled alignment materials.[2-5]

The optically controlled alignment process demonstrates high spatial and angular resolution of the local alignment of liquid crystals.[1] With the proper design of the alignment material, the process is reversible allowing for the potential of real-time write/rewrite control of the local liquid crystal director.

An immediate application is to use this noncontact method to align liquid crystal displays. The noncontact nature of this technology has the potential to decrease particulate contamination, reduce the number of processing steps, and prevent the build up of static charge which is a concern of active-matrix-liquid crystal display (AMLCD) manufacturers. For display applications, issues such as the pretilt angle and the dielectric properties of the optically controlled alignment polymer must be addressed. This paper will primarily focus on tilt angle requirements and briefly cover energy density requirements of optically controlled alignment layers.

Optically Controlled Alignment of Nematic Liquid Crystals

Our initial work demonstrated that guest-host liquid crystal mixtures could be realigned with polarized light.[6] We concluded from this work that the dichroic dye and the liquid crystal/aligning layer interface were important for the observed effect. As a consequence, liquid crystal cells were constructed that had a dichroic dye incorporated in the aligning layer instead of the liquid crystal. Localization of dye near the interface allows exposures in the absence of the liquid crystals and, thus, the process is not limited to guest-host liquid crystal systems.

An experiment was performed to demonstrate the concept of optical alignment. Prior to cell assembly, a polyimide/dye aligning layer[1] was scanned with linearly polarized laser light. A subsequent exposure was made through a metallized mask of a Hercules Logo and with the linearly polarized light rotated 90° to the first exposure. A cell was assembled with the exposed polyimide/dye and polyimide only coated substrates. The cell was filled with the guest-host mixture described previously.[6] The photograph of the cell as viewed through a single polarizer is depicted in Figure 1. It is important to reiterate that no electric field is applied to the cell and the background alignment and image were done optically. In addition, this example demonstrates

Mat. Res. Soc. Symp. Proc. Vol. 345. ©1994 Materials Research Society

the write/rewrite capability of this alignment process (background then image). The uniformity of the optically buffed background and subsequent image is comparable to or better than the quality of mechanical buffing techniques.

Figure 1. Optical buffing and realignment.

The high resolution of the optically controlled alignment technique is demonstrated in Figure 2. As with the Hercules Logo, a cell was assembled and, prior to filling, it was exposed with a linearly polarized optical interference pattern with a 10μm period.[1] After filling the cell with nematic liquid crystals, the cell was placed between crossed polarizers and viewed with a microscope. As shown in Figure 2, the local alignment of the liquid crystals was periodic and, as with the exposing beam, the period of the alignment was 10μm.

Figure 2. Liquid crystal grating.

Advantages of Optically Aligned Liquid Crystals

Optically controlled alignment of liquid crystals has several advantages over the existing techniques for aligning liquid crystals. These advantages include

Noncontact method of inducing macroscopic alignment;

212

- High resolution angular control of alignment;

- Reconfigurable by changing the linear polarization of the incident light;

- Potential for submicron resolution;

- Potential for real-time optical control of device.

As a consequence of these advantages, improved performance of traditional liquid crystal devices and some new applications in binary optics and optical data storage can be envisaged.[1,6] One important application of this technology is in the macroscopic alignment of liquid crystal displays (LCDs).

OPTICAL ALIGNMENT OF LCDS

LCD applications require an optically controlled alignment polymer that will improve on the performance of existing alignment polymers while preserving the desirable dielectric, thermal, uniformity, and thin film processing properties of existing alignment polymers. In addition, the alignment polymer must induce a pretilt angle to eliminate reverse tilt disclinations in twisted nematic applications.

Furthermore, the optically controlled alignment polymers must demonstrate good optical stability in the operating wavelength range (usually visible) and suitable optical energy densities for the alignment process. Multiple write/rewrite capability is not a requirement for the majority of existing LCD applications, but if present, will allow for the "repair" of poorly aligned regions of a completed display and the potential for real-time optical addressing of the display.

The alignment materials used for demonstrating the optical alignment of liquid crystal displays include a standard Huls America polyimide as a control, polyimide with 33wt% diazodiamine[1], and a variety proprietary polymers (PP1-PP4) with the active moieties covalently bonded to the backbone of the polymer.

The nematic liquid crystals used were purchased from E. Merck and are given in Table I with the relevant optical and physical parameters. Both liquid crystals are cyanobiphenyl based mixtures.

Table I			
Material	n_e	Δn	N→I (°C)
ZLI1982	1.640	0.14	91
ZLI2452	1.6368	0.1366	110

For comparison purposes and to offer insight into the interaction of the liquid crystal and optical alignment polymers, we first mechanically buffed cells and measured their tilt angle using the technique described in [7]. For carefully aligned systems, the tilt angle is accurate to ±0.1°. Mechanical buffing of the cells was performed by unidirectionally rubbing the alignment polymer with a fibrous polishing cloth. Fifty micron cells were manufacutured with the buffing directions anti-parallel and capillary filled with liquid crystal at room temperature. Table II summarizes the

213

values of the mechanically buffed cells studied. As a control, polyimide cells were constructed and their tilt measured as well.

Table II		
Material	**Liquid Crystal**	**Tilt Angle** ($^{\circ}$)
Huls America SPI-2000 Polyimide	ZLI1982	1.5-3.1
Nissan SE7210 Polyimide	ZLI1982	3.0
SPI-2000/ 33wt% Diazodiamine	ZLI1982	4.7-6.0
PP1	ZLI1982	-
PP2	ZLI1982	89.2
PP3	ZLI1982	21.6
PP4	ZLI1982 ZLI2452	16.7 6.8

The range of tilt angle values for SPI-2000 are due to processing and mechanical buffing differences. As can be seen in Table II, the addition of diazodiamine to the SPI-2000 polyimide increased the mechanically buffed tilt angle. PP1 did not provide uniform alignment when mechanically buffed, therefore, it was difficult to measure any tilt angle. PP1-PP4 all have the same polymer backbone but differ in the type of optically activated chromophore covalently bonded to the backbone. The type of chromophore greatly affected the magnitude of the tilt. In addition, as demonstrated with PP4, ZLI2452 had a smaller tilt than ZLI1982.

Table III summarizes the energy density requirements for two optically controlled alignment polymers discussed in this paper. The desired value is ≤ 3 J/cm^2 which is compatible with existing photopolymers and automated machinery. For example, if the energy density were 0.5 J/cm^2, ten 14inch X 14inch substrates can be optically aligned per minute using a 100 Watt source. Mechanical buffing techniques are limited to 5 to 6 14inch X 14inch substrates per minute and require an additional cleaning step after buffing.

Table III	
Alignment Material	**Energy Density (J/cm^2)**
Polyimide/Diazodiamine	50-2500
PP1	2

The energy density for the polyimide/diazodiamine material is strongly dependent on the processing conditions (cure temperature, atmosphere, etc.) of the thin film after spin casting onto a glass substrate. Table III demonstrates that the energy density values can be controlled by the material chemistry as well as the processing conditions of the material.

Optical alignment was performed using a scanning technique as depicted in Figure 3. The laser was operated in multiline mode. The polarized laser beam was focussed to a line and the substrate was scanned at rates of 0.5-30mm/s (depending on the material). To ensure high uniformity of the alignment, a step size of 1.5mm was used for each successive scan line.

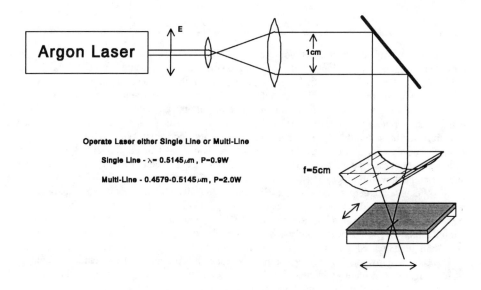

Figure 3. Scanning geometry for optically aligned materials.

To be useful for LCD applications, optical alignment techniques should allow for the creation of uniform pretilt angles. Table IV provides pretilt data on the alignment polymers as a function of process conditions and alignment technique.

It is clear from Table IV that optical alignment can provide pretilt angles in properly designed materials and with certain exposure conditions. However, it is unclear what physical mechanisms control the uniformity and magnitude of the pretilt angle. These parameters are currently being investigated.

Table IV			
Material	**Scan Speed**	**Liquid Crystal**	**Tilt Angle** (°)
SPI-2000/ Diazodiamine	0.75-12mm/s	ZLI1982 ZLI2452	0.0 0.0
PP1	5.00mm/s	ZLI2452	1.5
PP2	0.75mm/s	ZLI1982	78.2
PP3	1.50mm/s	ZLI1982	1.3
PP4	1.50mm/s 5.00mm/s	ZLI1982 ZLI1982	1.1 2.3

The tilt angle of the SPI-2000/diazodiamine alignment material was approximately 0° for all optical alignment conditions tried to date. However, it was measured to be 4.7-6.0° when buffed with a cloth (mechanical buffing). In general, we found for these alignment materials and exposure geometry that the optically aligned tilt was lower than the tilt generated with mechanical buffing. The uniformity of the alignment was good for all optically aligned cells except for those using PP2. Optically aligned PP2 had uniform alignment over 50% of the cell area with the remainder having a cloudy appearance due to many smaller domains. We also observed that the proprietary polymers gave different values for the pretilt angle as a function of scan speed as well as thin film processing conditions. Higher tilt angles were achieved (≤15°) with faster scan rates and different thin film processing but the uniformity of these cells was poor.

We have not demonstrated that the optically controlled alignment polymers satisfy all the requirements of liquid crystal display manufacturing. However, the preliminary data we have shown indicate that the potential for use in LCDs is good for these materials. The potential simplification of the alignment process with lower defect frequency and increased throughput could aid in increased yields for the LCD manufacturer. This is particularly important for AMLCDs where low yield affects the competitiveness of this product. Other potential advantages of this alignment technology include the ability to perform repairs on poorly aligned regions of a completed display and the simplification of multi-domain display manufacturing.

REFERENCES

1. W.M. Gibbons, P.J. Shannon, S.T. Sun and B.J. Swetlin, Nature, **351**, 49 (1991).
2. M. Schadt, K. Schmitt, V. Kozinkov and V. Chigrinov, Jpn. J. Appl. Phys., **31**, 2155 (1992).
3. Y. Iimura, J. Kusano, S. Kobayashi, Y. Aoyagi and T. Sugano, Jpn. J. Appl. Phys., **32**, 93 (1993).
4. K. Ichimura, Y. Hayashi and N. Ishizuki, Chem. Lett., 1063 (1992).
5. A.G. Dyadyusha, T.Ya. Marusii, Yu.A. Resnikov, A.I. Khizhnyak and V.Yu. Reshetnyak, JETP Lett., **56**, 17 (1992).
6. S.T. Sun, W.M. Gibbons and P.J. Shannon, Liquid Crystals, **12**, 869 (1992).
7. G. Baur, V. Wittwer, D.W. Berreman, Phys. Lett., **56A**, 142 (1976).

A NEW TYPE TFT WITH UNIQUE OPERATION AND SIMPLE FABRICATION PROCESS

REIJI HATTORI, YUKINOBU TANIDA AND JUNJI SHIRAFUJI
Osaka University, Department of Electrical Engineering, Suita, Osaka 565, Japan

ABSTRACT

A thin film transistor (TFT) with a new structure and a unique operation principle has been proposed. This TFT has Schottky barrier contacts at source and drain, and employs electron tunneling through the Schottky barrier. The first feature of this TFT is simplification of the production process because a self-aligned technique is applicable and an ion-implantation process is not necessary. These advantages are promising for low-cost production of active-matrix liquid crystal displays (AM-LCDs). In this letter, we propose of new type TFT and carry out 2-D device simulation on a simplified structure to show the fundamental characteristics of this transistor and to optimize impurity density, channel thickness, and barrier height.

INTRODUCTION

Low-cost production of AM-LCD is the most important issue to develop the further flat panel display (FPD) market. Drastic simplification of the production process for TFT array (reduction of numbers of photomask and deposition process) is required to realize the low-cost production. Recently, a self-aligned TFT structure using the ion-implantation method [1] draws attention as a promising technique. There is, however, a problem of the uniform ion-implantion over the large area substrates.

The TFT being proposed in this letter can be fabricated using the self-align technique and without the ion-implantation process, and is promising as LCD TFTs from the viewpoint of fabrication process, device dimension and leakage current. The operating principle is based on the electron tunneling through the Schottky barrier, which was originally proposed as Schottky barrier tunnel transistor (SBTT)[2, 3]. We designate the proposed TFT "SBTFT" in this letter.

We firstly explain the structure and the operation principle of SBTFT, and discuss the applicability to TFT of LCD. Next we show the device performance and the optimum design of SBTFT on the basis 2-D numerical analysis.

DEVICE STRUCTURE AND PROCESS

Figure 1 shows difference between conventional and Schottky barrier a-Si TFT structures. Although various structures can be suggested for SBTFT[3], the structure shown in Fig.1 is the most suitable one for FPD application at present.

The first difference from conventional TFT is Schottky barrier contacts at source and drain. In principle only Schottky source contact is essential for device operation. However, in order to emphasize simple fabrication process, Schottky contacts are located on the source and drain. The Schottky barrier contacts can be easily formed by evaporating a metal such

217

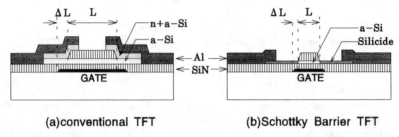

(a)conventional TFT   (b)Schottky Barrier TFT

Figure 1: Cross sectional view of (a) conventional inverted stagger TFT and (b) Schottky barrier TFT.

as Pd or Pt on a-Si. This feature gives a great advantage for device fabrication because a deposition process or an ion-implantation process to form n^+Si layer for ohmic contact can be eliminated. This structure allows us to apply a self-align process same as self-aligned TFT[1]. The self-aligned gate process reduces the gate/source overlap region, and contributes the lowering the parasitic capacitance, which influences much the picture performance. It is also possible to form the source and drain electrodes using self-align technique, in which channel passivation SiN can act as a mask for Schottky metal fabrication. After annealing at about 200 – 300 °C, the metal-silicon contact form a relevant metal silicide. As the metal on SiN forms no silicide, source and drain are easily formed by etching the unreacted metal. This low-resistivity silicide electrode reduces the series resistance and improve the contacts with a metal line.

The second point of differences is that the channel layer is moderately doped to n–type. The channel layer in conventional TFT is composed of undoped a-Si. The reason for the doped channel layer is that the electron tunneling occurs through the Schottky barrier. At the same time, this low resistivity channel layer can reduce short-channel effect because of narrow depletion width at source and drain junctions.

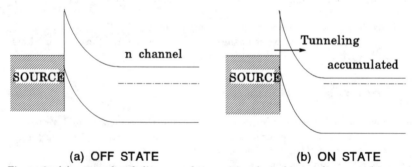

(a) OFF STATE   (b) ON STATE

Figure 2: (a) energy band diagram when positive drain bias and no gate bias are applied, and (b) energy band diagram when positive drain bias and positive gate bias are applied. Tunneling current is controlled by gate bias.

OPERATION OF SBTFT

The operating principle of SBTFT is entirely different from that of conventional TFT. The SBTFT employs tunnel injection of electrons through the source Schottky barrier which can be controlled by gate bias.

Figures 2(a) and (b) show the energy-band diagrams near the source Schottky barrier contact when a positive drain voltage is applied. At zero gate bias as shown in Fig.2(a), electrons can not be injected from the source electrode into the channel region because of the reverse direction of Schottky barrier at the source contact (off-state). When a sufficient positive gate bias is applied, the electric field at the Schottky barrier junction close to the gate insulator is enhanced enough to reduce the barrier width and thus electrons are emitted into the channel layer through the thinned Schottky barrier by tunnel- effect (on-state) as shown in Fig.2(b). SBTFT is expected to have a high transconductance, because tunneling current through Schottky barrier is highly sensitive to the electric field of the Schottky barrier which can largely modified by gate voltage.

SIMULATED DEVICE PERFORMANCES

Simulation Procedure

Two-dimensional simulator VENUS-2D/B (Fuji Research Institute Corporation) which was modified to include Schottky barrier junction was used to demonstrate the characteristics of SBTFT. This simulator can deal with trapped electrons in tail states of a-Si, but, for the simplicity, the effect of tail states was neglected in the present simulation. The electron drift mobility was assumed to be 0.2 $cm^2V^{-1}s^{-1}$. Only electron transport was taken into account, since the SBTT is basically a unipolar device and the hole mobility is smaller by about three orders of magnitude than electron one. The purpose of this simulation is to demonstrate the general characteristics of SBTFT. In order to obtain more elaborate and accurate information, we must consider the various effects such as tail states and hole transport.

Unfortunately, tunneling effect through the Schottky barrier has never been included in an conventional simulator, because few devices have used Schottky contact. We newly added the tunneling function to this simulator. Thermionic emission-diffusion theory[4] was installed in VENUS-2D/B for calculating current at the Schottky contact. The value of 0.04 $Acm^{-2}K^{-2}$[5] was taken for an effective Richardson constant in a-Si. In addition to this current, the tunneling current is newly considered. The tunneling current J_{tunnel} is given by

$$J_{tunnel} = \frac{A^*T^2}{k} \int_0^{\phi_{Bn}} (F_M - F_S) T(\varepsilon) d\varepsilon \qquad (1)$$

where F_M and F_S are the occupation probability in metal and semiconductor, respectively[4]. Assuming a triangular potential barrier, the tunneling probability $T(\varepsilon)$ is given as

$$T(\varepsilon) = \exp\left(-\frac{4(2m^*)^{1/2}(q\phi_{Bn})^{3/2}}{3q\hbar E_s}\right) \qquad (2)$$

where E_s is the electric field of the triangular potential, m^* the tunneling effective mass, $\hbar$ the reduced Planck constant. The details of the simulation procedures will be described elsewhere.

219

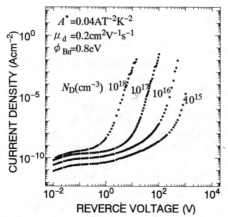

Figure 3: Calculated reverse current – voltage characteristics as a function of donor density.

Figure 3 is an example of the one dimensional simulation of the current–voltage relation in a reverse direction of the Schottky diode. The simulation shows an abrupt increase of the reverse current by tunneling effect, and the threshold voltage to the lower voltage region as the donor density is increased. The increase of the saturation current with increasing doping level is due to lowering of the effective barrier height by tunneling effect.

Figure 4 shows the device configuration used in the simulation. Only the channel region

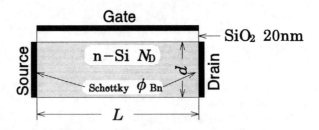

Figure 4: Device configuration used in the simulation

was calculated for reducing of the computing time. The thickness of the gate insulator SiN was fixed to 100 Å for each simulation. This value is desirable to be smaller for high transistor performance, but the thickness here was assumed to be the common value. The channel length was assumed to be 5 μm, which is the limit of the present lithography process on large area. For the boundary condition at the bottom of channel layer, the Neumann free boundary condition was used.

Dependence on barrier height and impurity density

First of all, we discuss the effect of barrier height of Schottky contact and donor den-

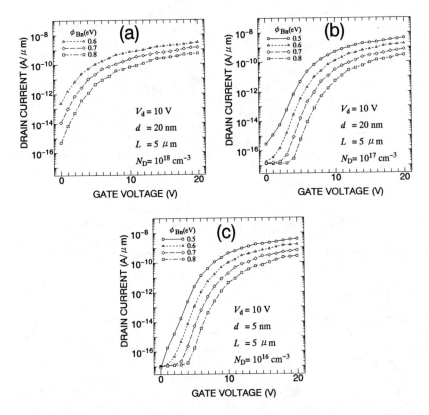

Figure 5: Transfer characteristics as a function of barrier height. (a) $N_D = 10^{18} \text{cm}^{-3}$, (b) $N_D = 10^{17} \text{cm}^{-3}$, (c) $N_D = 10^{16} \text{cm}^{-3}$

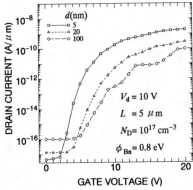

Figure 6: Transfer characteristics as a function of channel layer thickness

sity in channel layer on the gate voltage–drain current characteristics. Figures 5 (a), (b) and (c) show the drain current characteristics when the donor densities are chosen to be $10^{18}, 10^{17}$ and10^{16}cm^{-3}, respectively. The channel thickness is 20 nm for all simulations.

With regard to donor density, higher donor density is more advantagous from the viewpoint of on–current. However, higher barrier height is, however, required to suppress the off–current. The values of the drain current in on–state increase as the barrier height is lowered at each donor density. The off–current, however, also increases when the donor density is high (10^{16}cm^{-3}). Too high barrier height, for example 0.8 eV at 10^{17}cm^{-3}, increases the threshold voltage. After all, depending on the donor density the most suitable barrier height should be selected. For example, when the donor density is 10^{18}cm^{-3}, the 0.6 eV barrier height is the best choice with respect to the threshold voltage and the on/off current ratio.

Dependence on channel thickness

Figure 6 shows the dependence on the channel layer thickness. As can be seen from the figure, thick channel layer gives a poor transfer characteristic and a high threshold voltage. When the thickness is 5 nm, the best characteristics is obtained. This fact also gives an advantage of a high throughput of production, but deposition of such a thin layer may be difficult and results in a poor reliability.

SUMMARY

A new type of TFT with simple fabrication process and with a unique operation principle has been proposed. Schottky contacts at source and drain allow to employ self-align technique and eliminate ion-implantation process necessary for conventional self-align TFT. The 2-D device simulation shows the optimum value of barrier height, donor density and channel layer thickness. At each donor density Schottky contact has a different optimum value the of barrier height. For example, when the donor density is 10^{17}cm^{-3}, the best barrier height is 0.6 eV with respect to the threshold voltage and the on/off current ratio. The thinner layer thickness gives the better performance with respect to the threshold voltage and the on/off current ratio.

ACKNOWLEDGEMENTS

The authors wish to thank Fuji Research Institute Co. for the use of 2–D device simulator (VENUS–2D). This work was partly supported by the grant of Akai foundation.

REFERENCES

1. S.Nishida, H.Uchida, and S.Kaneko, Mat.Res.Soc.Symp.Proc. **219**, 303 (1991).

2. R.Hattori, A.Nakae, and J.Shirafuji, Jpn.J.Appl.Phys. **31**, L1467 (1992).

3. R.Hattori and J.Shirafuji, Jpn.J.Appl.Phys. **33**, 612 (1994).

4. C.R.Crowell and S.M.Sze, Solid State Electron. **9**, 1035 (1966).

5. Y.Mishima, M.Hirose, and Y.Osaka, Jpn.J.Appl.Phys. **20**, 593 (1981).

CHARACTERIZATION OF INORGANIC CONTAMINATION IN LIQUID CRYSTAL DISPLAY MATERIALS USING TOTAL REFLECTION X-RAY FLUORESCENCE (TXRF)

R. S. HOCKETT AND J. M. METZ
Charles Evans & Associates, 301 Chesapeake Drive, Redwood City, CA 94063

ABSTRACT

This work is a feasibility study for using Total reflection X-Ray Fluorescence (TXRF) to characterize inorganic contamination at the surface of, and in, liquid crystal display materials as a function of their processing. Five samples were taken from process steps called: Cr black mask, Cr pattern, RGB pattern, topcoat, and ITO, all on glass substrates. TXRF, a glancing angle XRF technique, is sensitive to inorganic elements and can be used to detect inorganic contamination at surfaces. In addition, increasing the glancing angle can lead to penetration of thin films, and thereby to some qualitative depth information for the detected elements. Elements detected in this study included: Al, Si, S, Cl, In/Sn, Ca, Ba, Cr, Fe, Cu, Ni and Zn.

INTRODUCTION

Inorganic contamination in the manufacture of liquid crystal displays (LCDs) may have an impact on yield or performance. This work is a feasibility study for using Total reflection X-Ray Fluorescence (TXRF) to characterize inorganic contamination at the surface of, and in, liquid crystal display materials as a function of their processing. A parallel feasibility study using TOF-SIMS to detect organic molecular information on the surface of these same samples is reported elsewhere in these proceedings [1].

The TXRF and TOF-SIMS are complementary techniques in that TXRF analyzes the inorganic elements and can detect several nanometers to several microns deep, while TOF-SIMS analyzes molecular (including organic molecules) and inorganic species but only in the top monolayer. Conventional XRF and electron probe techniques can analyze for inorganic contamination but their sample depth is generally several microns deep, so that near surface information in the region of the top few monolayers may be masked. AES and ESCA can analyze the surface top few monolayers, but sensitivity is limited to about 0.1 to 1.0 percent atomic. TXRF can analyze inorganic contamination in the top few monolayers, and for planar silicon samples, for example, the detection limits are about two orders of magnitude more sensitive than AES or ESCA.

In TXRF, x-rays impinge a planar sample at glancing angle, below the angle for total external reflection (about 0.18 degree for silicon or silicon oxide using a 10 keV x-ray source), so that the excitation depth is determined by the shallow penetration of the evanescent wave [2-5]. This penetration depth is typically a few nanometers for angles below the critical angle, and may reach several microns for angles much above the critical angle. A theoretical calculation of the penetration depth versus glancing angle for two x-ray sources (17.5 keV, 8 keV) impinging a planar silicon sample is shown in Figure 1 [6]. The excited fluorescence x-rays from the surface are detected

223

using an energy dispersive spectrometer, typically Si(Li). The analysis area is large, typically 10 mm in diameter, as determined by the area of the detector. By varying the glancing angle, one can qualitatively determine the depth distribution of the contamination.

EXPERIMENTAL

Five LCD samples listed below were analyzed by TXRF. The sample size was 100mm x 100mm. All materials were supported on glass.

#1 Cr Black Mask
#2 Cr Pattern
#3 RGB Pattern
#4 Cr+RGB+T/C
#5 Cr+RGB+T/C+ITO

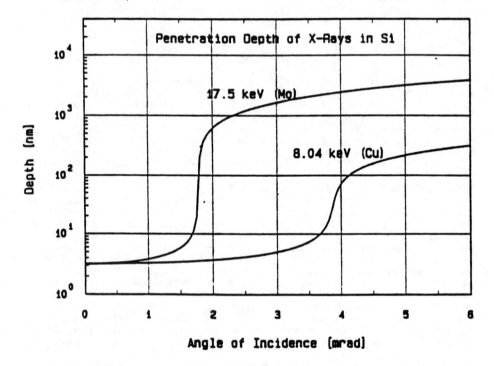

Fig. 1 Penetration depth of the primary X-ray beam in Si as a function of the incident angle for Cu (8.04 keV lower curve) and Mo (17.5 keV upper curve) radiation. [6]

The TXRF measurements were made using a TECHNOS TREX 610T, distributed by Philips Electronics Instruments outside of Japan. The TREX 610T is a dual x-ray source TXRF instrument: 9 kW rotating anode with a tungsten target, and 2 kW tube with a molybdenum target. Monochromators are used to select specific x-ray source lines. The glancing angle is determined by defining a zero angle plane and then using stepper motors to rotate the sample to the desired angle. The glancing angle range is typically 0.01 to 1.0°.

Two types of measurements were made.

TXRF surface analyses were completed under the conditions: 30 kV, 200 mA, W L-beta line source at 9.67 keV, 1000 sec, 0.02 degree glancing angle. The TXRF surface measurement was completed on all five samples and on the backside (at 0.05 degree) of a Sample #1 received at an earlier time. The purpose was to evaluate surface contamination. The backside measurement of Sample #1 provides information on the substrate elements and helps to avoid misinterpretation of the surface contamination.

TXRF anglescans (vary the glancing angle and detect fluorescence x-rays) were completed under the conditions: 30 kV, 30 mA, W L-beta line source, 500 sec, 15 different glancing angles (0.02°, 0.03°, 0.05°, 0.07°, 0.09°, 0.11°, 0.14°, 0.19°, 0.24°, 0.27°, 0.30°, 0.39°, 0.42°, 0.45°, and 0.50°). The instrument performs a new angle calibration for each angle in an anglescan.

The TXRF anglescan measurement was completed on Samples #2 and #5 only. Sample #2 was chosen because it had a surface pattern which may make the TXRF measurement difficult to understand due to scattering of the incident x-rays. Sample #5 was chosen because it had the largest number of layers which may create x-ray wave interference patterns. The purpose was to evaluate whether the TXRF measurement was working properly and to evaluate for any subsurface contamination of high level. Because the anode current is only 30 mA in the anglescan mode, sensitivity to contamination is less than with the surface analysis mode where the current is 200 mA.

RESULTS AND DISCUSSION

TXRF Surface Analysis

The TXRF surface analysis results are summarized in Table 1. The spectra are shown in Figures 2 to 6. There are several important points to note for Table 1. First, quantitative entries have been made in units of 10^{13} atoms/cm^2 (one monolayer of Si is about 100x this, or 10^{15} atoms/cm^2), but the quantitative numbers for the elements may not be accurate because the quantitative model is not valid for this type of sample. We have listed in the table quantitative numbers instead of count rates in order to remove the relative fluorescence yield effects in the comparisons of different elements.

Second, the Sn signal and the In signal in the ITO sample cannot be resolved, so the In reading includes the Sn signal. Third, a blank entry means the element was not detected, but detection limits are difficult to estimate here, because there are some interferences and unusual background signals in some cases. In spite of these caveats, the data show the samples to be very different from each other.

Table 1. TXRF Surface Analysis Results
(units of 10^{13} atoms/cm^2)

Al	Si	S	Cl	In	Ca	Ba	Cr	Fe	Cu	Zn	Ni
#1 CR BLACK MASK											
30	50	9	6		10	6	500	3	0.6	0.7	
#2 CR PATTERN											
200	400		30		80	50	4000			3	
#3 RGB PATTERN											
2000	2000	300	600		40	40	20	3	300		1
#4 CR+RGB+T/C											
	5000	40	60		20	20	40	2	20	3	0.1
#5 CR+RGB+T/C+ITO											
200	400		90	4000			4		1	0.8	

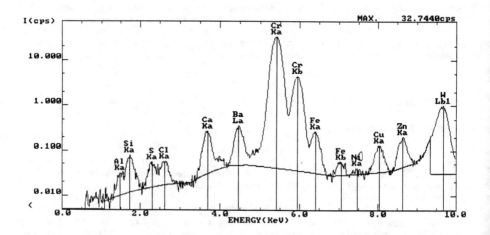

Fig. 2 TXRF spectrum of Sample #1 (Cr black mask)

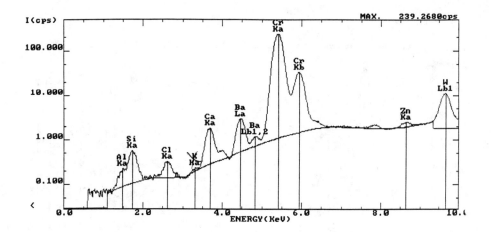

Fig. 3 TXRF spectrum of Sample #2 (Cr pattern)

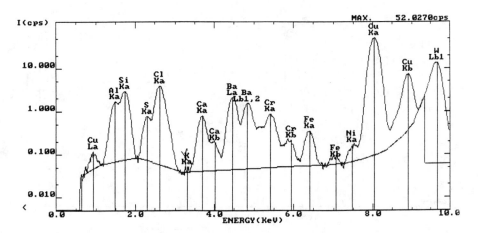

Fig. 4 TXRF spectrum of Sample #3 (Cr+RGB)

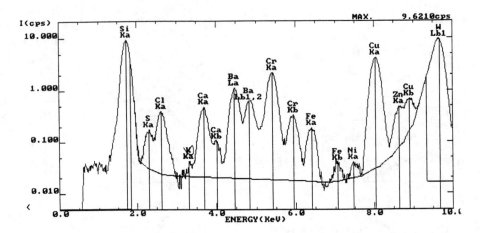

Fig. 5 TXRF spectrum of Sample #4 (Cr+RGB+T/C)

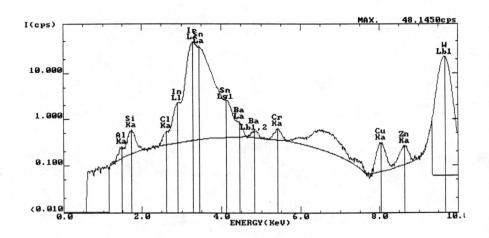

Fig. 6 TXRF spectrum of Sample #5 (Cr+RGB+T/C+ITO)

228

The <u>backside</u> of Sample #1 had signals for Si, Ca, Ba, Zn and a small signal for Fe; the Si, Ca and Ba may be part of the glass substrate and the Zn and Fe may be surface contamination. The <u>frontside</u> of Sample #1 has the Cr, as expected, and we are detecting at least several monolayers deep. There is contamination of Al, S, Cl, Fe, Cu and Zn. We are also picking up signals of Ca, Ba, and Si from the underlying substrate. We did not know the thickness or roughness of the Cr black mask film.

Sample #2 is patterned, which means some of the incident x-rays impinge pattern edge material above the critical angle while other x-rays impinge flat-tops below the critical angle. The x-rays impinging edge contours penetrate deeply into the film, while the others do not. We detect about 10x higher levels of Al, Si, Cl, Ca, Ba, and Cr compared to Sample #1, but we no longer detect Fe or Cu contamination. The Zn contamination for Samples #1 and #2 are about the same. The noted 10x increase in some signals is likely due to the pattern structure, because the x-rays will penetrate deeper on the pattern edges and produce higher signal levels from deeper in the surface. This is particularly evident because of the increased Ba signal, which should only come from the underlying substrate, and the increased Cr signal which means 10x more of the Cr film is being penetrated.

The RGB Sample #3 has higher (10X) levels of Al, Si, and Cl compared to #2. It has high levels of Cu, as was expected from the RGB material. It also has high levels of S contamination, and some Fe and Ni contamination. The reduction in the Cr signal while the Ca and Ba remain the same as Sample #2 is puzzling.

The T/C Sample #4 has high levels of Si but no detectable Al. There is S, Cl, Fe, Ni and Zn contamination, as well as the Cu supposedly from the underlying RGB layer. We are still detecting Ca and Ba, presumably from the substrate, and the same signal of Cr as for Sample #3.

The ITO Sample #5 has the expected In (and Sn) but also Al, Si, Cl, Zn and signals of Cr and Cu which may be subsurface. Ba and Ca signals are masked by the high In and Sn signals.

TXRF Anglescans

The TXRF anglescan of Sample #2 is shown in Figures 7 to 9. In Figure 7 we have plotted the fluorescence signals in counts per second (not quantitative) for the major constituent elements Ca, Ba, Cr, Zn and Si. In Figures 8 and 9 we have plotted fluorescence signals for the contamination elements Al and Cl respectively.

Our interpretation of these anglescans for Sample #2 is as follows. The fast rise in the Cr signal around 0.07 degree is indicative of total reflection occurring on the surface of the Cr film. As the angle is increased, the Cr film is penetrated, and the Cr signal slowly reduces. This anglescan of Cr is representative of a thin Cr film. The Cl signal follows the Cr signal (except at about 0.23 degree) and therefore appears to be contamination in the Cr film. If the Cl were only on the surface of the Cr film, we would expect the Cl signal to drop sharply by a factor of 2X around 0.10° to 0.14° and then level off.

The Ca, Ba, Si, Zn and Al anglescans are similar to each other and suggest these elements are similarly located in another film of higher electron density than the Cr film, because the rise in signals is at a higher angle than for the Cr. The conclusion that there is a film is due to the drop in signals at the higher angles (greater than 0.25 degree).

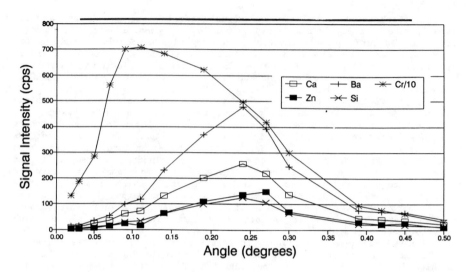

Fig. 7 TXRF anglescan for Sample #2 (Cr pattern): Ca, Ba, Cr, Zn and Si.

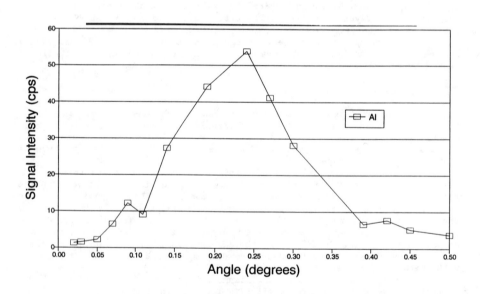

Fig. 8 TXRF anglescan for Sample #2 (Cr pattern): Al.

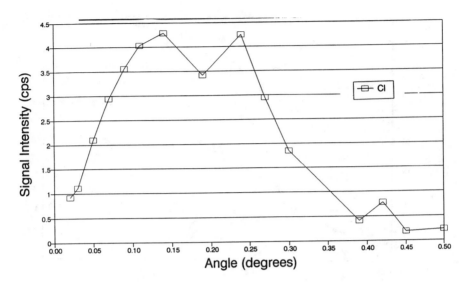

Fig. 9 TXRF anglescan for Sample #2 (Cr pattern): Cl.

        Since we did not expect there to be a second <u>film</u> (Ca, Ba, Zn, Si, Al)
but expected these elements (at least the Ca and Ba) to make up the bulk
substrate, we have tried to look for another explanation for the drop in
signal above 0.25 degree. One possible explanation is a count rate effect on
the detector efficiency due to a rise in deadtime at the higher angles
(plotted in Figure 10). We do not have experience with this effect on the
TREX 610T. Normally, our anglescans at the high angles are dominated by the
Si signal from the bulk Si wafer and the fluorescence yield of Si is low
enough to not reach these high dead times. One way to check this possible
explanation would be to run the anglescan of this sample at a lower anode
current, however, the samples are no longer available.
        The TXRF anglescan of Sample #5 is shown in Figures 11 and 12. In
Figure 11 we have plotted the fluorescence signals for the major constituent
elements Si, In, Cr, Cu and Zn. In Figure 12 we have plotted fluorescence
signals for the elements Al and Cl. A deadtime versus angle plot is shown in
Figure 10.
        Our interpretation of these anglescans is as follows. The ITO film is
shown by the rise and drop of the In signal. (Note the Sn signal is included
in the In signal because we cannot resolve them.) The ITO film may be rough
because we do not see a sharp rise in In signal indicative of a clear x-ray
reflection transition. As the x-rays finally penetrate the ITO film, there is
a second reflection occurring off the Cr subsurface film, shown by the rise
and inflection of the Cr signal at high angles. The Cu and Zn signals do not
track the Cr signal, and the Si signal tracks none of the others. The Al
signal is also complex. The Cl appears to be in the ITO film, with possibly
some segregation toward the surface of the ITO film. Sample #5 is a very
complex sample for TXRF anglescan because of the multiple layers and the
possibility of multiple reflections of the x-rays.

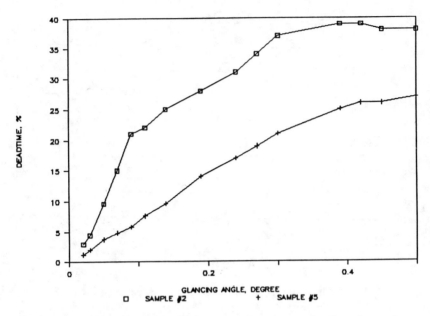

Fig. 10 Si(Li) detector dead-time versus glancing angle for the anglescans of Sample #2 and Sample #5.

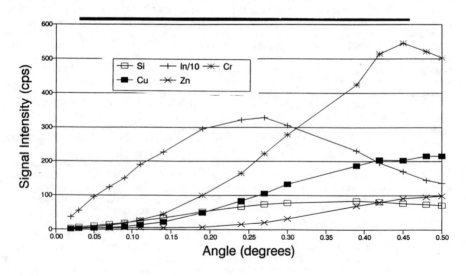

Fig. 11 TXRF anglescan for Sample #5 (Cr+RGB+T/C+ITO): Si, In, Cr, Cu and Zn.

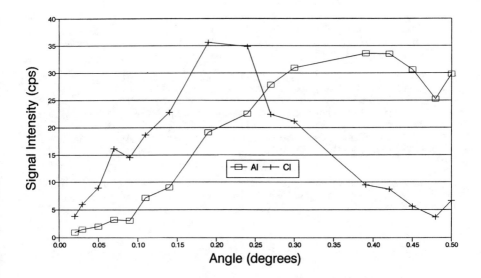

Fig. 12 TXRF anglescan for Sample #5 (Cr+RGB+T/C+ITO): Al and Cl.

One point of interest is that the Cr, Al, Cu, and Zn signals do not drop off at the higher angles. The deadtime for this sample remains below 30% at all angles as shown in Figure 10, so we do not expect there is a deadtime problem.

CONCLUSIONS

We conclude it is possible to perform TXRF on large LCD samples and to detect inorganic contamination. Interpretation and quantification are possible if the samples are planar; interpretation is difficult and qualitative for patterned samples. Layers of films result in more difficulty in interpretation.

We add that if there were particulate contamination on the surface of one of the LCD samples and if the particulate contamination had elements detectable by TXRF, then we think TXRF could indicate the particulate nature of the contamination. The contaminants detected in this study did not appear to be particulates.

References

[1] J. J. Lee, P. M. Lindley and R. W. Odom, "Surface Analysis of LCD Materials in Various Stages of Production by Time-of-Flight Secondary Ion Mass Spectrometry (TOF-SIMS)," this Materials Research Society Symposium, San Francisco, April 1994.

[2] R. S. Hockett, "High Sensitivity Characterization of Contamination on Silicon Surfaces Using TXRF," IES 1993 Proceedings Volume 1, published by Institute of Environmental Sciences (Mount Prospect, IL), pp. 432-459, (1993).

[3] A. Iida, K. Sakurai, A. Yoshinaga, and Y. Goshi, "Grazing incidence X-ray fluorescence analysis," Nuclear Instruments and Methods in Physics Research, A246, 736 (1986).

[4] R. S. Hockett, "TXRF Semiconductor Applications," Advances in X-Ray Analysis, Vol. 37, Plenum Press (1994)

[5] P. Eichinger, H. J. Rath and H. Schwenke, "Application of Total Reflection X-Ray Fluorescence Analysis for Metallic Trace Impurities on Silicon Wafer Surfaces," Semiconductor Fabrication: Technology and Metrology, ASTM STP 990, D. Gupta editor, American Society for Testing and Materials, pp. 305-313 (1989).

[6] U. Weisbrod, R. Gutschke, J. Knoth, and H. Schwenke, "X-ray fluorescence spectrometry at grazing incidence for quantitative surface and layer analysis," Fresenius J Anal Chem, 341, pp. 83-86, (1991).

STRUCTURAL, OPTICAL AND ELECTRONIC PROPERTIES
OF SEMI-INSULATING TIN OXIDE THIN FILMS

A. DE ACUTIS, M. C. ROSSI and M. BARBETTI
Dipartimento di Ingegneria Elettronica, Università di Roma "La Sapienza", Via Eudossiana 18,
00184 Roma, Italy.

ABSTRACT

Bismuth doped SnO_2 films with reproducible optical and electronic properties were deposited by spray-pyrolysis on quartz and glass substrates. Deposition temperatures in the range 300°C-360°C were selected and resistivity values in the range 10^4-$10^{11}\Omega$/square were obtained. Scanning Electron Microscope (SEM) analysis and X-ray diffractometry showed that samples grown at low temperature are amorphous, while at higher deposition temperature the material structure becomes microcrystalline. The spectral transmittance of the films was measured in the UV-VIS range. The absorption coefficients were interpreted to give values of both direct and indirect band gap. The slope of Tauc's plot, which is commonly related to the degree of disorder in the material, confirmed the SEM observations. Conduction mechanisms were also studied through resistivity measurements as a function of deposition temperature. Results obtained for undoped tin oxide were also investigated for comparison.

INTRODUCTION

Conductive tin oxide films have been extensively studied and are widely used as transparent electrodes in various optoelectronic devices such as photovoltaic cells and liquid crystal panels. Moreover, semi-insulating SnO_2 films are used for gas sensing devices and can be adopted to build both new liquid crystal panels with invisible interpixel gaps, and new cells based on oblique electric fields. Tin oxide films have been prepared by various techniques like sputtering [1], chemical vapour deposition [2], spray-pyrolysis [3], vacuum evaporation [4] and by dc glow discharge [5]. The properties of the films have been found to depend strongly on the mode of preparation. Among these, spray pyrolysis is one of the best suited to obtain good film uniformity on large area substrates. Its cost effectiveness also constitute a great economic advantage. Undoped tin oxide is a n-type semiconductor, due to the presence of oxygen vacancies which forms a donor level within the band gap [6]. Most of the scientific literature on spray deposited tin oxide films deals with doping by fluorine [7] and antimony [8], which provides additional electrons in this n-type semiconductor thereby leading to an increase of the electrical conductivity. We tried to obtain semi-insulating tin oxide films with sheet resistance in the range 10^6-$10^7\Omega$/square, transparent and stable up to 200°C.

In this paper we report the structural, electrical and optical properties of undoped and bismuth doped tin oxide thin films, deposited at different temperatures in the range 300-360°C.

EXPERIMENTAL

The films were deposited on glass and quartz substrates by spray-pyrolysis,on a hot plate held at temperatures ranging between 300-360°C. The substrate temperature during the spray process was maintained constant within ±5°C by a temperature controller. A solution of stannic chloride in isopropilalchol was sprayed by using compressed air as carrier gas. For bismuth doping, one tenth in weight of the stannic chloride was replaced by an equal weight of bismuth chloride. The thickness of the film was measured by a Talystep instrument and confirmed by ellipsometry. All the measured samples had the same thickness of 1550±60Å.

Structural analysis were carried out using the X-ray diffraction technique, Co60 as radiation source with λ=1.78892Å, and the surface morphology of the film was performed by scanning

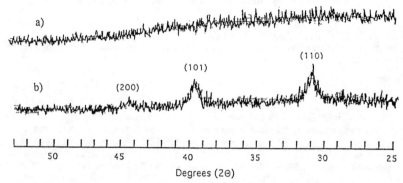

Fig.1. X-ray diffraction spectra of Bi doped SnO_2 films. Deposition temperatures:
a) 300°C , b) 350°C

electron microscopy (SEM). SnO_2 films were characterized for electrical properties by sheet resistance measurements. Temperature dipendence of resistivity was also measured in a vacuum of 10^{-3} Torr. The optical characterization was carried out by trasmittance measurement in the UV-VIS wavelength range by a Perkin Elmer dual beam spectraphotometer.

STRUCTURAL PROPERTIES

Fig.1a and 1b shows the diffraction spectra of bismuth doped tin oxide films, grown at 300°C and 350°C respectively, versus X-ray incident angle (Θ). At the lowest deposition temperature diffraction peaks are completely absent, due to the amorphous structure of films. On the contrary they appear at higher temperature for $\Theta_1 = 15.5°$, $\Theta_2 = 19.8°$ and $\Theta_3 = 22.1°$. Using the relationship

$$\lambda = 2d\sin(\Theta) \qquad (1)$$

where d is the distance between two contigous reticular planes, we obtain $d_1 = 3.1$Å, $d_2 = 2.634$Å and $d_3 = 2.370$Å. These values correspond to the distance between (110) planes, (101) planes and (200) planes of SnO_2. Correspondently, a structural change from amorphous to microcrystalline takes place in the material. This structural change is further confirmed by scanning electron micrographs as shown in Fig.2 for doped and undoped tin oxide films, prepared at three different substrate temperature, 300°C, 330°C and 360°C respectively. At the lower deposition temperature the surface topography is smooth and homogeneous, due to the amorphous nature of the material. With increasing deposition temperatures films become microcrystalline; further increase of the deposition temperature only produces an enlargment of the grain size up to a dimension of 1000Å. Comparing doped and undoped surface topography of the films, incorporation of bismuth seems to lead to an appreciable increase of the grain size.

OPTICAL PROPERTIES

For the determination of the fundamental absorption edge of undoped and doped films, which lies in ultraviolet range, only the films deposited on quartz substrates could be used. The spectral dependence of the absorption coefficient α of these films near the ultraviolet range has been

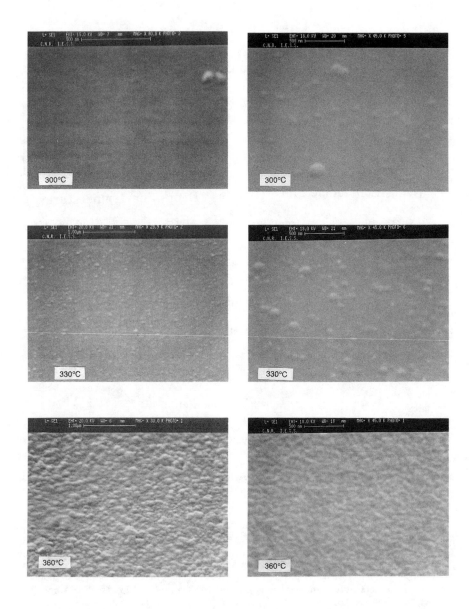

Fig.2. SEM micrographs of Bi doped and undoped SnO$_2$ films grown at 300°C, 330°C and 360°C. Left column refers to doped films while right column refers to undoped ones.

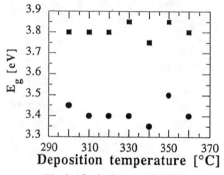

Fig.3. Optical gap of Bi doped SnO$_2$ films versus deposition temperature. Squares refer to the direct band gap from α^2 plots, circles to the indirect band gap from Tauc's plots.

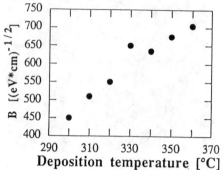

Fig.4. Value of B versus deposition temperature for Bi doped SnO$_2$ films.

computed from transmission data. The nature of the transition involved can be determined on the basis of the dependence of α on the photon energy hv. For amorphous films, due to the loss of the selection rules for the wavevector k, it is not possible to distinguish between direct and undirect transitions. Instead, the optical band gap E_g of amorphous and mycrocristalline films is often determined according to Tauc's relationship [9]

$$(\alpha h v)^{1/2} = B(h v - E_g) \qquad (2)$$

where B is a constant. For microcrystalline films, also direct transition can be considered and the energy gap can be evaluated according to the relationship:

$$\alpha^2 = C(h v - E_g) \qquad (3)$$

where C is a constant.Values of the gap can be derived extrapolating the linear portion of the $(\alpha h v)^{1/2}$ and α^2 vs hv plots to $\alpha = 0$. The corresponding results are shown in Fig.3 for bismuth doped samples. Both direct and indirect band gap do not change with the deposition temperature, their values being in agreement with those reported in literature [10] Fig.4 depicts the obtained values of the costant B versus deposition temperature. As reported in Fig.4, B is an increasing function of the deposition temperature, going from 450(cm eV)$^{-1/2}$ to about 700(cm eV)$^{-1/2}$. Although the physical meaning of B is still controversial, its value has been related to the inverse width of conducting tail states [11], which in turn depend to the amount of structural and compositional disorder. According to this interpretation the two-fold observed increase of B could be due to the decreased structural disorder which takes place when the deposition temperature is raised. This trend confirms the SEM and X-ray diffraction results, previously reported in Fig.1 and Fig.3.

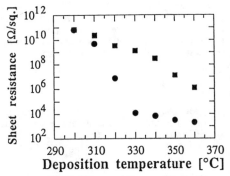

Fig.5. Sheet resistance of SnO₂ film versus deposition temperature. Squares refer to Bi doped films, circles refer to undoped ones.

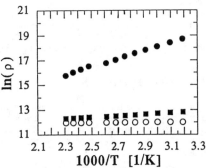

Fig.6. Resistivity versus temperature for Bi doped SnO₂. Temperature deposition of samples: black circles 310°C, black squares 340°C, white circles 360°C.

ELECTRICAL PROPERTIES

Fig.5 shows resistivity values as a function of deposition temperature for undoped and bismuth doped samples. In the case of undoped SnO₂, the electrical properties of the films would depend on the quality of the material, stoichiometry and structural properties while, for bismuth doped films, the electrical contribution of doping should be observable. Actually, in both cases a gradual decrease of the resistivity occurs when raising the deposition temperature from 300°C to 360°C.

More details on the transport properties can be gained by studying the resistivity dependence on temperature, which can be described according to the following relationship:

$$\rho = \rho_0 \, e^{\, E_i/KT} \qquad (4)$$

where K is the Boltzmann factor and E_i is the activation energy. It can be related to (E_C-E_F), i.e. to the energy difference between the conduction band edge E_C and the Fermi level E_F. Measurements were performed in the range 40°C-150°C and Fig.6 shows the results, for bismuth doped SnO₂ films grown at 310°C, 340°C and 360°C. We can find the value of E_i from the slope of the plots, ln(ρ) versus 1000/T. For samples deposited at low temperature, the resistivity decreases with temperature giving an activation energy of 0.3eV. This value of E_i corresponds to the donor level of the oxygen vacancies [12]. As the deposition temperature increase, the temperature dependence disappears, giving a value of E_i close to zero and a conductivity metallic in character. In fact, increasing the deposition temperature the number of oxygen vacancies also increase till to form a shallow donor band overlapping with the fundamental conduction band.

CONCLUSION

Undoped and bismuth doped tin oxide thin films have been deposited by spray-pyrolysis at a temperature within the range 300°C-360°C. Their structural, optical and electronic properties have been investigated as a function of deposition temperature.

We suggest that, in the selected temperature range, bismuth does not behave as substitutional impurity. The higher resistivity for doped versus undoped film could then be interpreted as a result of the incresead compositional disorder, leading to poorer transport properties. Anyway, the decrease of resistivity with deposition temperature is in good agreement with the observed structural change from an amorphous film structure to a mycrocristalline one, SEM and X-ray spectroscopy. Moreover, from the electrical point of view, this behaviour can also be attribuited to the increase in number of oxygen vacancies, which determine an increase of carrier concentration, but no effect of compensation can be seen. In order to better understand the effect of bismuth doping on SnO_2, further investigation on carrier concentration and mobility are necessary.

ACKNOWLEDGMENTS

The authors are truly indebted towards Prof. P. Maltese, of the Department of Electronic Engineering, University of Rome "La Sapienza", for helpful discussion and support and towards Ing. A. Bearzotti, of the C.N.R.-I.E.S.S., for SEM micrographs and X-ray diffraction measurements. Finally, special thanks are due to Ing. F. Sciarra for helping in samples deposition.

REFERENCES

[1] B. Stjerna and C. G. Granqvist, Sol. Energy Mater. **20**, 225 (1990)
[2] S. Raghunatah Reddy, A. K. Malik, and S. R. Jawalekar, Thin Solid Films **143**, 113 (1986)
[3] Chitra Agashe, M. G. Takwale, B. R. Marathe, and V. G. Bhide, Sol. Energy Mater. **17**, 99 (1988)
[4] H. Watanabe, Jpn. J. Appl. Phys. **9**, 1551 (1970)
[5] D. E. Carlson, J. Electrochem. Soc. **122**, 1334 (1975)
[6] J. A. Aboaf, V. C. Marcotte, and N. J. Chou, J. Electrochem. Soc. **120**, 701 (1973)
[7] J. Bruneax, H. Cachet, M. Forment, and A. Messad, Thin Solid Films **197**, 129 (1991)
[8] A. I. Oniya and C. E. Okeke, J. Phys. D: Appl. Phys. **22**, 1515 (1889)
[9] J. Tauc, R. Grigorovici, A. Vancu, Phys. Stat. Sol., **15**, 627 (1966).
[10] E. Shanti, V. Dutta, A. Banerjee, and K. L. Chopra, J. Appl. Phys. **51**, 6243 (1980)
[11] J. Bullot and M. P. Schmidt, Phys. Stat. Sol. (b), 143 (1987)
[12] E. Leja, Acta Physica Polonica, **A38**, 165 (1970)

TRANSPARENT CONDUCTING FILMS OF GaInO₃ BY SPUTTERING

J. KWO, S. A. CARTER, R. J. CAVA, S. Y. HOU, J. M. PHILLIPS,
D. H. RAPKINE, G. A. THOMAS, and R. B. VAN DOVER
AT&T Bell Laboratories, Murray Hill, NJ 07974.

ABSTRACT

One of the critical components used in the display device is the transparent conducting electrode. A new candidate for the transparent conductor, GaInO₃ containing a tetrahedrally coordinated Ga site was identified recently, and shows good promise of improved optical transmission in the blue wavelength over ITO due to a high band gap ~3.3 eV. Thin films of GaInO₃ with cation dopants Ge for Ga, and Sn for In, respectively, have been prepared using dc reactive magnetron sputtering. Among the growth parameters, oxygen partial pressure plays the decisive role in affecting the film quality. A post-anneal in H_2-rich atmosphere at 300C effectively reduced the oxygen content and lowered the resistivity to ~3.0 mΩ-cm; however, the final resistivity appears to be insensitive to cation dopant concentrations. Concurrently, Hall measurements indicated a carrier concentration in the mid 10^{19} range for all films. Our structural analysis by x-ray and SEM has suggested that a limited Sn solubility in the film to less than 5 %. Doping appears to be due both to oxygen vacancies and aliovalent ion substitutions. The optical transmission of this new material is indeed superior to ITO over the entire visible spectrum, especially in the green and blue wavelengths. More work is underway to identify appropriate dopants for attaining better film conductivity.

INTRODUCTION

Transparent conductors have been used as one important component as the transparent electrode in liquid crystal display (LCD). Generally speaking, optical transparency and metallic conductivity are the properties of solids virtually in antinomy. There are, however, a few materials which do share both properties simultaneously. The most widely known example is tin doped indium oxide (ITO).[1] Materials of improved transparency or better conductivity than those commercially available are now in demand in order to develop high performance photoelectronic devices. For instance, in the development of large area, colored, active matrix liquid crystal displays (AMLCD), low surface resistivity and high transparency of visible lights are required for full color and rapid response.

241

One major drawback of the ITO materials is the much reduced transparency less than 50% at green and blue lights due to a band gap of only 2.7 eV. Identification of new materials with a band gap of at least 3.3 eV or larger is expected to improve greatly the transmission of blue light and the overall optical performance. Furthermore, typical ITO films have a sheet resistance of 30-50 $\Omega/\square$ for 1000 Å thick films which satisfies the 50 $\Omega/\square$ requirement for thin film transistor technology currently used in AMLCD. However, future designs of the color filter panel will require a sheet resistance as low as 1 $\Omega/\square$. This cannot be accomplished simply by increasing the thickness of the ITO, since the thicker film would have unacceptably poor transmission characteristics. These challenging goals thus call for materials research to identify new candidates of n-type wide band gap semiconductors. Ueda et al. recently reported that several spinel oxides with a band gap near 3.5 eV showed substantially better optical transparency than ITO and quite reasonable electrical conductivity.[2]

In this work, we report our efforts of synthesizing $GaInO_3$ thin films by using dc magnetron sputtering.[3,4] We present the results of film growth, transport, and optical characterizations. Films of greatly improved optical transmission in green and blue lights than ITO have been demonstrated. The film conductivity is comparable to the bulk materials data, and satisfies the 50 $\Omega/\square$ requirement if thick films can be used.

GROWTH

$GaInO_3$ is a recently identified transparent conductive material by Cava et al.[5] It has a β $GaInO_3$ layered structure with the Ga site tetrahedrally coordinated and the In site octahedrally coordinated as shown in Figure 1. Aliovalent elements such as Ge or Sn substituting Ga or In with typical concentrations less than 20 % were introduced as n-type dopants. Additional doping from oxygen vacancies also contributes to the overall conductivity reaching as high as 300 $(\Omega-cm)^{-1}$ in bulk polycrystalline form. The high band gap of 3.3 eV leads to superior light transmission, particularly in the blue wavelength region of the visible spectrum, and enhanced index matching with glass substrates used in the flat panel displays.

The sputtering targets employed for film growth were prepared by standard ceramic processing methods described previously.[5] $GaInO_3$ films nominally doped with Sn varying from 5 to 15 % on the In site (denoted as IGTO films) were deposited by dc reactive sputtering using both on-axis and off-axis sputtering configurations. The placement of substrates outside the plasma plume in the so-

Figure 1 The crystal structure of GaInO$_3$ showing a β Ga$_2$O$_3$ structure.

-called 90° off-axis geometry avoids the bombardment of negative oxygen ions and gives tighter control of the stoichiometry, resulting in better film conductivity. However, it also tends to yield a higher degree of thickness nonuniformity than the on-axis sputtering configuration. The total pressure (Ar + O$_2$) during growth is kept in the range of 5 - 10 in both cases. Our studies have shown that the oxygen partial pressure during growth plays the most critical role in governing the phase stability and film quality. The optimal O$_2$ pressure is about 0.5 - 1.0 mTorr. Higher O$_2$ partial pressure produces transparent, yet more resistive films, indicative of underdoping. In contrast, depositions in pure Argon pressure with no O$_2$ added yield black insulating films due to formation of other oxygen deficient phases. Crystalline films of the correct phase form even at room temperature; however, as-grown films with the lowest resistivity are usually obtained at substrate temperatures in the range of 350-400 C. After growth, post anneals in formic gas flow (15% H$_2$ +85% N$_2$) at 300C for 4-5 hours are found to reduce the film resistivity effectively.

CHARACTERIZATIONS

Sample characterizations were carried out including the optical, transport properties, and microstructures. Transmittance spectra of GaInO$_3$ films have been measured for films of various Sn doping concentrations under a variety of deposition conditions. As shown by representative spectra in Figure 2, the absorption coefficients in the far-infrared and the visible spectra of IGTO films are indeed much lower than typical commercial ITO films. The low absorption in the green and blue portion of the spectrum of IGTO is due to the large band gap near

3.3 eV. The weak absorption in the far infrared is due to smaller carrier numbers corresponding to a low dc conductivity of IGTO. In general, films with higher dc conductivity show consistently higher optical absorption. The transmittance spectrum exhibits Fabry-Perot oscillations that allow a determination of the index of refraction as 1.65. The enhanced matching of the index of refraction with the glass substrate (n ~ 1.5) compared to the ITO case (n ~ 2.0) offers the advantage of reducing the reflection loss at the interface with the glass.

The temperature-dependent resistivity as well as the room temperature Hall constant were measured by the standard four-probe method. The film conductivity was maximized by post H_2 anneal, and the degree of improvement depends on the initial oxygen content in the films. However, the final resistivity tends to saturate at ~ 3.0 mΩ-cm comparable to the bulk samples, and appears to be insensitive to the exact cation (Sn) dopant content as shown in Figure 3. The removal of oxygen through reduction thus has a larger effect on the conductivity than changing the concentration of a cation dopant. The temperature coefficient of resistivity (TCR) is slightly positive below 300K, indicating the weakly metallic nature of the material. Below about 120K the TCR changes sign, which may reflect either localization or inhomogeneity (e.g., increased resistivity at grain boundaries). In contrast, the resistivity of typical ITO films is about one order of magnitude lower, and shows stronger metallic temperature dependence.

The sign of the Hall constant is negative in all samples indicating electron conduction, as expected for oxygen-vacancy doping or Sn, Ge doping. Typical carrier densities inferred from the Hall constant vary from mid 10^{19} to low 10^{20} cm^{-3}, about one order of magnitude lower than the expected value~mid 10^{21}cm^{-3} based on the nominal metal cation compositions. The absence of systematic dependence of the magnitude of the Hall constant with the nominal cation dopant stoichiometry suggests that the presence of oxygen vacancies with concentration depending on synthetic conditions could be the principle source responsible for the n-type charge carriers. Moreover, it is conceivable that some compensation mechanisms exist and that tend to trap free carriers.

The cause for the ineffective doping of $GaInO_3$ by the metal dopant like Sn may be related to the lowered Sn solubility in the materials as evidenced in scanning electron microscopy (SEM). The film morphology of $GaInO_3$ appeared to be very smooth on the 1 μm scale, although the precipitate density is notably high for films with Sn dopant contents greater than 5 %. In comparison, ITO films with 20 % Sn doping showed little evidence of precipitates. In addition, the tendency toward dopant segregation increases drastically with the relative Ga ratio to In in the pseudo binary $Ga_{1+x}In_{1-x-y}Sn_yO_3$ compound. The results suggest

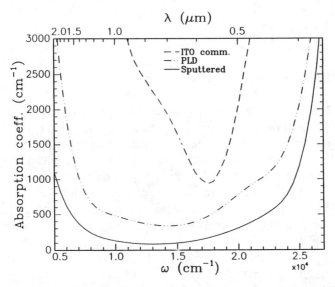

Figure 2 Absorption coefficients of an off-axis sputtered film with $\sigma \sim 170 \ (\Omega\text{–cm})^{-1}$, a pulsed laser deposited[3] film with $\sigma \sim 280 \ (\Omega\text{–cm})^{-1}$, and a commercial $In_{0.8}Sn_{0.2}O_3$ film with $\sigma \sim 2000 \ (\Omega\text{–cm})^{-1}$.

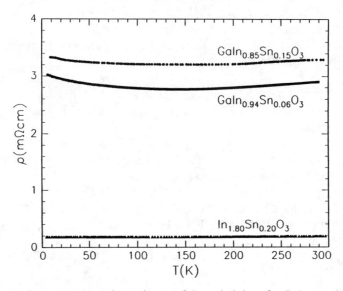

Figure 3 Temperature dependence of dc resistivity of a $GaIn_{0.95}Sn_{0.06}O_3$, a $GaIn_{0.85}Sn_{0.15}O_3$, and a $In_{1.80}Sn_{0.2}O_3$ films.

that the cation doping by Sn in $GaInO_3$ may have a solubility limit less than 5 % as opposed to 20 % in In_2O_3 , and such reduction may arise from tetrahedral coordination of the Ga site.

CONCLUSIONS

In summary, our thin film synthesis by the sputtering technique has demonstrated that $GaInO_3$ is a promising candidate for transparent conductors. The optical transmission characteristics are significantly better than those of ITO throughout the visible spectrum. The n-type carriers result mainly from oxygen vacancies, and some come from substitution of aliovalent elements such as Ge or Sn. Further research is needed to identify effective dopants for the Ga site to increase total carrier concentrations. Although our research was motivated initially by technological needs, our present findings have · suggested new scientific opportunities of investigating the doping issues for wide band gap semiconductors in order to achieve decent metallic conductivity, while preserving the already excellent optical transparency.

REFERENCES

1. For a review, see G. Haacke, Ann. Rev. Mater. Sci. **7**, 73 (1977); C. G. Granqvist, Appl. Phys. A. **52**, 83 (1991), and references therein.

2. N. Ueda, T. Omata, N. Hikuma, K. Ueda, H. Mizoguchi, T. Hashimoto, and H. Kawazoe, Appl. Phys. Lett, **62**, 499, (1993), and references therein.

3. J. M. Phillips, J. Kwo, G. A. Thomas, S. A Carter, R. J. Cava, S. Y. Hou, J. J. Krajewski, J. H. Marshall, W. F Peck, D. H. Rapkine, and R. B. van Dover, Appl. Phys. Lett, (submitted).

4. J. Kwo, G. A. Thomas, S. A. Carter, R. J. Cava, S. Y. Hou, J. M. Phillips, D. H. Rapkine, and R. B. van Dover (in preparation).

5. R. J. Cava, J. M. Phillips, J. Kwo, G. A. Thomas, R. B. van Dover, S. A. Carter, J. J Krajewski, W. F. Peck, Jr., J. H. Marshall, and D. H. Rapkine, Appl. Phys. Lett. (submitted).

MECHANISMS OF LIQUID CRYSTAL ALIGNMENT ON BUFFED POLYIMIDE SURFACES

HIROTSUGU KIKUCHI, J. A. LOGAN, AND DO Y. YOON
IBM Research Division, Almaden Research Center, 650 Harry Road, San Jose,
California 95120-6099

ABSTRACT

The surfaces of poly(amic acid) and cured polyimide films, subjected to different buffing and cure profiles, have been examined by atomic force microscopy (AFM). The ability of these buffed polymer surfaces to align nematic and chiral smectic C liquid crystals were also investigated. These studies show that the presence of microgrooves on buffed polymer surfaces are not necessary for alignment of liquid crystals. Rather, it is concluded that the liquid crystal alignment is mainly caused by the anisotropic intermolecular interactions between liquid crystal molecules and the polymer chains oriented by buffing. For the alignment of smectics, both the degree of order and mechanical properties of polyimide films are found to be important factors.

INTRODUCTION

Uniform alignment of liquid crystals over a large area is essential to the fabrication of flat panel liquid crystal display devices. It is well known that the direction of average molecular orientation, the so-called "director", of a liquid crystal phase can be controlled by a proper treatment of surfaces in contact with the liquid crystal.[1] Unidirectionally rubbed or buffed polymer surfaces can strongly anchor the director to a specific direction in the surface plane. Such a buffing technique has been put to practical use for liquid crystal display devices in order to achieve a homogeneous or twisted alignment.

Two possible mechanisms why the buffed polymer surface provides good alignment of nematic directors have been proposed. One is based on microgrooves[2-5] and the other is on the oriented polymer molecules.[6-8] However, the detailed physical mechanisms controlling the alignment of liquid crystal molecules are not understood yet. In this paper, a detailed investigation of the morphology of buffed polyimide surfaces by the atomic force microscopy (AFM) is presented, and a possible mechanism of buffing-induced alignment for nematic and chiral smectic C liquid crystal molecules is discussed.

EXPERIMENTAL

For the preparation of the poly(p-phenylene biphenyltetracarboximide) (BPDA-PDA) films, the precursor BPDA-PDA poly(amic acid) solution ("PYRALIN" PI-5810D from DuPont Co.) was dissolved in N-methylpyrrolidone. The solution was filtered through a 1 μm Teflon filter and spin-coated onto a Si-wafer or a glass plate. The coated films were roughly dried in the air at 350 K for 30 min, and then further dried in vacuum overnight at 350 K. The thermal conversion of the poly(amic acid) to polyimide, as shown schematically in Figure 1, was performed at 670 K for one hour under nitrogen. The film thickness was from 50 to 100 nm.

247

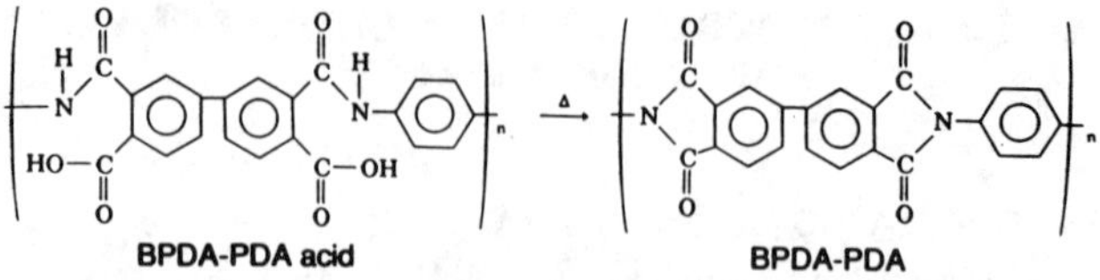

Figure 1. Schematics of BPDA-PDA poly(amic acid) and polyimide.

4-cyano 4'-pentyl biphenyl (5CB, Aldrich) and CS-1016 (Chisso Co.) were used as a nematic and chiral smectic C phase materials, respectively. 5CB exhibits phase transitions from crystal to nematic at 296.6 K and from nematic to isotropic at 308.3 K. CS-1016 shows phase transitions from crystal to chiral smectic C, chiral smectic C to smectic A, smectic A to chiral nematic and chiral nematic to isotropic at 252.1, 328.7, 340.2 and 345.3 K, respectively.

The buffing was carried out by pressing the sample down onto a rayon cloth under 2 or 20 g/cm^2 load, and the cloth was moved unidirectionally over a known distance, usually 300 cm, at a velocity of 1 cm/s. The surface of cloth used was covered with velour-like brush made of many fibers with the length, diameter and fiber density of 1.3 mm, 15 μm and 90 fibers/mm^2, respectively.

Atomic force microscopy (AFM) was carried out with NanoScope III from Digital Instruments, using the normal scanning mode as well as the tapping mode. Practically identical images were obtained for both modes, thereby assuring that the polymer surfaces were not damaged by the scanning AFM probes.

In order to evaluate the alignment of liquid crystals, cells made of a pair of buffed substrates were assembled with buffing axes parallel to each other. Cell gaps were set at about 6 μm and 2 μm by using PET film spacer for 5CB and CS-1016, respectively. The alignment of liquid crystals sandwiched by buffed polymer surfaces was investigated by polarizing microscopic observations.

RESULTS AND DISCUSSION

Mechanical and Thermal Properties of Polyimide and Rayon

Figure 2 shows a dynamic mechanical response of the BPDA-PDA film, prepared by thermal imidization of precursor, BPDA-PDA acid, on a glass substrate. The BPDA-PDA film exhibits a high modulus (about 10 GPa) near room temperature. The relaxation at 600 K reflects a some softening of the material, but the films still remains pretty solidlike above this transition. The melting point or flow temperature of BPDA-PDA is higher than the thermal decomposition temperature. The BPDA-PDA is, namely, a high modulus and heat-resistant polymer material. On the other hand, the mechanical modulus and thermal stability of the rayon cloth used to rub the BPDA-PDA surface are much lower than those of BPDA-PDA. The rayon used in this study has a melting point around 370 K and decomposes completely upon heating at 670 K.

Therefore, it is very surprising that the BPDA-PDA surface buffed by the rayon cloth provides a good alignment for nematics even after the buffed BPDA-PDA has been annealed at 670 K for one hour. Some rayon may be deposited on the BPDA-PDA surface by buffing since it is softer than BPDA-PDA. However, the above observation suggests that the rayon deposited on the BPDA-PDA surface does not contribute to the nematic alignment, but the BPDA-PDA surface itself undergoes permanent deformation which hardly recovers by annealing at 670 K. We will discuss this point later.

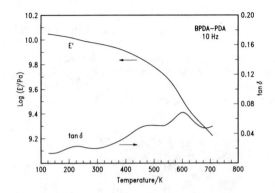

Figure 2. Dynamic mechanical properties of BPDA-PDA film versus temperature.

<u>Atomic Force Microscopy</u>

Figure 3 shows an AFM image of the surface of the BPDA-PDA acid film buffed under 20 g/cm^2 load. Though there were some slight scratch marks along the buffing direction, the surface was basically quite smooth within several nm. The number of observable scratch marks was about 10 lines in the 25 μm^2 area. However, from a calculation based on the number of fibers in contact with film surface per unit area and the distance of buffing process, the number of fibers which buffed on the film surface should be more than 1000 for the area shown in Figure 3. Therefore, the observed marks on the buffed surface was not drawn by cloth fibers but by some small hard dust particles.

The AFM image after thermal imidization at 670 K of the buffed BPDA-PDA acid film is shown in Figure 4. Many well-aligned grooves were created along the buffing direction. They

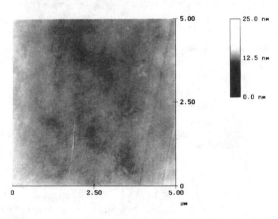

Figure 3. AFM image of the surface of buffed BPDA-PDA poly(amic acid) film.

were not observed before thermal imidization. What has happened during the thermal imidization?

The aggregation state of the as-cast BPDA-PDA acid is nearly amorphous. However, it has been reported that BPDA-PDA after thermal imidization has a crystalline-like structure (or highly ordered smectic state).[9] The wide angle X-ray diffraction photograph of the BPDA-PDA film prepared in this study is shown in Figure 5(a). Since many sharp Debye-Scherrer rings were

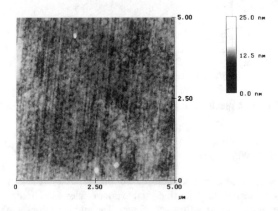

Figure 4. AFM image of the surface of BPDA-PDA, cured after buffing in the poly(amic acid) state.

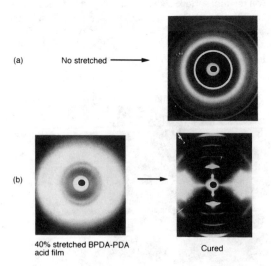

Figure 5. X-ray diffraction photographs of BPDA-PDA acid and imidized films:
(a) normal cure; (b) amic acid film stretched by 40% and cured subsequently under constraint by a metal frame.

250

observed, there existed crystalline-like domains in the BPDA-PDA film. The BPDA-PDA acid film can be stretched uniaxially up to 40%. A little anisotropy in the amorphous halo was observed in the X-ray diffraction photograph for the stretched BPDA-PDA acid film as shown in Fig.5(b, left side). However, highly oriented, much more than expected from 40% stretching, X-ray diffraction pattern was obtained for the BPDA-PDA film which was fixed with a metal frame after uniaxial stretching in the amic acid state and then cured at 670 K for one hour. The degree of orientation is comparable to that for a cold drawn poly(ethylene) which was stretched several hundred %. Namely, the orientation of ordered regions in the imidized film was markedly enhanced by slight stretching of the precursor amic acid. If there remained stretched chains induced by buffing on the BPDA-PDA acid film surface, they might result in highly oriented crystalline-like regions. The grooves might consist of such oriented crystalline-like domains.

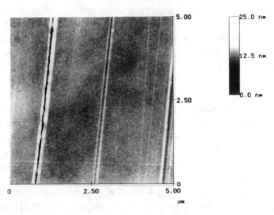

Figure 6. AFM image of the surface of BPDA-PDA buffed under 20 g/cm^2 load.

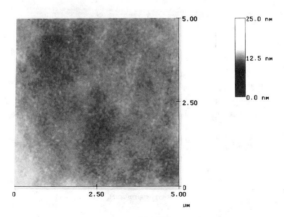

Figure 7. AFM image of the surface of BPDA-PDA buffed under 2 g/cm^2 load.

Perhaps, this is the reason why there were many grooves on the BPDA-PDA film which was prepared by thermal imidization of a buffed BPDA-PDA acid film.

The BPDA-PDA surface cured without any prior buffing was much rougher compared with the BPDA-PDA acid case. When the buffing procedure was performed only after curing, some steep scratch lines were observed as shown in Figure 6. Those lines might be marked by hard dust particles as discussed above. The number of those lines was remarkably reduced by decreasing the buffing pressure and a groove-free surface was achieved by buffing under 2 g/cm^2 load as shown in Figure 7.

Alignment Characteristics of Nematic and Chiral Smectic C Liquid Crystals

All of the buffed surfaces, regardless of cure, whether buffed after or before cure, aligned the nematics homogeneously along the buffing direction. Even a surface which showed no grooves exhibited excellent alignment of nematics. Furthermore, after the buffed BPDA-PDA acid was cured, we buffed it again in the direction perpendicular to the initial buffing direction. The microgrooves were created along the initial buffing direction. However, the nematics aligned parallel to the final buffing direction. That is, nematics could align in the direction perpendicular to the microgrooves. Therefore, it is concluded that the microgrooves are not necessary for alignment of nematics on buffed polymer surfaces, though they might be helpful.

It is more difficult to provide a good alignment of smectics than that of nematics. Actually, the smectics could not always be aligned by the buffed surface which aligned nematics very well. Both of the buffed BPDA-PDA acid and buffed BPDA-PDA (cured at 670 K) yielded poor alignment for smectics. The BPDA-PDA film cured after buffing also showed poor alignment for smectics, despite the presence of well-aligned microgrooves (see Figure 4). However, the buffed BPDA-PDA which had been cured at 420-470 K gave good smectic alignment. From the AFM measurement, there were no grooves on those surfaces. The final cure temperature dependence of the dynamic mechanical modulus and tan δ was investigated to understand these results, and summarized in Figure 8. The temperature range of 420-470 K corresponds to the

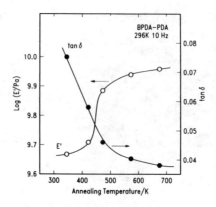

Figure 8. Dynamic mechanical modulus and tan δ versus the final heating temperature of BPDA-PDA.

transition region in that BPDA-PDA acid is getting thermally imidized into BPDA-PDA around this temperature and the mechanical modulus is still much lower compared with fully imidized films cured at higher temperatures. Therefore, the combination of appearance of ordered polyimide structure and the soft mechanical properties may be responsible for these soft cured films to provide the good alignment of smectics after buffing

Concerning the effect of buffing on the BPDA-PDA surfaces, we have estimated that a large local stress sufficient to cause plastic deformation of BPDA-PDA films is applied to the buffing interface. It will be reported elsewhere.

CONCLUSIONS

The liquid crystalline molecules are spontaneously oriented with their long axes approximately parallel. Since the orientation of a director is arbitrary in space, it is controlled by very minor forces. This property makes it difficult to know what is the major mechanism for influencing the nematic alignment on polymer surfaces. It has been shown both experimentally and theoretically that the nematics tend to align parallel along the microgrooves to minimize their elastic distortion free energy. However, our results show that on buffed polyimide surfaces the microgrooves are not necessary for nematic alignment. Rather, it is concluded that the nematic alignment is mainly caused by the anisotropic intermolecular interactions between liquid crystal molecules and the polymer chains oriented by buffing. Moreover, for the alignment of chiral smectic C materials, both the degree of order and mechanical properties of buffed polyimide films are found to be important factors.

ACKNOWLEDGEMENT

We acknowledge the postdoctoral fellowship granted by IBM Japan to H. K.. We thank T. Russell, H. Brown, and K. H. Yang for technical discussions, and B. Fuller for help with the mechanical measurements.

REFERENCES

1. J. Cognard, Mol. Cryst. Liq. Cryst., **51**, 1 (1982).
2. D. W. Berreman, Phys. Rev. Lett., **28**, 1683 (1972).
3. D. W. Berreman, Mol. Cryst. Liq. Cryst., **23**, 215 (1973).
4. U. Wolff, W. Grenbel, and H. Kruger, Mol. Cryst. Liq. Cryst., **23**, 187 (1973).
5. L. T. Creagh and A. R. Kmetz, Mol. Cryst. Liq. Cryst., **24**, 59 (1973).
6. J. A. Castellano, Mol. Cryst. Liq. Cryst., **94**, 33 (1983).
7. J. M. Geary, J. W. Goodby, A. R. Kmetz, and J. S. Patel, J. Appl. Phys., **62**, 4100 (1987).
8. K. Nakajima, H. Wakemoto, S. Sato, F. Yokotani, S. Ishihara, and Y. Matsuo, Mol. Cryst. Liq. Cryst. **180B**, 223 (1990).
9. D. Y. Yoon, W. Parrish, L. E. Depero and M. Ree, MRS Symp. Proc. **227**, 387 (1991).

TRANSPARENT CONDUCTING FILMS GROWN BY PULSED LASER DEPOSITION

JULIA M. PHILLIPS, R. J. CAVA, S. Y. HOU, J. J. KRAJEWSKI, J. KWO, J. H. MARSHALL, W. F. PECK, JR., D. H. RAPKINE, G. A. THOMAS, AND R. B. VAN DOVER
AT&T Bell Laboratories, Murray Hill, NJ 07974

ABSTRACT

We have studied the properties of two types of transparent conducting oxides grown by pulsed laser deposition (PLD) on quartz substrates. We have grown films of ITO with resistivity as low as 250 $\mu\Omega$-cm and with absorption coefficient < 600 cm^{-1} throughout the visible spectrum. Even films deposited at room temperature can have ρ < 500 $\mu\Omega$-cm, although the optical transmission characteristics are worse than those of commercially available ITO. Important parameters governing film quality include the oxygen partial pressure during film deposition and substrate temperature. $GaInO_3$ is a recently identified transparent conducting material which is structurally distinct from ITO. Films have been grown with no intentional dopants and with either Ge substitution for Ga or Sn substitution for In. Doping concentrations as high as 10 at. % have been studied. There is no evidence for dopant segregation. Films with resistivities as low as 3 $m\Omega$-cm have been achieved, and the absorption coefficient can be less than 500 cm^{-1} throughout the entire visible spectrum.

INTRODUCTION

Indium tin oxide (ITO) has been the transparent conducting material of choice for a wide variety of applications from solar cells to flat panel displays for at least 20 years.[1] Typical ITO films have a sheet resistance of 10 Ω/sq (i.e., a resistivity of about 200 - 400 $\mu\Omega$-cm). A drawback of ITO, however, is its relatively strong absorption in the green-blue portion of the visible spectrum (absorption coefficient of several thousand cm^{-1}) which leads to both loss of display brightness and to a greenish cast of the ITO films. There is a need for a conductor with better transparency across the visible spectrum, especially in the green-blue region. This challenging goal requires a major improvement in the materials used as transparent conductors. In this paper we report our work on pulsed laser deposition

Mat. Res. Soc. Symp. Proc. Vol. 345. ©1994 Materials Research Society

(PLD) of ITO films with improved optical characteristics as well as studies of GaInO3, a new transparent conducting material.

GaInO$_3$ is a recently identified transparent conductive material.[2] It is structurally distinct from ITO (shown in Figure 1a), with the β-Ga$_2$O$_3$ structure shown in Figure 1b. The Ga site is tetrahedrally coordinated, and the In site is octahedrally coordinated. Aliovalent elements such as Ge or Sn and/or oxygen vacancies dope these materials to achieve resistivities as low as ~3 mΩ-cm as discussed below.

[a]

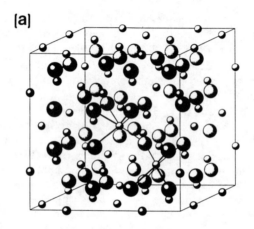

[b]

Figure 1.   Crystal structures of: (a) ITO and (b) GaInO$_3$.

EXPERIMENTAL CONDITIONS

We have used pulsed laser deposition (PLD) to deposit thin films of ITO and GaInO$_3$. Two ITO targets, both with 10% weight substitution of Sn for In were used. One was obtained commercially, while the other was fabricated in house by standard ceramic processing methods analogous to those used for the GaInO$_3$ targets. Both types of target gave the same results. Starting materials for the GaInO$_3$ targets were powdered Ga$_2$O$_3$, In$_2$O$_3$, GeO$_2$, and SnO$_2$ mixed in the appropriate molar proportions to yield Ga$_{1-x}$Ge$_x$InO$_3$ or GaIn$_{1-x}$Sn$_x$O$_3$, for $0 \leq x \leq 0.20$. Powders were initially fired for two 15 hour periods in air at 1300°C with intermediate grindings. Targets of the appropriate size were pressed in steel dyes and then fired for an additional 15 hour period at 1300°C in air. Two different final firing steps were found to be satisfactory in chemically reducing the samples from their air-fired state to the yield the desired high conductivity material before use as targets. In one, the targets were heated at 1200°C in Zr-gettered flowing N$_2$ at 1200°C for 15 hours. In the other, a 1 hour treatment at 550-600°C in a more reducing 15%H$_2$-85%N$_2$ mixture was found to yield equivalent or slightly superior results.

PLD deposited films were grown using a target of the desired film composition. Up to 10% Sn for In in either compound or 10% Ge for Ga in GaInO$_3$ was used. A KrF excimer laser operating at 248 nm with a repetition rate of 10 Hz was used with an incident energy density of 2 J/cm^2 energy density on the target. The deposition chamber had a base pressure of 1 X10^{-7} Torr. During growth, the O$_2$ pressure was maintained between 0 and 100 mTorr. The temperature of the quartz substrate was varied between room temperature and 400°C. Both the oxygen pressure and substrate temperature are important parameters in dictating film transparency and conductivity as will be discussed at length elsewhere.[3] Films with highest conductivity and only slightly sub-optimum transparency were grown at a substrate temperature of 250°C in an oxygen pressure of 1 mTorr. X-ray diffraction shows only GaInO$_3$ or ITO peaks in these films. The results on ITO films are generally consistent with those previously reported by Zheng and Kwok for PLD films of this material.[4]

RESULTS

Films were characterized for their morphology, optical, and conducting properties. As seen in Figure 2, scanning electron microscopy

(SEM) shows ITO films deposited at either room temperature or 250°C to be very smooth except for a few precipitates. The GaInO$_3$ films deposited in 1 mTorr O$_2$ show a somewhat granular microstructure but no evidence for precipitates at any dopant concentration up to 10%, as reported previously.[5]

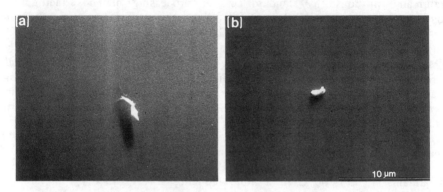

Figure 2. SEM micrographs showing the morphology of ITO films grown at: (a) room temperature in 10 mTorr O$_2$ and (b) 250°C in 1 mTorr O$_2$, the conditions found to give the lowest resistivity.

The temperature-dependent resistivity as well as the room temperature Hall constant and magnetoresistance were measured in the van der Pauw configuration using chopped dc at ~1 A/cm^2. For example, GaIn$_{.95}$Sn$_{.05}$O$_3$ deposited at 250°C by PLD in 1 mTorr O$_2$ yields a room temperature resistivity of 3.6 mΩ-cm. ITO films deposited under the same conditions have $\rho \sim 250$ μΩ-cm while those deposited at room temperature in 10 mTorr O$_2$ have $\rho \sim 470$ μΩ-cm. The sign of the Hall constant is negative in all samples, indicating electron conduction, as expected for oxygen-vacancy doping or Sn (or Ge) doping. Thermoelectric measurements are consistent with electron-like carriers. Typical carrier densities inferred from the Hall constant are in the range 1 X 10^{19} - 4 X 10^{20} cm^{-3} for GaInO$_3$ and 5 - 8 X 10^{20} cm^{-3} for ITO.

The transmittance spectra of ITO and GaInO$_3$ films have been measured for films of various doping concentrations grown under a variety of deposition conditions. In general the far-infrared absorption and the dc conductivity vary together with the O$_2$ pressure during deposition.[6] The visible and near infrared transmittance shows Fabry-Perot oscillations that allow a determination of the index of refraction or GaInO$_3$ as 1.65 ± 0.1. This is a much closer match to the index of refraction of glass than for ITO, which has n = 2.0. ITO films deposited at room temperature in 10 mTorr O$_2$ have a significantly higher absorption coefficient throughout most of the visible spectrum (except for the longest wavelengths) than do commercially available films. Figure 3 shows the absorption coefficient of PLD-deposited ITO and GaIn$_{.95}$Sn$_{.05}$O$_3$ films that were deposited at 250°C in 1 mTorr O$_2$, the conditions that have been found to give the lowest film resistivity, as discussed in the previous paragraph. The same data for a commercially available ITO film are also included for comparison. The absorption of both PLD-deposited films is significantly lower than that of the commercially available film throughout the visible spectrum. The high frequency absorption of GaInO$_3$ shows an energy gap near 3.3 eV (380 nm).

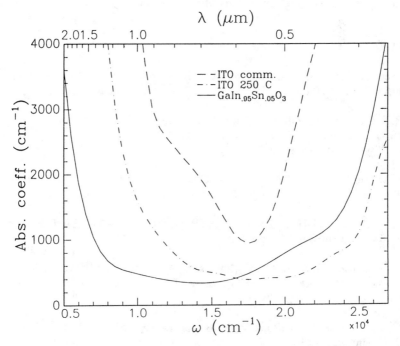

Figure 3. Absorption coefficients of three transparent conducting films: commercially available ITO (dash line - ITO comm.), a PLD-deposited ITO film grown at 250°C in 1 mTorr O$_2$ (dot-dash line - ITO 250 C), and a PLD-deposited GaIn$_{.95}$Sn$_{.05}$O$_3$ film grown at 250°C in 1 mTorr O$_2$ (solid line).

CONCLUSIONS

We have shown that PLD is a promising technique to grow transparent conducting films of both an established material, ITO, and a new material for this application, $GaInO_3$. Doping results from oxygen vacancies and/or substitution of aliovalent elements such as Ge or Sn. The optical transmission characteristics of both materials grown by PLD are considerably better than those of commercially available ITO. While the resistivity of $GaInO_3$ is higher than that of ITO, its superior transparency compared with that of commercially available ITO and its better index match to glass make it possible to consider the use of thicker films to compensate for this shortcoming. Alternatively, we have shown that it is possible to use PLD to deposit low resistivity ITO with excellent transmission across the entire visible spectrum.

REFERENCES

1. See, for example, G. Haacke, Ann. Rev. Mater. Sci. *7*, 73 (1977); C. G. Granqvist, Appl. Phys. A *52*, 83 (1991) and references therein.

2. R. J. Cava, J. M. Phillips, J. Kwo, G. A. Thomas, R. B. van Dover, S. A. Carter, J. J Krajewski, W. F. Peck, Jr., J. H. Marshall, and D. H. Rapkine, Appl. Phys. Lett. (in press).

3. J. M. Phillips, G. A. Thomas, S. A. Carter, R. J. Cava, S. Y. Hou, J. Kwo, D. H. Rapkine, J. H. Marshall and R. B. van Dover (in preparation).

4. J. P. Zheng and H. S. Kwok, Appl. Phys. Lett *63*, 1 (1993); J. P. Zheng and H. S. Kwok, Thin Solid Films *232*, 99 (1993).

5. J. M. Phillips, J. Kwo, G. A. Thomas, S. A. Carter, R. J. Cava, S. Y. Hou, J. J. Krajewski, J. H. Marshall, W. F. Peck, Jr., D. H. Rapkine, and R. B. van Dover, Appl. Phys. Lett. (submitted).

6. G. A. Thomas, D. H. Rapkine, R. B. van Dover, J. M. Phillips, J. Kwo, and R. J. Cava (in preparation).

Room Temperature Laser Deposited Indium Tin Oxide Films for Display Applications

W.C. Yip, A.Gururaj Bhat, and H.S. Kwok

Department of Electrical and Electronic Engineering, Hong Kong University of Science and Technology, Clear Water Bay, Hong Kong.

Abstract

Indium tin oxide is the most basic transparent electrode material for all flat panel displays. Commercial ITO glass is manufactured mostly by sputtering. Here, we report the use of pulsed laser deposition to produce ITO thin films on glass at room temperature. Several interesting properties of such films were observed. (1) It was found that the resistivity of 0.5mΩ-cm compared very well with the best published values produced at high deposition temperatures. Room temperature deposition affords the possibility of using plastics and other flexible substrates for displays. (2) The microstructure of these ITO films were quite different from those of commercial ITO glasses. (3) By passing a strong current through the film, a large thermally induced Δnl could be observed. This change was due to lateral stress and could be as large as 1μ m for a 1-μm thick film. An electro-optic shutter can easily be designed with such films. Applications of this electronically controlled Δnl to display technology are discussed.

Introduction

Since the use of plastic substrates for displays may find many useful applications, low-temperature deposition of ITO thin films has become quite important, for example, in the fabrication of polymer based electro-luminescence devices[1-4]. Recently it was shown that laser deposited ITO thin films could be obtained at room temperature without post-annealing and exhibited the properties of low resistivity (as low as 0.28mΩ-cm) and high transmission (90% over the visible spectrum)[5]. In this paper, we shall explore further the optical properties of these ITO thin films deposited at oblique angles. In Pulsed Laser Deposition (PLD), highly energetic atoms and ions are ejected from the target as a result of laser-target interaction. A densed laser plume is formed which is influenced by the background oxygen pressure and other process parameters. It is believed that this plume activates the surface and allows low temperature deposition. By depositing at an oblique angle, it was hoped that some anisotropy in the crystalline structure could be produced and exploited.

The results showed that a sheet resistance of 12.1Ω/sq could be obtained. An interesting transmission change was observed when a current was passed through the ITO sample. The maximum optical transmittance change at 632.8nm was more than 24% when the applied voltage was varied from 4.6V to 4.8V for laser deposited ITO.

261

Experimental

The ITO thin films were prepared at room temperature with laser pulses of 200mJ, 15Hz, and 193nm generated by a Lambda Physik LPX200. The base pressure was 2×10^{-6} Torr. The oxygen pressure was kept at 20mTorr during deposition. The deposition time was 1hr8min. and the target-substrate distance was 45mm. The target was a 2.5cm diameter Indium Tin Oxide (10 mole% Sn) sintered ceramic and the substrates were Corning cover glass cleaned with $H_2SO_4:H_2O_2$ (10:1) and deionized water. During deposition, the glass substrate was masked with a square window of 4mm long. Afterwards, a pair of aluminum contact electrodes were evaporated on the masked ITO film for resistivity and optical transmittance measurements. The electrode separation was 4mm and the electrode size was 4mmx3.2mmx100nm. The film thickness was measured by an Alpha step 200 profiler. To measure how the transmittance depended on the applied voltage, an optical system as shown in Fig.1 was used. The polarization of the HeNe was aligned so that detector D1 received maximum power; while detector D2 showed none. Any change in the reflectance or rotation of polarization could thus be detected.

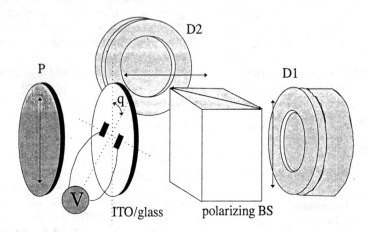

Fig.1 Experimental setup for transmittance measurement

Results and Discussion

1. *Electrical properties*

Since the film deposited at an oblique angle was not very uniform, the sheet resistance was measured (Fig.2). It was found that the sheet resistance of ITO increased monotonically with the deposition angle. At the smallest angle studied (18°), the sheet resistance was 12.1Ω/sq. The corresponding mean thickness was measured to be 280nm, giving rise to a resistivity of about 0.34mΩ-cm. This value is larger than that for normal deposition as reported previously [5] and follows the same trend. Presumably, this increase in resistivity has to do with the degradation of the grain structures and connectivity.

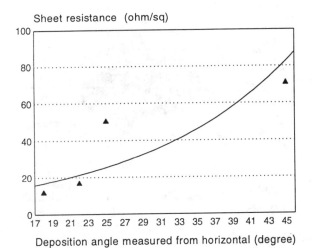

Sheet resistance (ohm/sq)

Deposition angle measured from horizontal (degree)

Fig.2 Sheet resistance of ITO thin films deposited by PLD against the deposition angle. (room temp., oxygen pressure: 20mTorr, 1hr8min and target-substrate distance: 45mm)

2. Surface morphology and X-ray diffraction analysis

The X-ray diffraction results showed a board peak which was primarily due to the glass substrate. The ITO film was therefore either amorphous or composed of crystals of very small grains. A specimen deposited at an angle of 25° and 20mTorr oxygen pressure was investigated by SEM (JOEL 6300F) and STM (TopoMetrix TMX2000). The surface was found to be very smooth and flat (Fig.3a), and the surface roughness was 30nm (Fig.3b).

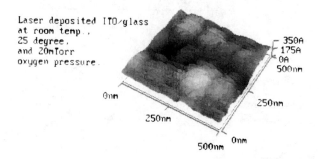

Laser deposited ITO/glass
at room temp.,
25 degree,
and 20mTorr
oxygen pressure.

350A
175A
0A
500nm
Onm
250nm
250nm
500nm   Onm

Fig.3 The (a) SEM and (b) STM micrographs of ITO thin film, deposited at 25°, 20mTorr, 45mm and 1hr8min.

3. *Optical transmittance*

Referring to Figure 1, the optical transmittance was measured at 632.8nm, and the results were shown in Figure 4. It can be seen that a voltage difference of 0.2V produces a 15% transmittance change, for both the laser deposited and commercial ITO films. In some cases, this change can be as high as 24% for the laser deposited film. This change in transmittance could be accounted for partially by a thermal effect. It was proved by observing a similar change in the transmittance when the film was heated up at an applied voltage of 4V.

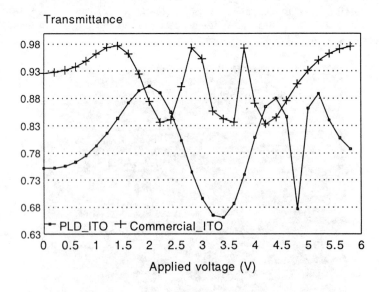

Fig.4 Transmittance @632.8nm of ITO thin film against applied voltage.

The oscillatory behaviour in Fig.4 is due to Fabry-Perot interference. From the interference fringes, the change in Δnl can be calculated. It can be seen that Δnl is as large as 1μm. This change in optical transmission as a function of applied voltage has potential applications in display technology. Admittedly, it is a thermal effect and is therefore quite slow and requires considerable electrical power. However, these drawbacks may be remedied by patterning the ITO into small pixels. Additionally, reflective coatings can be applied to the ITO film to enhance the contrast ratio. It is indeed possible to improve the on/off transmission contrast ratio to more than 100:1 by a simple 82% reflective coating on the ITO instead of using the nascent Fresnel reflection. This 100:1 contrast is quite suitable for display devices.

Conclusions

The properties of ITO films deposited at room temperature and oblique angles were studied. The sheet resistance was 12.1Ω/sq at a deposition angle of 18°. X-ray diffraction revealed the amorphous structure of the room temperature laser deposited ITO film. The surface was very smooth and flat, which was related closely with the resistivity. The optical transmittance at 632.8nm gave a large change of 24% when a voltage was applied. This was due to the lateral stress caused by heating. We believe that this effect can be used to control the transmittance of an electro-optic shutter for display applications.

The authors would like to thank Mr. W.S. Au, Mr. C.C. Leung ,Mr. T.F. Hung and Mr. J.Q. Zheng of Materials Characterization and Preparation Centre (HKUST) for their help in analyzing the ITO films. This research was supported by a Research Infrastructure Grant from The Hong Kong University of Science and Technology and Varitronix Inc.

References

1. B.S. Chiou and S.T. Hsieh, *Thin Solid Films*, **229** (1993) 146-155.
2. J.A. Dobrowolski, F.C. Ho, D. Menagh, R. Simpson, and A. Waldorf, *Appl. Opt.* **26** (1987) 5204-5210.
3. T. Karasawa and Y. Miyata, *Thin Solid Films*, **223** (1993) 135-139.
4. C.C. Wu, J.K.M. Chun, P.E. Burrows, J.C. Sturm, M.E. Thompson, and S.R. Forrest, to appear in *MRS Sym. Proc.* vol. **344**, (1994).
5. J.P. Zheng and H.S. Kwok, *Thin Solid Films*, **232** (1993) 99-104.

PART II

Liquid Crystal Display
Materials and Processes

CHALLENGES FOR FLAT PANEL DISPLAY PHOSPHORS

H.P. MARUSKA, T. PARODOS, N.M. KALKHORAN, AND W.D. HALVERSON
Spire Corporation, One Patriots Park, Bedford, MA 01730-2396

ABSTRACT

Phosphors are a class of materials which emit visible light when impacted by either electrons or photons. Phosphors are the critical material in all self-emissive displays. The major display technologies which depend on phosphors are cathode ray tubes, flat cathode ray tubes (especially, field emission displays), thin film electroluminescent displays, and gas discharge plasma displays. Each of these technologies started with phosphors prepared in powder form, sprayed or screen printed onto a faceplate suitable for viewing. Electroluminescent displays have largely converted to thin film phosphors. It can be expected that, for many applications, the other competing technologies will also come to rely on more robust, high definition, thin film phosphors. Presently, full color displays must utilize several deposition and etching procedures to prepare the red, green, and blue pixels. Ion implantation of color centers is now paving the way for producing full color displays in a single host phosphor. We shall discuss the present limitations that compromise full color self-emissive displays, and present state-of-the-art solutions based on thin films and ion implantation.

INTRODUCTION

Phosphors are a group of materials capable of hosting specific impurity atoms which can emit visible light upon excitation either by photons or electrons which impinge upon and enter the phosphor. Such a phosphor material may be placed in an evacuated vessel, or positioned as a layer or film in an all solid state manifestation. In an evacuated vessel, excitation of the phosphor may be accomplished by a beam of electrons ("cathode rays"): this is cathodolumines-cence. Alternatively, a low pressure gas may be introduced into an evacuated vessel containing the phosphor, and the gas may emit high energy (usually ultraviolet) photons which can excite the phosphor: this is photoluminescence. Finally, the phosphor may be placed as a layer between laminated solid materials which supply a stream of electrons due to the application of an electric field across the sample, and these electrons excite the phosphor while traversing it: this is electroluminescence.

In general, the light-emitting phosphor is the key material in a display system that serves as the interface for transferring information (including entertainment) between machines and humans. The most common display system is the cathode ray tube (CRT) which is used both in televisions and in monitors for computers. Because the CRT is so bulky, there are many efforts to replace it with a flat panel display of some kind. There are essentially two classes of flat panel displays, those which are self-emissive, and those which require separate external illumination. All self-emissive displays, including CRTs, rely on phosphor materials to generate the light. We shall concentrate on the problems inherent in creating phosphors that can provide full color self-emissive displays. We shall describe several very promising approaches for overcoming the problems with phosphor materials. The field of non-emissive displays, such as liquid crystal light valves, will not be discussed herein.

269

Most phosphors are inorganic sulfides or oxides with relatively wide bandgaps (> 3 eV), and elements from all regions of the periodic table have been identified as luminescence centers. There are combinations of phosphor hosts and luminescence centers which will emit each of the six major colors of the spectrum: red, orange, yellow, green, blue, and violet. Therefore it is relatively simple to produce a monochrome display of virtually any one color. However, it is difficult to identify a single phosphor host that can accommodate three different luminescence centers which emit the three primary colors red, green, and blue (RGB). If the display can emit red, green, and blue, then it can produce white, and hence various intermediate colors. Thus there have been continuous efforts to produce full color, and hence white-emitting displays, but identifying efficient phosphors have proven to be difficult. The basic challenge is to identify a phosphor or, if necessary, a group of phosphors, which will emit the RGB colors with sufficient relative intensities to appear white to a human observer. This light must be sufficiently bright overall to be seen comfortably in a lighted room, the brightness of the light emission must remain constant over time, and the cost of the display must be low enough for widespread consumer acceptance.

SELF-EMISSIVE DISPLAYS

There are four major types of self-emissive displays, $viz.$, the cathode ray tube, the flat cathode ray tube, laminated electroluminescent materials, and the gas plasma discharge tube. The first three use high energy electrons to stimulate the luminescence centers in the phosphor, while the fourth is based on photoluminescence. We shall mainly concentrate on phosphors which are excited by electrons. However, let us briefly describe each type of display.

Cathode Ray Tube

The first cathode ray tube was demonstrated by Karl Braun in 1897, so this venerable instrument is almost 100 years old. The phosphor material is deposited on the faceplate in the form of dots or stripes to form the picture elements, or pixels. For a full color CRT display, there must be three subpixels, one red, one green, and one blue. The original monochrome CRTs were either green, blue, or white; adjacent blue and yellow subpixels appear white to the human eye. The workhorse phosphor was always zinc sulfide, ZnS, although many other CRT phosphors have also been investigated. Doping with copper provides bright green while silver gives excellent blue cathodoluminescence. Manganese in ZnS can give yellow. Red has always been a challenge for ZnS; the problem has never been properly solved. In the end, full color CRTs have typically used europium-doped Y_2O_2S as the red emitting phosphor. The phosphors are prepared as powders, which are sequentially deposited onto the faceplate. Photolithography is used for defining the proper areas for each color. Exposure of the photoresist is accomplished through the CRT shadow mask, using a light positioned where each color electron gun will be placed. The entire process has become highly automated. The majority of displays presently in use are CRTs, mainly because CRTs are so inexpensive.

Flat Cathode Ray Tube

The traditional CRT is bulky, occupies a large volume, and operates at tens of kilovolts. Because it is a vacuum tube, the glass envelope must withstand atmospheric pressure. This means thick glass plates must be used in large CRTs. Thus a large CRT, as might be desired for High Definition Television (HDTV), becomes extremely heavy, too heavy for an average human to lift. Efforts are underway to produce a flat, two-dimensional CRT. The standard CRT relies on a scanned electron beam to excite the phosphor elements in the pixels. It is very difficult to scan an electron beam in a flat tube. Therefore, a large number of electron guns (cathodes) are usually supplied in a flat CRT, one or more for each pixel. The cathodes may be heated wires, like the traditional CRT cathode (this is usually called a vacuum fluorescent device, or VFD). However, a multitude of heated cathodes is very undesirable because of the enormous waste heat problem. Therefore, most current work in this area is focussed on developing cold cathode field emitters.[1]

The recent emphasis in flat CRT development has been focussed on efforts to develop cold cathode field emitters suitable for field emission displays (FEDs).[2] These cathodes are usually narrow (~10 micron diameter) pins or wires mounted on the backplate and formed from molybdenum or silicon.[3] A particularly exciting aspect of the work is the development of thin-film diamond field emission cathodes.[4] Operation of the FED relies on the application of a relatively modest potential between the cathode and a closely spaced grid to supply electrons into a vacuum space about one millimeter wide; the anode, located on the faceplate, is usually coated with cathodoluminescent phosphors in powder form.[5] Unfortunately, problems have been encountered with preparing acceptable cathodoluminescent phosphors for full color FED displays, especially when high resolution is required, such as in high quality graphics monitors or head mounted displays. It is clearly difficult to use thick film techniques (the same type as typically employed in the CRT industry)[6] to create powder lines having widths much less than 100 microns in a production environment: this limits a full color display to 80 lines per inch or less. Furthermore, powder material with 5 to 10 micron grain size produces lines with excessive thickness (~20 microns), while electron penetration depth is less than a micron;[6] this excess non-functional powder material scatters light into nearby pixels (cross talk). The thick material also impedes light transmission through the faceplate[7] and can inhibit charge conduction, unless a conductor such as indium tin oxide (ITO) is mixed together with the phosphor; this dilutes the phosphor, lowering emission intensity. Finally, a major source of cathode degradation comes from contamination with particles released from the powdered phosphors during operation.

As in a conventional CRT, the phosphor layer for an FED is typically made up of loosely bound crystallites ranging in size from 1 to 10 µm. Such layers are first held together by screen printing onto ITO coated glass with an organic binder before sintering at elevated temperatures. The layers tend to be on the order of 20 µm thick. The most common phosphor material is ZnO, but only a greenish color is available with this compound; ZnS-CdS alloy-based red, green, and blue (RGB) phosphors have been demonstrated.[8] The most popular phosphors for FEDs appear to be $ZnS:Ag,Al$ for blue, $Zn_{0.65}Cd_{0.35}S:Ag,Cl$ for green, and $Zn_{0.20}Cd_{0.80}S:Ag,Cl$ for red. However, these three different phosphors require separate deposition steps to place the RGB pixels next to each other. Consequently, an improved approach for preparing the cathodoluminescent phosphors for FED faceplates would be highly desirable. The introduction of thin film phosphor materials promises to alleviate several of these shortcomings.

271

Solid State Electrically-Excited Luminescent Structures

High Field Electroluminescence

Electroluminescent displays are the solid state analog of the cathodoluminescent vacuum tubes. For these field excited luminescence displays, the electrodes, phosphor material, and other layers are sequentially laminated onto a transparent faceplate. The high energy electrons that serve to excite the phosphor originate internally at interfaces or from electrode films, rather than as an impinging beam. The most popular phosphor material is ZnS, sandwiched between two insulating films, and driven in an AC mode.[9] This is termed a "thin film electroluminescent" or TFEL device. There is also a powder form of electroluminescent device, which appears to rely on a copper sulfide film to form a heterojunction with the ZnS particles, allowing minority-carrier charge injection across a form of pn junction.[10] Such devices usually suffer from limited operating lifetime, and we will not pursue a detailed discussion of powder electroluminescence.

Commercial TFEL displays start with a glass substrate coated with a transparent conductor such as indium tin oxide configured as stripes for matrix addressing. This substrate is then completely covered with a thin insulating film such as SiO_2, Al_2O_3, Y_2O_3, or Si_3N_4. The phosphor layer is deposited either by physical or chemical vapor deposition, coated with a second insulator, and finally with a second set of electrodes, orthogonal to the first. The insulating films prevent untrammelled avalanche breakdown under the high field excitation. With AC electric fields applied, charges that originate at the interface between the dielectric and the phosphor enter the phosphor, where they are accelerated to high energies. These electrons undergo collisions with the luminescence centers that have been incorporated into the phosphor film, exciting them. The charges travel back and forth across the film, as the polarity of the field is reversed.

The most efficient luminescence center for these devices is manganese.[11] Mn emits broadband yellow light, and ZnS:Mn TFEL displays are commercially available. For example, Sharp has introduced a yellow 17 inch (diagonal) TFEL display with brightness as high as 65 fL with VGA resolution.[12] No other transition metal is an effective luminescence center in ZnS. Other colors are obtained by doping with rare earths.[13] Unfortunately, the ionic diameter of all of the rare earth elements greatly exceeds the size of the zinc ion for which they must substitute. Therefore, their solubility is limited. The exception is terbium, which is a very efficient green emitter in electroluminescent ZnS.[14] Although thulium is a bright blue emitter when excited by cathode rays, it is very weak in a solid state electroluminescent film.[15]

There are two alkali earth sulfides that have the rock salt structure and can better accommodate rare earth impurities in the lattice, viz., CaS and SrS. CaS doped with Eu emits red, while SrS doped with Ce gives a greenish blue.[16] Neither is bright enough, and the materials are unstable with respect to moisture. Recently, the first blue emitting electroluminescent phosphor with reasonable efficiency and correct chromaticity was announced by Planar Systems: $CaGa_2S_4$ doped with Ce.[17] The emission peak is at 459 nm with a brightness of 3 fL. For the first time, a full color RGB electroluminescent display has been demonstrated.

Injection Luminescence

We do not include pn junction light-emitting diodes (LEDs) under the general topic of electroluminescence, because the internal electric field is essentially zero in an operating LED when forward bias is applied. Therefore LEDs are always low voltage, high current devices. III-V compounds such as AlGaAs and GaP are used for most junction LEDs. These materials are capable of emitting red, yellow, and green, with very high efficiencies. Blue has always been a problem for LEDs, although recent results with blue GaN LEDs are very encouraging.[18] To obtain multiple colors, it is necessary to mechanically assemble individual LED dice next to each other, a tedious and costly task. Therefore large LED displays appear to be unlikely.

There has been much recent interest, however, in light emission from porous silicon films.[19] This material is prepared by electrochemical etching of crystalline silicon, a process which forms angstrom-sized particles and wires. Quantum confinement effects move the silicon bandgap into the visible, and Spire has prepared yellow LEDs by making contact to the porous silicon layers with transparent indium tin oxide films.[20] Although the characteristics of these devices indicate that they operate by the minority-carrier injection mechanism,[21] surface recombination problems have thus far limited luminescence efficiencies.[22] Further work to improve contacts should improve operation, and since the etching procedure determines the color, full color display might be prepared by masking and etching procedures without the necessity of mechanical assembly of dice.

Gas Discharge Displays

All plasma display panels (PDPs) are based on the original neon glow discharge principle. A sealed glass envelope is filled with a combination of noble gases, which become ionized when sufficient voltage is applied across electrodes adjacent to the gas. The ionized gas molecules recombine, giving off light.[23] It is obvious that such a simple device can only emit a single color. However, if the light emitted by the gas is in the UV, it can be used to generate photoluminescence in a phosphor located in the tube.[24] The most common gas mixture for PDPs consists of 93% He + 5% Kr + 2% Xe. The simplest PDPs are operated with a DC voltage applied to their electrodes, and clearly such electrodes must be located within the glass container. For a full color display, phosphor dots are deposited onto or near the anode material.[25] Recently, NHK (Japan Broadcasting Corporation) has announced the fabrication of a 40 inch DC plasma display with white areal luminance of about 20 fL.[12]

There is a basic problem with DC panels arising from contamination of the electrodes. This difficulty can be overcome in principle by changing to an AC driven design.[26] AC PDPs can be driven at frequencies as high as 250 kHz, which helps to increase brightness. With an AC display, both row and column electrodes can be insulated from the discharge. Placement of the phosphor in color AC panels becomes a critical issue. For example, the phosphor dots might be deposited on the inner surface of the faceplate, with both the cathode and the anode electrodes positioned on the backplate, insulated from each other. Fujitsu now markets a 21 inch AC plasma display with an impressive 60 fL white areal luminance.[12]

The UV excitation from the gas discharge must be confined in cells to define the pixels. Since the phosphors are located within the glass envelope, they are in direct contact with the plasma. Therefore, in both the DC and AC versions, usual powder phosphors deposited by thick film techniques[27] are subject to damage during operation, as are the very sensitive MgO secondary emitting layers. These problems may be reduced or eliminated with a much more adherent thin film approach.[28]

THE PROBLEM WITH CREATING FULL COLOR DISPLAYS

Two major problems plague the self-emissive display efforts: the inability to prepare phosphors which emit red, green, and blue with sufficient brightness to satisfy luminance requirements for television or computer monitors, and the inability to provide displays with sufficient longevity, due to the instabilities of powder phosphors. The physical instability problems can be largely overcome by converting to highly adherent thin film phosphors. However, there remains the high cost of depositing and etching several films when all three colors are required. A solution to this impasse has been presented by the use of ion implantation of luminescent centers into a single host phosphor layer.[29] We shall describe recent results with the implantation of luminescence centers into thin film phosphors which are eminently suitable for either electroluminescent or cathodoluminescent displays. Although the particular patterning of the phosphors that is usually employed for gas discharge displays tends to be three dimensional, there may also be niche applications for ion implanted thin films in plasma displays as well.

THIN FILM ELECTROLUMINESCENCE: FULL COLOR BY ION IMPLANTATION

Monochrome TFEL panels are now an established commercial product, based on ZnS phosphor films doped with Mn during deposition. Full color TFEL displays are difficult to manufacture because of the patterning and etching of phosphor films. The complex processing sequence involves three phosphor deposition steps, with photolithography and etching required to position the RGB sub-pixels side by side.[30] Considerable cost savings can be achieved by introducing all three color centers into a single thin film phosphor by ion implantation.

We have implanted a wide range of luminescence centers into partially finished TFEL panels provided by Norden Systems and by Planar Systems; Norden and Planar then completed the panels. Yellow electroluminescence with luminance approaching 50 fL at 60 Hz has been achieved with Mn implantation in thin film ZnS. Bright green panels are produced with Tb; alternating yellow and green stripes have been made using Mn and Tb with a shadow mask to define the rows. Blue, green, and orange electroluminescence has been demonstrated by implanting Ce, Eu, and Mn, respectively, in calcium thiogallate films deposited by Planar. Proper annealing and implantation of co-activators has been shown to be essential for high brightness.

In order to improve the brightness of blue electroluminescence, we have deposited $Mg_xZn_{1-x}S$ films by MOCVD and then implanted Ce. Because Mg ions are larger than Zn, it is anticipated that the lattice of the alloys will better accommodate the large cerium ions. By ion implanting Mg into ZnS prior to Ce implantation, which produced a very dilute Mg content, we enhanced the blue Ce peak, yielding 1931 CIE parameters $x = 0.148$, $y = 0.233$, and a luminance of 0.25 fL at 1 kHz.

A list of typical ion implantation parameters for preparing ZnS electroluminescent displays is given in Table I.

Our studies have indicated that every added cation (luminescence center) must be balanced by an additional anion. Otherwise, anion vacancies which limit luminescence efficiency are created. Damage to the lattice which results from the implantation has been repaired by a combination of rapid and extended time thermal annealing procedures. SIMS analysis has indicated that proper annealing conditions allow diffusion of the implanted species throughout the volume of the phosphor.

Table I *Typical ion implantation parameters for full color TFEL displays.*

Ion	Host	Function	Color	Energy (keV)	Dose (x 10^{15} cm^{-2})
Mn	ZnS	Color center	Yellow	190	0.1-10
Tb	ZnS	Color center	Green	190	1-50
Eu	CaGa$_2$S$_4$	Color center	Green	190	5-10
Sm	ZnS, CaGa$_2$S$_4$	Color center	Red	190	1-10
Tm	ZnS	Color center	Blue	190	1-5
Ce	CaGa$_2$S$_4$, Mg$_x$Zn$_{1-x}$S	Color center	Blue	190	5-10
S	ZnS, CaGa$_2$S$_4$	Charge balance	-	70-110	0.1-20
O	ZnS	Charge balance	-	30	1-100
F	ZnS	Charge balance	-	30	1-100

Figure 1 shows the measured brightness (@ 180 Hz) of ZnS:Mn pixels as a function of the dose of implanted Mn. When there is no anion compensation, brightness levels fall below 5 fL. Sulfur compensation and a standard one-hour furnace anneal at 500°C brings the brightness over 40 fL. Finally, a rapid thermal anneal at 625°C for 1-2 minutes for compensated samples gives brightness levels exceeding 120 fL, which is state of the art for coevaporated ZnS:Mn panels.

A study was performed to provide green emission from ZnS panels. Tb was implanted at an energy of 190 keV and doses ranging from 10^{15} to 10^{16} ions/cm^2. It was determined that anion compensation was again vital, and thus S,O, and F were also implanted into the samples. The brightest samples were found to have the dose of (O + S) equal to Tb, plus F = Tb. A pixel brightness of 10 fL at 180 Hz has been measured. Furthermore, green and yellow panels have been prepared using both Mn and Tb, while the implantation of Sm and Tm into the same panel allowed the demonstration of red and blue.

We have also implanted rare earth luminescence centers into CaGa$_2$S$_4$, with the phosphor layers prepared by Planar Systems. Ce implantation has yielded blue electroluminescence with a brightness of almost 1 fL. Eu gave green emission at 2.5 fL. Red emission, although relatively weak, was provide by Mn. The emission spectra are shown in Figure 2. We expect that optimization of the implantation and annealing sequences will give significant improvements in these brightnesses.

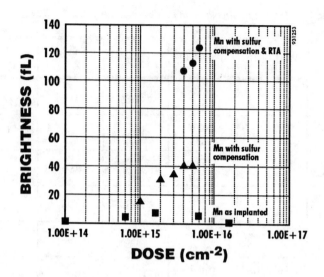

Figure 1 *Brightness dependence on manganese dose for ZnS electroluminescent display panels. Brightness is controlled by anion compensation and the repair of damage to the lattice.*

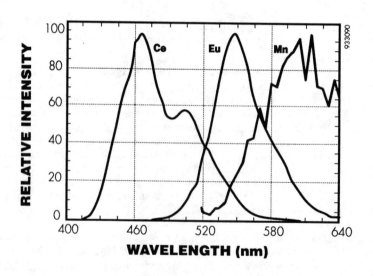

Figure 2 *Normalized spectral radiance of CaGa$_2$S$_4$ thin film phosphors implanted with Ce, Eu, and Mn.*

THIN FILM CATHODOLUMINESCENCE: FULL COLOR BY ION IMPLANTATION

We have demonstrated very bright blue and green luminescence by ion implantation of Cu and Al in ZnS, based on activation and co-activation of color centers.[31] Green cathodoluminescence was demonstrated with Mn implanted in Zn_2SiO_4 films (P1 phosphor). After a high temperature anneal, a brightness of 17 fL at 1 mA/cm^2 (1,500V) was measured. Photoluminescence was measured in-house, while cathodoluminescence studies were performed at the Army Research Laboratory, Fort Monmouth.[32] Efforts in this study were focussed on demonstrating the feasibility of producing full color displays using thin films of ZnS prepared by metalorganic chemical vapor deposition (MOCVD).[33] The starting materials for the MOCVD depositions were dimethyl zinc and hydrogen sulfide. For comparison, bulk and evaporated samples of ZnS were also investigated. Rutherford backscattering spectroscopy (RBS) showed that the thin films were indeed stoichiometric ZnS. The depth of penetration of the implanted ions was carefully analyzed by SIMS. Final Al depth profiles can be adjusted by proper annealing procedures.

Specifically, copper can give either green or blue photoluminescence or cathodoluminescence in ZnS. Copper will only emit blue or green light if a co-activator (donor ion) is present; aluminum is an excellent donor. The copper emission color is determined by the Cu/Al ratio. In the program, the Cu emission color was determined by adjusting the dose of the Al donor, a process which allows us to define green and blue subpixels. In regions with no Al donor implant, there was no light emission, even though Cu was present. In these regions, implanted Mn was found to emit yellow. The yellow can be filtered with redeposited $CdSe_{1-x}S_x$ to provide red subpixels.

The ZnS samples were implanted with various doses of copper and aluminum ions at 200 keV. Manganese was implanted at a dose of 2 x 10^{15} Mn^{2+}/cm^2. After the implantation procedure was completed, samples were annealed for 0.5 to 3 hours at temperatures of 500 to 700°C in nitrogen. The post implantation anneals served to remove implantation damage and to redistribute the dopants by diffusion. The double emission peak shown in Figure 3 is characteristic of the copper luminescence center. Blue emission was obtained when the Al dose was 10^{15} cm^{-2}, while green was found when the Al dose was 10^{17} cm^{-2}. The basis for these color changes is discussed below. Areas of samples which were not doped with Al showed absolutely no photolumines-cence, an essential property if other centers such as yellow Mn (described above) are also desired.

The observations of blue and green emission from Cu/Al impurities in ZnS can be explained as follows.[34] When the valency of an incorporated impurity deviates from the valency of the host element of the pure compound which it replaces, then there is a tendency in wide bandgap semiconductors to form native defects (vacancies and/or interstitials) to provide charge compensation. In ZnS, the most common luminescence centers are the so-called "activators" Cu, Ag, and Au, which substitute for Zn. However, since they possess only a single bonding electron, they give rise to an empty level situated in energy above the valence band of ZnS. Therefore, they function as acceptors, in that they can accept a second electron to complete the bond, perhaps supplied from the valence band. This lack of an electron (*i.e*, a hole) can also be compensated by the formation of an associated sulfur vacancy. Such an anion vacancy will have an electron (from a neighboring Zn) identified with it, and therefore can be considered a donor. Hence the concept of a donor-acceptor pair as a luminescence center.

On the other hand, charge compensation can also be provided by the incorporation of so-called "co-activators," *viz*., Cl, Br, I, Al, Ga, or In. If a halogen is substituted for S, the seventh electron is not required to complete the valence bond and, in fact, this electron forms a state just below the conduction band. If any of the group III elements such as Al, Ga, or In is substituted

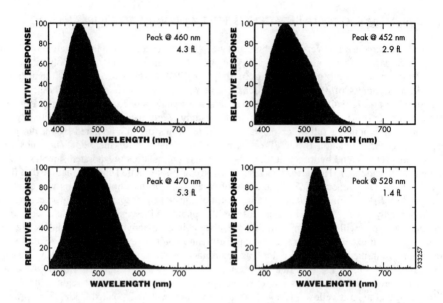

Figure 3 *Spire's blue and green luminescence from ZnS by implantation of low and high doses of aluminum co-activator.*

for Zn, an extra electron is again available. Thus co-activators all function as donors. If the donor concentration is equal to that of the acceptors, then there is exact charge compensation. If not, then native defects form to complete the compensation. For example, the third Al electron forms a shallow donor when substituted for Zn in ZnS, and thus Al tends to promote the creation of a Zn vacancy to compensate it.[35]

The energy levels associated with Cu and Al impurities in ZnS were discussed in great detail by Van Gool, and are shown in Figure 4.[36] Notice that there exists various paths for radiative recombination in ZnS doped with donors and acceptors, especially when lattice vacancy formation is also favored. Without copper or vacancies, Al donors give rise to the ultraviolet SAL (self-activated low) emission at 390 nm.[37] If the sample is annealed sufficiently to form Zn vacancies, then the blue SA (self-activated) emission is seen at 470 nm.[38] Copper associated with a sulfur vacancy provides red emission at 670 nm. Cu associated with Al is capable of exhibiting two distinct emission colors, blue at 460 nm, or green at 520 nm. The color of Cu+Al depends on their concentration ratio.[39] This was discussed by Kroger and Dikhoff,[40] who added CuNO$_3$ and Al(NO$_3$) as dopants to ultrapure ZnS samples. They determined that the luminescence shifted from blue to green when the Al concentration exceeded that of Cu.

It has long been recognized that there is no green or blue emission from any acceptor-type of luminescence center in ZnS unless a charge compensator is also present. For example, in 1956 Prener and Williams doped ZnS with copper by growing the material with radioactive zinc which transmuted to copper; no increase in green photoluminescence was observed after transmutation.[41] They showed that an element such as Cl on a sulfur site or Al on a Zn site is necessary to provide an extra electron which can compensate for the deficit of an electron caused by Cu situated in place of Zn. The Spire sample areas without Al implant showed no photoluminescence, in agreement with this work.

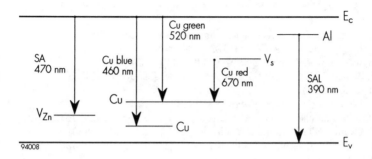

Figure 4   *Transitions in ZnS:Cu,Al leading to emission colors from red to ultraviolet.*

SUMMARY AND CONCLUSIONS

An overview of requirements for phosphors used in self-emissive flat panel displays has been presented. Problems that are encountered due to present reliance on powdered phosphors have been given. A detailed discussion of the merits of thin film phosphors was presented, and the advantages of employing ion implantation to introduce luminescence centers for full color displays into a single phosphor host were provided. The enhancements in performance were shown to be particularly applicable to cathodoluminescent and electroluminescent displays, although there are also certain circumstances where the thin film/ion implantation approach may be useful for cathode ray tubes and gas discharge plasma displays.

ACKNOWLEDGEMENT

I wish to acknowledge the help of Themis Parodos, Ward Halverson, and Nader Kalkhoran of Spire Corporation, Russel Budzilek and Dominick Monarchie of Norden Systems, Richard Tuenge of Planar Systems, David C. Morton of the Army Research Laboratory, and Timothy Anderson and Balu Pathangey of the University of Florida, all of whom contributed to various phases of the work. The work was supported in part under several contracts from the Advanced Projects Research Agency.

REFERENCES

1.   R.A. Millikan and C.F. Eyring, *Phys. Rev.*, <u>27</u>, 51 (1926).
2.   C. Curtin, *Proc. IDRC*, San Diego, Oct 15-17, 1991, page 12.
3.   C.A. Spindt, C.E. Holland, *IEEE Trans. Electron Dev.*, <u>ED38</u>, 2355 (1991).
4.   M.W. Geis, N.N. Efremow, J.D. Woodhouse, M.D. McAleese, M. Marchywka, D.G. Socker, J.F. Hochedez, *IEEE Electron Dev. Lett.*, **12**, 456 (1991).
5.   S. Matsumoto, <u>Electronic Display Devices</u>, John Wiley, publ., p.219, (1990).
6.   F. Levy and R. Meyer, *1991 International Display Research Conf.*, San Diego, Oct 15-17, 1991, page 20.

7.   T. Okajima, Y. Sano, N. Koyama, T. Ota, and K. Nunomura, *Proc. IEEE Conf. Electronic Devices*, (1991).

8.   K. Morimoto, *Proc. Electrochem. Soc.*, **87**, 1677 (1987).

9.   P.M. Alt, *Proc. of the SID*, **25**, 123 (1984).

10.   A.G. Fischer, *J. Electrochem. Soc.*, **110**, 733 (1963).

11.   A. Zeinert, P. Benalloul, J. Benoit, C. Barthou, J. Dreyhsig, H.E. Gumlich, *J. Appl. Phys.*, **71**, 2855 (1992).

12.   K. Werner, *Information Display*, **9**, 10 (1993).

13.   M.K. Jayaraj and C.P.G. Vallabhan, *J. Electrochem. Soc.*, **138**, 1512 (1991).

14.   K. Okamoto, T. Yoshimi, S. Miura, *Appl. Phys. Lett.*, **53**, 678 (1988).

15.   B.T. Collins, J. Kane, M. Ling, R.T. Tuenge, S.S. Sun, *J. Electrochem. Soc.*, **138** 3515 (1991).

16.   S. Tanaka, H. Deguchi, Y. Mikami, M. Shiiki, H. Kobayashi, *SID Digest*, 29-32 (1986).

17.   W.A. Barrow, R.C. Coovert, E. Dickey, C.N. King, C. Laakso, S.S. Sun, R.T. Tuenge, R. Wentross, *SID 93 Digest*, 761-764 (1993).

18.   I. Akasaki, H. Amano, M. Kito, K. Hiramatsu, *J. of Lumin.*, **48 & 49**, 666 (1991).

19.   A.G. Cullis and L.T. Canham, *Nature*, **353**, 335 (1991).

20.   F. Namavar, H.P. Maruska, N.M. Kalkhoran, *Appl. Phys. Lett.*, **60**, 2514 (1992).

21.   H.P. Maruska, F. Namavar, N.M. Kalkhoran, *Appl. Phys. Lett.*, **61**, 1338 (1992).

22.   H.P. Maruska, F. Namavar, N.M. Kalkhoran, *Appl. Phys. Lett.*, **63**, 102 (1993).

23.   A. Sobel, *IEEE Trans. Electron Dev.* **24**, 835 (1977).

24.   T. Kamagaya, H. Matsusaki, M. Yokozawa, *IEEE Trans. Electron Dev.*, **25**, 1094 (1978).

25.   H.J. Hoehn and R.A. Martel, *IEEE Trans. Electron Dev.* **20**, 1081 (1973).

26.   T. Shinoda, Y. Miyashita, Y. Sugimoto, K. Yoshikawa, 1981 *SID* symposium, New York, 164-165.

27.   G.H.F. de Vries, 1982 *SID* symposium, San Diego, 164-165.

28.   C.H. Perry, Extended Abstracts, Electrochemical Society meeting, Los Angeles, 783-784 (1979).

29.   T. Parodos, H.P. Maruska, W. Halverson, R.A. Budzilek, D. Monarchie, E. Schlam, *SID 93 Digest*, 777-779 (1993).

30.   W.A. Barrow, R.E. Coovert, C.N. King, M.J. Ziuchkovski, *Conf. of 1988 SID*, 284.

31.   DARPA Contract DAAH01-90-C-0536,,"MOCVD of Low-Cost TFEL Flat Panel Display Manufacturing," Final Report, December 1990.

32.   D.C. Morton, private communication.

33.   J. Fang, P.H. Holloway, J.E. Yu, K.S. Jones, B. Pathangey, E. Brettschneider, T. Anderson, *Appl. Surf. Sci.*, **70/71**, 701 (1993).

34.   M. Aven and J.S. Prener, <u>Physics and Chemistry of II-VI Compounds</u>, North Holland Publishing, 1967.

35.   R.H. Bube, *J. Chem. Phys.*, **20**, 708 (1952).

36.   W. Van Gool, "Fluorescence Centers in ZnS," thesis, University of Amsterdam, Jan. 1961.

37.   R.W.A. Gill and S. Rothschild, *Enlarged Abstracts, Electrochemical Society Meeting,* 72, (1960).

38.   F.A. Kroger and J.E. Hellingman, *J. Electrochem. Soc.*, **93**, 156 (1948).

39.   F.A. Kroger, J.E. Hellingman, and N.W. Smit, *Physica*, **15**, 990 (1949).

40.   F.A. Kroger and J. Dikhoff, *Physica*, **16**, 297 (1950).

41.   J.S. Prener and F.E. Williams, *J. Electrochem. Soc.*, **103**, 342 (1956).

LASER-DEPOSITION OF HIGH LUMINANCE THIN FILM PHOSPHORS

J. A. Greer, H. J. Van Hook, M. D. Tabat, H. Q. Nguyen, G. Gammie, and P. F. Koufopoulos*
Research Division, Raytheon Company, Lexington, MA,
*Missile Systems Division, Raytheon Company, Quincy, MA

INTRODUCTION

High luminance (brightness) thin-film phosphor materials have potential use in a variety of applications including heads-up, helmet-mounted, and electroluminescent displays, as well as in emerging flat-panel displays based on field emitter technology. Phosphor materials in thin film form offer several advantages over conventional powder phosphor screens. Since the film is nearly fully dense and in intimate contact with the underlying substrate, thin film phosphors transfer heat to the face plate much quicker than conventional, more porous, powder phosphor materials. This allows thin film phosphor screens to be driven at higher power levels, and therefore produce higher luminance, assuming the efficiency of the powder and film are the same. Fully dense phosphor films have smaller surface area, and will outgas less than conventional powder phosphor materials. Thin film phosphors have smaller grain sizes than conventional powder phosphor materials which will provide for smaller spot size, and thus, higher resolution. Furthermore, in applications such as field-emitter displays, powder phosphor particles can be physically dislodged from the screen due to the high electric fields produced by the large potential difference between the anode screen and gate electrode (or cathode), or dislodged by arcing which may occur if a powder particle protrudes significantly above the screen surface. Dislodged particles or damage produced by arcing could degrade display performance. Dense, thin-film phosphor materials which are well adhered to transparent substrates will provide much smoother surface morphologies, and should be able to withstand significantly higher electric field strength without arcing or screen degradation due to the dislocation of particles.

Thin-film Yttrium Aluminum Gallium Garnet (YAGG) phosphor materials have previously been deposited by conventional techniques such as sputtering[1] and Liquid Phase Epitaxy[2]. More recently, thin-film phosphors of Mn doped ZnS have been deposited by Pulsed Laser Deposition (PLD)[3]. PLD has become a routine laboratory tool with which to deposit a wide variety of complex chemical compounds due to its unique ability to accurately replicate the target stoichiometry in the laser-deposited film[4]. Here we report on the properties of YAGG films doped with rare earth cations of Eu (red), Tb (green), and Tm (blue) laser-deposited onto sapphire substrates. The results obtained to date indicate that PLD is capable of producing dense, polycrystalline, thin-film phosphor materials with high efficiencies and high luminance for Eu and Tb doped YAGG films. However, the efficiency of the Tm:YAGG phosphor films will need improvement for most applications.

MATERIALS AND METHODS

The large area PLD technique used to deposit the phosphor materials has been described previously[5]. Ablation targets of the desired compositions were fabricated in-house using standard ceramic processing techniques. Target compositions consisted of $Y_{2.80}Eu_{0.20}Ga_2Al_3O_{12}$, $Y_{2.82}Tb_{0.18}Ga_2Al_3O_{12}$, and $Y_{2.80}Tm_{0.20}Ga_2Al_3O_{12}$ for red, green, and blue phosphors, respectively. Ablation targets, 50 mm in diameter, were placed into the deposition chamber with the target center offset by 25.4 mm from the rotation axis of the substrate. Using this offset with a rastered laser beam allowed uniform depositions over rotating substrates larger than that of the targets[4]. The target-substrate distance was set at 12.7 cm. The phosphors were deposited onto 75 mm diameter, 0.625 mm thick, $(1\bar{1}02)$ sapphire substrates with an epi-polish on both surfaces. Typical laser parameters for deposition included a wavelength of 248 nm (KrF), a fluence of 3.7 J/cm^2, and a repetition rate of 100 pulses per second. Using these conditions an average uniform

281

($\pm$ 3 %) growth rate of 1 μm/hour was readily obtained over a 75 mm diameter substrate in O_2 background pressures ranging from 0.2 to 5 mTorr. Film thicknesses ranging from 0.3 to 8.0 μm were deposited depending on the application.

After deposition the substrates were diced into small samples and annealed at temperatures ranging from 1,400 to 1,650°C in oxygen. After annealing a 0.2 μm Al film was evaporated onto the phosphor surface for charge dissipation. For thin phosphor samples only 100 Å of Al was deposited. The combination of thin phosphor and Al produced translucent phosphor screens which were useful for studying the emission properties of field emitter cathode structures. In some cases, the full 75 mm diameter substrates were annealed, metallized, and then diced into 50.8 mm squares for testing. RGB color screens were fabricated on sapphire substrates using photolithography to first define one set of pixels, each pixel measuring 60 μm on a side. Using PLD, 2 μm of the desired phosphor was deposited, and the unwanted material was removed using a lift-off technique. This process was then repeated for each of the remaining two colors in succession. The as-deposited three color screen was then annealed in oxygen at a temperature of 1,400°C for 3 hours, metallized with 0.2 μm of Al, and diced to size. In order to study the dependence of the luminous efficiency on film thickness, Tb:YAGG was deposited onto a 75 mm diameter sapphire substrate using a metal mask in order to obtain four distinct quadrants with phosphor film thickness of 2, 4, 6, and 8 μm.

The phosphor's extrinsic efficiency was measured in an evacuated bi-potential electro-static focus type CRT with a special fixture designed to hold the 50.8 mm substrates in front of the CRT's glass face plate (phosphor side towards the electron gun). Electron beam deflection was accomplished through a standard magnetic deflection yoke. The anode (phosphor) voltage and current could be varied independently from 8 to 20 kV and 10 to 1,600 A, respectively. Standard raster generators were used to scan the beam at a 525 line horizontal rate with a 60 Hz vertical refresh rate. A Photo Research Spectralscan (PR-702AM) and Gamma Scientific Digital Radiometer are used to measure the spectral distribution and phosphor luminescence, respectively. It should be mentioned that since the phosphor screen is placed completely inside the CRT tube the emitted light reaching the detector has necessarily passed through the front face plate of the CRT. Since about 4 percent of the incident light energy will be reflected at both vacuum/glass and glass/atmosphere interfaces, the measured efficiencies are actually only 92 percent of the true values. The data presented in this report has not been corrected for this measurement error. Film morphology was studied by SEM both before and after a high temperature post-deposition anneal, and film crystallinaty was evaluated using X-ray powder diffraction with Cu K_α X-radiation.

RESULTS AND DISCUSSION

Figure 1 displays the X-ray powder diffraction scans of laser deposited Tb, Eu, and Tm doped YAGG films annealed in O_2 at 1,575°C for 15 hours. Also shown in the Figure 1 is the expected powder diffraction profile for an un-doped polycrystalline Yttrium Aluminum Garnet (YAG) film, since a standard for YAGG does not exist. However, the crystalline structure is the same for the YAG and YAGG garnets, with only a small variation in lattice constant due to the substitution of Ga for Al. As noted, all three annealed PLD YAGG materials display un-oriented polycrystalline texture when deposited on sapphire, and no secondary phases are present. Similar scans were obtained for films annealed at temperatures ranging from 1,400 to 1,650°C. The lattice constants of the (10 42) peak were obtained using Cu $K_{\alpha 1}$ radiation, and found to be 12.067 $\pm$ 0.018 Å, 12.058 $\pm$ 0.007 Å, and 12.046 $\pm$ 0.012 Å, with corresponding FWHM values of 0.15°, 0.12°, and 0.13°, for the Eu:, Tb:, and Tm:YAGG films annealed at 1,575°C, respectively. These results compare with a lattice constant of 12.10 Å for YAGG, and are in agreement with expected lattice distortions due to the relative sizes of the three rare-earth cations used.

Figure 2 shows a series of SEM photomicrographs obtained from 8 μm thick PLD films, of the Eu, Tb, and Tm doped YAGG material annealed at temperatures ranging from 1,400 to 1,650°C for various times. SEM micrographs of the as-deposited phosphors (not shown in the

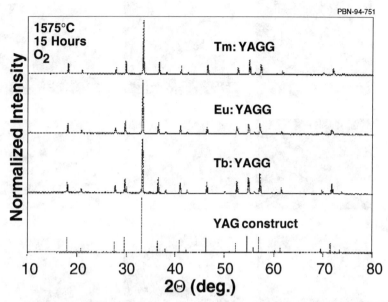

Figure 1. X-ray Powder Diffraction Scans of Laser-Deposited Tm:, Eu: and Tb:YAGG Films Annealed in O_2 at 1,575°C for 15 Hours.

figure) display small particulates which are incorporated to some degree in all PLD films. The Normalized Particle Density[6] (NPD) for this material was found to be about 75 particles/cm²/Å for films grown at pressures below 5 mTorr. As the pressure is increased the NPD also increases. However, after the high temperature anneal cycle thermaly driven migration was sufficient to remove any trace that these laser-generated particulates existed. As noted in Figure 2, the average grain size of each doped-YAGG material grows as the anneal temperature increases. For instance, the grain size of the Tm:YAGG material remains about 0.5 μm until the anneal temperature reaches 1,537°C, where the grains grow in size dramatically (note the change in scale for the 1,600°C micrograph). Micrographs of films annealed at a 1,575°C for 15 and 60 hours indicate that the grains have doubled in size, reaching average values of ~3, 2, and 3 μm for the Eu, Tb, and Tm:YAGG films, respectively. Cross sectional micro-graphs indicate that the annealed films are ~90 % dense and well adhered to the substrate. The peak to peak surface roughness of several PLD phosphor films was measured using a stylus profilometer. The surface roughness was found not to vary by more than ± 1 μm for as-deposited films and films annealed at 1,400°C. Annealing these films at higher temperatures reduces the average surface roughness to ± 0.5 μm. This compares well with powder phosphor screens, which may have particles or agglomerations of over 30 μm in size which protrude well above the screens surface.

Figure 3 shows the extrinsic luminous efficiency versus anode (screen) voltage at a beam current of 25 μA/cm², obtained from a Tb:YAGG (green) PLD screen. This screen was deposited in an oxygen pressure of 5 mTorr over four quadrants of the substrate in successive depositions using metal masks to obtain YAGG thicknesses ranging from 2 to 8 μm. This screen was then annealed at 1,400°C in oxygen. As noted, the extrinsic efficiency increases with film thickness, almost doubling when the thickness is increased from 2 to 8 μm at 20 kV. The efficiency also increases with increasing anode potential for the two thicker films. As the anode potential increases above 16.5 and 18.5 kV for the 2 and 4 μm thick films, respectively, a portion of the electron beam completely penetrates the film and deposits a fraction of its energy in the substrate, thus reducing efficiency. Figure 4 displays the efficiency versus luminance for the same Tb:YAGG (green) screen. Luminance levels of 3,000 fL were readily achieved with

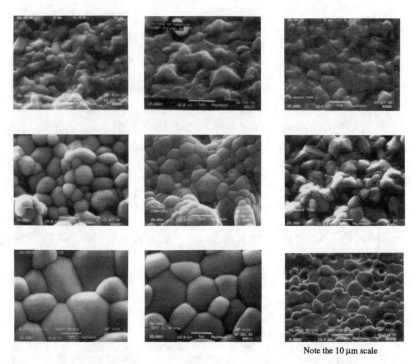

Note the 10 μm scale

Figure 2. Photomicrographs of 8 μm Thick PLD Films of a) Eu:YAGG, Tb:YAGG, and Tm:YAGG Films Annealed at 1400°C for 3 Hours; b) Annealed at 1500°C for 3 Hours; and c) Annealed at 1625°C for 3 Hours. All scales are 1 μm, except for the Tb film annealed at 1,625°C which is 10 μm.

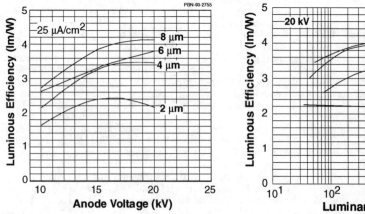

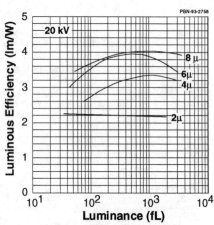

Figure 3. Extrinsic Luminous Efficiency vs. Anode Voltage at a Beam Current of 25 A/cm^2 for a Tb:YAGG (Green) PLD Screen.

Figure 4. Efficiency Versus Luminance for a Tb:YAGG (Green) PLD Screen.

efficiencies of 4 lm/W for the 8 μm thick phosphor film. Conventional P-53 (Tb:YAGG) powder phosphors can provide 3,000 fL at 20 kV with an efficiency of 30 lm/W. Figure 5 displays the spectral distribution from 8 μm thick PLD screens, annealed at 1,400°C for Eu:, Tb:, and Tm:YAGG, respectively. The Universal Color Scale coordinates (U', V') obtained from of the three laser-deposited phosphor compositions as determined with the spectrophotometer were (0.391, 0.541), (0.159, 0.558), and (0.155, 0.255), for the red, green, and blue phosphors, respectively. Thus, about 25 % of the color scale would be obtainable with screens produced using this combination of phosphor materials. For reference, the CIE U' V' coordinates for white are (0.210, 0.316).

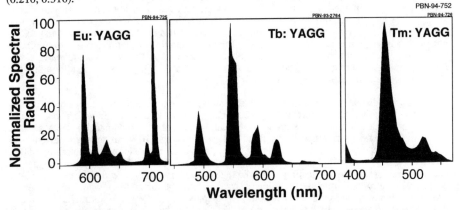

Figure 5. Spectral Distributions of 8 μm Thick Eu:, Tb:, and Tm:YAGG Films Annealed at 1,400°C.

Figure 6 is a photograph of a 5 cm square, 2 μm thick, three color, RGB screen fabricated using PLD and a lift-off process. Figure 7 shows the external efficiency of this screen (annealed at 1,400°C in O_2) as a function of screen brightness. A maximum efficiency of 1.2 lm/W is obtained at 20 kV and a luminance level of 200 fL. A screen brightness of 900 fL was obtained at 20 kV with an efficiency of 1 lm/W. However, Figure 3 indicates that the screen efficiency increases significantly with film thickness, thus it is plausible to assume that this color screen's

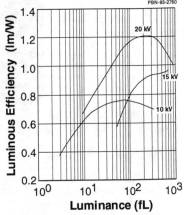

Figure 6. Photograph of a 2 μm Thick, Three Color, RGB Screen Fabricated Using PLD and a Lift-off Process.

Figure 7. External Efficiency vs. Screen Luminance of the Screen Shown in Figure 6

efficiency could be doubled to about 2.4 lm/W, with a significant increase in brightness, simply by increasing the PLD film thickness to 8 μm. The maximum luminance obtained for the three 8 μm thick PLD phosphor screens annealed at 1,400°C were 500 fL at 0.73 lm/W; 3,500 fL at 3.9 lm/W; and 2 fL at 0.002 lm/W, each at 20 kV for the red, green, and blue phosphors, respectively. It should be realized that the fractional photopic luminance content of a standard white screen TV consists of approximately 20%, 70%, and 10% coming from the red, green, and blue phosphors, respectively. Thus, a white screen with a luminance of 2,000 fL would consist of 400 fL for red, 1,400 fL of green, and 200 fL of blue. To date, the luminance levels for the Eu: and Tb:YAGG phosphors are readily achievable with high efficiencies. However, the efficiency and brightness levels obtained with the Tm:YAGG material are still very low, and improvements of about two order of magnitude in brightness are needed. The uniformity of screen luminance was measured across the 70 mm diagonal of the 5 cm square, 8 μm thick, PLD Eu: and Tm:YAGG phosphor screens, both annealed at 1,400°C. The maximum total variations in screen luminance were 12 and 10 percent for the Eu: and Tm: doped screens, respectively. The human eye is relatively insensitive to gradual spatial luminance variations of up to 25 percent, although it is sensitive to color variations.

Figure 8 displays a photograph of the emission pattern obtained from a PLD thin-film Tb:YAGG phosphor screen irradiated by a cold-cathode field-emission chip which was fabricated with 80,000 Mo tips. The screen and test chip were spaced 1 mm apart in a UHV chamber for testing. The field emitters were operated at a grid voltage of 70 V, an emission current of 20 μA, and the screen was held at a potential 4.4 kV. Individual pixels (consisting of about 650 Mo tips) can clearly be seen, the pitch between the largest pixels being 500 μm. Monitoring the chamber pressure during the testing of this laser-deposited phosphor screen indicated significantly less electron-stimulated desorption of gas than was obtained with powder P-53 screens. This low outgassing was evident right from FEA display turn-on, and was maintained for the duration of chip testing which lasted over 1 week. Furthermore, there was no evidence of dislodged particulates, which were typically found when using standard powder P-53 phosphor screens under identical test condtions.

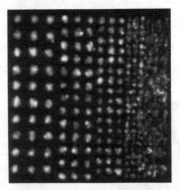

Figure 8. Photograph of the Emission Pattern Obtained From a PLD Thin-film Tb:YAGG Screen Irradiated by a Cold-cathode Field-Emission Chip.

CONCLUSIONS

PLD has been used to deposit Eu:, Tb:, and Tm:YAGG phosphor materials onto sapphire substrates. Once annealed the phosphors form highly dense, polycrystalline films which are well adhered to the underlying substrate. Annealing temperatures near 1,575°C greatly increase the grain size of the phosphor materials, and it has been previously suggested that efficiencies increase with increased grain size[1]. The efficiencies of films annealed at 1,400°C are presently adequate for forming green or red monochrome displays with luminance levels of 3,000 or 500 fL, respectively. The blue phosphor efficiency needs to be improved significantly before full color, high-quality high-brightness thin-film screens are available. These results are preliminary, and efficiences of films annealed at higher temperatures, with significantly larger grain sizes as noted in Figure 2, may well yield improved efficiency and luminance. Higher efficiencies and luminance might also be obtained by varying both the dopant concentration as well as the anneal cycles. Such experiments are currently underway in our laboratories, and will be presented in future publications[7].

The results presented here indicate that PLD is capable of depositing high quality phosphor materials onto refractory substrates such as sapphire. These screens can provide low outgasing rates, and no emitter damage due to disloged particulates obtained with powder phosphors when used in field emitter displays. Commercial applications utilizing thin-film phosphors, such as lap-top computers based on FE technology, will not require the high brightness needed for many high performance military or sun-light-readable applications. Lower luminance displays will certainly use less expensive and lower temperature transparent substrates for the phosphor screens, and thus will require different phosphor materials than those described in this report. However, given the wide range of low voltage phosphor materials available, and the ease in which PLD can deposit these complex compounds, it is likely that pulsed-laser-deposition will play a key role in emerging flat-panel display technology.

REFERENCES

1)   J. Shmulovich and D. F. Kocian, Proceedings of SID, Vol. 30/**4**, pps. 297-302, 1989.
2)   J. M. Robertson and M. W. van Tol, Thin Solid Films, Vol. **14**, pp. 221, (1984).
3)   M. McLauglin, H. F. Sakeek, P. Maguire, W. G. Grahm, J. Molloy, T. Morrow, S. Laverty, and J. Anderson, Appl. Phys. Lett., Vol. **63** (14), pps. 1865-1867, 1993.
4)   J. A. Greer, J. Vac. Sci. Technol., **A**, Vol. 10(4), pps. 1821-1826, 1992.
5)   "Pulsed Laser Deposition of Thin-films", Ed. by D. B. Chrisey and G. K. Hubler, John Wiley and Son, In press.
6)   J. A. Greer and H. J. Van Hook, Mat. Res. Soc. Symp. Proc., Vol. 191, pps. 171-176, 1990.
7)   To be published in Proc. of SID, San Jose CA., June 1994.

BLUE AND YELLOW LIGHT EMITTING PHOSPHORS
FOR THIN FILM ELECTROLUMINESCENT DISPLAYS

Paul H. Holloway[*], J.-E. Yu[*], Phillip Rack[*], Joseph Sebastian[*], Sean Jones[*], Troy Trottier[*], K. S.Jones[*], B. Pathangey[#], T.J. Anderson[@], S.-S. Sun[&], R. Tuenge[&], E. Dickey[&] and C.N. King[&]
*--Dept. of Materials Science and Engineering, #--MICROFABRITECH, @--Dept. of Chemical Engineering, University of Florida, Gainesville, FL 32611
&--Planar Systems Inc., 1400 NW Compton Drive, Beaverton, OR 97006

ABSTRACT

Following a description of the purpose and participating members in the Phosphor Technology Center of Excellence, research on the growth and characterization of modulation doped ZnS:Mn and of $Ca_{0.95}Sr_{0.05}Ga_2S_4$:6%Ce are reported. ZnS:Mn has been grown using MOCVD and incorporation of Mn in 1 to 5 layers from 5 to 20 nm thick separated by layers of pure ZnS from 5 to 50 nm thick. This is shown to result in lower threshold voltages for ACTFELD displays. The luminescence spectra from sputter deposited, cerium-doped thiogallate thin films were measured and the diffusion of thin ZnS passivation layers versus temperature of heat treatment was discussed.

INTRODUCTION and PHOSPHOR TECHNOLOGY CENTER OF EXCELLENCE

It is now recognized that the flat panel display (FPD) technologies are critical to the future economical well being of the United States. Therefore there is renewed interest in all of the flat panel technologies ranging from the different varieties of liquid crystal displays (LCD's) to the lesser developed technologies of plasma displays (PD's), electroluminescent displays (ELD's), and field emission displays (FED's).[1] To support the development of these technologies, federal funding agencies are supporting research programs in all aspect of development, including materials synthesis, manufacturing technology, data handling and compression, and display properties and evaluation. Included in this effort is research and development of PD, ELD and FED phosphors for full color, high brightness, long lifetime, and high efficiency. Since the activity is noticeably lacking in research, development and manufacturing of such phosphors in the United States because television manufacturers have moved off shore, the Advanced Project Research Agency (ARPA) solicited proposal to support a phosphor research center. A consortium of universities, a not-for-profit research institute, and a flat panel manufacturers consortium jointly proposed to form the Phosphor Technology Center of Excellence (PTCOE) in response to this solicitation. The PTCOE is headquartered at Georgia Institute of Technology, and the founding university members are the University of Florida plus the University of Georgia, Oregon State

University, and Pennsylvania State University. The David Sarnoff Research Center is a founding member along with the American Display Consortium.

The PTCOE was officially funded in August, 1993, with the objectives stated in Table I. A prime objective is to develop applied and fundamental research programs to evaluate the current and to develop new phosphors for ELD, FED and PD's. There are also discussions as to the needs of LCD's for new, efficient phosphors for backlighting of displays. And finally there are new developments in cathode ray tube (CRT) displays which could benefit from new phosphors and phosphor processing. The amount of effort planned to support CRT's is limited. Instead our start-up efforts have largely been in the ELD, PD and FED areas, with the prioritization of effort determined by strong input from the American Display Consortium members. Thus the lack of effort in LCD backlighting and CRT's represent a lack of prioritization by our industrial collaborators. The PTCOE is intended to serve the industry for times longer than five years, therefore a procedure has been defined for companies to become a member who will both prioritize research directions, as well as help support the center and university research.

Besides the applied and fundamental research on phosphors, the PTCOE will facilitate and organize new education programs and will provide educated students to support the developing FPD industries. Finally, a database is being established at the PTCOE headquarters at Georgia Tech which will incorporate the existing papers and performance data on phosphors. Members of the PTCOE will be able to access the database and determine in real time the reported properties of a particular phosphor for a particular application with specified operating conditions. This will be an important benefit of membership in the PTCOE.

At the University of Florida, six faculty members participate in this Center. The prime objective of our research is to develop new and improved phosphors for ELD's and FED's. To date our primary activities have been in the area of EL phosphors, and this will be the focus of the balance of this paper. The ELD's of interest to our research has been the alternating current, thin film ELD's (ACTFELD) devices shown schematically in Fig. 1. This device is driven by an

Table I:
OBJECTIVES OF THE PHOSPHOR TECHNOLOGY CENTER OF EXCELLENCE

1. Develop a program of fundamental and applied research of phosphors for flat panel displays: CRT, EL, LCD, FED, and PD.

2. Collaborate with industry on applied research and shorten the technology utilization time.

3. Develop academic programs and provide educated personnel to address issues for phosphor development.

4. Develop a database on phosphor expertise, technology and processing.

alternating potential applied to front and rear contact electrodes. Thin film ELD-based flat panel displays are becoming competitive in both device performance and production technology. Currently, the most efficient TFELD's use ZnS:Mn as a monochrome (yellow) phosphor material. The polycrystalline phosphor thin films are deposited by various techniques, including electron beam evaporation, sputtering, and atomic layer epitaxy.

ACTFELD's performance would be considerably enhanced with brighter, more efficient phosphors emitting in the red, green and especially blue. Many studies have been performed to understand how to accomplish these improvements, including studies of new dopants, new growth techniques (e.g. metal-organic chemical vapor deposition [MOCVD] instead of atomic layer epitaxy [ALE] or sputter deposition), doping after growth by ion implantation rather than during growth, and studies of new host materials (e.g. CaS or SrS instead of ZnS).[2-5] In the present work, we have characterized the microstructure of ZnS grown by MOCVD as a function of thickness and growth conditions. We have also characterized the performance of ACTFELD's where one or five layers of Mn rich sulfide was grown sandwiched between wider layers of ZnS. Finally, we have examined the effects of changing the host from ZnS to a Ca-Ga sulfide with Ce dopants. These results are summarized below.

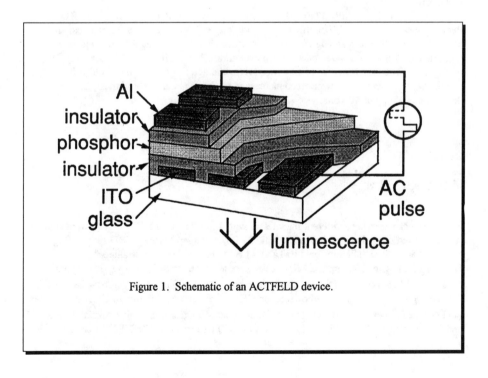

Figure 1. Schematic of an ACTFELD device.

EXPERIMENTAL

A modified Spire Model SPI-MOCVD 450 system was used for the growth of ZnS thin films. The system is a 4 gas-4 bubbler unit equipped with a fast switching run-vent manifold. The reactor is a horizontal design with an RF-heated tilted susceptor. A turbopumped, load-lock system allows substrate insertion without exposing the reactor to air. The parameters used to grow ZnS thin films were as follows:

• growth temperature: 250-400°C.
• reactor pressure: 50-80 Torr.
• VI/II ratio: 50-200.
• film thickness: 100nm-2μm.

$BaTa_2O_6$/ITO/glass substrates were used for the MOCVD growth of ZnS thin films. The 0.3μm polycrystaline $BaTa_2O_6$ insulating layer and the 0.2μm ITO electrode layer were sputter deposited. In the case of the $Ca_{0.95}Sr_{0.05}Ga_2S_4$:Ce, the 0.5 μm phosphor films were sputter deposited onto 0.3 μm thick ALE grown Al_2O_3-TiO_2 insulators over ITO on a glass substrate (with a glass transition temperature > 750°C). The ACTFELD devices were finished by sputter deposition of a top 0.3 μm layers of $BaTa_2O_6$ insulator followed by sputter deposition of an Al film electrode.

In this study, an APD 3720 diffractometer was used for X-ray diffraction (XRD), a Perkin-Elmer Lamda 9 UV/VIS/NIR spectrophotometer (UVS) was used for bandgap analysis, and a JEOL JSM-6400 scanning electron microscope (SEM) was used for studying the topography. Auger data were collected using a Perkin-Elmer PHI Model 660 scanning Auger microprobe. The EL properties of all devices were characterized by the threshold voltage, V_{th}, defined as the onset voltage for a steep increase in brightness, and the brightness, L_{40} (cd/m^2), determined at V_{th} plus 40 volts.

RESULTS

Manganese doped zinc sulfide

Samples grown to different thicknesses with T_{sub} = 350°C and VI/II = 100 were studied with XRD and optical absorption measurement of the bandgap.[6] These XRD spectra (Fig. 2) showed that the ZnS thin films on a $BaTa_2O_6$ / ITO / glass were polycrystalline. Under a thickness of 200 nm, the XRD peaks were mainly from the $BaTa_2O_6$ /ITO /glass substrate. When the film thickness was in the range of 200-700 nm, the peak near 28.5° (2θ) was very strong indicating a preferred orientation. This peak can be attributed to either the 3C cubic (111) or the 2H hexagonal (002) planes.[6] Besides this strongest ZnS peak, peaks at 2θ's of ~56° and 95° are also evident in Fig. 2. However, the XRD patterns from ZnS did not change with

292

thicknesses over the range of 200-700 nm. As the thickness of the film increased to $2\mu m$, additional diffraction peaks were detected at 2θ's of $33°$, $47°$, $59°$, $69°$, $74°$ and $88°$. The diffraction peaks often can be assigned to either the cubic or the hexagonal crystal structure. The exceptions to dual assignment are the three peaks at about $27°$, $33°$, and $69°$. The peak at $27°$ corresponds to a ZnS hexagonal (100) reflection[6] and cubic ZnS does not have a peak at this position. The other two peaks at $\sim 33°$ and $69°$ correspond to ZnS cubic (200) and (400) reflections[6] and hexagonal ZnS does not have peaks at these positions. The XRD pattern from a $2\mu m$ ZnS film matches the cubic structure, although a small fraction of a hexagonal phase still exists as evident from the relatively small (100) peak at $\sim 27°$.

The photoabsorption edge of these ZnS films was determined to be near 350 nm and it shifted to longer wavelengths as the film thickness increased. This indicates that the bandgap energy of the ZnS films decreased as the film thickness increased, as shown in Fig. 3. The bandgap energy of ZnS has been reported to be 3.54 eV for the cubic phase and 3.80 eV for the hexagonal phase.[6] For ZnS exhibiting mixed cubic and hexagonal phases, the bandgap energy has been reported to decrease as the fraction of the cubic phase increased.[6] The data in Fig. 3 demonstrate that a larger portion of the cubic phase was present in thicker films which resulted in a lower bandgap. As the film thickness increased to $2\mu m$, the bandgap energy decreased from

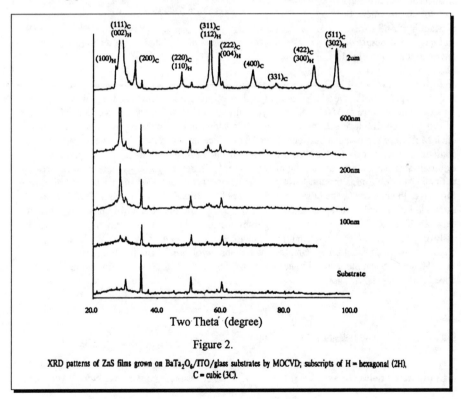

Figure 2.

XRD patterns of ZnS films grown on $BaTa_2O_6$/ITO/glass substrates by MOCVD; subscripts of H = hexagonal (2H), C = cubic (3C).

3.70 to 3.61 eV and XRD data show that the cubic crystal structure dominates. Thus, a transition in crystal structure from initially hexagonal at thicknesses < 700 nm to cubic at 2μm thickness is indicated by the XRD and photoabsorption data. It was also observed by SEM that the surface became rougher as the thickness of ZnS films increased.

To test whether growing layers of ZnS free from Mn might allow greater electron acceleration and therefore more efficient excitation of ZnS:Mn, a multilayered structure was grown as shown in Fig. 4.[7] The ZnS was grown using diethylzinc and H₂S at 400°C.

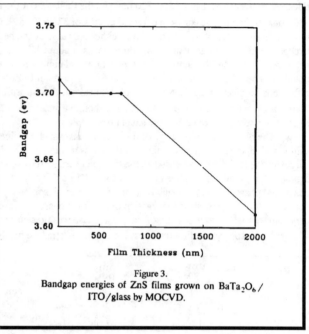

Figure 3.
Bandgap energies of ZnS films grown on $BaTa_2O_6$/ ITO/glass by MOCVD.

In order to grow MnS layers, tricarbonyl-(methylcyclopentadienyl)-Mn and H₂S was used at a substrate temperature of 550°C. Single layers of equivalent MnS thicknesses of 5 or 20 nm were grown between ZnS layers 25 or 50 nm thick. In addition, five repeated layers of 5 or 20 nm thick MnS were sandwiched between 20 or 50 nm thick layers of ZnS, in a second sample configuration. Later data have shown that the Mn can diffuse several tens of nanometers in these materials at these temperature during growth times.[8] Therefore, the layers labeled MnS are normally Mn rich ZnS, although XRD peaks from MnS were detected from samples with greater MnS layer thicknesses.[7] The brightness versus applied voltage for single MnS layer devices is shown in Fig. 5, and excellent brightness was observed from the 20 nm MnS layer sandwiched between 50 nm ZnS layers. Similarly, brightness versus voltage data are shown in Fig. 6 for a uniformly Mn doped ZnS versus multilayer samples of equivalent thickness. While the V_{40} brightness is about equal for all samples, the threshold voltage for the five multilayer 5 nm MnS/50 nm ZnS sample showed lower threshold voltages. Work is continuing on modulation doped ZnS samples.

Cerium doped calcium-strontium thiogallate

The luminescent spectrum from $Ca_{0.95}Sr_{0.05}Ga_2S_4$:Ce films and powders excited by photons (PL) or electric fields (EL) are shown in Fig. 7.[9] The emission from the precursor powder for a sputter target is slightly red shifted from the PL or EL from sputter deposited films. The PL and EL spectra from deposited films are improved by annealing to higher temperatures. To provide chemical protection for the thiogallate film at higher temperatures, a film of ZnS (up to 100 nm) at the ATO/phosphor interface has been found to be necessary.[10] The location of this interface layer is evident in the Auger depth profile shown in Fig. 8 (note the Zn peak at about 12 min. of sputtering). The Auger depth profile after annealing is shown in Fig. 9, and the

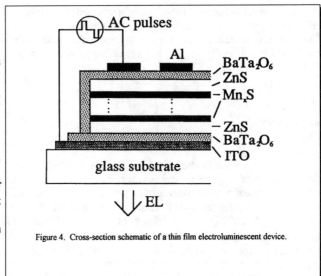

Figure 4. Cross-section schematic of a thin film electroluminescent device.

interfacial Zn peak is severely attenuated. Initially we interpreted this to indicate that the ZnS had completely diffused into the thiogallate film, however subsequent data from cross section TEM

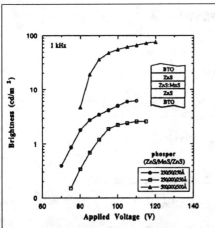

Figure 5. Brightness vs. voltage characteristics of three single modulation doped samples consisting of a single MnS-doped region with a thickness of 50 or 200 Å bounded by two ZnS layers either 250 or 500 Å thick.

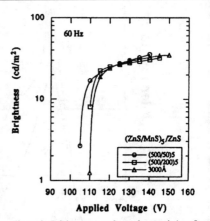

Figure 6. Brightness vs. voltage characteristics of two multiple modulation doped samples consisting of five MnS-doped regions either 50 or 200 A thick bounded by six 500 A thick ZnS layers, and a uniformly doped sample of the same overall thickness.

showed an intact ZnS layer. Therefore we are forced to conclude that heat treatment has seriously degraded the interfacial resolution of the Auger depth profile, due to a roughening of the film. This is consistent with the breadth of the interface of the polycrystalline film (4 minutes in Fig. 9 vs. 1 minute in Fig. 8). The role of the ZnS layer in chemical protection of the thiogallate film is still under study.

SUMMARY

A Phosphor Technology Center of Excellence (PTCOE) has been formed to support the development of a flat panel display industry. Research at the University of Florida within the PTCOE is focused on improvement of phosphors for electroluminescent displays (ELD's) and field emission displays (FED's). Research into Mn doped ZnS was reported, and the crystal structure of MOCVD grown films changed from initially hexagonal for thin films to cubic for films 2μm thick. ELD's consisting of MnS sandwiched between ZnS films showed good brightness and reduced threshold voltages. The PL and EL spectra from $Ca_{0.95}Sr_{0.05}Ga_2S_4$:Ce films

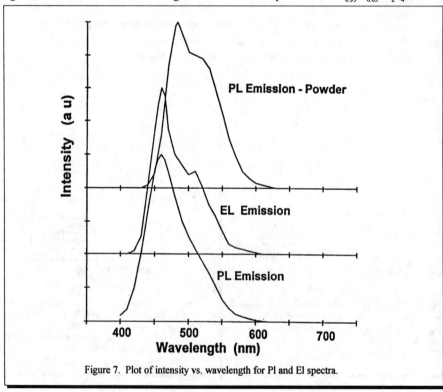

Figure 7. Plot of intensity vs. wavelength for Pl and El spectra.

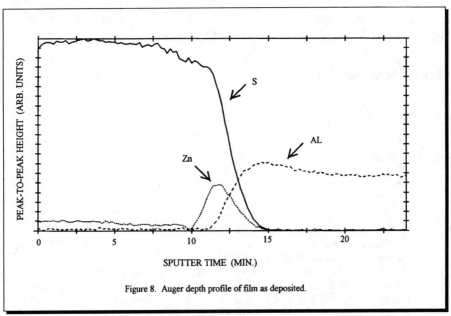

Figure 8. Auger depth profile of film as deposited.

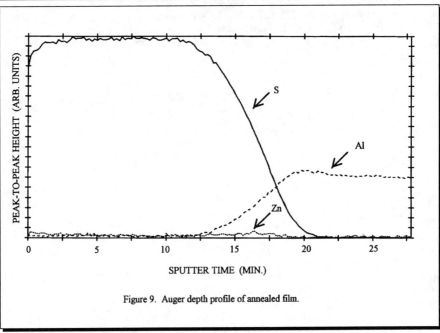

Figure 9. Auger depth profile of annealed film.

297

are maximum near 450 nm in the blue. Sputter deposited thiogallate films are smooth, and a ZnS layer helps to chemically protect them at higher temperatures. Auger depth profiles of these films are influenced by increased surface roughness after heat treatment.

ACKNOWLEDGEMENT

This work was supported by ARPA grant #MDA 972-93-1-0030 .

REFERENCES

1. L.E. Tannas, Jr., <u>Flat-Paned Displays and CRTs,</u> (Van Nostrand Reinhold Co. Inc., New York, 1985).
2. R. Mach and G.O. Muller, phys.stat. sol. (a) **69**, 11 (1982).
3. V.P. Tanninen, M. Oikkonen, and T. Tuomi, Thin Solid Films **109**, 283 (1983).
4. P.J. Dean, phys. stat. sol. (a) **81**, 625 (1984).
5. V.V. Ushakov and A.A. Gippius, J. Crystal Growth **101**, 458 (1990).
6. J. Fang, P.H. Holloway, J.-E. Yu and K. Jones, Appl. Surf. Sci. **70/71**, 701 (1993).
7. J.E. Yu, K.S. Jones, P.H. Holloway, B. Pathangey, E. Bretschnieder, T.J. Anderson, S.-S. Sun and C.N. King, J. Elect. Materials **23**, 299 (1994).
8. J.E. Yu, K.S. Jones, and B. Pathangey, to be published.
9. R.Tuenge and S.-S.Sun, J. Electrochem. Soc., in press.
10. S.-S. Sun, R. Tuenge, J. Kane, C.N. King and P.N. Yocom, U.S. Patent No. 5 309 070 (3 May 1994).

ELECTROPHORETIC DEPOSITION OF PHOSPHORS
FOR DISPLAY TECHNOLOGY

MICHAEL J. SHANE*, JAN B. TALBOT*, ESTHER SLUZKY**, AND K. R. HESSE***
*University of California, San Diego, Materials Science Program 0310, 9500 Gilman Drive, La Jolla, CA 92093-0310
**Hughes Aircraft Co., 6155 El Camino Real, Carlsbad, CA 92008
***Consultant, 1221 La Paloma Glen, Escondido, CA 92026

ABSTRACT

Electrophoretic deposition is a process used in producing display screens, in particular high-resolution CRT screens. The deposition of phosphor particles from isopropanol suspensions is investigated. It is shown that two materials deposit during electrophoretic deposition on a cathode: the phosphor particles, and hydroxides formed by chemical and electrochemical reactions occurring at the cathode. A simple model to predict the deposition rates of these two materials, given the particle and ion concentrations and mobilities, is developed. Finally, the microstructure of the resulting deposited screen is investigated using scanning and transmission electron microscopy.

INTRODUCTION

Electrophoretic deposition on a cathode has been used for the manufacture of specialized cathode ray tubes (CRTs) since the 1950's[1] and is presently employed for CRTs for advanced display applications. High resolution screens require a processing technique to produce densely packed thin screens consisting of small particles, in the range of 0.5 to 6 μm. Electrophoretic deposition offers several potential advantages over conventional gravity settling, centrifugal settling, and slurry screening processes in both quality of the screens produced and control of the production of high-resolution screens.[2] Other advantages include the ability to deposit onto curved screen surfaces and a more economical use of phosphor by the reduction of waste material.

The electrophoretic coating bath of interest in this study consists of phosphor particles suspended in a solution of isopropanol (IPA) which contains dissolved salts, such as $Mg(NO_3)_2$, similar to that used by McGee et al.[3] During the deposition process, two materials are deposited on the cathode: the phosphor particles deposit under the influence of the electric field and magnesium hydroxide, formed by hydroxide ions from the electrolysis of water which react with the magnesium ions as follows:[4,5]

$$2H_2O + 2e^- = H_2(g) + 2OH^- \tag{1}$$
$$Mg(NO_3)^+ + 2OH^- = Mg(OH)_2 \tag{2}$$

The magnesium hydroxide binds the phosphor particles to the substrate;[6] however too much adhesive material in the screen can adversely affect the CRT screen appearance and light output. Typically, for each type of phosphor particle to be used the bath composition and processing conditions to produce the desired screen characteristics are chosen empirically. One goal of our research is to understand the fundamentals of electrophoretic deposition in order to a design a process for any given type of particle to achieve the quality of coating desired.

In addition to the measurement of the relative amounts of the phosphor and hydroxide in a deposit, the distribution of these components is also of importance. This distribution may influence the adhesion properties of the deposited film and the light output from the screen. In particular, it is of interest whether the hydroxide is deposited as a thin layer near the cathode, leaving the outer regions of the deposited film with little hydroxide, or whether the hydroxide is uniformly distributed throughout the deposited film.

The objectives of our research were to systematically investigate the electrophoretic deposition of phosphor by: (a) measuring the electrophoretic properties (zeta potential) of phosphor particles, (b) measuring the dissociation behavior of the added salts, (c) developing a model to predict both phosphor and hydroxide deposition rates, and (d) investigating the microstructure of the deposited screens.

ELECTROPHORETIC DEPOSITION MODEL

A model was developed to relate process parameters, such as deposition time and applied voltage, to the amount of material depositing.[7] The mass of material depositing, M_{calc}, can be determined from the following integral relationship:

$$M_{calc} = \int_0^t \alpha CvA \, dt = \frac{\alpha C \mu i_{avg} t}{\sigma} \tag{3}$$

where α is the fraction of particles which adhere to the substrate, C is the concentration of material in the suspension, v is the velocity of the depositing material under the influence of the electric field, A is the cathode area, μ is the mobility, i_{avg} is the average current during the deposition, σ is the specific conductivity of the solution, and t is the deposition time. Eq. 3 is integrated assuming constant parameter values during deposition. This model can be applied to both phosphor and hydroxide deposition by using the appropriate concentration and mobility. For calculating the hydroxide deposition, C is the concentration of $Mg(NO_3)^+$ at a particular $Mg(NO_3)_2$ concentration, multiplied by the molecular weight of the depositing material, $Mg(OH)_2$. The mobility can be calculated using:

$$\mu_+ = \frac{\Lambda_o t_+}{F} \tag{4}$$

where Λ_o is the molar conductivity at infinite dilution and t_+ is the transference number for the cation. The value for Λ_o of 18 mho cm^2/mole, which corresponds to the first dissociation of $Mg(NO_3)_2$,[8] was used in performing calculations, while t_+ was estimated from the aqueous transference number of Na^+ in $NaNO_3$, which is 0.41.[9] For the phosphor particles, the concentration is simply the mass of phosphor particles per unit volume of suspension, while the mobility can be calculated using the Smoluchowski equation:

$$\mu = \frac{\zeta \varepsilon}{\eta} \tag{5}$$

where ε and η are the liquid permittivity and viscosity, respectively, and ζ is the particle zeta potential, which was measured previously.[8]

EXPERIMENTAL

The electrophoretic coating process of interest utilizes ZnS:Ag (P-11, 4.77 μm average diameter) phosphor particles suspended in isopropyl alcohol (IPA) with dissolved magnesium nitrate. A typical bath consists of approximately 4 g/l phosphor and various concentrations of $Mg(NO_3)_2$ in IPA. Zeta potentials were measured using a Pen Kem Inc. Model 501 Lazer Zee Meter.[8] The zeta potential can be measured with a precision of ±5 mV using this instrument.

To determine the dissociation behavior of $Mg(NO_3)_2$ in IPA, the molar conductivity of $Mg(NO_3)_2$ salts in IPA was measured at 25.0°C using a Yellow Springs Instrument (YSI) Model 34 conductivity meter using concentrations from approximately 10^{-7}M to 10^{-2}M.[8]

Deposition experiments were performed within a glove box to allow deposition to occur without effects of atmospheric water absorption by the IPA solution. The variables studied were electric field strength, duration of deposition, and nitrate salt concentration. The deposition apparatus consisted of two vertical, parallel electrodes suspended in a beaker of IPA containing phosphor suspension, placed inside the box. The electrodes were connected to a high voltage power supply and ammeter. After deposition, the sample was weighed and the film was dissolved in a mixture of hydrochloric and nitric acid. The acid solution was then analyzed for Zn and Mg using atomic absorption (AA) spectroscopy. From this analysis, the amount of P-11 phosphor (ZnS) and magnesium hydroxide which had deposited was calculated.

The samples for scanning electron microscopy (SEM) were prepared by electrophoretically depositing a phosphor film, and then depositing under the same conditions a film of only magnesium hydroxide, onto microscope slides which were coated on one side with approximately 1000Å of evaporated aluminum. The anode was an aluminum plate with dimensions identical with the slide. The depositions were carried out in IPA suspensions with 10^{-2}M $Mg(NO_3)_2$, using 200 V for 5 minutes with a 3 cm electrode separation. Lower $Mg(NO_3)_2$ concentrations were not used as very small amounts of hydroxide were produced, making it difficult to distinguish the phases in the SEM. After deposition, the microscope slides were fractured, coated with carbon or gold, and the cross section viewed in the SEM.

The samples for transmission electron microscopy (TEM) were prepared by depositing phosphor and hydroxide directly onto a nickel TEM grid, using 10^{-2}M $Mg(NO_3)_2$ in the IPA suspensions, with an applied voltage of 100V for 10 s, with an electrode spacing of 2 cm. This was sufficient to deposit approximately a monolayer of particles. The anode was a 0.635 cm. diameter stainless steel rod, with an exposed area approximately equal to that of the TEM grid. The deposition occurred on all exposed surfaces of the TEM grid. After deposition, the grid was placed in the TEM with no additional treatment and areas viewed which showed the region between particles.

RESULTS AND DISCUSSION

The zeta potential of P-11 (ZnS:Ag) phosphor as a function of $Mg(NO_3)_2$ in IPA was measured previously.[8] The zeta potential is constant at approximately -45 mV at concentrations less than 10^{-7}M, becomes positive above a concentration of approximately 10^{-6}M, and reaches a maximum of +50 mV at 10^{-5}M. Further increases in concentration result in a gradual decrease in the zeta potential.

In liquids of low dielectric constant such as IPA, dissociation of salts is small, as considerable ion pairing occurs. The dissociation of $Mg(NO_3)_2$ occurs as a two-step process:

$$Mg(NO_3)_2 = Mg(NO_3)^+ + NO_3^- \qquad K_{DI} = \frac{[Mg(NO_3)^+][NO_3^-]}{[Mg(NO_3)_2]} \qquad (6)$$

$$Mg(NO_3)^+ = Mg^{2+} + NO_3^- \qquad K_{DII} = \frac{[Mg^{2+}][NO_3^-]}{[Mg(NO_3)^+]} \qquad (7)$$

The dissociation constants were determined from the conductivity measurements by using the Ostwald dilution law, which relates molar conductivity at a finite concentration to molar conductivity at infinite dilution and dissociation constant, the following values were found for $Mg(NO_3)_2$ in IPA:[8]

$\Lambda_{oI} = 18$ mho cm^2/mole $K_{DI} = 5.9 \times 10^{-5}$ mole/l
$\Lambda_{oII} = 123$ mho cm^2/mole $K_{DII} = 1.9 \times 10^{-7}$ mole/l

From these values the concentrations of the dissociation species were calculated. It was determined that in the concentration range of 10^{-6} to 10^{-3}M $Mg(NO_3)_2$ of interest for charging of the phosphor particles, the dominant species is $Mg(NO_3)^+$ from the first dissociation of the salt. Above 10^{-3}M $Mg(NO_3)_2$ very little dissociation occurs.

A series of deposition experiments was conducted and the results were compared to the predictions of Eq. 3, assuming α equals unity. The experiments performed used a P-11 phosphor concentration of 4.0 g/l and $Mg(NO_3)_2$ concentrations from 10^{-5} to $10^{-2}M$ with applied voltages of 100-800V and deposition times from 1-10 minutes. While the $Mg(NO_3)_2$ concentration was varied, the voltage was held constant at 200V and the deposition time was held constant at 5 minutes. A $Mg(NO_3)_2$ concentration of $10^{-3}M$ and 5 minute deposition time was used during variable voltage experiments, and a $Mg(NO_3)_2$ concentration of $10^{-3}M$ and 200 V applied voltage was used during variable time experiments.

The ratios of measured to calculated deposited weight for P-11 were calculated for each of the deposition experiments in which concentration, voltage, and deposition time were varied.[7] The results showed that in each experiment in which voltage and time of deposition were varied, the actual amounts agreed with the prediction from Eq. 3. When the concentration of $Mg(NO_3)_2$ was varied however, there was disagreement at low concentrations (10^{-5} and $10^{-4}M$). At these low concentrations, the phosphor particles are unable to adhere to the substrate due to low amounts of $Mg(OH)_2$ formation.

The ratios of measured to calculated deposited weight for $Mg(OH)_2$ were also determined. Again the data was in good agreement with the calculations from Eq. 3. Finally, the weight percent of $Mg(OH)_2$ in the deposited film was measured for each condition. The percent of $Mg(OH)_2$ in the films deposited from $10^{-3}M$ $Mg(NO_3)_2$ suspensions was fairly constant at 1.5%, independent of applied voltage and deposition time. Only in the cases where the concentration of $Mg(NO_3)_2$ changed did the percent of $Mg(OH)_2$ in the deposited film vary, from an immeasurably small amount at $10^{-5}M$ to over 6% at $10^{-2}M$.

Microstructural Analysis of Deposited Films

Figure 1 shows the results of a deposition experiment in which no phosphor is present in the suspension. The result is a uniform film of $Mg(OH)_2$ approximately 5μm thick, which appears to grow in a columnar fashion. Figure 2 shows the results of a deposition experiment in which 4g/l phosphor was present in the suspension. The deposition time and voltage used were identical to that used to prepare the sample shown in Figure 1. Note that the hydroxide is not present as a uniform film; rather, it appears to be surrounding each of the particles. This implies that the hydroxide is preferentially depositing on the particle surface. It is possible that the magnesium ions adsorbed on the particle surface react with the hydroxide ions near the cathode, thereby nucleating the deposition of a hydroxide layer on the particle surface.

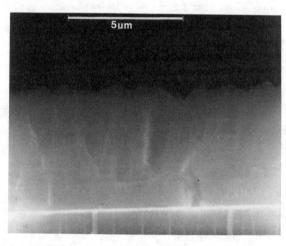

Figure 1: SEM image of $Mg(OH)_2$ deposited onto a microscope slide from $10^{-2}M$ $Mg(NO_3)_2$ solution in IPA.

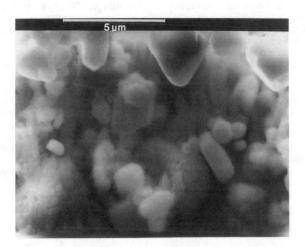

Figure 2: SEM image of P-11 phosphor and $Mg(OH)_2$ deposited from suspension containing 4g/l P-11 and $10^{-2}M$ $Mg(NO_3)_2$ in IPA.

Figure 3 is a TEM image near the contact point between two particles. Note that each of the particles again appears to be coated with a layer of hydroxide, and that the hydroxide is present between the particles and as a neck in the interparticle region. This shows that the hydroxide acts as a binding agent between the particles.

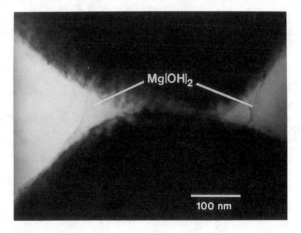

Figure 3: TEM image of two particles, with $Mg(OH)_2$ shown in the neck region between the particles.

CONCLUSIONS

Our investigation of the electrophoretic deposition of phosphor has significantly increased our knowledge of the basic mechanism of the process. The amount of free ions in the bath suspension is small. The roles of the ions in the bath are to charge the phosphor positively and to form the adhesive hydroxide matrix to bind the phosphor to the substrate. The amount of the adhesive needed to bind the phosphor is relatively small.

A series of deposition experiments was conducted in which the $Mg(NO_3)_2$ concentration, applied voltage, and deposition time were independently varied. For all of the experiments in which voltage and time of deposition were varied, the actual amounts deposited agreed well with the predictions of a simple deposition model. However, for experiments in which the concentration of $Mg(NO_3)_2$ was varied, the phosphor particles are unable to adhere to the substrate at low concentrations of $Mg(NO_3)_2$ due to low amounts of $Mg(OH)_2$ formation. The percent of $Mg(OH)_2$ in the films was approximately 1.5%, independent of applied voltage or deposition time. Only in the cases where the concentration of $Mg(NO_3)_2$ changed did the percent of $Mg(OH)_2$ vary, from immeasurably small amount at $10^{-5}M$ to over 6% at $10^{-2}M$.

The microstructural analysis showed that the hydroxide is uniformly distributed throughout the deposited film. The TEM images showed that the hydroxide coats the particles and acts to bind the particles together.

ACKNOWLEDGEMENTS

This research was supported by Hughes Aircraft Company and the University of California MICRO Program. The authors would like to acknowledge the assistance of Colette L. Ross, Huda Aldahhan, Benjamin Kinney, and Ruth Schreiber in performing various measurements and experiments.

REFERENCES

1. N. F. Cerulli, U.S. Patent No. 2 851 408 (9 September 1958).
2. P. F. Grosso, R. E. Rutherford, Jr., and D. E. Sargent, J. Electrochem. Soc. **117**, 1456 (1970).
3. J. D. McGee, R. W. Airey, and M. Aslam, Adv. Electron. Phys. **22A**, 571 (1966).
4. J. A.Siracuse, J. B. Talbot, E. Sluzky, T. Avalos, and K. R. Hesse, J. Electrochem. Soc. **137**, 2336 (1990).
5. J.A. Siracuse, M.S. Thesis, University of California, San Diego, 1989.
6. J. A. Siracuse, J. B. Talbot, E. Sluzky, and K. R. Hesse, J. Electrochem. Soc. **137**, 346 (1990).
7. M. J. Shane, J. B. Talbot, B. G. Kinney, E. Sluzky, and K. R. Hesse, J. Coll. Interface Sci., to be published.
8. M. J. Shane, J. B. Talbot, R. D. Schreiber, C. L. Ross, E. Sluzky, and K. R. Hesse, J. Coll. Interface Sci, to be published.
9. J. S. Newman, Electrochemical Systems, 2nd. ed. (Prentice Hall, Englewood Cliffs, NJ, 1991), p. 255.

NOVEL THIN FILM LIGHT EMITTING DIODE DISPLAY MADE OF AMORPHOUS SILICON-BASED SEMICONDUCTORS

DUSIT KRUANGAM, WIROTE BOONKOSUM[*], SOMSAK PANYAKEOW AND BANCHERD DeLONG[**]
Semiconductor Device Research Laboratory, Department of Electrical Engineering, Faculty of Engineering, Chulalongkorn University, Bangkok 10330, Thailand.

ABSTRACT

A novel Thin Film Light Emitting Diode (TFLED) flat panel display was developed. The TFLED is a carrier injection-type electroluminescence and made of hydrogenated amorphous silicon-based semiconductor p-i-n junctions. The amorphous layers employed in this work are for example, $a\text{-}Si_{1-x}C_x{:}H$ and $a\text{-}Si_{1-x}N_x{:}H$. The TFLED has two basic structures; 1) glass substrate/ITO/amorphous p-i-n layers/Al and 2) metal sheet substrate amorphous n-i-p layers/ITO. The typical thicknesses of the amorphous p-i-n layers are 150 Å, 500 Å and 500 Å, respectively. The color of the emission can be changed from red to white-blue by increasing the optical energy gap (2.5-3.5 eV), that is the atomic fraction x, in the i-layer. The brightness of the TFLEDs are of the order of 1-10 cd/m^2 with injection current density of 100-1000 mA/cm^2 and applied voltage of 8-15 V.

INTRODUCTION

A light-emitting diode (LED) is now an electronic component in everyday use such as in pocket calculators, alphanumeric displays, indicator lamps on stereo equipment and computers. Most of the LEDs fabricated so far are made of expensive direct band gap crystalline semiconductors, e.g., GaAs and other III-V compound materials. The reasons why LEDs are so popular are, e.g., long life, compatible with integrated circuits, small size and weight, ruggedness, fast switching times, low drive voltage, etc. However, the crystalline LEDs still have some disadvantages, e.g., made of expensive and small area materials, operation in a small single chip, etc.

In this work novel thin film LEDs (TFLEDs) made of inexpensive amorphous silicon alloys were developed. Amorphous silicon (a-Si:H) and its alloys do not have the same selection rules for optical transitions as the crystals, so that it is feasible to make TFLEDs from amorphous silicon alloys (e.g., a-SiC:H, a-SiN:H) [1]. Moreover, The larger band gap and range of alloys give the possibility of TFLEDs spanning the visible spectrum. In this paper a series of the technical data on the device fabrication technology and device characteristics are presented. Some new ideas of the applications of the amorphous TFLEDs are proposed.

ADVANTAGES OF AMORPHOUS THIN FILM LED (TFLED)

Amorphous Thin Film LEDs (TFLEDs) have various advantages over conventional crystalline LEDs, such as :

---

[*] On leave from Telephone Organization of Thailand, Electronic Equipments Repair Center, Bangkok, Thailand.
[**] Visiting researcher from Premier Global Corporation Limited, Bangkok, Thailand.

Mat. Res. Soc. Symp. Proc. Vol. 345. ©1994 Materials Research Society

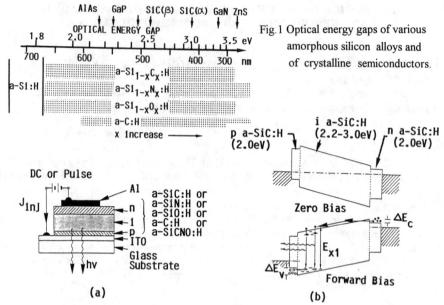

Fig.1 Optical energy gaps of various amorphous silicon alloys and of crystalline semiconductors.

Fig.2 Structure of amorphous silicon alloys thin film LED (TFLED) used in this work (a), and its band diagram (b).

- The optical energy gap of amorphous silicon based alloys, e.g, a-SiC:H, a-SiN:H, a-SiO:H can be widely varied from 1.7 eV up to more than 4 eV, by changing the composition Si/C or Si/N in the film (see figure 1). While the optical energy gaps of crystalline semiconductors are mostly constant.
- Because of the feature of amorphous network, a-SiC:H, a-SiN:H films can be deposited on large area foreign substrates, e.g., glass, stainless steel, ceramic, polymer sheets.
- The TFLED fabrication process does not require a high temperature condition. This leads to a low cost LED, and ease of mass production.
- The TFLED can emit light having any pattern by designing the pattern of the transparent ITO and Al electrodes or by inserting insulating layer in the device. [2].
- The TFLED can be operated at a low voltage (<20 V).

BASIC STRUCTURE & FABRICATION OF AMORPHOUS THIN FILM LED

The amorphous thin film light emitting diode (TFLED) has a structure of p-i-n junctions of amorphous silicon alloys deposited on a glass/ITO substrate as shown in Fig. 2. The rear electrode is aluminum thin film. The p- and n- layers act as holes and electrons injection layers, respectively, and the i-layer acts as a luminescent active layer. The TFLED will emit light when it is forward biased through the ITO (+) and aluminum (-) electrodes. Since the luminescence in amorphous silicon alloys arises from the radiative recombination of electrons and holes through the deep localized states in the gap (Fig. 2(b)), the optical energy gap of the i-layer must be larger than about 2.0 eV so that visible light can be observed. The amorphous materials that are

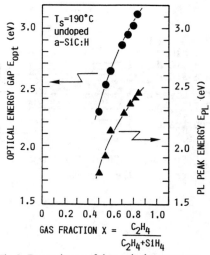

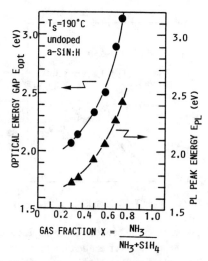

Fig.3 Dependence of the optical energy gap
and the peak energy of PL spectrum
on the C_2H_4 gas fraction for the
preparation of a-SiC:H film.

Fig.4 Dependence of the optical energy gap
and the peak energy of PL spectrum
on the NH_3 gas fraction for the
preparation of a-SiN:H film.

Table I Preparation conditions for
amorphous p-i-n layers by RF plasma
enhanced CVD

RF frequency	13.56 MHz
Substrate temperature	190 °C
Total gas pressure	1.0 Torr
Gases for	
p a-SiC:H layer	$SiH_4 + CH_4 + B_2H_6$
i a-SiC:H layer	$SiH_4 + C_2H_4$
a-SiN:H layer ·	$SiH_4 + NH_3$
a-SiO:H layer	$SiH_4 + CO_2$
a-C:H layer :	C_2H_4
n a-SiC:H layer	$SiH_4 + CH_4 + PH_3$

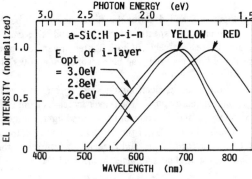

Fig.5 Electroluminescent spectra of a-SiC:H TFLEDs.

considered to be available for visible light emissions are for example, a-SiC:H, a-SiN:H, a-SiO:H,
a-C:H, and perhaps the combination of the Si-C-N-O-H atoms. In this paper the results on the
utilization of a-SiC:H and a-SiN:H are described. The ITO electrode was prepared by an electron
beam evaporator at the substrate temperature of 250 °C. The amorphous p-i-n layers were
prepared by a conventional RF plasma enhanced CVD method. The typical preparation conditions
for the amorphous layers are summarized in Table I. In this work, to ensure dark conductivity
higher than 10^{-8} (S.cm^{-1}), p- and n- type a-SiC:H having the optical energy gaps constant at 2.0
eV were selected as the carrier injection layers in the TFLEDs [3-5].

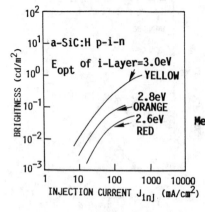

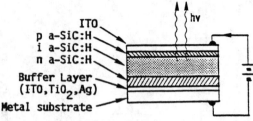

Fig.7 Structure of a-SiC:H TFLED deposited on a metal sheet substrate.

Fig.6 Relationship between the brightness and the injection current density for the a-SiC:H p-i-n TFLEDs. The parameter is the optical energy gap of the i a-SiC:H layer.

BASIC CHARACTERISTICS OF AMORPHOUS MATERIALS & TFLEDs

Figures 3 and 4 show the dependences of the optical energy gaps and peak energies of photoluminescent spectra on the C_2H_4 and NH_3 gas fractions for undoped a-SiC:H and a-SiN:H materials, respectively. In both figures, it can be clearly seen that the optical energy gaps and PL peaks of both materials can be widely changed over visible light regions by adjusting preparation conditions.

Figure 5 shows electroluminescent spectra of p a-SiC:H/i a-SiC:H/n a-SiC:H TFLEDs. When the optical energy gap of the i-layer increases from 2.6 eV to 3.0 eV, the spectra move to shorter wavelengths and the color of the emitted light changes from red to yellow.

The brightness (B) of the TFLEDs varies with the injection current density (J_{inj}) as $B \propto J_{inj}$ at the low current regions, and B seems to saturate at the high current regions, as shown in Fig. 6. The highest brightness obtained in the a-SiC:H and a-SiN:H TFLEDs is about 1-10 cd/m² so far.

IMPROVEMENT OF BRIGHTNESS OF TFLED BY USING METAL SUBSTRATE

The brightness of amorphous TFLEDs obtained so for is too low for an application as a display. It is necessary to improve the brightness of the device. One of various factors that limit the brightness might arise from the thermal quenching effect of the internal quantum luminescent efficiency due to the bad thermal conductivity of the glass/ITO substrate. In this work, an effort has been made to improve the brightness of the a-SiC:H TFLED by using highly-thermal conductive metal (SUS, Cu, Al, Cr, Zn) sheet substrates as shown in Fig. 7. The preliminarly experiment has shown that the brightness measured at room temperature was increased from 1 Cd/m² for a glass substrate to about 5 Cd/m² for a SUS substrate [6].

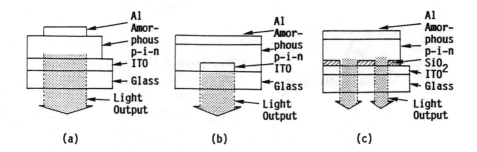

Fig.8 Structures of amorphous TFLEDs having desired emission patterns. (a) Making the pattern of the Al electrode, (b) Making the pattern of the ITO electrode, and (c) Making the pattern of the insulating layer inserted in the TFLED.

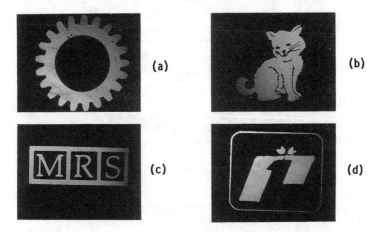

Fig.9 Examples of real emissions from the yellowish-orange a-SiC:H TFLEDs. (a) a gear (18 mm height), (b) a cat (14 mm height), (c) Premier Company's symbol (14 mm height), and (d) MRS's symbol (7 mm height).

FABRICATION OF AMORPHOUS TFLED DISPLAY

In an actual display the emitted light must have a desired pattern. This can be realized in amorphous TFLED by utilizing any one of the techniques shown in Fig. 8. (a) is to make the pattern of the Al electrode. (b) is to make the pattern of the ITO electrode. (c) is to make the pattern of an insulating layer inserted in the TFLED [2]. Fig. 9 shows some examples of the real emissions of orange a-SiC:H TFLEDs in which the emission patterns were performed by using technique in Fig. 8 (c). Fig. 10 shows an example of the real emission of white-blue a-SiN:H TFLED.

Fig. 10 Example of real emission from a-SiN:H TFLED.
The height of the a-SiN:H pattern is 6 mm.

DISCUSSIONS & SUMMARY

An amorphous silicon-based semiconductor thin film LED flat panel display was fabricated. At present the external efficiency of the device is as low as 10^{-3} % and the brightness is several cd/m^2. The device still needs further improvements, for example, carrier injection efficiency and lifetime. The typical rise-time of the TFLED is of the order of μsec [7]. Therefore, the switching time of the device is fast enough to be operated in a scanning mode having frequency of several tens kHz. Recently, the authors also succeeded in the development of the amorphous photocoupler (optocoupler) in which the light emitting device and the light detecting device were made of a-SiC:H TFLED and a-Si:H photodiode, respectively [6].

ACKNOWLEDGEMENT

This work was supported by Research Division of Chulalongkorn University and the Premier Global Corporation Limited, Bangkok, Thailand.

REFERENCES

1. D. Kruangam, in Amorphous & Microcrystalline Semiconductor Devices : Optoelectronic Devices, edited by Jerzy Kanicki (Artech House, Boston, London, 1991), p. 195.
2. Patent submitted.
3. W. Boonkosum, D. Kruangam and S. Panyakeow, Jpn. J. Appl. Phys. **32**, No. 16, 1534 (1993).
4. W. Boonkosum, D. Kruangam and S. Panyakeow, Int. Symp. Physical Concepts and Materials for Novel Optoelectronic Device Application II, Trieste, Italy, SPIE **1985** 40 (1993).
5. W. Boonkosum, B. DeLong, D. Kruangam and S. Panyakeow, 1st Int. Symp. Laser & Optoelectronics Technology & Applications, Singapore, 300 (1993).
6. W. Boonkosum, D. Kruangam, S. Panyakeow and B. DeLong, Mat. Res. Soc. Symp. A, Spring (1994).
7. D. Kruangam, W. Boonkosum and S. Panyakeow, J. Non-Crys. Sol. **164-166** 809 (1993).

NANOCRYSTALLINE SILICON FILMS FOR LARGE AREA DISPLAYS: PREPARATION AND PROPERTIES

S. Veprek, H. Tamura[*], M. Rückschloss and Th. Wirschem
Institute for Chemistry of Information Recording, Technical University Munich, Lichtenbergstr. 4, D-85747 Garching/Munich, Germany; [*] on leave from the Res. Lab. of Engineering Materials, Tokyo Institute of Technology, Nagatsuta, Midori, Yokohama, Japan

Abstract

We discuss the possible preparation techniques of the light emitting nanocrystalline silicon for large area electroluminescence (EL) displays and the control and optimization of the EL properties of the material. Some open problems are addressed and their possible solutions briefly discussed.

Introduction

Single crystal silicon is an indirect band gap material and, therefore, not suitable for optoelectronic applications. However, decreasing the crystallite size to a few nanometers leads to increasing mixing of the quantum states in the momentum space resulting in an increase of the optical transition probabilities [1]. Such material shows an efficient photoluminescence (e.g. [2][*]). The electroluminescence from the nanocrystalline silicon (nc-Si) has so far a relatively low efficiency of the order of $\leq$ 0.1 %, but an improvement is being currently achieved [3,4].

There are essentially two different theoretical models explaining the phenomena: The "quantum confinement" [2] and "surface state" [5] model. Both are based on the well documented fact that the bang gap of a semiconductor increases with decreasing crystallite size in the range of a few nm. Although the band gap of the silicon nanoparticles remains indirect [6], the transition probability between the bonding and antibonding states increases due to the above mentioned momentum assisted mixing of the quantum states [1]. Consequently, the absorption coefficient increases. In the framework of the "quantum confinement" model the light emission occurs due to the recombination of an electron-hole pair confined within the nanoparticle [5], whereas the "surface state" model assumes a trapping of the electron and/or hole in a surface state from where the radiative recombination occurs. From the point of view of the application of this material in AM LPD it is important to realize that, whereas the quantum confinement model predicts a blue shift of the emitted light with decreasing crystallite size, the photon energy remains determined by the nature of the surface states in the second model, i.e. it might also increase or remain constant with decreasing particle size. Experimentally, the blue shift has been found in isolated particles (e.g. [6]) and in "porous silicon" (PS) [4], but not in compact films [7].

311

Preparation of the Thin Films

Most of the work so far deals with the porous silicon which is prepared by anodic etching of single crystal silicon wafers in solution of hydrofluoric acid in ethanol [2-5]. The advantage of this technique is its simplicity. Therefore, various optoelectronic devices have been already demonstrated using PS, including small area electroluminescence (EL) displays (e.g.[3,4]). The disadvantage lies in the high porosity and brittleness of the material as well as in the limitation of the device area by the size of the available silicon wafers.

For these reasons we have been developing the preparation of the nanocrystalline silicon via a plasma induced CVD technique (see [7] and references therein). This technique is very similar to that used for the fabrication of thin film transistors (TFT) based on amorphous silicon (a-Si) which is currently being used for the fabrication of AM LPD. Only the deposition conditions for nc-Si differ from those of a-Si in the sense that the nc-Si is obtained from silane strongly diluted with hydrogen to a few mole % [8]. Alternatively, we have deposited a-Si at low temperature of $\leq 50°C$ which has been subsequently carefully recrystallized in order to obtain the necessary crystallite size [9]. The best control of the crystallite size provides the technique of chemical transport of silicon in a hydrogen glow discharge plasma which has been developed some time ago [10] and used for the preparation of light emitting nc-Si recently [7,9]. All these techniques are suitable for scaling up to large areas which are needed for essentially any size of AM LPD. Therefore, in the following part of the paper we shall concentrate on the control of the optoelectronic properties of the films which are important for such applications.

With all these techniques an efficient luminescence requires an appropriate passivation of the surface of the small crystallites in order to avoid non-radiative recombinations. This is achieved either by the passivation of the surface by chemisorbed hydrogen (e.g. during the anodic etching of the silicon wafer in HF) or by oxidation. A significant improvement of the efficiency of the luminescence results from annealing the oxidized nc-Si in forming gas at about $\leq 870°C$ which decreases the density of defects and mechanical strain in the nc-Si/SiO$_2$-films [7].

Control of the Optoelectronic Properties of the CVD nc-Si Films

The possibility of the application of nc-Si for the LPD has to be discussed in the context of other alternative materials and LPD designs, such as addressable liquid crystal displays and electroluminescence displays based on different materials (EL-polymers and compound semiconductors). With this in mind we concentrate on the following questions: Control of the efficiency of the luminescence, stability of the films, efficiency of the EL and the possibility of the control of the colour of the emitted light. Most of the data will be based on the measurement of the photoluminescence because it is much easier and faster than the preparation of the samples for EL which involves a rather complicated technology of the fabrication of stable and efficient electrical contacts.

312

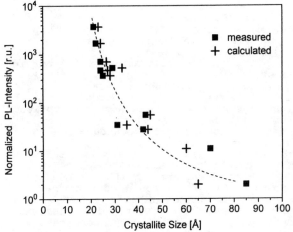

Fig. 1: Dependence of the photoluminescence intensity on the crystallite size for the nc-Si/SiO$_2$ films. The PL intensity has been normalized to the same fraction of the nc-Si component in the films.

Theoretical considerations predict [1] and our recent experimental results confirm [7] that the efficiency of the luminescence strongly increases by almost three orders of magnitude with crystallite size decreasing from about 70 Å to 20 Å. This is seen in Fig. 1 which reproduces these data together with some new results which will be discussed below. Accordingly, optimization of the luminescence requires films with a small crystallite size of ≤ 20 Å and a high fraction of the silicon nanocrystalls. The calculated data in Fig. 1 corresponds to a simple "surface state" model in which the PL intensity is proportional to the fraction of the Si atoms at the Si/SiO$_2$ interface, i.e. I_{PL} = Const./R_{at}, where R_{at} is the atomic radius.

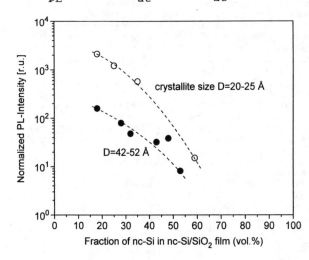

Fig. 2: Example of the effect of the packing density of the nc-Si, i.e. of the thickness of the SiO$_2$ intergrain layers on the PL efficiency.

313

For an efficient EL the films have to possess a sufficiently high electric conductivity in order to allow an efficient charge injection. Because of the necessity of the surface passivation of the crystallites by a dielectric material, such as SiO_2, the thickness of this dielectric matrix should be as small as possible. On the other hand, a defect-free passivated surface of the crystallites requires a sufficient thickness of the SiO_2 intergrain layers in order to allow for the relaxation of the strain which arises due to the structural mismatch of the crystalline silicon and amorphous silica network. Such relaxation of the grain boundary strain in various materials typically occurs within three to four monolayers. Thus, we expect the optimum thickness of the SiO_2 intergrain layers for PL to be around $\geq$ 15 Å. This limits the maximum fraction of nc-Si to about 15 - 25 %, depending on the shape of the crystallites.

The preparation of thin nc-Si/SiO_2 films with a controlled size of the crystallites and the thickness of the SiO_2 dielectric interfaces is a difficult task which we are currently conducting. The limited number of the samples which could be prepared and characterized so far supports the above estimate. Indeed, for a given crystallite size the luminescence efficiency decreases when the amount of nc-Si increases (Fig. 2). Obviously, more data are needed to optimize the nc-Si/SiO_2 films in terms of both, luminescence efficiency and electric transport simultaneously. Nevertheless the data show which way to go: The optimum thickness of the dielectric interface should be a compromise between the high efficiency of the radiative recombination of the electron-hole pairs (which calls for a thick interface, see Fig. 2) and an efficient charge transport through the film which requires a thin interface. As the transport is due predominantly to tunnelling through the dielectric barrier, the optimum thickness of the dielectric interface should be around 10 Å or less.

The stability of the films and the control of the colour of the emitted light are another important criterion for the choice of the material and of the preparation procedure. The hydrogen terminated surface is unstable upon prolonged exposure to air and, in particular, under the EL conditions. Indeed, Lang et al. have demonstrated the possibility of the control of the colour of the EL between blue and orange by controlling the porosity of the PS during its preparation, but even the red EL turned to green/blue one upon the EL operation for more than about 60 second [4]. This green/blue luminescence appears to be fairly stable upon both PL and EL operation. As we shall show later, it is associated with silanol groups in the silica matrix. Although the available data do not allow to drow any final conclusions regarding the long term stability of the EL from the nc-Si, they seem to well justify the view that only the nc-Si/SiO_2 or other refractory composites may meet these requirements. For this reason we restrict our further considerations to such films.

As already mentioned, there is no blue shift observed in compact films with decreasing crystallite size. Also the above mentioned change of the red EL to the green/blue in the EL experiments of Lang et al. [4] is due to a decay of the red component and appearance of the new one. In our recent work we could show that the green/blue luminescence is associated with the presence of silanol groups in the silica matrix and not with the nc-Si. This is illustrated by an example shown in Fig. 3 where the PL from several samples on nc-Si/SiO_2 with a various amount of crys-

talline component and various exposure to humid air or to boiling
ultrapure water is shown. For comparison, the PL spectra of
several silica glasses are shown as well. One can see that the
spectral distribution of the intensity of the green/blue PL in
the nc-Si/SiO is identical with that of silica glasses, and that
it is independent of the PL in the yellow/red spectral range. The
latter PL is observed only in samples with a sufficient content
of nc-Si but not in the silica glasses. The intensity of the
green/blue PL in that glasses scales with the density of structural defects as seen in the optical absorption in the
violet/UV-spectral region [11]. In all samples which show the
green/blue PL its intensity depends on the presence of silanol
groups ≡Si-O-H and it reaches maximum under conditions where the
concentration of the **isolated** silanol groups is maximal (about
350 to 400°C annealing temperature) [11].

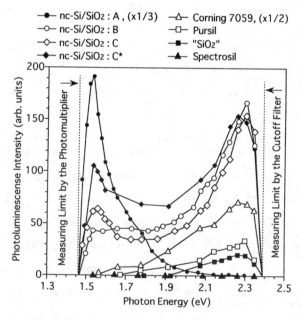

Fig. 3: Comparison
of PL spectra of
various samples:

Conclusions

The available data show that nc-Si/SiO thin films prepared by
plasma CVD and posttreatment represent an interesting material
for electroluminescence displays. The technique used for their
preparation is compatible with the present plasma CVD technique
used for the AM LPD. The relatively high thermal budged needed in
our present work for the oxidation and annealing of the films in
forming gas has to be reduced. This could be achieved by anodic
oxidation [12] and, possibly shorter annealing in FG at lower

temperature. The control of the colour of a stable electroluminescence represents an interesting challenge. Only a more detailed understanding of the PL and EL mechanism can allow one to decide if this is possible.

Acknowledgement

This work has been supported in part by the Volkswagen-Stiftung and by the Federal Ministry for Research and Technology. One of the authors (H.T.) thanks the Yamada Science Foundation for the grant which allowed him to participate in this work as visiting scientist.

References

*⁾ For lack of space we quote only some typical recent papers where the reader can find also further, earlier references.

[1] B. Delley and E.F. Steigmeier, Phys. Rev. **B 47**, 1397 (1993)
[2] P.D.J. Calcott, K.J. Nash, L.T. Canham, M.J. Kane and D. Brumhead, J. Luminescence 57, 257 (1993)
[3] H. Koyama and N. Koshida, J. Luminescence 57, 293 (1993)
[4] W. Lang, P. Steiner and F. Kozlowski, J. Luminescence 57, 341 (1993)
[5] F. Koch, V. Petrova-Koch and T. Muschik, J. Luminescence 57, 271 (1993)
[6] L. Brus, J. Phys. Chem. 97, 1493 (1993)
[7] M. Rückschloss, O. Ambacher and S. Veprek, J. Luminescence 57, 1 (1993);
M. Rückschloss, B. Landkammer and S. Veprek, Appl. Phys. Lett. **63**, 1474 (1993)
[8] S. Veprek, Z. Iqbal and F.-A. Sarott, Phil. Mag. **B 45**, 137 (1982)
[9] M. Rückschloss, B. Landkammer, O. Ambacher and S. Veprek, Mater. Res. Soc. Symp. Proc. **283**, 65 1992
[10] S. Veprek and V. Marecek, Solid State Electron. **11**, 683 (1968)
S. Veprek, F.-A. Sarott and Z. Iqbal, Phys. Rev. **B 36**, 3344 (1987)
[11] H. Tamura, M. Rückschloss, Th. Wirschem and S. Veprek, Appl. Phys. Lett., submitted March 1994
[12] F. Muller, R. Herio, M. Ligeon, F. Gaspard, R. Romestain, J.C. Vial and A. Bsiesy, J. Luminescence 57, 283 (1993)

OPTICAL PROPERTIES OF SILICON CLUSTERS
DEPOSITED ON THE BASAL PLANE OF GRAPHITE

L. N. Dinh*#, L. L. Chase#, M. Balooch#, L.J. Terminello#,
R. J. Tench**, F. Wooten*
*Department of Applied Science,
#Chemistry and Material Science Department,
**Materials Fabrication Division,
University of California, Lawrence Livermore National Laboratory, Livermore, CA 94551

ABSTRACT

Laser ablation and post annealing was employed for the synthesis of silicon (Si) clusters on highly oriented pyrolytic graphite surfaces in an ultra high-vacuum environment. The size distribution of the clusters was determined as a function of annealing time and temperature using an *in situ* scanning tunneling microscope (STM). Pure Si clusters with sizes ranging from 1 to 10 nm showed no detectable photoluminescence (PL) in the visible range. Exposure of these clusters to oxygen at 10^{-6} Torr and for up to 8 hours showed adsorption of oxygen on the surface of the clusters without Si oxide formation and no detectable PL. Hydrogen termination of these clusters was accomplished by exposing them to atomic hydrogen beam but did not result in any detection of the PL spectra either. Prolonged exposure of these clusters to ambient air, however, resulted in strong PL spectra with color ranging from red to greenish-blue depending on average cluster size. Auger electron spectra (AES) revealed the existence of partially oxidized Si clusters for these samples. This PL could be due to either an oxide phase or to quantum confined Si inner cores.

INTRODUCTION

Due to its small and indirect band gap, the use of Si in optical applications is very limited. However, according to the theory of the quantum confinement effect, when the dimension of a semiconductor is significantly reduced, its electronic energy levels are quantized, which results in an enlargement of the energy gap and a quantization of the electronic density of states [1, 2, 3]. Recent theoretical calculation also predicted a direct gap for surface passivated Si nanoclusters [4]. Si nanoclusters may, therefore, become a promising material for optical applications if their electronic and optical properties are well understood.
In this paper, we show how Si nanoclusters can be made in a well controlled environment. Surface passivation of these clusters and their optical spectra will then be discussed. Finally, a suggestion for future experiments on these clusters will also be mentioned.

EXPERIMENTAL

In order to have a control over the surface reaction rate which may be important in these small clusters, we proceeded to make them in an ultra high vacuum (UHV) chamber with a base pressure of $< 5 \times 10^{-10}$ Torr, by laser ablation from a cleaned Si target onto highly oriented

Mat. Res. Soc. Symp. Proc. Vol. 345. ©1994 Materials Research Society

pyrolytic graphite surfaces. **The graphite substrates were cleaved in laboratory air by pealing off layers of graphite with a piece of tape, and transferred into the UHV chamber through a load lock.** The substrates were then heated to 900 °C for 2 minutes to remove any adsorbed surface contaminant. The laser employed was an excimer laser producing output at a wavelength of 308 nm and a pulse duration of 20 nanoseconds. The laser's output of about 0.5 Joules/pulse was focused down to a spot of about 1 millimeter square on the surface of the Si target. The Si target was cleaned by laser ablation, then the graphite substrate was moved to face the Si target. A few laser shots at a target sample distance of about 3 cm could produce an equivalent of one to a few monolayers of Si on the substrate, although the Si distribution was very nonuniform and tended to peak around the normal to the Si target. In our experiment, the basal plane of graphite was chosen as substrate because all the carbon bonds in this plane are satisfied, and the well known structure of these graphite rings can be used as a calibration for subsequent STM images of the clusters.

Figure 1a shows an Auger spectrum of the as-deposited Si on graphite. The peak near 270 eV was from the carbon KLL Auger transition. The peak near 90 eV was from the Si LMM Auger transition . Less than 1% of adsorbed oxygen is seen near 500 eV. Figure 1b shows the Auger spectrum of the same sample after post annealing to 500 °C for 5 minutes. Here a reduction in the Si Auger peak is observed. **A reduction in this Auger peak implies a reduction in the surface covered by Si, which is consistent with the formation of bigger Si clusters through surface diffusion.** Figure 2a shows an STM image of as-deposited Si on graphite, which is observed to have no definite shape and a wide distribution of sizes. After post annealing for 5 minutes at 500 °C, a tendency to form aggregations of Si atoms of average size of 3.0 ± 1.0 nm in diameter can be observed in figure 2b **(although images in figure 2b may not be at the same location as those in figure 2a, due to the inability of our STM tip to come back to the same location after being withdrawn, for heat treatment of the sample).** However, as the substrate temperature was raised to 800 °C, a surface wetting (SiC interface formation) was evidenced by an increase in the Si Auger peak (hence increasing the surface area covered by Si) as shown in figure 3, and by "pancake shape" clusters observed by STM in figure 4 **(left picture is a line-out plot of the marked cluster in the right top-view picture)**. Clusters with pancake shape were expected at this temperature as a result of bonding of Si dangling bonds with broken π-bonds in the graphite rings. We were not interested in the clusters with pancake shape, due to its bonding to the graphite substrate and will not discuss any further this type of clusters in this paper.

PL was measured *in-situ* with a 15 mW, 325 nm continuous wavelength He-Cd laser, a grating spectrometer and an Oriel Instaspec IV cooled CCD. No detectable PL from the as-deposited clusters was observed, due to the PL quenching effect of the Si dangling bonds [5,6]. Surface passivation is necessary if these clusters are to be of any use in optical applications.

First, we introduced atomic hydrogen at 10^{-6} Torr into our UHV chamber (by passing molecular hydrogen through a white hot platinum mesh at about 2000 °C, with the sample located at about 3 cm behind the mesh), so as to passivate the surface. That did not result in any detectable visible PL from the clusters. For many other samples **which had not been exposed to atomic hydrogen** , we carried out surface passivation by flowing oxygen at up to 10^{-6} Torr into the UHV chamber for up to 8 hours. Auger spectra shows adsorption of oxygen on the surface of the clusters without Si oxide formation. **This was evidenced by a lack of Si LMM Auger peak shift from 92 eV toward lower energy (about 60 eV for SiO_2 and 80 eV for partially oxidized Si)** . Again, no visible PL was detected. **Similar results were found with samples which had been exposed to atomic hydrogen, then heat treated to 450 °C prior to oxygen exposure.**

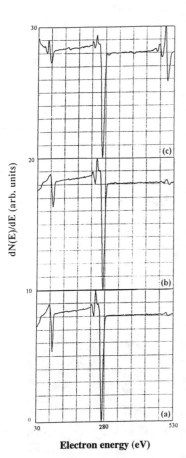

dN(E)/dE (arb. units)

Electron energy (eV)

Fig. 1. Auger electron spectra of
a.) as-deposited silicon on graphite;
b.) the same sample after post
annealing to 500 C for 5 minutes;
c.) the same sample after prolonged
air exposure. The peaks around 60 eV
and 80 eV were from fully and partially
oxidized silicon clusters respectively.

As-deposited

Heated to 500 C

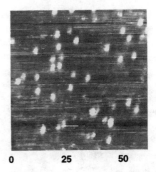

Fig. 2. STM image of a.) as-
deposited silicon on graphite;
b.) the same sample after post
annealing to 500 C for 5
minutes.

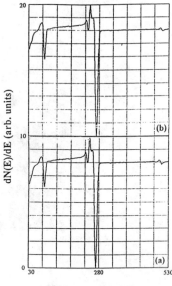

Electron energy (eV)

Fig. 3. Auger electron spectra of
a.) as-deposited silicon on graphite;
b.) the same sample after post
annealing to 800 C for 5 minutes.

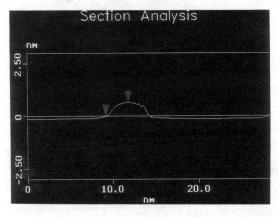

Fig. 4. STM image of a cluster with a
pancake shape after post annealing to 800 C
for 5 minutes. The horiz. and vert. distances
between the two pointers are 2.646 nm and
0.646 nm respectively.

320

Photoluminescence intensity (arb. unit)

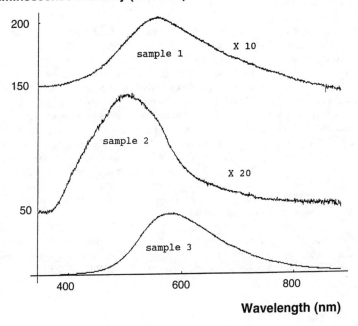

Fig. 5. Photoluminescence intensity spectra of silicon clusters after prolonged air exposure. No STM work has been done on sample 1. Samples 2 and 3 contained clusters with average size of 3 nm and 5 nm ($\pm$ 1 nm) respectively.

However, subsequent removal of the samples out of the UHV chamber and ambient air exposure for prolonged period of time (months) resulted in strong PL spectra with color ranging from red to greenish-blue (figure 5). Auger electron spectra revealed the existence of partially oxidized Si clusters for these samples (figure 1c).

Spectra similar to figure 5 have also been observed from clusters obtained by ultrasonicating thin sections of anodized porous Si [7]. These orange-to-blue emission components had shorter lifetimes (several nanoseconds), than the infrared-red emission bands of porous Si. X-ray photoabsorption measurements on the sample studied in reference [7] showed the presence of only oxidized Si, suggesting that the shorter wavelength emission components originated **either** from defect centers in an oxide phase **or from oxygen passivated Si inner cores**.

SUMMARY and ACKNOWLEDGEMENT

In summary, we have made Si nanoclusters on the basal plane of graphite. The size distribution and shape of the clusters could be determined as a function of annealing time and temperature. Surface oxidation of these clusters was very difficult to obtain with an oxygen background of pressure up to 10^{-6} Torr. The pristine clusters did not show any visible PL, but prolonged exposure of these clusters to ambient air produced strong visible and broad PL spectra.

At this time, the dominant mechanism for the observed visible and broad PL spectra from these clusters cannot be clearly determined. *In-situ* surface passivation of these clusters with oxygen at elevated temperature (600 °C) and higher background pressure (300 Torr, for example) will be carried out in our laboratory. *In-situ* PL spectra as a function of oxidation time will be obtained and compared with optical absorption spectra (in reflection mode). Efforts to observe the quantization of electronic density of states (if any) of these individual clusters as a function of sizes will also be performed. From these experiments, we expect to tell whether the observed visible photoluminescence spectra from our clusters is a manifestation of the quantum confinement effect or a result of some interfacial PL.

We would like to express our special thanks to Dr. A. V. Hamza, and Dr. W. J. Siekhaus for helpful discussions. This work was supported by the Division of Materials Sciences, Office of Basic Energy Science, and performed under the auspices of the U.S. Department of Energy by Lawrence Livermore National Laboratory under contract No. W-7405-ENG-48.

REFERENCES

[1] L. Banyai, S. W. Koch, *Semiconductor quantum dots* (World Scientific, 1993).
[2] P. Butcher, N. H. March, M. P. Tosi, *Physics of low dimensional semiconductor structures* (Plenum Press, 1993), pp. 95-188.
[3] C. Weibuch, B. Vinter, *Quantum semiconductor structures: fundamentals and applications* (Academic Press, 1991), pp. 189-191.
[4] B. Delley, E. F. Steigmeier, Physical Review B **47**, 1397 (1993).
[5] G. A. Somorjai, *Principles of surface chemistry* (Prentice-Hall Inc.,1972), p. 155.
[6] L. Brus, Advanced Materials **5**, 286 (1993).
[7] S. Berhane, S. M. Kauzlarich, K. Nishimura, R. L. Smith, J. E. Davis, H. W. Lee, M. L. S. Olsen, and L. L. Chase, Mat. Res. Symp. Proc., vol. 298, 99 (1993).

STRESS IN MOLYBDENUM FILMS USED FOR FEA DISPLAY TECHNOLOGY

James A. Greer and Guy F. Pagliuca
Raytheon Company - Research Division, Lexington, MA

INTRODUCTION

Flat-panel displays based on cold-cathode field emission are actively being developed in a number of laboratories world-wide. Once fully developed, Field Emitter Displays (FEDs) will compete directly with Liquid Crystal Displays (LCDs). FEDs offer several significant advantages over LCDs including higher screen brightness, wider viewing angle, lower power consumption, and operation over a broader temperature range, making FEDs desirable for applications such as lap-top computers. Presently, several materials are being evaluated for use as cold-cathode field emitters including molybdenum[1], silicon[2], and DLC[3]. At this time it is unclear which material (or materials) will ultimately be incorporated into commercial or military flat-panel display products. Each potential cathode material has its own set of advantages and disadvantages, and the ultimate choice will depend on the particular display requirements and architecture.

Currently, the most advanced FEDs are based on glass substrates, with Mo base metal, Mo cold-cathode tips, a Low Temperature Oxide (LTO) dielectric spacer, and either a Mo or Nb gate layer[4]. The advantages of using Mo for the base electrode, the emitter, and/or gate structure include the following: 1) Mo has a low resistivity and high melting point, thus high currents and temperatures can be sustained without failure of tip or gate metal; 2) Mo has a very low sputter yield which may be more important for high brightness displays. Low sputter yields will allow operation at high screen potentials where back-bombardment of tip or gate metal by ions (produced by electron-impact ionization of residual gas or electron-stimulated desorption from the anode) could degrade device performance. This latter feature coupled with Mo's refractory nature may minimize damaging effects due to arcing which can occur during initial burn-in of the display; 3) Mo has a relatively low work function, ϕ, of 4.37 eV, and will not form a native oxide at low temperatures; and 4) Mo is compatible with standard semiconductor process technology. Molybdenum films have been deposited by several Physical Vapor Deposition (PVD) techniques including electron beam evaporation, ion beam[5], cylindrical[6], and planar magnetron sputtering to name just a few. Each of these processes yield Mo films with varying degrees of stress which if large enough could be deleterious to subsequent display processing steps. For instance, under certain conditions, Mo films sputter deposited onto 75 mm diameter Si can significantly warp the substrate making it impossible to complete the subsequent photolithography steps needed to define emitter locations. As substrate sizes scale up to those used for lap top computers and larger, the effects of film stress on substrate warping will become even more problematic unless such stress can be minimized. Furthermore, the stresses induced when depositing Mo to form the cold-cathode emitter structures can physically lift the gate-layer metallization off of the underlying LTO dielectric.

Here we report on the stress in Mo films deposited onto oxidized (100) silicon substrates by a number of PVD techniques including electron beam evaporation, evaporation with simultaneous low energy (E< 150 eV) argon ion beam bombardment, and planar DC and RF magnetron sputtering. Other film properties including the resistivity, crystallographic nature, and morphology are presented. The results of this study indicate that Mo films can be deposited with modest amounts (~ 100 MPa) of either compressive or tensile stress and low resistivity depending on the deposition technique used.

MATERIALS AND METHODS

Molybdenum films were deposited by several techniques in either one of two chambers. First, a commercially available load-locked Perkin Elmer 4400 sputter system with a 200 mm diameter Mo target (99.99% pure) was used for planar DC magnetron sputtering onto unheated substrates which were electrically grounded during deposition. This system is cryo-pumped and has a base pressure of 2×10^{-7} Torr. Substrates positioned on a water cooled platen located 6.5 cm below the target were back sputtered with Ar using an RF power of 500 Watts for 5 minutes prior to film deposition. The Mo target was similarly precleaned before each run using 500 Watts DC. The platen which can hold 12 substrates was rotated at a rate of 4 RPM through the diode region during deposition.

The second deposition system was a custom designed load-locked UHV chamber used to deposit Mo films by electron beam evaporation, ion beam assisted evaporation, or RF magnetron sputtering as shown in Figure 1. The base pressure routinely obtained in this deposition chamber is 1×10^{-9} Torr using a 3,000 l/sec cryopump with H_2 and CO as the predominant residual background gases. After a bake-out at 450°C at 5×10^{-10} Torr the substrates are shuttled from the prep-chamber into the main chamber and inserted into an electrically grounded MBE manipulator (VG/Fisons). Programmable controllers were used to heat the substrate during deposition to temperatures in excess of 800°C, and to rotate the substrate about its normal (4 RPM for this study), as well as change the substrates azimuthal angle, θ, defined in Figure 1, by ± 75 degrees. This latter feature allows the substrate normal to be set to any desired angle with respect to either the Mo evaporant, sputtered, or Ar ion fluxes. The system has two 30 cc, four pocket electron guns (TFI Telemark Model 281), each with a 6 kW power supply. All four pockets of one gun are charged with vacuum zone refined Mo slugs (99.99% pure). The linear distance from the substrate to the crucibles is 92 cm. Deposition rate and control of the evaporant is accomplished by either a quartz crystal micro-balance and IC4+ controller, or a dual channel optical electron Impact Emission Spectrometer (IES) (Leybold/Inficon). A low energy (E < ~170 eV) gridless

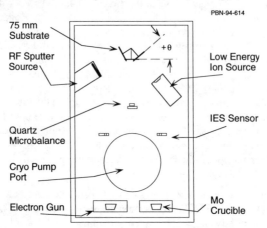

PBN-94-614

Figure 1. Custom UHV Deposition System Used to Deposit Mo Films by Electron Beam Evaporation, Ion Beam Assisted Evaporation, and RF Magnetron Sputtering.

ion source (Commonwealth Scientific) can be used for either presputtering the substrate, or for Ion Beam Assisted Deposition (IBAD) during evaporation. The chamber pressure increases to between 1 and 2 X 10^{-4} Torr while the ion source is operational. The source is located 20 cm from the substrate center when $\theta = +40°$, i.e., the ion flux is incident normal to the substrate surface, as seen in Figure 1. Finally, a 600 Watt planar RF magnetron source (US Inc.) with a 76 mm diameter Mo target (99.99% pure) is located 152 mm from the substrate when $\theta = -60°$ (the incident sputtered flux is normal to the substrate). During RF sputtering a capacitance manometer is used to control the argon gas pressure by adjusting a programmable gate valve.

The substrates used in this study were 0.381 mm thick, (100) oriented p-type, 75 mm diameter silicon with a nominal resistivity of 15 Ω-cm. These vendor supplied substrates were annealed in flowing O_2 and H_2 at 1,000°C to form a "wet" oxide layer of 3,500 Å, and no special cleaning procedures were used either before or after the oxidation. The Mo films which were grown over the oxide measured between 2,000 to 4,000 Å. After deposition several film properties were evaluated. Molybdenum film stress was obtained using a Flexus Model F2320 stress measurement system. This unit measures the change in the radius of curvature of the substrate both before and after film deposition. Assuming that the change in substrate radii is caused entirely by the total force induced by the deposited film, the average film stress, σ, can then be calculated if the modulus of the substrate is known. Film resistivity was measured using a standard four point probe. Film thickness was measured using a stylus profilometer after chemically etching lines in the Mo films. X-ray powder diffraction scans were obtained from several Mo films using CuK_α radiation with a Rigaku diffractometer. Accurate measurements of the diffraction angles and line widths from the (110) and (211) peaks of the Mo films provided a measure of the films lattice constant in the growth direction as well as defect density. Film morphology was evaluated using SEM.

RESULTS AND DISCUSSION

Figure 2 displays the stress measured as a function of power for three different Ar gas pressures obtained from Mo films deposited by DC magnetron sputtering onto unheated and grounded substrates. As noted, all the DC sputtered films displayed tensile stress, and the stress magnitude increases with increased power and/or reduced pressure. Target bias and currents for the DC magnetron ranged from -260 V and 2.3 amps, 600 W at 20 mTorr, to 330 V and 6.1 amps at 2,000 Watts at 5 mTorr. Figure 2 also shows the measured stress obtained as a function of power at 20 mTorr pressure for Mo films deposited at room temperature using RF magnetron sputtering at power levels of up to 500 W. Target bias increased from -360 to -485 V over the RF power range tested. In contrast to Mo films deposited using DC magnetron sputtering, low levels of compressive film stress were measured for all but one of the RF magnetron sputtered films. The film deposited at 300 W and 20 mTorr displayed a small tensile stress of +18 MPa. The resistivities of DC sputtered Mo films ranged in value from 18 $\mu\Omega$-cm with 5 mTorr and 2 kW to 130 $\mu\Omega$-cm with 20 mTorr and 0.6 kW. The resistivities of the RF sputtered films ranged in value from 90 to 190 $\mu\Omega$-cm using 20 mTorr and 300 and 500 W, respectively. The RF sputter deposition rate obtained at 500 W and 20 mTorr was comparable to that of the the DC rates obtained at 600 W and 20 mTorr (~2 Å/s). However, DC sputtering at higher power provided for deposition rates of up to 6 Å/sec.

Figure 3 displays both the stress and resistivity from oxidized Si substrates with Mo films deposited at 3 Å/sec by electron beam evaporation as a function of substrate temperature. An angle of $\theta = 7°$ was used such that the evaporated Mo flux was incident normal to the substrate

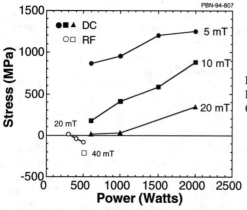

Figure 2. Mo Film Stress Vs. Power for Planar DC and RF Magnetron Sputtering Onto Unheated and Grounded Substrates.

surface. During deposition the chamber pressure remained below 1 x 10⁻⁸ Torr. The evaporated films display only moderate levels of tensile stress, and the stress magnitude increased with increasing substrate deposition temperature. It should be mentioned that during evaporation without intentional heating of the substrate, the manipulator thermocouple located directly behind the substrate indicated a temperature rise of about 50°C due to thermal radiation from the Mo source. It is likely that the substrate surface is in fact hotter than that recorded by the thermocouple, and thus a substrate temperature of 100°C has been assumed for these wafers. The tensile stress noted in Figure 3 at elevated temperatures is directly related to the difference in the thermal coefficients of expansion between the Mo film and Si substrate, 5.1 versus 2.5 PPM/°C, for Mo and Si, receptively. As the film and substrate cool down after deposition the Mo film would like to contract twice as much as the substrate. However, since the film adheres to the substrate surface its contraction is limited; thus the Mo is left with modest amounts of extrinsic tensile stress. Comparing the magnitude of tensile stresses obtained by DC diode sputtering to

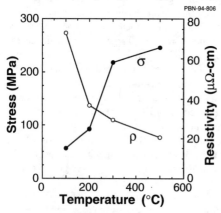

Figure 3. Stress (●) and Resistivity (○) vs. Substrate Deposition Temperature for Mo Films Deposited by Electron Beam Evaporation.

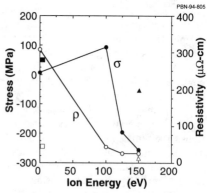

Figure 4. Stress (●) and Resistivity (○) vs. Incident Ar Ion Energy for Mo Films Grown by Ion-Beam Assisted Evaporation at a Substrate Temperature of 100°C, ▲ and Δ at 300°C, and ■ and □ at 100°C and 1 X 10⁻⁸ Torr.

those obtained using evaporation at elevated temperatures it is clear that the sputtered stresses are predominantly intrinsic and not due to significant substrate heating during the sputter deposition process. As noted in Figure 3, the Mo film resistivity decreases by a factor of 2 when the temperature is increased from 100°C to 500°C where it reached a value of 20 $\mu\Omega$-cm.

Figure 4 shows the stress and resistivity of Mo films deposited onto grounded substrates by electron beam evaporation at 3 Å/sec with simultaneous Ar+ ion bombardment, as a function of the incident ion energy. Again, for these depositions θ was set to +7° such that the evaporant flux was normal to the substrate, and thus ions were incident at an angle of 33°. The ion beam current density ranged from 1.2 to 0.9 mA/cm^2 for energies of 100 to 150 eV, respectively. At ion energies of 100 eV tensile stress was found in the Mo films. At ion energies between 100 and 125 eV the film stress goes through a sharp transition, and changes to compression. The stress ($\bullet$) and resistivity ($\circ$) of a Mo film deposited at 100°C and an Ar background pressure of 1 X 10^{-4} Torr without ion bombardment is shown in Figure 4 at 0 eV. As noted, the tensile film stress in this case was lower than that obtained for Mo films evaporated at pressures below 10^{-8} Torr. This film displayed extremely high resistivity (305 $\mu\Omega$-cm). Figure 4 also shows the stress ($\blacktriangle$) and resistivity ($\triangle$) obtained from a Mo film evaporated onto a substrate heated to 300°C with simultaneous ion beam bombardment at 150 eV. In this case the intrinsic compressive film stress produced by ion bombardment is offset by the extrinsic tensile stress induced by the differences in thermal coefficients of expansion yielding a stress of -60 MPa. The resistivity of this film, 11.5 $\mu\Omega$-cm, was the lowest value obtained in this study, and compares to that of 5.3 $\mu\Omega$-cm for bulk Mo. Also shown in this figure are stress ($\blacksquare$) and resistivity ($\square$) values obtained from a Mo film evaporated at a pressure below 10^{-8} Torr at 100°C. Figure 4 clearly shows that a low energy ion beam significantly alters the stress of the Mo film, changing it from tension to compression, as well as reducing the films resistivity by about an order of magnitude. Evaporated films deposited with IBAD displayed lower resistivities than those of all the other techniques studied except evaporation of Mo onto substrates with temperatures of 500°C.

X-ray powder diffraction scans obtained from Mo films grown by all the PVD techniques indicated strong polycrystalline texture for this bcc material. The lattice constants and FWHMs obtained from both the (110) and (221) peaks are listed in Table I. X-ray diffraction of a Mo foil yielded a FWHM of 0.12° (using just the CuK$_{\alpha 1}$) of the (211) peak, and a lattice constant of 3.1467 ; 0.0009 Å which compares favorably with the standard value of 3.1472 Å. It should be

Table I

Deposition Conditions	(110) Lattice Parameter (Å)	(110) FWHM (Deg)	(211) Lattice Parameter (Å)	(211) FWHM (Deg)
Mo Foil: CuK$_{\alpha}$1	N.A.	N.A.	3.1467±.0009	0.12
Evap. (100°C UHV)	3.153±.015	0.50	3.150±.022	1.18
Evap. (500°C UHV)	3.136±.004	0.40	3.137±.006	0.88
Evap. (100°C 10^{-4}T)	3.143±.012	0.62	3.152±.015	1.36
Evap. (100°C 150eV)	3.185±.014	0.64	3.175±.020	1.54
Evap. (300°C) 150eV)	3.156±0.13	0.74	3.155±.016	1.40
DC (600W 20 mTorr)	3.156±.014	0.64	N.A.	N.A.
DC (2kW 5 mTorr)	3.136±.006	0.34	3.140±.008	0.80
RF (300W 20 mTorr)	3.152±.015	0.60	N.A.	N.A.
RF (500W 20 mTorr)	3.155±.015	0.70	3.157±.075	1.76

N.A. – not available. Mo standard = 3.1472 Å

realized that the stress is measured in the plane of the film, while the lattice constant obtained by x-ray diffraction is measured in a direction normal to the film surface. Thus, due to the Poisson effect, the lattice constants agree well with the measured stress values being larger/smaller than the unstressed value for compressive/tensile stress, respectively. SEMs of several Mo films obtained from normal and cross sectional views of fractured substrates are shown in Figure 5. The Mo film evaporated at a pressure of 1×10^{-4} Torr without ion bombardment displayed severe cracking which accounts for the very low stress and high electrical resistivity noted above. The surface morphology of evaporated Mo films deposited with ion beam bombardment had the least surface roughness and displayed a dense columnar structure typical of zone T (transition zone) in the standard T/T_m model[7]. Planar DC sputtered films showed dense colum-

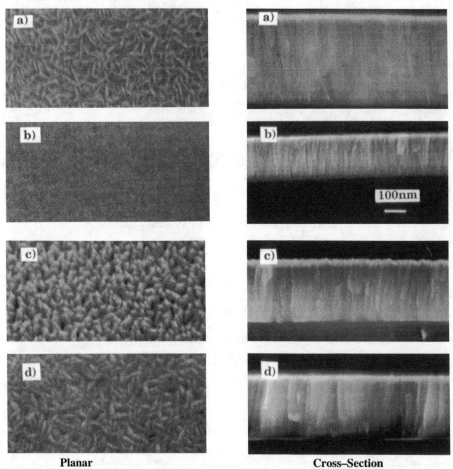

Planar   **Cross–Section**

Figure 5. Planar and Cross-Sectional Views of Mo Films Deposited Using: a) Evaporation at 100°C Substrate Temperature; b) Ion Beam Assisted Evaporation at 100°C and 150 eV Ar+ Energy; c) Planar DC Magnetron Sputtering at 600 W and 20 mTorr; and d) 2 kW and 5 mTorr. The Scale is the Same For All of the SEMs.

nar structure with rougher surface morphology, especially films deposited with low power and high pressure. RF sputtered films displayed surface roughness similar to the low power DC sputtered films with columnar structure typical of Zone 1. Evaporated films deposited at low temperatures showed similar surfaces to that of the high power DC sputtered films, but the cross sectional views indicated a smaller grain sizes. Heating the substrates to 500°C tended to produce Mo films with larger grains and a rough surface morphology.

CONCLUSIONS

Molybdenum films have been deposited onto oxidized Si substrates by a variety of physical vapor deposition techniques. The Mo film stress can be made to vary over a wide range of either tension or compression depending on the deposition technique and conditions used. For field emission displays, Mo films with low amounts of internal stress are clearly preferable, as such films will simplify further processing steps, especially as the display sizes increase.

The highest stresses ($\sigma > 1$ GPa) produced in this study were obtained using planar DC magnetron sputtering at low pressure and high power, which also produced Mo films with low resistivity. However, high pressure in conjunction with low power produced DC sputtered films with very low tensile stress ($\sigma < 0.05$ GPa), but relatively high resistivity. Also, planar RF magnetron sputtered films displayed low amounts of compressive film stress, but high film resistivity. Electron beam evaporation onto heated substrates produced Mo films with lowest amounts of extrinsic tensile stress and low electrical resistivity. Electron beam evaporation with simultaneous low energy ion bombardment produced dense Mo films with low compressive stress, low electrical resistivity, and excellent surface morphology. Heating the substrates during ion beam assisted evaporation offset the intrinsic compressive stress with thermally induced extrinsic tensile stress, and at the same time reduced the films resistivity. While ion beam assisted evaporation produced Mo films with the lowest resistivity, low compressive stress, and smoothest surface morphology, the technique is probably not practical for a production line where, ideally, several large substrates would be coated simultaneously. On the other hand, using either evaporation at modest substrate temperatures, or planar DC magnetron sputtering with a high gas pressure and medium power, would yield Mo films with low amounts of stress and resistivity, and good surface morphology. These deposition approaches are capable of handling batch processing of large substrate sizes required for future FEA flat-panel display needs.

REFERENCES

1) C.A. Spindt, C.E. Holland, A. Rosengreen, and I. Brodie, IEEE Trans. on Electron Devices, Vol. **38**(10), pps. 2355-2363, 1991.
2) C.E. Hunt, J.T. Trujillo, and W.J. Orvis, IEEE Trans. on Electron Devices, Vol. **38**(10), pps. 2309-2313, 1991.
3) B.C. Djuba and N.N. Chubun, Trans. on Electron Devices, Vol. **38**(10), pps. 2314-2316, 1991.
4) A. Ghis, R. Meyer, P. Rambaud, F. Levy, and T. Leroux, IEEE Trans. on Electron Devices, Vol. **38**(10), pps. 2320-2322, 1991.
5) S. Sun, J. Vac. Sci. Technol., **A 4**(3), pps. 572-576, 1986.
6) D.W. Hoffman and J.A. Thornton, J. Vac Sci. Technol., Vol **16**(2), pps. 134-137, 1979.
7) J.A. Thornton and D.W. Hoffman, Thin Solid Films, Vol. **171**, pp. 5, 1989.

SOLID-STATE LUMINESCENT COLOR DISPLAYS

EDWARD J. A. POPE
Matech, 31304 Via Colinas, Suite 102, Westlake Village, CA 91362

ABSTRACT

By the end of 1994, flat-panel displays for lap-top computers and televisions will exceed $4.0 billion in total sales. Currently, most such displays are based entirely upon an advanced liquid crystal technology requiring several precisely aligned LC layers. A new technology for flat-panel displays, based upon the solid-state luminescence of sol-gel derived microspheres has been proposed. Silica gel-derived microspheres can be prepared at near ambient temperatures, doped with either optically-active organic dye molecules or lanthanide ions. Microspheres doped to give red, blue, and green luminescence can be arranged in a pixel pattern to form the basis of a display screen. A single monochrome LC layer is used to modulate the excitation light, or pump source, that activates the fluorescence of each pixel.

INTRODUCTION

In 1968, Stöber demonstrated the preparation of monodisperse silica microspheres from dilute base-catalyzed solutions [1]. Others have continued to study this process for the production of microspheres [2,3]. The maximum diameter achievable with this process is a few microns. More recently, microsphere formation under dilute acidic conditions has been demonstrated [4].

A new method of microsphere formation has been developed, based upon solution immiscibility, which renders microspheres from a few microns to a few millimeters in diameter [5,6]. Microsphere diameter is controlled by the mixing rate, or stirring speed, of two immiscibile liquids [7]. Microspheres are formed by suspending acid solution droplets in tetraethoxysilane (TEOS) by stirring [5,6]. Hydrolysis occurs at the interface between the TEOS and the acid solution, thereby allowing the hydrolyzed TEOS to diffuse into the aqueous droplet.

The ability to fabricate large microspheres of silica, or other compositions, could be useful for both technological applications and basic scientific study. Useful applications might include: 1) raw materials for high purity glass melting; 2) porous glass filters; 3) catalyst supports; 4) fillers for plastics; 5) chemical sensors; 6) controlled release agents for medicines, chemical reactants, and fragrances, and; 7) flat-panel displays.

Silica microspheres, doped with optically-active organic dye molecules or lanthanide elements, can be used in the development of flat-panel displays. Unlike conventional displays, in which light is simply transmitted through color filters, this new approach uses optically active microspheres as luminescent radiators.

Mat. Res. Soc. Symp. Proc. Vol. 345. ©1994 Materials Research Society

Table I: Fluorescence peak wavelength for selected organic dye molecules and inorganic ions when incorporated into sol-gel derived silica microspheres.

DOPANT SPECIES	PEAK WAVELENGTH (nm)	COLOR
Example Organics:		
7-amino-4-methylcoumarin	440	blue
fluorescein	520	green
rhodamine-B	625	red
Example Inorganics:		
europium (2+)	450	blue
uranium (6+)	530	green
europium (3+)	615	red

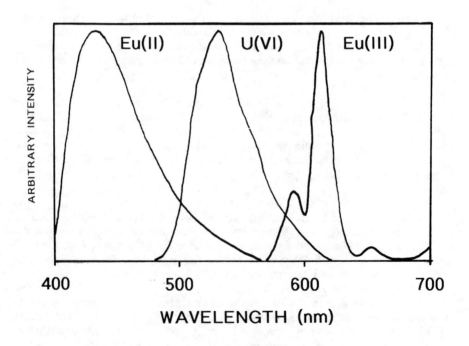

Figure 1: Fluorescence emission spectra of selected ions,

EXPERIMENTAL

Microspheres were produced by mixing tetraethoxysilane (TEOS) with 0.1 molar HCl solution and stirring. The relationship between microsphere formation and the TEOS to HCl solution ratio have been previously investigated [5,6]. The optimum ratio was determined to be 10.0 ml HCl solution to 85.0 ml TEOS. The average microsphere diameter was controlled by stirring frequency, in which the logarithm of the average diameter is proportional to the inverse stirring frequency.

Dopants were incorporated by dissolution in the 0.1 molar HCl solution. Organic dyes were added directly as solid powders. Europium was added as europium nitrate and uranium was added as uranium (III) chloride. In addition to europium and uranium, erbium and neodymium have also been incorporated into silica gel microspheres. Dye-doped microspheres were dried at 65°C, while inorganic ion-doped microspheres were heat treated at 800°C for one hour. Fluorescence behavior was measured on a Hitachi F2000 fluorescence spectrophotometer.

OPTICALLY-ACTIVE MICROSPHERES

Fluorescent organic dyes can be incorporated into porous gels [8], and composites [9]. More recently, lasing has been observed in dye-doped gels [10] and composites [11]. Rhodamine-B, rhodamine-6G, fluorescein, coumarin 314T, thionin, and pyranine have all been successfully incorporated into silica gel microspheres [5,12]. It was shown that a pronounced red shift of the fluorescence spectra, by as much as 66 nm, is observed between the initial liquid solution and the dried gel microsphere [5]. Part of this fluorescence shift may be attributed to compressive stress exerted upon the organic dye molecule by the collapsed gel network. Another component of this shift may be ascribed to the change in the local chemical environment.

Inorganic ions have been incorporated into silica gel microspheres by doping the initial solution with metal salts, followed by drying and high temperature heat treatment. In the case of ions which exhibit multiple valence states, such as europium and chromium, the valance state can be controlled by initial solution chemistry and heat treatment conditions, such as oxidizing vs. reducing atmosphere [13].

For the application to flat-panel displays, microspheres which fluoresce red, blue, and green are desirable. In table I, the fluorescence peak wavelengths for selected organic dye molecules and inorganic ions doped into silica gel microspheres are presented. In principle, color display screens might be fabricated from either organic or inorganic dopants. In figure 1, the fluorescence spectra for selected inorganic ion doped microspheres are presented.

FLAT-PANEL COLOR DISPLAYS

In figure 2, a schematic diagram illustrates the operation of a luminescent flat-panel color display. An ultraviolet source, such as an electroluminescent panel or UV tube light,

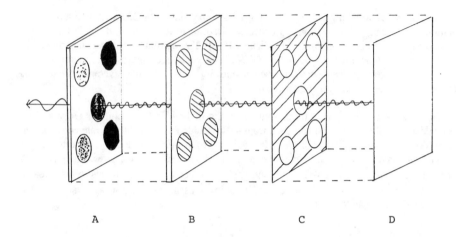

Figure 2: Schematic diagram of luminescent solid-state flat
          panel color display; (A) optically-active microsphere
          array; (B) monochromatic (B/W) liquid crystal shutter;
          (C) pin hole mask, and; (D) UV light source.

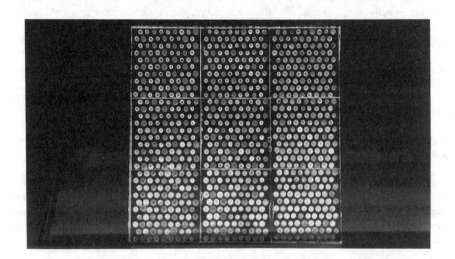

Figure 3: Photograph of 1,000 pixel dye-doped silica gel
          microsphere array. This prototype has been used to
          produce simple images.

"pumps" the luminescence of an array of optically-active microspheres. The light source is modulated by a single layer, monochromatic liquid crystal shutter array[14]. This design differs significantly from the conventional approach, in which liquid crystal multilayers are doped with dye molecules that act as filters. The reliance upon only a single LC layer may significantly reduce alignment difficulties during fabrication. Given the high luminescent conversion efficiencies of fluorescent dye molecules, this can lead to a calculated increase in brightness of 50 - 100 percent.

Unlike conventional flat-panel displays, the emitted light is non-polarized. The initially polarized UV pump source stimulates fluorescence of depolarized red, blue, and green emission of the doped microspheres. In figure 3, a "prototype" 1,000 pixel color display screen is shown. Simple images have been produced by this screen [11].

SUMMARY

A new method of fabricating transparent silica gel microspheres has been developed based upon the solution immiscibility of TEOS and acid-catalyzed water solutions. The low temperature processing of these materials permits the incorporation of a wide variety of optically-active organic dye molecules.

Luminescent inorganic ions, such as europium and uranium, can also be doped into silica gel microspheres. Both europium and uranium are strongly fluorescent when incorporated into silica gel-glass microspheres.

A prototype flat-panel color display has been demonstrated through the formation of a microsphere array of sequentially alternating red, blue, and green fluorescing silica microspheres.

ACKNOWLEDGEMENTS

The author gratefully acknowledges the assistance of Mr. Alex Almazan in sample preparation and Mrs. Barbara M. Pope (author's mother) in manuscript preparation. The advice and consultation of Mr. W. Edward Johansen is greatly appreciated.

REFERENCES

1. W. Stöber, A. Fink, and E. Bohn, J. Colloid. Interf. Sci., **26**, 62 (1968).

2. G. H. Bogush and C. F. Zukoski, in Ultrastructure Processing of Advanced Materials, edited by J. D. Mackenzie and D. R. Ulrich (Wiley Interscience, New York, 1988) p. 477.

3. E. C. Ruvolo, H. L. Bellinetti, and M. A. Aegerter, J. Non-Cryst. Sol., **121**, 244 (1990).

4. B. Karnakar, G. De, D. Kundu, and D. Ganguli, J. Non-Cryst. Sol.,**135**, 29 (1991).

5. E. J. A. Pope, J. Amer. Ceram. Soc., in press; patent pending.

6. E. J. A. Pope, in Sol-Gel Optics II, edited by J. D. Mackenzie, (SPIE Vol. **1758**, Bellingham, WA, 1992) pp. 360-371.

7. N. Easwar, Phys. Rev. Lett., **68** (2), 186 (1992).

8. D. Avnir, D. Levy, and R. Reisfeld, J. Phys. Chem., **88**, 5956 (1984).

9. E. J. A. Pope and J. D. Mackenzie, Mater. Res. Soc. Bulletin, **12** (3), 29 (1987).

10. B. Dunn, et al., in Sol-Gel Optics, edited by J. D. Mackenzie and D. R. Ulrich, (SPIE Vol. **1328**, Bellingham, WA, 1990) p. 174.

11. E. J. A. Pope, J. Sol-Gel Sci. and Tech., in press; presented at the 7th International Workshop on Glasses and Ceramics from Gels, Paris, France (1993).

12. E. J. A. Pope, in press.

13. E. J. A. Pope, in Sol-Gel Optics II, edited by J. D. Mackenzie, (SPIE Vol. **1758**, Bellingham, WA, 1992) pp. 26-39.

14. patents pending.

Author Index

Subject Index

amorphous
  photocoupler, 305
  silicon, 3, 11, 23, 29, 35, 59, 65, 81, 93, 123, 175
    double layer films, 111
    germanium alloys, 149
    stability, 11
atmospheric pressure CVD, 29, 35
atomic force microscopy, 247

crystallization, 41, 59, 81, 111, 123, 149
  rapid thermal, 93

defect passivation, 135
degradation, 155
deposition
  electrophoretic, 299
  low temperature, 53, 71
  rate, 3, 35, 65, 175
disilane, 123

electrical stress, 155
electroluminescent displays, 269, 289, 311
electron cyclotron resonance, 81, 135
  CVD, 117
  distributed, 87

field emission displays, 269, 281, 323

glass substrate, 163
  thermal expansion, 163
grain
  boundary, 141, 155
  growth, 81
  size, 41, 111

hydrogen
  bonded, 53
  diffusion, 135
hydrogenation, 117, 135, 155

incubation time, 81
indium tin oxide, 191, 255, 261
interface reaction, 191
ion doping, 3, 35, 269

laser
  processing, 41, 105, 255, 261, 281, 317
  repair, 185
leakage current, 129, 141
light emitting diode, 305
  amorphous silicon based, 305
liquid crystal display, 65
  active matrix, 71, 163, 185, 197
  alignment, 205, 211, 247
    optically controlled, 211
  contamination, 223
  materials, 197

low pressure CVD, 93
luminescence, 331
  microspheres, 331

microcrystalline silicon, 47, 53
mobility, 53, 65, 87, 129
molybdenum, 323

nanocrystalline silicon, 311

phosphors, 269, 281, 289, 299
photoluminescence, 317
plasma
  displays, 269
  enhanced CVD, 3, 29, 65, 87, 111, 175
    excitation frequency, 65, 175
    remote, 53
  exposure, 29, 81, 99
polycrystalline silicon, 41, 71, 87, 93, 99, 117, 123, 129, 135, 141, 155

Schottky barrier, 217
secondary ion mass spectroscopy, 197
  time of flight, 197, 223
selective deposition, 47
silicon
  clusters, 317
  dioxide, 29, 53
  nitride, 23, 53, 105, 175
sputtering, 241
surface analysis, 197

thin film(s), 23, 241, 269
  stress, 323
  transistor, 23, 29, 35, 41, 47, 53, 59, 65, 71, 87, 93, 99, 129, 135, 141, 155, 217
    LDD structure, 129
    offset structure, 99, 141
    self aligned, 3, 71, 217
    top gate, 47
thiogallate, 289
tin oxide
  properties, 235
  spray-pyrolysis, 235
total reflection x-ray fluorescence, 223
transmission electron microscopy, 117
transparent conductors, gallium indium oxide, 241, 255
tunneling current, 217

ultra high vacuum CVD, 123

XPS, 29, 105

yttrium aluminum gallium garnet, 93

zinc sulfide, 289